SUPERVISORY AND COLLEGE
MANAGEMENT
THE ART OF WORKING WITH AND THROUGH PEOPLE
2D EDITION

DONALD C. MOSLEY, PH.D.
Professor of Management
College of Business and Management Studies
University of South Alabama

LEON C. MEGGINSON, PH.D.
J.L. Bedsole Professor of Business
Mobile College

PAUL H. PIETRI, JR., D.B.A.
Professor of Management
College of Business and Management Studies
University of South Alabama

GZ66BA
PUBLISHED BY
SOUTH-WESTERN PUBLISHING CO.
CINCINNATI   WEST CHICAGO, IL   CARROLLTON, TX   LIVERMORE, CA

ISBN: 0–538–80026–7

Library of Congress Catalog Card Number: 87–61618

5   6   7   Ki   4   3   2

Printed in the United States of America

CONTENTS

PART II   ORGANIZING

PART III   LEADING

PART V   CONTROLLING

PREFACE

We dedicate this Second Edition of *Supervisory Management: The Art of Working with and through People* (Stock No. GZ66BA) to the thousands of line supervisors and managers we have worked with through the years from manufacturing companies, hospitals, banks, public service companies, and governmental organizations. We recently heard a CEO of a large company address the company's supervisory club. As he put it, members of his audience were the key management players because, as supervisors, they functioned "where the rubber hits the road" in getting people to directly achieve the organization's objectives. This theme is reinforced throughout this textbook: *The essence of supervisory management is working with and through people.*

As in the First Edition, we have maintained a solid theory base and a practical, applied, hands-on approach to make the material relevant and exciting.

ORGANIZATION OF THE TEXT

The text is organized along the framework of the basic management functions that supervisors must perform. Following an introduction to the role of the supervisor, Part I (Planning) focuses on the fundamentals of planning and decision-making/problem-solving processes. Part II (Organization) deals with the fundamentals of organizing and the delegation of authority. Part III (Leading) focuses on communication, group dynamics, conducting meetings, motivating employees, and leadership. Part IV (Managing Human Resources) includes selecting and training, appraising and compensating, discipline, and labor relations. Part V (Controlling) addresses the controlling process, productivity, quality and safety, management information systems, and the computer. Finally, Part VI (Current Challenges and Opportunities) zeroes in on the supervisor's role in team building and managing change, changing to a participative management culture, managing stress, time management, and careers in supervisory management.

HIGHLIGHTS OF THE SECOND EDITION

A number of changes in the Second Edition have been made to provide a text attuned to the ever-changing world of supervisory management. These changes include the following:

1. Two entirely *new* chapters have been added: Chapter 17, Management Information Systems and the Computer, and Chapter 19, Changing to a Participative Management Culture and Developing Creativity.
2. New coverage has been added to a number of topics such as group dynamics, training and developing employees, leadership, and motivation.
3. Material throughout the text has been updated to reflect recent trends and developments.
4. Seven *comprehensive* cases have been added, which appear at the end of each Part of the text.
5. There are 9 *new* chapter-opening cases and 17 *new* Learning Exercises.
6. The First Edition's "application" orientation has been balanced to include a blend of manufacturing, service, and public-sector industries in the chapter-opening cases, examples, and Learning Exercises.

INSTRUCTOR'S RESOURCE MANUAL

An excellent *Instructor's Resource Manual* (Stock No. GZ66BX) is available free of charge to those who adopt the text for class use. Written by Gayle M. Ross of Copiah-Lincoln Junior College, the manual contains the following for *each chapter*:

1. The learning objectives of the text.
2. A comprehensive lecture outline, with recommendations for using transparency masters at various points in each lecture.
3. Answers to the review and discussion questions in the text.
4. Suggested answers to the Learning Exercises in the text.
5. Suggested films and audiovisuals, with a brief overview of each. The addresses of the audiovisual distributors are listed after the preface in the manual.
6. A test bank of true–false, multiple choice, and essay questions, accompanied by answers and text page references. This test bank is also available in microcomputer (MICROSWAT II) versions.

7. A set of transparency masters.
8. Suggested answers to the Comprehensive Cases in the text.

STUDY GUIDE

Also available for use with this textbook is the Second Edition of the *Study Guide* (Stock No. GZ66BD), authored by Professor Marcia Ann Pulich of the University of Wisconsin at Whitewater. Each chapter in the *Study Guide* contains the following sections:

1. An expanded discussion of core concepts based on chapter outlines in the text.
2. Fill-in-the-blank and matching questions to help the student in mastering vocabulary.
3. Exercises that prod the student to develop and/or analyze the key text concepts.
4. True–false and multiple choice questions to aid the student in practicing for exams.

ACKNOWLEDGMENTS

A number of people have played highly supportive roles in helping us prepare this Second Edition. Our reviewers' comments and ideas were especially helpful. The reviewers included:

Janice E. Brandt
Southern Illinois University

Alvar Debaca
Southwestern Community College

Dr. Benjamin F. Findley, Jr.
Amarillo College

Dr. Jonathan S. Monat
California State University,
Long Beach

Dr. Wayne Nelson, Chair
Central Missouri State University

Kenneth R. Prolo
San Jose State University

Dr. Robert L. Qualls
Baldor Electric Company

Milton D. Rumsey
Kerr-McGee Chemical Corporation

Lyle B. Smith
Shawnee State Community College

Naomi W. Walker
Mt. San Antonio College

Suzanne Barnhill provided overall final-draft typing and editorial assistance. Typing support was also provided by Sharon Chandler, Kay Emanuel, and Rosemary Fittje. Teresa Blakney, Lyne McMullen, and Sharon Mitchell were also extremely helpful. A special thanks must also go to Dr. Warren Beatty of the University of South Alabama (our resident MIS expert) for his assistance in writing the MIS chapter of the Second Edition. We also acknowledge our colleagues and administrators at the University of South Alabama and Mobile College for their support.

Finally, our thanks go to the practicing and potential supervisors and managers with whom we've used the First Edition of this text. Their feedback and willingness to share with us their experiences have helped us create an upgraded, updated, practical text that we hope will continue to meet the needs of instructors and students of supervisory management.

Donald C. Mosley
Leon C. Megginson
Paul H. Pietri

1
THE ROLE OF
SUPERVISORY
MANAGEMENT

OBJECTIVES

After reading and studying the material in this chapter, you should be able to:

- Explain why management is needed in all organizations.
- Describe what management is and how it differs by levels.
- Discuss the five functions performed by all managers.
- Describe the many roles played by managers.
- Explain the four basic skills required by managers to operate effectively.
- Trace the changing role of supervisory management.
- Explain the different relationships supervisory managers have with others.

IMPORTANT TERMS

organization
organizational activities
operations
distribution
financing
management
human resources
physical resources
financial resources
authority
responsibility
chief executive officer (CEO)
top management
middle management

supervisory management
managerial functions
planning
organizing
staffing
leading
controlling
roles
conceptual skills
human-relations skills
administrative skills
technical skills
intermediaries

CHAPTER OUTLINE
CASE 1-1. BILL MORROW: NEW-STYLE SUPERVISOR

The supervisory manager has become a critical figure in industrial management.
John N. Yanouzas

CASE 1–1
BILL MORROW:
NEW-STYLE SUPERVISOR

Supervisor Bill Morrow has worked for Ciba-Geigy, a multinational chemical manufacturer, for 17 years. He joined the company's largest American production operation, in McIntosh, Alabama, as a production engineer. Bill's responsibilities increased, and he was promoted regularly to his current position of area supervisor. He is a classic example of today's new supervisory manager (see Figure 1–1).

FIGURE 1–1   WILLIAM W. MORROW, NEW-STYLE SUPERVISOR

Photo courtesy CIBA-GEIGY, McIntosh Alabama Plant.

In his present job, Bill supervises 50 employees and has total responsibility for an entire production unit. (See Figure 1–2 for his relationship to others in the plant.) "Our unit must manufacture the chemical products within a set framework of time and money," Morrow said. "In order to produce, we must properly consume the raw materials, labor, utilities, and other items associated with the manufacture of a particular product—and do it on time and within budget."

Morrow's supervisory duties range from housekeeping and maintenance of the production unit to the initiation of capital projects to keep the multimillion-dollar facility up to date. He is also responsible for the safety of his employees and the protection of the surrounding south Alabama environment.

"Many changes have occurred since I first joined Ciba-Geigy," said Morrow. "Processes have been updated, equipment has been modernized, and computers are now used to control most of the chemical processing." But Bill is quick to point out that automation does not replace people. "The single most striking change I've seen since I began working here has been the manner in which we manage people," said Morrow. "In years past, the workers and supervisor were like two different companies that worked

FIGURE 1–2 PARTIAL ORGANIZATION CHART OF CIBA-GEIGY'S MCINTOSH PLANT

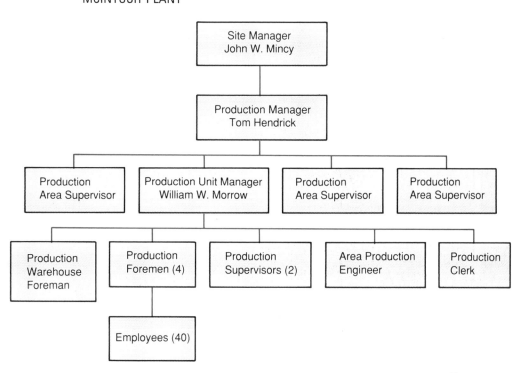

against each other." Such differences are no longer the case, as managers are rapidly working to reduce barriers between hourly and salaried workers and managers. Discrepancies such as designated parking lots for labor and management and differently colored hardhats are becoming a thing of the past.

Morrow says that today there is more of a spirit of cooperation. "Employees see the value of working together," he said, "to insure that the company, and their paychecks, can and will survive. People make things happen and they do it best in a climate of mutual respect, commitment, and trust."

Morrow has wide discretion in making decisions. He can recommend hiring and firing workers, salary increases, and promotions, and he can generally choose appropriate discipline for subordinates and make performance appraisals. He determines how his area of the plant is run, and he can shut it down without prior approval, as needed, from either a process or equipment viewpoint.

Morrow's position requires not only a technical background—he has a B.S. in chemistry—but also a variety of other disciplines, such as human-resource management, industrial relations, and computer science. Morrow has kept current in these areas and has even expanded his knowledge by attending at least eight technical, professional, and management courses. Currently he's enrolled in a night MBA program at a local college.

In summary, Ciba-Geigy is fortunate to have supervisory managers such as Bill Morrow. They're largely responsible for making the company into one of the world's largest industrial corporations.

This case shows some of the fundamental changes taking place in today's organizations. Supervisors are becoming more important to both employees and higher levels of management.

The opening case also indicates some of the roles played by supervisors and implies some of the relationships that supervisors have with others. Supervisors maintain relationships with employees, with the union and its leaders, and with other managers. Also, supervisors play interpersonal roles, informational roles, and decision-making roles. All these will be discussed later in the chapter.

What managers have you come in contact with during the past week—either in person or on the phone, TV, or radio? What were their titles? What did they do?

THE NEED FOR MANAGEMENT

Whenever a group of people work together to achieve a common objective, they form an **organization.** That organization may be a business firm, a religious group, a governmental institution, a military unit, a sports team, and so on. The main objective of these organizations is to produce a product and/or to provide a service. Other organizational objectives are to provide employment and satisfaction to employees, benefits to the public, and a return to the owners of the business (usually in the form of a profit). To reach these objectives, management must perform three basic **organizational activities**. These are (1) **operations**, or producing the product or service, (2) **distribution**, or marketing and distributing the product, and (3) **financing**, or providing and using funds. These activities must be performed in almost all organizations.

Organizations are the means by which people get things done. People form organizations simply because they can accomplish more working together than they can achieve alone. But the process of management is needed to combine and coordinate the efforts of the members of the organization. Management is needed because, without it, people in the group would go off on their own and try to reach the organization's objectives independently of other group members. Without management in small organizations, the members' efforts would be wasted. If management were absent in the larger, more complex organizations, objectives would not be reached and chaos would probably result.

What Is Management?

Management can be defined as the process of working through people to achieve objectives by means of effective decision making and coordination of available resources. The basic resources of a business firm are **human resources**, which are the people involved; **physical resources**, which include buildings, furnishings, machinery, equipment, tools, materials, and supplies; and **financial resources**, which include money, capital, and credit.

The term management is also used to describe the group of people within the organization who are responsible for making decisions and coordinating the available resources. In this sense, management and managers mean the same thing. Figure 1–3 shows the vital task of management in combining resources into a productive system to attain organizational objectives.

Levels of Management

Except in very small organizations, there are usually different levels of management based on the amount of responsibility and authority required to perform the job. Therefore, individuals at higher levels of the organization have more authority and responsibility than those at lower levels. **Authority** is the right to command others to act or not act in order to reach objectives. **Responsibility** is the obligation that is created when a subordinate accepts a manager's delegated authority.

FIGURE 1–3 HOW MANAGEMENT COMBINES THE ORGANIZATION'S RESOURCES INTO A PRODUCTIVE SYSTEM

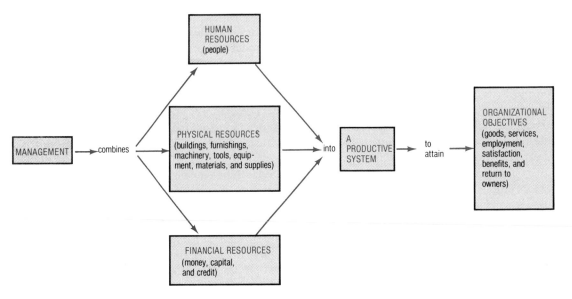

In large organizations, there are usually at least four levels of management. These levels are usually referred to as (1) the chief executive officer (CEO), (2) top management, (3) middle management, and (4) supervisory management. In larger organizations, there are many more levels.

Notice in Figure 1–2 that there are at least four levels of management at the Ciba-Geigy plant, not including others at the corporate level.

Figure 1–4 shows that authority and responsibility, as well as titles and designations, increase as one moves into the managerial ranks and then into the higher managerial levels. The titles and designations shown are only a few of those actually used in organizations.

While the duties and responsibilities of the various management levels vary from one organization to another, they may be summarized as follows: the **chief executive officer (CEO)** is responsible for the overall operations of the entire organization; **top management** is responsible for a major segment of the organization, or a basic organizational activity; **middle management** is

FIGURE 1–4   HOW MANAGEMENT AUTHORITY AND RESPONSIBILITY
INCREASE AT HIGHER LEVELS

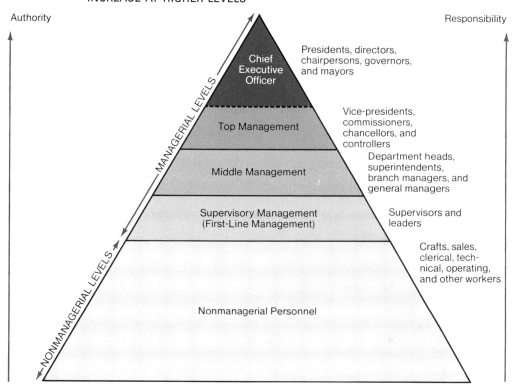

responsible for a substantial part of the organization (perhaps a program, project, division, plant, or department); and **supervisory management** has control over the operations of smaller organizational units (such as a production line, operating unit, office, or laboratory). Managers in this last group are in charge of other managers, supervisors, and nonmanagerial, or rank-and-file, employees. They are the "managers" that most employees are able to relate to, as shown in the following example.

Bob Malone, the administrator of a large hospital, and Peter Chen were college classmates who remained close friends after graduating. Peter's son Billy enrolled at a college near Bob's hospital. He and his father were guests in Bob's home for a couple of days while Billy moved into a dormitory and got a part-time job at Bob's hospital.

During Billy's first visit home, his father asked, "How's Bob Malone?" Billy replied, "I never see him. The only manager I ever see is the head nurse."

Did you notice in Figure 1–2 that Bill Morrow supervises other "supervisors," "foremen," and nonmanagerial professional and clerical employees? And notice that Billy Chen referred to the head nurse as his "manager," and perceived the administrator of the hospital as a manager, too.

Another difference between managers at different levels is the amount of time they spend carrying out various activities. Figure 1–5 shows how one group of managers of an electrical appliance manufacturer spend their time. The terms and titles used are different from those used in this text, but the figure does illustrate the point that the importance of the activities differs according to managerial level.

Notice that the manufacturer's supervisory managers spend around 70 percent of their time working with people. Compare that with Bill Morrow's estimate of the importance of people under his supervision at Ciba-Geigy.

Did you notice in Figure 1–5 that the president and group executives spend the greatest percentage of their time "thinking ahead" and "doing work which cannot be delegated," while "working with people on lower levels" took most of the time of supervisory managers? Do you think this allocation of time is logical and reasonable? Why?

This book deals primarily with the bottom group of managers, who may be called supervisory managers or simply supervisors.

WHAT DO MANAGERS DO?

It is now time to see what managers do that makes them so needed. There are two ways of doing this. First, we will show what the functions of management are. Then we will look at some roles managers play. It should be noted at this point, however, that not all managers spend the same amount of time performing each management function or playing each role.

FIGURE 1–5   HOW MANAGERS SPEND THEIR TIME

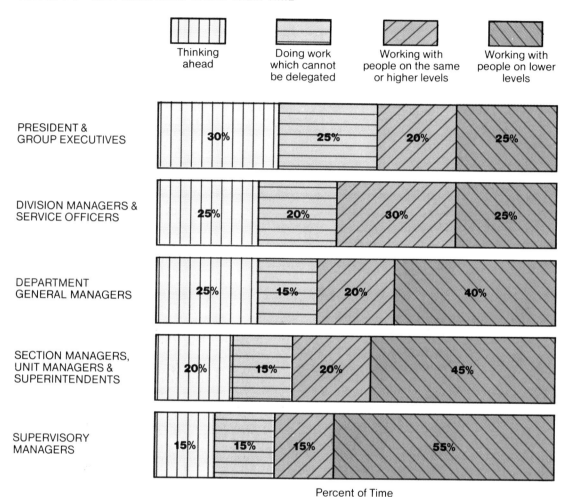

Percent of Time

Source: Based on a 1974 study of executives of an electrical appliance manufacturer, which asked to remain anonymous.

Functions Performed by Managers

Managerial functions are the acts or operations expected of a manager in a given situation. There is no single generally accepted classification of the functions of management. However, we believe that there are at least five separate, but inter-related, basic functions that must be performed by any manager at any level in any organization. Successful managers—whether at the top, middle, or supervisory level—perform these functions efficiently and effectively; unsuccessful ones do not. The functions are

1. Planning.
2. Organizing.
3. Staffing.
4. Leading.
5. Controlling.

PLANNING. The **planning** function means thinking ahead. It involves selecting future courses of action for the organization as a whole and for each of its subunits and deciding how to achieve the desired results. It also involves gathering and analyzing information in order to make these decisions. Through planning, goals and objectives are established and methods of attaining them are determined. All other basic managerial functions depend on planning, because it is unlikely that they will be successfully carried out without sound and continuous planning. Chapters 2 and 3 are devoted to some of the more important aspects of planning.

What happens to managers' need to plan (thinking ahead) as they move up in an organization, as illustrated in Figure 1–5? Why does this happen?

ORGANIZING. Deciding what activities are needed to reach goals and objectives, dividing human resources into work groups, and assigning each group to a manager are the tasks that make up the **organizing** function. Another aspect of organizing is bringing together the physical, financial, and human resources needed to achieve the organization's objectives. More will be said about the organizing function in Chapters 4 and 5.

STAFFING. The process of recruiting, selecting, training and developing, promoting, and paying and rewarding people to do the organization's work is called **staffing**. Laying off and terminating employees are also included. This basic managerial function is sometimes regarded as a part of the organizing function, but we think it is important enough to be considered separately. Chapters 10 through 14 will elaborate on this function.

LEADING. The **leading** function involves directing, guiding, and supervising subordinates in the performance of their duties and responsibilities. It consists of exercising leadership; communicating ideas, orders, and instructions; and motivating employees to perform their work effectively and efficiently. Some authorities refer to it as the "people" function of management. As shown in Figure 1–5 on page 11, middle managers and supervisory managers are more heavily involved in leading than are top managers. Chapters 6 through 9 provide more details about this function.

CONTROLLING. The **controlling** function involves comparing actual performance with planned performance and taking corrective action, if needed, to ensure that objectives are achieved. Control can be achieved only by setting up standards of performance in advance, checking to see whether they have been achieved, and then doing what is necessary to bring actual performance in line with planned performance. The successful execution of this function is needed to make certain that the other management functions are efficiently and effectively performed. Chapters 15, 16, and 17 deal with various aspects of this function.

HOW THE FUNCTIONS ARE RELATED. We should emphasize that the management functions are basically the same in different types of organizations and at different management levels. But while all of them must be performed by all managers, the functions may be performed in a different way and be given different emphases by various managers. One or more functions may be emphasized more than others when performed at different levels. For example, planning is done more by top management. Leading is more common among supervisory managers. And controlling seems to be the job chiefly of middle managers. Yet the functions are interrelated, interacting, and interdependent, as shown in Figure 1–6. While they *may* be performed in any order, they tend to be performed in the sequence shown by the lines and numbers shown in the figure.

Roles Played by Managers

Another way to explain what management is and why it is so important is to explore the different roles played by managers in performing the management functions. The discussion of these functions might lead you to believe that the manager's job is orderly, well-organized, systematic, and harmonious. But this is just not so. Instead, in performing these functions, managers engage in a great many varied, disorganized, fragmented, and often unrelated activities. Also, these activities may last for only a very short time or may take much longer periods.

In carrying out these activities, managers play **roles** as if they were actors, and those roles change quickly and frequently. Ten of these managerial roles have been identified and defined. These specific roles can be classified into three groups: (1) interpersonal roles, (2) informational roles, and (3) decision-making roles. Table 1–1 shows how the roles are grouped, describes what each one involves, and gives an example of each.

FIGURE 1–6   HOW THE MANAGEMENT FUNCTIONS ARE RELATED

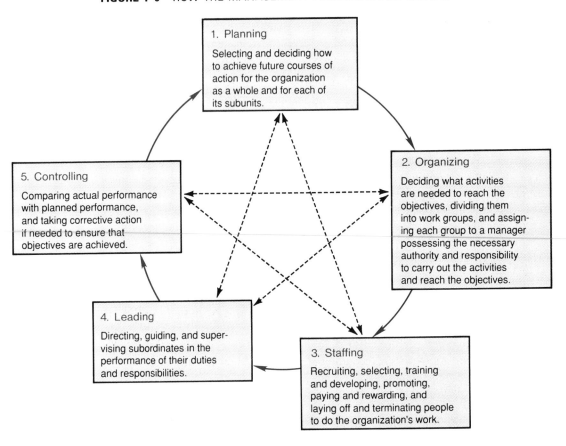

TABLE 1–1   ROLES PLAYED BY MANAGERS

Role	What Is Involved	Examples
INTERPERSONAL ROLES		
Figurehead	Representing the organization as its symbolic head.	Serving on public boards and charitable groups; attending public ceremonies.
Leader	Helping people achieve organizational and personal goals.	Leading, guiding, directing motivating, and evaluating employees.
Liaison	Maintaining relationships between the organization and outsiders in order to increase its knowledge and benefits.	Attending conferences and business-related meetings; developing contacts with helpful outsiders.

TABLE 1–1   (continued)

Role	What Is Involved	Examples
INFORMATIONAL ROLES		
Monitor	Seeking beneficial information about and for the organization which is especially relevant to developing trends, ideas, and government actions.	Reading trade journals and related publications; taking outside trips; entertaining visitors and groups.
Disseminator	Providing pertinent information to appropriate organization members.	Routing articles, reports, and periodicals; sending letters and memos to employees.
Spokesperson	Representing subordinates to superiors and vice versa, and representing the organization to outsiders and groups.	Speaking to professional and trade groups; appearing as an expert witness before various groups.
DECISION-MAKING ROLES		
Entrepreneur	Conceiving and initiating new opportunities and introducing systematic change into the organization—especially for growth.	Helping develop new products or programs; encouraging research and development; encouraging others to take calculated risks.
Disturbance Handler	Solving or resolving interorganizational or interpersonal conflicts or destructive competition.	Helping resolve employee complaints or grievances; trying to resolved "personality conflicts" among organization members.
Resource Allocator	Allocating the organization's scarce resources and setting priorities.	Helping prepare budgets; deciding which machines and equipment to replace; making retirement decisions.
Negotiator	Representing the organization in negotiations with individuals or groups.	Helping negotiate union contracts; arranging terms of stock issues.

Source: Adapted from *The Nature of Managerial Work* by Henry Mintzberg. Copyright 1973 by Henry Mintzberg. Reprinted by permission of Harper & Row Publishers, Inc.

Like managerial functions, these roles are given varying emphasis by managers in various organizations and at different levels in the same organization. The roles vary in the length of time they take to play and in their importance to each manager and different managers may interpret them differently—but the roles must be played.[1]

BASIC SKILLS REQUIRED OF MANAGERS

You are probably wondering at this point what basic skills managers need in order to perform the managerial functions and play the managerial roles most effectively. While many skills are needed, a few of the most common ones are

1. Conceptual skills.
2. Human relations skills.
3. Administrative skills.
4. Technical skills.

The relative importance of these skills varies according to the type of industry the managers are in, the organization to which they belong, their level in the managerial ranks, the job being performed, and the employees being managed.

Conceptual Skills

Conceptual skills involve the ability to acquire, analyze, and interpret information in a logical manner. Managers need to understand the internal and external environments in which they operate. They also need to understand the effects of changes in one or more of these environments on the organization for which they work. Another way of putting this thought is that managers should be able to "see the big picture." Top managers particularly need strong conceptual skills, because changes affecting the organization tend to be more important at their level than at the middle and supervisory levels of management. Well over a third of their time is spent using these skills.

Human-Relations Skills

Human-relations skills consist of the ability to understand other people and to interact effectively with them. These skills are most needed in performing the leading function because they involve communicating with, motivating, and leading employees, as well as relating to other people. These skills are important in dealing not only with individuals, but also with people in groups and even with the relationship of groups to one another. These skills are important to managers at all levels, especially to supervisory managers, who spend about 45 percent of their time using these skills.

Administrative Skills

Administrative skills are those that permit managers at all levels to use the other skills effectively in performing the managerial functions. These skills include the ability to establish and follow policies and procedures and to process paperwork in an orderly manner. In fact, the terms *coordination*, *order*, and *movement* are quite useful in helping us to understand what these skills are used for. These skills entail the ability some people have to "make things happen" and to "get things done." Around 15 percent of all managers' time is spent using these skills.

In summary, managers use the conceptual skills to make decisions, the human-relations skills to get people to carry out the decisions, and the administrative skills to assure that the decisions are carried out correctly.

Technical Skills

Technical skills include understanding and being able to supervise effectively the specific processes, practices, or techniques required of specific jobs in the company. Top managers should possess sufficient technical skills to keep their companies competitive, but supervisory managers should have enough of these skills to see that day-to-day operations are performed effectively. These skills are relatively more important for supervisors than for top managers, since supervisors are closer to the actual work being performed. They must often tell—or even show—employees how to perform the job, as well as know when it is done properly. Around a third of their time is devoted to activities involving these skills.

For example, the owner-manager (or another manager) of a men's clothing store would need the technical skills required to select the appropriate clothing styles, fabrics, and details. These skills may be obtained through experience as a buyer of men's clothing. On the other hand, supervisors would need such technical skills as the ability to program a computer, operate a machine (such as a lathe, typewriter, or printing press), or prepare financial statements.

A word of caution is needed here. Do not assume that an operative employee who is highly skilled and who has been able to perform technical jobs also has the requirements and characteristics to become an effective supervisor or manager. This is an invalid assumption because a *good producer is not necessarily a good supervisor or executive*.

To what extent do you think Bill Morrow needs each of these four kinds of skills? Does he appear to be using them properly?

THE CHANGING ROLE OF SUPERVISORS

Now let us concentrate on the supervisor's place in management and see how the role of supervisors has changed. At one time, supervisors had autocratic power over subordinates. Figure 1–7 shows that employees at that time either produced efficiently or were fired. The new concept today is one of *leading* rather than driving. In essence, it is a compromise between exercising too much authority and being a "rubber stamp" for higher managers. Yet the supervisor's goal is still the same—getting out production, maintaining quality, holding down costs,

FIGURE 1–7   SUPERVISORS ONCE HAD AUTOCRATIC POWER

We have a great incentive program here...

One mistake and you're fired.

maintaining high morale, and otherwise serving as management's representative as well as a spokesperson for employees. Although the knowledge required to perform most jobs has greatly increased and the methods used are different, the central objective has remained the same—obtaining quality and quantity production while maintaining "good human relationships."

Historical Downgrading of the Supervisor's Position

Until about 100 years ago, "lead men" and "foremen" were essentially subcontractors acting as agents between the owner of a business and the workers. As such, they listened to what workers had to say, used the workers' ideas, and focused on problem solving. But, as an unwanted result of increasing corporate size and power, these supervisors became more powerful and autocratic. They had complete authority to hire and fire workers on the basis of personal bias. They could determine work loads and product quality, schedule work, set wages and production quotas, and otherwise be "a law unto themselves."

Then their position began to change as many of their duties were shifted to personnel departments. Technical and professional jobs replaced blue-collar jobs. Union leaders and government authorities became the workers' advocates. Technological developments required higher-level qualifications for employees and their supervisors. Consequently, supervisors found themselves with reduced authority and changed responsibilities. They suffered a relative decline in their position because, at the same time, subordinates' positions were improving as a result of increasing employee rights.

Present Improved Position of the Supervisory Manager

Experts agree that the role of supervisory management is drastically changing. This thought was expressed by Barry Stein, president of a consulting firm, when he said that supervisors aren't going to control people any more. Instead, they have to "coach them, help do the planning, approve organizational direction, and make sure the directions are clear. It will be an enabling function rather than a control function."[2] We think, though, that supervisors must do both "enabling" and "controlling" if they are to be effective.

Today supervisors are viewed as **intermediaries**, or go-betweens, acting as mediators between their employees and higher levels of management. According to this concept, supervisors stand between and among groups and have a feeling of both belonging and not belonging to those groups. Thus, supervisors are caught between having to report to their superiors and at the same time being representatives of management in relations with subordinates. Therefore, supervisors are transmitters of decisions made by superiors, but they also have authority for making recommendations to those managers.

To what extent does this description fit Bill Morrow?

SUPERVISORY RELATIONSHIPS

If we are to understand the role of supervisory managers in organizations, we must understand some of the relationships they have with different groups. Any study of the supervisory position must recognize that there are separate sets of interactions and interrelationships that are potential sources of several problems. For example, supervisors are legally a part of management and interact upward with other members of management. But they are not accepted as peers by those managers, who usually have more education, come from outside the organization, and have high social status and position. At the same time, supervisors are typically promoted from among the subordinates they supervise but with whom they formerly worked as peers.

There are three major types of relationships that require supervisors to play different and demanding roles, as shown in Figure 1–8. These are personal relationships, organizational relationships, and external relationships.

Personal Relationships

At one time it was believed that managers, as well as other employees, left their personal problems at home when they entered the workplace. We now know this

FIGURE 1–8 THE SUPERVISOR'S RELATIONSHIPS

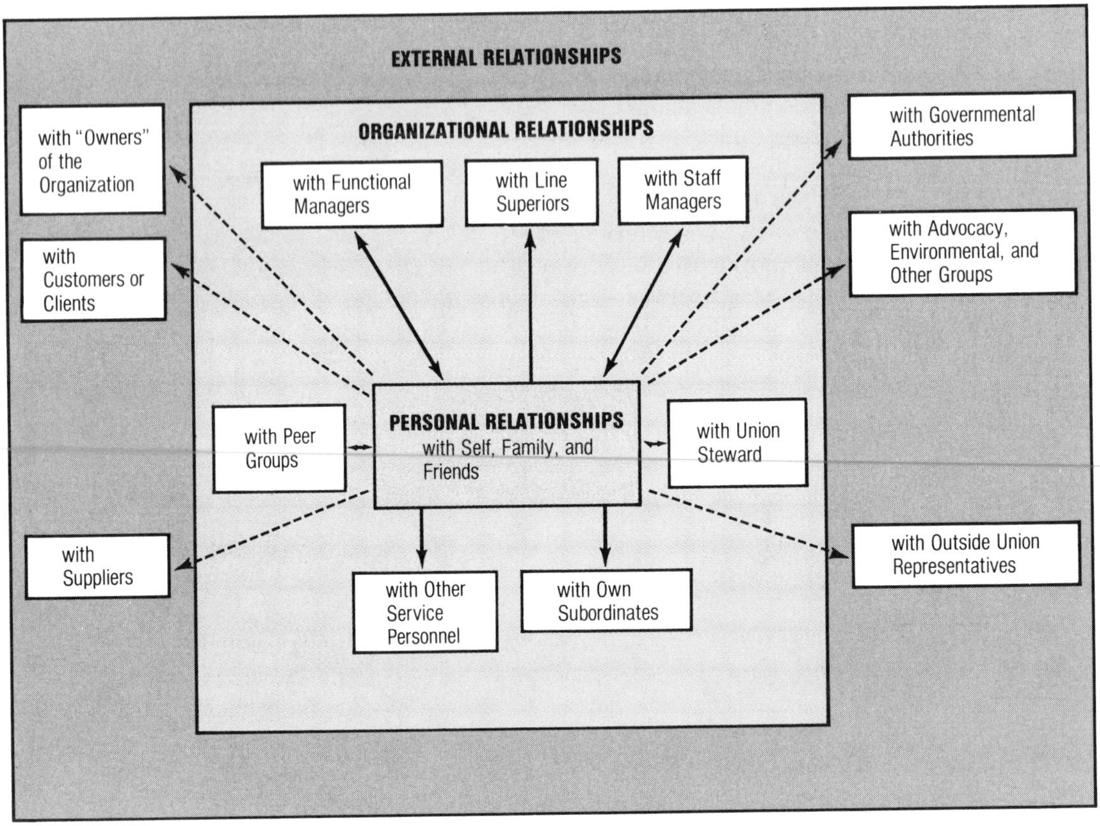

EXTERNAL RELATIONSHIPS

ORGANIZATIONAL RELATIONSHIPS

with "Owners" of the Organization

with Customers or Clients

with Suppliers

with Functional Managers

with Line Superiors

with Staff Managers

with Peer Groups

PERSONAL RELATIONSHIPS
with Self, Family, and Friends

with Union Steward

with Other Service Personnel

with Own Subordinates

with Governmental Authorities

with Advocacy, Environmental, and Other Groups

with Outside Union Representatives

is not so because people bring their troubles—and pleasures—to their jobs. These relationships that supervisors have with themselves, with their families, and with friends determine their attitudes and frame of mind as they perform managerial duties. Their attitudes, in turn, influence the relationships they have with other people, both inside and outside the organization.

Organizational Relationships

Within the organization, supervisory managers have many varied and often conflicting relationships. The flow of these relationships takes three directions: from superior to subordinate, horizontal (or between peers), and from subordinate to superior.

SUPERIOR-TO-SUBORDINATE RELATIONSHIPS. Supervisory managers must relate to their own employees and with people from other units who perform some type of service for them. As Figure 1–9 illustrates, a superior-subordinate rela-

FIGURE 1–9   THE SUPERVISOR-SUBORDINATE RELATIONSHIP

tionship exists where the supervisor is the "boss" over nonmanagerial personnel. It provides a sense of importance.

HORIZONTAL RELATIONSHIPS. There are essentially two sets of horizontal relationships: those with other supervisory managers and those with the union steward or other representative(s) of the employees. Supervisors need the feeling of support and reinforcement that comes from associating with fellow supervisors (see Figure 1–10), who are considered their equals, or peers. Yet the relationship can result in competition or even conflict if they seek to be promoted to the same job at the next higher level.

FIGURE 1–10   THE SUPERVISOR WITH PEERS

While the union steward is a supervisory manager's peer—legally, if not organizationally—the union steward represents the supervisor's subordinates. Therefore, the association between the supervisory manager and the union steward may be competitive, or even conflicting. This association provides supervisors with a challenge but can also be frustrating. For example, a supervisor will probably attempt to motivate employees to improve productivity, while a union steward may encourage them not to perform better for fear of losing their jobs.

SUBORDINATE-TO-SUPERIOR RELATIONSHIPS. Supervisors also have a *reverse* superior-subordinate relationship with managers at higher levels, as you can see from Figure 1–11. This is a position where the supervisors are subordinate to, must take orders from, and are accountable to their "boss." Also, staff executives in other departments, such as legal and research, tell supervisors what to do. Functional executives, such as the controller and personnel director, tell supervisors how to handle certain activities. In this association, supervisors are the subordinates. They must support and reinforce their superiors.

External Relationships

Supervisory managers must also deal with people outside the organization. Some of the people who must be served or catered to are the owners of the business, customers or clients, suppliers, union representatives, governmental authorities, and leaders of environmental and advocacy groups. These relationships can be quite difficult and frustrating for supervisors who represent their organizations but usually do not have the authority needed to make demands and enforce them (see Figure 1–12).

FIGURE 1–11   THE SUBORDINATE-SUPERIOR RELATIONSHIP

FIGURE 1–12   EXTERNAL RELATIONSHIPS CAN BE DIFFICULT

CHAPTER REVIEW

Management is needed wherever people form and operate in organizations. An organization is a group of people in a structured situation with a common purpose. People form organizations because they realize that they can achieve more by working together than they can alone.

Management is the art of working through people to achieve objectives through effective decision making and by coordinating the development and use of scarce human, financial, and physical resources. There are usually at least four levels of management in large organizations. The CEO is responsible for the total organization; top management is responsible for a major segment of the organization or one of the basic organizational activities; middle management is responsible for a smaller part, such as a division or department; and supervisory management oversees and controls smaller organizational units. Yet all these managers perform the same functions; namely, planning, organizing, staffing, leading, and controlling.

In performing these functions, managers engage in many varied and often unrelated activities that require them to play different roles. In playing the inter-personal roles, a manager may act as a figurehead, as a leader, or as the liaison between different groups. The manager also plays informational roles by being a monitor, disseminator, and spokesperson. Finally, the decision-making roles require the manager to be an entrepreneur, disturbance handler, resource alloca-tor, and negotiator.

Effective managers need different skills in order to perform their functions and play their roles. Conceptual skills require acquiring, interpreting, and analyzing information in a logical manner. Human-relations skills involve understanding other people and interacting effectively with them. Administrative skills provide the ability to get things done by using other skills effectively. Technical skills consist of understanding and being able to perform the processes, practices, or techniques required by specific jobs in the organization.

The concept of supervision has changed from that of foremen having autocratic power over subordinates to that of supervisors leading people to be more productive. Until about 100 years ago, supervisors were essentially subcontractors who tended to understand and relate to workers. Then, with growing corporate size and power, supervisors gained almost complete authority over their units. Now they are considered intermediaries between their subordinates and higher levels of management.

Supervisory managers are involved in at least three sets of relationships. First, they have personal relationships with themselves, their families, and their friends. Second, they have conflicting organizational relationships with lower-level employees, with fellow supervisors, and with higher levels of management. Third, they have external relationships with outsiders such as business owners, customers or clients, suppliers, union representatives, governmental authorities, and leaders of environmental and advocacy groups.

QUESTIONS FOR REVIEW AND DISCUSSION

1. Why is management needed in organizations?
2. Why do people form organizations?
3. How would you define these terms?
   a. organization
   b. management
   c. planning
   d. organizing
   e. staffing
   f. leading
   g. controlling
   h. conceptual skills
   i. human-relations skills
   j. administrative skills
   k. technical skills
4. What are the four levels of management found in large organizations? Describe each, giving its responsibilities.
5. What are some of the roles that managers play?
6. What are the skills needed by managers? Describe each.
7. What are the three types of supervisory relationships? Explain.
8. Trace the changing concepts of supervision. Why did these changes occur?

LEARNING EXERCISE 1–1
THE YOUNG SUPERVISORS

Roberta Bradley, Frances Friedmann, and James Jacinto were first-line supervisors for the Computer Software Company (CSC). They had been hired as technicians in different departments and had only recently been promoted to supervisory positions. Now they were attending a supervisory development program conducted by Southern State University.

After dinner on the first day of the course, they were discussing some of the points made by the professors and comparing the ideas with their own experiences at CSC. The professors had asked such questions as: "What factors distinguish managers from nonmanagers?"; "What do you hope to achieve as a supervisor?"; and "What are you doing to train and develop your own people?"

The three supervisors were quite impressed with one professor's conclusion that, "While many individuals have the title of 'manager,' they are in fact doers, not managers. Sometimes these people are so insecure that they just can't 'turn loose' and let employees do their jobs properly."

This statement led Roberta to say that when she was a technician, her supervisor did not delegate enough authority to her and the other employees. Instead, the supervisor had told them that he intentionally kept close control over the activities of the unit in order not to be replaced. The supervisor seemed to be afraid that the subordinates would become so knowledgeable that his boss, the general manager, would want to replace him with one of them.

Frances and James recalled that they had had similar experiences with their supervisors.

Answer the following questions:

1. What does this exercise show about the difficulty some managers have in delegating authority?
2. What does it show about the progression up the management ladder?

LEARNING EXERCISE 1–2
EFFECTIVE AND INEFFECTIVE SUPERVISORS

Think of all the supervisors for whom you've worked—part-time or full-time. If you have not worked for a supervisor, try to observe one in action in some organization, or consider a teacher or parent instead. Try to pick out the one who was *most effective* as a supervisor. Then try to (1) list the reasons why he or she was effective, and (2) make a list of the qualities that led to the effective performance. Do the same things for the *least effective* supervisor you can think of.

ENDNOTES

1. For more details, see Henry Mintzberg, "The Manager's Job," *Harvard Business Review* 53 (July–August 1975): 49–61.
2. "The Old Foreman Is on the Way Out, and the New One Will Be More Important," *Business Week*, April 25, 1983, pp. 74–75.

SUGGESTIONS FOR FURTHER READING

Child, John, and Bruce Partridge. *Lost Managers: Supervisors in Industry and Society*. Cambridge, England: Cambridge University Press, 1982.

Drucker, Peter. "Management: The Problems of Success." *Academy of Management Executive* 1 (February 1987): 13–18.

Johnston, R. W. "What You Need to Know to Be a Supervisor." *Supervisory Management* 28 (March 1983): 35–42.

LaForge, R. Lawrence, and Lester R. Bittel. "A Survey of Production Management Supervisors." *Production and Inventory Management* 24 (Fourth Quarter 1983): 99–112.

Lippert, F. G. "Responsibilities of a Supervisor: On the Level?" *Supervision* 45 (March 1983): 16–17.

Pearce, John A. II. "Problems Facing First-Time Managers." *Human Resource Management* 21 (Spring, 1982): 35-38.

Teas, R. K. "Supervisory Behavior, Role Stress, and the Job Satisfaction of Industrial Salespeople." *Journal of Marketing Research* 20 (February 1983): 84–91.

Whitely, William. "Managerial Work Behavior: An Integration of Results from Two Major Approaches." *Academy of Management Journal* 28 (June 1985): 344–62.

Williams, Harry E. "The Elements of Supervision." *Supervision* 43 (May 1981): 3–6.

Part I

PLANNING

2
FUNDAMENTALS
OF PLANNING

OBJECTIVES

After reading and studying the material in this chapter, you should be able to:

- Explain some important points about planning.
- Discuss why supervisory managers tend to slight the planning function.
- Explain how planning differs at top, middle, and supervisory management levels.
- Discuss the important guidelines in setting performance objectives.
- Identify the five steps used in management by objectives (MBO).
- Differentiate among policies, procedures, and rules.

IMPORTANT TERMS

"Siamese twins" of management
contingency planning
objectives
goals
hierarchy of objectives
unified planning
performance objectives
management by objectives (MBO)

standing plans *or* repeat-use plans
policy
rules
procedure
single-use plans
program
project
budget

CHAPTER OUTLINE
CASE 2–1. CHANGES AT DIXON

I. SOME IMPORTANT POINTS ABOUT PLANNING
    A. Planning precedes other management functions
    B. Planning is most closely related to controlling
    C. Avoid the tendency to slight planning
    D. Contingency planning anticipates problems

II. PLANNING AT DIFFERENT MANAGEMENT LEVELS

III. IMPORTANCE OF SETTING OBJECTIVES
    A. What are objectives?
    B. Objectives as a stimulus for motivation and effort
    C. Hierarchy of objectives
    D. Objectives permit unified planning
    E. Guidelines for setting performance objectives

IV. THE SUPERVISOR AND MBO
    A. Steps in MBO
        1. Step 1. Discussing the supervisor's responsibilities and objectives
        2. Step 2. Discussing the employee's job
        3. Step 3. Setting objectives jointly
        4. Step 4. Reviewing progress periodically
        5. Step 5. Reviewing end-of-period performance
    B. Advantages of MBO
    C. Disadvantages of MBO

V. TYPES OF PLANS
    A. Standing plans
        1. Policies
        2. Rules
        3. Procedures
    B. Single-use plans
        1. Programs
        2. Projects
        3. Budgets

Chapter Review

Questions for Review and Discussion

Learning Exercise 2–1. Setting Performance Objectives

Learning Exercise 2–2. Differing Perceptions of Priorities

Learning Exercise 2–3. MBO Role Play

Suggestions for Further Reading

CASE 2-1
CHANGES AT DIXON

Harold Marshall, newly promoted plant manager of the Dixon Plant of Computronix, Inc., was addressing a meeting of the plant's 35 department heads, superintendents, and supervisors. The Dixon Plant was one of the oldest in the Computronix system and one of the least cost-effective. In fact, there were rumors that it would gradually be phased out of operation.

For most people at the meeting, it was the first time they had seen Marshall, although his reputation had preceded him. At age 32, he had gained widespread exposure as plant manager of the company's "experimental" plant in Fresno, California. That plant utilized totally new technology and many radically innovative management techniques. Marshall began:

Ladies and gentlemen, it's good to meet many of you for the first time. We are faced with an important challenge—to increase the efficiency of this plant—and it's going to take dedication and commitment. I've promised Mr. Alexander [the vice-president] that I'll give it my all, and together we can show progress that will make top management commit itself to capital spending which will again make our plant the top producer in the company.

If we're going to improve, our management system must change drastically. At Dixon, as well as at most other plants in our system, we have been practicing "defensive" management. That is, we react to problems *when* or *after* they occur. We've been good at doing that. But to be effective today, we must become far better at planning our future—setting goals and objectives, developing ways to reach them, and making sure we get there. Our industry cannot fly by the seat of its pants as we've done in the past. Each and every one of us is going to have to become adept at planning—for the plant, for each department, and for each work unit. This is especially true of our supervisory level, for that is where the rubber meets the road, so to speak. In the past, top management has done most of your planning for you—in fact, we're the ones responsible for your becoming "fire fighters." Things will have to change. Under the new system, you will have a major planning role in the plant—developing departmental and work unit plans that will result in fewer and smaller fires. Better planning must be done at all of our management levels.

Marshall's talk went on for 15 minutes on topics such as objectives, delegation, communication, and the need for all employees to feel that they were an important part of the Dixon team.

We wish Marshall well in his attempts to turn the Dixon Plant around. Note the important emphasis he placed on effective planning. He is quite correct in his assessment of the role of supervisory management. Indeed, many of the managers do see their jobs as being strictly "fire fighting"—handling first this problem, then another, and then another. But he's also correct in his view that supervisors today must become more proficient at planning—perhaps the most neglected function of management—regardless of the management level.

This chapter builds on the ideas presented in Chapter 1. There, the need for management, what it is, the managerial functions performed by managers, the skills they need, and the changing role of supervisory management were discussed. We now focus on one of these management functions—planning—for greater emphasis.

SOME IMPORTANT POINTS ABOUT PLANNING

As stated in Chapter 1, planning means deciding what will be done in the future. It's forward-looking. Because of this, it takes a lot of discipline for a manager to take the time needed to solve present problems and to plan for the future. Moreover, much planning is intellectual; it is a "between the ears" activity that is hard work. Do you recall the conceptual, human-relations, administrative, and technical skills used by managers that were discussed in Chapter 1? Planning is normally an example of the conceptual skills needed by managers. But it also requires use of the other skills, especially in getting the plans adopted and implemented.

Planning Precedes Other Management Functions

Ideally, planning should precede a supervisor's performance of the other management functions of organizing, leading, staffing, and controlling. For this reason, it is called the *primary* function of management. Let's see how this works:

Charlene Romero, department manager at a large retail department store, just learned in a managers' meeting that the store is planning a huge special weekend sale in four weeks. Charlene's department consists of eight full-time and six part-time sales personnel. An average of six persons work in the department at a given time.

Because of the strong advertising and sales promotion to be used, record crowds are expected. Charlene's boss indicated that department heads should plan to staff at average strength plus 50 percent, which in Charlene's case would be a total of nine employees working in the department at all times during the sale.

Charlene is asking herself these questions: Whom should she select to work? How should she proceed in making the choices? What if fewer than nine people want to work?

As Charlene ponders and seeks out answers to these questions, she is doing managerial *planning*. However, when she considers having a proper mix of full-time and part-time people, as well as veteran and less experienced personnel, she is doing managerial *organizing*. When she selected the sales personnel and oriented them to their job, she was performing the *staffing* function. When she actually discusses with each person what his or her work schedule will be, she will perform the managerial function of *leading*. And when she takes steps to assure that the nine people selected will be on hand, she will perform managerial *control*. But note how *planning* precedes the other managerial functions.

Planning Is Most Closely Related to Controlling

Of the various managerial functions, planning is probably most closely related to controlling. As you will see in more detail in Chapter 15, the steps in controlling are

1. Setting performance goals, or norms.
2. Measuring performance.
3. Comparing performance with goals.
4. Analyzing results.
5. Taking corrective action as needed.

Carefully note the first step in the controlling process. It is planning! Because planning is such an integral part of controlling, these two functions are sometimes called the **"Siamese twins" of management**.

Avoid the Tendency to Slight Planning

Poor planning often results in activities that are disorganized and uncoordinated, thus wasting time, manpower, and money. Since thinking is often more difficult than doing, many managers, including supervisors, tend to slight planning. It is very tempting to forego thinking about the future in order to get busy performing a task or solving present work problems. The result is frequently unsatisfactory, as shown in Figure 2–1.

Just as Harold Marshall, the new Dixon plant manager in Case 2–1, pointed out, it's not unusual at all for a supervisor to spend his or her day "fighting one fire after another"—seemingly never caught up. Consider the following example:

Hank Green, a supervisor, had a hectic schedule and was about to be driven up a wall. He said: "Today I had three no-shows because of the weather, and my department is absolutely swamped. I'm pitching in myself, but I've

FIGURE 2–1   LACK OF PLANNING

also got to conduct a plant tour for some of our home office staff personnel after lunch. I'm supposed to meet with our industrial relations people on a case that goes to arbitration next week. To cap it off, Barbara Brown wants a transfer out of the department and wants to talk about it today. She and two of the other workers can't get along. This afternoon, I've got to have those figures ready for the cost accounting department. On top of all this, I'm supposed to supervise my 19 people, three of whom are new hires and being broken in. What a day! But they all seem to be like this."

Is it any wonder that this supervisor would forego planning if his typical daily schedule is so demanding? Perhaps not. But, ironically, many of the short-run crises that confront supervisors can be greatly eased by proper planning. As shown in Figure 2–2, when a supervisor devotes too little time to planning, the result is any number of short-run problems—including such things as impossible deadlines, unforeseen obstacles, crises, and crash programs. These problems preoccupy the supervisor, leaving little time to devote to planning—and the cycle goes on.

Contingency Planning Anticipates Problems

It is important for a supervisor to remain flexible by having contingency plans. **Contingency planning** means thinking in advance of problems or changes that may arise so that we are prepared to deal with them smoothly when they do arise. Consider the following examples:

When the X-ray unit in the radiology department went down, Nurse Ratchett knew exactly whom to contact and how to divert patients to the X-ray machine in the hospital's emergency room.

FIGURE 2–2 THE NONPLANNER'S CYCLE

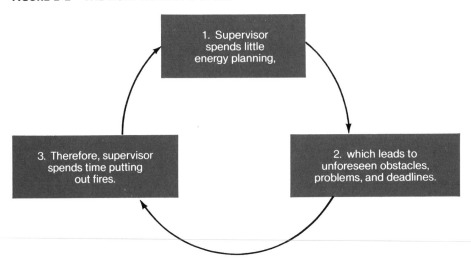

Charlie Fay had been trained as a backup forklift operator three weeks ago. While not the expert Willie Burns is, Fay performed smoothly on the forklift when Burns was absent twice in one week.

Contingency planning separates effective managers from ineffective ones. The proper anticipation of a crisis may prevent it from happening. You will need to ask yourself the following questions and find answers to them if you are to be a good contingency planner:

1. What events might happen that are likely to cause problems within my department?
2. What can I do to prevent these events from happening?
3. If these events do occur, what should I do to minimize their effect?
4. Have similar situations occurred in the past? If so, how were they handled?

What are some examples of contingency planning that Charlene Romero can perform regarding the personnel schedule for her department during the big store sale?

PLANNING AT DIFFERENT MANAGEMENT LEVELS

As shown in Table 2–1, middle- and lower-level managers plan on a different scale than top managers. Their planning deals with shorter time frames. Also,

TABLE 2–1 PLANNING AT THREE MANAGEMENT LEVELS

Level	Planning Period	What is Planned for
Top managers	Strategic long-term and inter-mediate-range plans of 1 to 5 or more years	Growth rate Competitive strategies New products Capital investments
Middle managers	Intermediate- and short-range plans of 1 month to 1 year	How to improve scheduling and coordination How to exercise better control at lower levels
Supervisors	Short-range plans of 1 day, 1 week, 1 to 6 months	How to implement new poli-cies, work methods, and work assignments How to accomplish perfor-mance objectives How to increase efficiency (in costs, quality, etc.)

the activity planned for by these supervisory managers is narrower in scope than that planned for at higher levels. As one first-line manager related:

Planning? Sure, I spend time planning. But most of my department's goals, objectives, and schedules are handed down to me from others. My planning is more along the lines of, How can I get better performance in my department? How can I cut down turnover and absenteeism? Given my department's workload for the week, or for the day, what's the best way to attack it? Whom should I assign to various jobs? Take last week, for example. Four of my people were out – two sick and two on vacation – and I had a lot of planning to do figuring who'd work where and when. Things seemed to go a lot more smoothly because I'd put in some time anticipating the problems. I've learned to plan on a few people always being "sick" on the opening day of the hunting season!

As you can see, all managers need to plan, regardless of their position in the hierarchy. While planning at the supervisory level is generally less complex and involves less uncertainty, it is still crucial that it be done effectively.

What are other examples of things that supervisory managers must plan for?

IMPORTANCE OF SETTING OBJECTIVES

Objectives are very important to effective planning. As implied in the opening quotation in this chapter, only if you first know where you are heading can you effectively plan to get there.

What Are Objectives?

Objectives tell you where you are going or what you want to do. They respond to the question, "What do I want to accomplish?" Objectives become the focus toward which plans are aimed.

Is there a difference between an "objective" and a "goal"? Most management experts think not, but some do differentiate between the two. We will not try to make a distinction. Since the terms **goal** and *objective* are often used interchangeably, we will treat them alike in this book.

Which objectives are you accomplishing by reading this book? Can you list several? Might they be different for other people?

Objectives as a Stimulus for Motivation and Effort

If you follow organized sports, you know that people who play them are very much involved in the game of "objectives." Baseball players strive to hit .300; basketball players, to average 20 points; and football quarterbacks, to average 50 percent pass completions. Others get into the same game, though. A weekend golfer steps up to the first tee with an 85 in mind (not on the first hole, but for the entire 18!). A Friday-night league bowler shoots for a 150 average. Just as these individuals in sports are motivated toward goals or objectives, so are people in the world of work.

Ann Casey really felt good. In her second week as a sales rep for Dover Apparel, she had sold over $12,000 worth of merchandise to retail stores in her southern Illinois territory. Her boss, too, was quite pleased. "We had set a goal for Ann of $15,000 for the entire month. She's likely to pass that next week, the way she's going. Ann's doing a great job."

Objectives provide a stimulus for worker motivation and effort; they give people something to strive for. If Ann had no set goal—if she simply planned to go out and sell—she'd have no benchmark to tell whether she was doing well or poorly.

Hierarchy of Objectives

In any organization, objectives are first needed at the top-management level. Once top management determines broad objectives or goals, other levels of the organization, including supervisory management levels, reflect these with objectives or goals of their own, thus creating a **hierarchy of objectives.** Figure 2–3 presents a hierarchy of objectives for Computronix, the firm described in Case 2–1.

Given Computronix's overall organizational objectives, the division objectives of the Dixon Plant are set at 50,000 production units within a budget of $214 million. At the department level, the various departments, such as production, maintenance, engineering, and purchasing, each have objectives that reflect the plant's objectives. Work units in each department will have objectives that reflect the department objectives. Finally, within each work unit, each worker will have job objectives that reflect the work unit's objectives. This illustrates in a simplified way how any organization achieves its objectives.

FIGURE 2–3   HIERARCHY OF OBJECTIVES FOR COMPUTRONIX

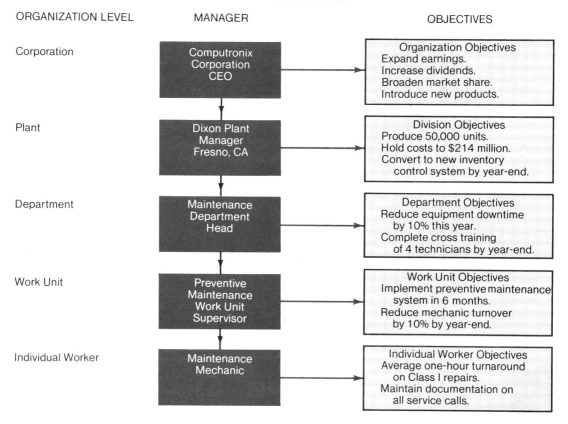

Objectives Permit Unified Planning

A major advantage of organizational objectives is that they give managers at lower levels guidance for developing their own plans and coordinating their own activities. Ideally, these plans at lower levels should have unity of purpose in accomplishing top management's objectives. **Unified planning** means that plans at all organizational levels should be in harmony, rather than at cross purposes, with one another. Unified planning is especially important where coordination among departments or work units is concerned. Many supervisors are extremely dependent on other departments in accomplishing their own objectives. As shown in the example below, lack of unified planning in the Dixon Plant (recall Case 2–1) has led to difficulties!

> *"This is ridiculous! Those #$%¢&* are trying to cut me down," stormed Fred Adkins, supervisor of the processing department at the Dixon Plant. The plant was under the gun to reach its monthly production quota, and Fred's department absorbed a lot of the pressure. Fred continued: "If we don't process quota, the plant doesn't make quota. It's as simple as that. But those jerks in maintenance are killing me. Last week, they were supposed to shut me down for PM [preventive maintenance]. But what happened? Absolutely nothing! They couldn't get to me because they were caught shorthanded. You tell me why they had to send three of their technicians to a training school last week. I built my whole departmental schedule around last week's being slack. They knew I was scheduled for PM last week. There's no way they're shutting me down for even one minute during the next three weeks. Somebody needs to straighten those jerks out!"*

So we have a problem here! Fred seems to be between a rock and a hard place, doesn't he? He doesn't want to shut down for maintenance, but he may risk some downtime later if his equipment doesn't receive the proper preventive maintenance. The lack of unified planning at lower levels may cost Dixon its objectives. It has already strained the relationships among personnel in the plant.

What action would you take now if you were Fred Adkins? What should be done to prevent this type of situation in the future?

As you will shortly see, other types of plans may also be established to aid in unified planning at lower levels. These types of plans, policies, procedures, and rules are more specific than objectives and spell out the methods used at lower levels.

Guidelines for Setting Performance Objectives

Since all supervisors should set **performance objectives** in their departments, the following guidelines which are relevant for all management levels should prove helpful. *Performance objectives* tell employees what is expected of them to make their performance acceptable.

1. *Select key performance areas for objectives.* Since objectives focus attention and effort, having too many objectives means that the more important areas will suffer. For example, instead of having 15 objectives, select those four or five key areas of performance, such as quality, quantity, customer relations, or cost controls, that really count!

2. *Be specific, if possible.* For example, "to have good quality" probably means different things to you and to an employee. "To produce parts with a 99 percent acceptance rate by the inspection department" is more specific, and it gives the worker a tangible measure of progress.

3. *Set challenging objectives.* Objectives should not be set so low that they can be met through "average" effort. While they should have some stretch in them, they should not be so difficult to achieve that an employee is discouraged from commitment to them.

Do you think the goal set for the month for Ann Casey was an appropriate one? If she had sold $12,000 before the end of her second week, couldn't she probably sell more than $15,000 for the entire month?

4. *Keep objective areas in balance.* Effort expended in one performance area frequently affects another. The quality of work required influences the quantity of work, and the quantity of work may affect employee safety. Objectives may be required in each of these areas so as to balance them properly.

Note the quality objective in Number 2 above: "to produce parts with a 99 percent acceptance rate by the inspection department." If this were the only objective established, do you see any problems? Explain.

5. *Involve subordinates in setting objectives.* What do they consider the key performance area of their job? What do they think is a challenging but fair objective in a given area? There are times, however, especially during periods of financial difficulties and other crises, when it is not feasible or desirable to involve subordinates.

6. *Follow up.* Once objectives are set, supervisors tend to let up. Frequently, only the supervisor knows the results of a worker's performance. Discuss progress with employees. Sharing the results and discussing employees' progress will improve their commitment and demonstrate your own.

THE SUPERVISOR AND MBO

Management by objectives (MBO) is also commonly called *management by results, joint target setting, key performance area management,* and other terms. Its popularity has grown greatly since its introduction in the 1950s, especially in large organizations. **Management by objectives (MBO)** is defined as a system whereby managers and their subordinates jointly establish objectives and develop a systematic approach for monitoring results.

Do you recall the "hierarchy of objectives" concept mentioned earlier? Usually, MBO refers to an organizational system that ties together all levels of the organization's hierarchy. However, even a first-line manager may establish an MBO approach within his or her own unit. That's why the principles of MBO will be important to you as a supervisor even if MBO is not used in your organization as a whole. The following example shows how this can work.

> *Ann Phillips, sales supervisor for a large cosmetics firm, said: "My boss doesn't believe in joint target setting or MBO or anything like that. She tells me what my group's goal is for the next year, and I have very little, if any, input into what the figure is. Once that's established, though, I meet with my salespeople. Then we come up with individual objectives for each of them as to sales volume, number of new accounts, timeliness in filing sales reports, average number of calls a day, and so on. I find that when I involve my people, they push themselves more. MBO has been very helpful to me."*

Steps in MBO

While the approaches to MBO vary in detail, they usually involve several important steps. Figure 2–4 shows that there are five distinct steps that comprise the MBO cycle. As you will see later, the broken arrows labeled "6" can have several meanings. But first, let us explain each of the five distinct steps.

STEP 1. DISCUSSING THE SUPERVISOR'S RESPONSIBILITIES AND OBJECTIVES. The first MBO step attempts to assure effective communication and understanding between the supervisor and the employees. To illustrate the importance of this step, we invite you to take a simple test. How would you rank these items in order of importance for *your job*?

FIGURE 2–4   STEPS IN THE MBO PROCESS

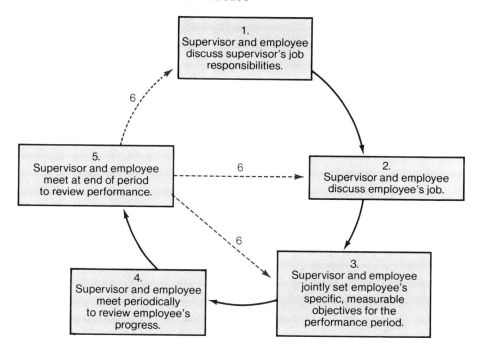

_____ Safety of employees
_____ Quality of output
_____ Quantity of output
_____ Cost control
_____ High employee morale
_____ Reduction of equipment downtime
_____ Good housekeeping (clean work environment)

Now consider what priority _your boss_ would say you should give to these items. The extent to which you and your boss would agree reflects the accuracy of understanding between you. If the two of you ranked these items pretty much the same, this would mean that you were directing your energy and efforts in the right direction (at least from your boss's viewpoint). But is there always such a clear understanding?

At a recent seminar, 17 line supervisors were asked by the trainer to rank-order in priority the objectives on the above list. The 17 supervisors ranked quantity of output, quality of output, and cost control as the three most important areas. The plant manager, present as an observer at the back of the room, was astounded by their response. Why? Because the plant had the poorest safety record of any of the six plants in the company system. In *the industry, this plant ranked the third-poorest in safety record among 60 plants in the entire Southwest. For the past four months, at weekly meetings with his supervisors, the plant manager had been emphasizing safety as the primary objective in the plant. Obviously, the line supervisors hadn't gotten the message. They were, in effect, working on the wrong priorities!*

If you were the plant manager, what action would you take to assure that the line supervisors "got the message"? What might explain the difference in the way the plant manager and his 17 supervisors ranked safety?

The first step of MBO, properly taken, would have cleared up the misunderstanding in the example given above. By discussing your own responsibilities and objectives with your employees, you allow them to understand where their own jobs fit into the bigger picture.

STEP 2. DISCUSSING THE EMPLOYEE'S JOB. This step is an eye-opener for many supervisors. As the plant manager in the above-mentioned example learned, subordinates' priorities may be quite different from those of their supervisor. Sometimes workers take on responsibilities outside the normal job description or spend more time on duties that, from the supervisor's viewpoint, are not important. Step 2 of the MBO cycle permits clear communication and agreement as to just what the employees' jobs should entail.

STEP 3. SETTING OBJECTIVES JOINTLY. The joint selection of key performance objectives is the heart of MBO. Table 2–2 illustrates some statements of specific, measurable objectives.

If you are presently a supervisor, what measurable performance areas would be appropriate for your workers? Explain.

Note that we said that the specific performance targets should be set *jointly*. Does this mean that you have to accept anything the employees come up with? Certainly not! It is crucial that the employees' ideas be reflected; however, as

TABLE 2–2   EXAMPLES OF STATEMENTS OF SPECIFIC, MEASURABLE
OBJECTIVES IN THE MBO PROCESS

Performance Area	Specific and Measurable Objective
Safety	Number of safety warnings issued by safety inspector to employee
Quality of work	Acceptance/rework ratio of parts produced by employee as determined by quality control department
Cost of scrap	Weight, bulk, or cost of scrapped material
Work flow	Minutes lost by coordinating departments in waiting for completed work-in-process by employee
Attendance	Days employee is absent from job
Training and development	Number of hours of completed training to improve job or personal skills
Customer satisfaction	Number of formal complaints by clients about quality or speed of service
Quantity of work	Number of units produced, number of sales, number of clients processed

supervisor, *you* have the final say. Where there is a big disagreement, it must be reconciled in a way acceptable to both parties. Remember, employees are more highly committed to objectives that they have helped to set. Our experience shows that most subordinates set their own objectives higher than their supervisors would set them!

STEP 4. REVIEWING PROGRESS PERIODICALLY. It is important that, as supervisor, you meet periodically with employees to discuss the progress being made toward achieving the objectives. Perhaps weekly or monthly meetings are appropriate. However, if these meetings are held too frequently (unless the worker is new), you'll defeat the purpose of allowing employees to manage their own work and make their own decisions. You should, however, make known your support and availability to discuss major problems at any time.

During the discussion of progress with an employee, if performance is below par, play the role of a helper rather than a critic. Ask yourself these questions: Why is performance deficient? What are the employee's ideas? What can be done to get back on the track? Are there factors beyond the employee's control, such as deficient parts or machine breakdowns, that have caused substandard performance? If this is the case, perhaps you will need to modify the original objective. The periodic reviews are important because you can learn about unanticipated problems that have developed.

STEP 5. REVIEWING END-OF-PERIOD PERFORMANCE. At the end of the performance period, both the employee and the supervisor generally know whether the employee's objectives have been reached. It is important for the supervisor to play again the role of helper in reviewing the overall performance during the period. What accounted for the success or failure in reaching objectives? What might have been learned? What might be done to better prepare the employee for improved performance? What might the supervisor have done to provide more help?

Now refer back to Figure 2–4 on page 41. The broken arrow connecting Step 5 to Step 1 means that the MBO process for a particular period has been successfully completed, and a new MBO cycle for another period can now be established. The broken arrows connecting Step 5 to either Step 2 or Step 3 mean that some circumstances have changed during the performance period in question. Perhaps Step 2 or Step 3, or both, should be repeated before beginning the next cycle.

Advantages of MBO

Among the advantages of MBO are these:

1. *It improves communication between supervisor and employees.* MBO requires goal-oriented communication that may not otherwise occur.
2. *It increases employee morale.* Since employees play an active part in goal setting and can measure their own progress, they feel greater ownership of their jobs and higher commitment to results.
3. *It encourages individuality.* All employees don't have equal talents. Under MBO, the goals and objectives set for one person may cover aspects of that person's job that are unlike another's. Moreover, performance targets may be set to reflect each individual's talents.
4. *It allows supervisors to assume a helper's role.* Since employees know whether or not they are on target, criticism is built into the system. In the traditional system, the supervisor rather than the system plays the role of critic. MBO frees the supervisor to be a helper or coach instead of a critic.
5. *It targets key performance areas.* Instead of every aspect of an employee's job being weighed equally, key objectives channel effort toward narrower goals. If a worker's attendance has been poor, for example, an objective based on attendance will have a strong effect on focusing on the employee's behavior for the performance period.

Disadvantages of MBO

Perhaps we have given you the impression that MBO is a perfect system. If that were the case, all organizations and managers would be using it. However, MBO has many disadvantages, including the following:

1. *MBO is time-consuming.* It takes a lot of the supervisor's time to go through the MBO process. The greater the number of employees, the greater the time commitment required.

2. *MBO dilutes supervisory authority.* When you ask employees to help set their own objectives, you are sharing some authority that you previously had alone. Presumably, in the traditional system a supervisor could say, "Here's what I expect from you." In the MBO system, the supervisor would say, "Let's determine together what to expect from you."

3. *MBO creates difficulty in tying results to rewards.* Since MBO reflects performance, it is normally tied to rewards. However, MBO doesn't replace the need for judgment. Suppose that Worker *A* is more talented than Worker *B* and sets higher goals than *B* but doesn't reach them. Worker *B*, less talented, has lower goals but does reach them. Who should receive what reward? The supervisor must still use judgment to determine a reward system.

4. *MBO requires greater supervisory skill.* Supervisors who practice MBO must use a number of skills. Conceptual skills are required to find specific, measurable performance areas and a way to provide feedback to the subordinate. This can be very challenging. In addition, the human relations skills of empathy, listening, and counseling are also crucial in conducting the one-to-one meetings required in the system.

5. *MBO doesn't suit all jobs.* Because of the need for measurable, verifiable performance objectives, MBO is not easy to use for all types of jobs. Some jobs are much easier to quantify and verify than others.

Can you think of some types of jobs that are difficult to quantify and verify? Explain.

Should you use MBO? We cannot answer that question for you. Perhaps your organization is already committed to it and you are required to use it. Even if your own manager does not use it, however, you may want to consider using it among your own employees.

TYPES OF PLANS

Once objectives have been set to determine *what* needs to be accomplished, plans can be developed to outline *how* the objectives can be attained. Basically, these plans fall into two categories: standing plans and single-use plans.

Standing Plans

Standing plans, or **repeat-use plans**, are those that are used many times over a period of time. Three types of standing plans are policies, rules, and procedures.

POLICIES. A **policy** is a guide to decision making—a sort of boundary (see Figure 2–5). It's a way to provide consistency among decision makers. For example, assume that an *objective* of Computronix (recall Case 2–1) is "to operate our plants so as to achieve high safety." Note that this objective tells the "what." A *policy* to achieve this objective at the various plants could be: "All flammable substances will be stored and handled in a manner consistent with federal, state, and local regulations." Another policy might be: "Each plant shall emphasize safety performance of employees through a well-designed promotional campaign."

FIGURE 2–5 EXAMPLE OF A POLICY

Within the Dixon Plant described in Case 2–1, an overall policy established by Marshall might be: "Each operating department shall hold regular safety meetings to encourage adherence to rules and solicit employee safety suggestions." Other examples of policies are shown in Figure 2–6.

Supervisory managers fit into the policy picture in two key ways. First, they play an important part in implementing organizational policies that have been established by higher management. Second, they also establish or create policies within their departments as guides to their own work groups. Here are some examples:

1. *Absence notification.* "Employees who will be absent should notify me in advance, assuming this is feasible."
2. *Decision making.* "You are encouraged to make decisions on your own as long as these fall within the realm of your job description."

FIGURE 2–6   OTHER EXAMPLES OF POLICIES

Compensation policy: "This company shall establish and maintain wages on a level comparable to those found for other positions in other firms in the community."

Overtime policy: "Supervisors shall offer overtime opportunities to the most senior employees in the department."

Grievance policy: "Each employee shall have an opportunity for due process in all disciplinary matters."

Purchasing policy: "Where feasible, several sources of supply shall be utilized so as not to be solely dependent on one supplier."

Supervisory policy: "Managers should periodically hold group meetings with employees for the purpose of discussing objectives, discussing new developments that may affect employees, responding to questions, and, in general, encouraging more effective and accurate communications within the organization."

What are some other examples of supervisory policies that you can come up with? Can you think of any examples of policies established by the teacher of this course?

Policies established by upper-level managers should be put into writing by supervisory managers since the policies must be applied at operating levels that are farther down the chain. However, policies may also be communicated orally, as is likely the case with the supervisory policies mentioned above. Some policies, however, may be unwritten, implied, or based on past practices because "that's the way things actually happen."

Mary Hicks was new on the job, this being her first week. Her supervisor, Terri Shaw, had been very helpful in showing her the ropes. Each day, Mary had shown up for work a few minutes before starting time—just to make sure she was on time. She noticed, however, that at least a third of the employees drifted in five to ten minutes late. This was true not only in her department, but also in others throughout the building. On asking one of her co-workers about this, she was told, "Yeah, they pretty much don't get really upset about five or ten minutes, just so it's not the same person all the time."

The above example is not a policy but a practice that has become so widespread in use that supervisors may treat it as a policy. Supervisors must keep in mind that action or even inaction may come to be thought of as policy by subordinates and serve as a guide to their behavior.

Finally, policies are relatively permanent but should not be set in stone. Circumstances change, and management must from time to time reexamine the appropriateness of its policies.

RULES. Like policies, rules also provide guidance. But **rules** are stronger than policies in that the guidance given by rules is final and definite. Rules are inflexible. If you work in a plant that has the rule, "No smoking on the premises," you cannot smoke, and that is that. Note the difference between a policy and a rule as shown in the examples below:

1. *Policy.* "Employees who violate the no-smoking rule *are subject to* discharge."
2. *Rule.* "Employees who violate the no-smoking rule *are automatically discharged.*"

Why distinguish between rules and policies, especially when the distinction is sometimes such a fine one? First, as a supervisor you must know *when* you do not have flexibility. Second, too many rules can result in "overmanagement." Taking too much discretion away from the employees to use their own judgment leads them to say, "Well, let me look in the rule book and see what I'm supposed to do," as Figure 2–7 suggests.

FIGURE 2–7   A CASE OF OVERMANAGEMENT

What are some examples of rules that you can think of? Can a supervisor establish his or her own rules? Give an example.

When there are too many rules, supervisors lose their individualism and may use the rules as crutches. Or they may offer weak, apologetic reasons when they are enforcing the rules. For example, consider the following dialogue given below. While rules have an important place in organizations, their overuse can lead to problems.

"Catherine, I'm sorry to have to write you up for punching in three minutes late."

"But you know I was actually here ten minutes early and just forgot to punch in. I was at my desk all the time. I can't afford to get laid off half a day for being written up."

"Sorry, Catherine. It doesn't seem fair to me, either, but I've got to stick by the rule book. A rule's a rule."

PROCEDURES. The need for procedures arises when an organization or one of its departments requires a high degree of consistency in activities that occur frequently. Procedures are established to avoid "reinventing the wheel" and assure an effective sequence. A **procedure** outlines the steps to be performed when taking a particular course of action. Organizations have procedures for such matters as obtaining leaves of absence, ordering parts through central purchasing, taking weekly inventory, processing an employee's grievance, and so on.

Can you think of a procedure for a regular activity that takes place in each of the following organizations: airline, hospital, retail store, high school?

Single-Use Plans

Single-use plans are developed to accomplish a specific purpose and are then discarded. Unlike policies, rules, and procedures, single-use plans detail courses of action that won't be performed on a repetitive basis. Examples of single-use plans are programs, projects, and budgets.

PROGRAMS. We hear and read about programs daily—the U.S. space program, your city's pollution-control program, a voter-registration program, and so on. A **program** is a large-scale plan that involves a mix of objectives, policies, rules, and small projects. A program outlines the specific steps to be taken to achieve its objectives, including the time, money, and human resources required to complete it. It is essentially a set of single-use plans that are carried out over a period of time. Other examples of programs are:

1. A program undertaken by a hospital to build a new wing.
2. A research and development program undertaken by a drug manufacturer to find a cure for a certain disease.
3. A quality-improvement program undertaken by an auto manufacturer.

PROJECTS. A **project** is a distinct, smaller part of a program. A quality-improvement program of an auto manufacturer involves a number of projects such as upgrading equipment, revising inspection methods, raising standards, motivating personnel, and so on. Each project has its own objectives and becomes the responsibility of personnel assigned to it.

BUDGETS. Every individual, family, or organization uses some form of budgeting. A well-planned budget serves as both a planning and a controlling tool. Simply stated, a **budget** is a forecast of expected financial performance over a period of time. A departmental budget covers such items as supplies, equipment, scrap, overtime, and personnel payroll. We will discuss budgets in more detail in Chapter 16.

CHAPTER REVIEW

Planning is deciding what will be done in the future. Properly done, it helps managers accomplish the four other management functions of organizing, leading, staffing, and controlling. Of these functions, planning is most closely linked to controlling.

Because it is a difficult and time-consuming process, many supervisors tend to neglect planning. Instead of planning, they scurry about solving one problem, then another, seemingly too busy to plan anything. Effective planning anticipates many problems so that they are more easily handled when they occur.

Planning differs for the top-, middle-, and first-level management. Top managers spend a greater proportion of their time in planning and focus on strategic long-term and intermediate-range plans of one to five or more years. Middle managers focus on intermediate- and short-range plans of one month to one year. Supervisory managers zero in on short-range daily, weekly, or up to six-month plans.

Objectives are crucial to effective planning. But, once established, objectives provide a stimulus for individual effort. The network of objectives set at one management level reflects the objectives of the next operational level. This is called a hierarchy of objectives. Objectives permit unified planning and coordination at lower management levels.

Management by objectives (MBO), also commonly known as "management by results" and "joint target setting," is a system whereby managers and subordinates jointly establish objectives and develop a systematic approach for achieving results. MBO typically involves five steps: (1) supervisor and each employee discuss supervisor's responsibilities and objectives; (2) supervisor and employee discuss employee's job; (3) supervisor and employee jointly set specific, measurable objectives for a given performance period; (4) supervisor and employee meet periodically to review employee's progress; and (5) supervisor and employee meet at end of period to review performance. The supervisor and the employee can then begin a new cycle.

Among the advantages of MBO are that it improves communication between a supervisor and employees, increases employee morale, encourages individuality, focuses effort on key performance areas, and allows the supervisor to be a "coach" or helper rather than a critic. The disadvantages of MBO are that it is time-consuming, requires the supervisor to share authority with employees, may be difficult to tie to a reward system, requires greater supervisory skill, and is less applicable to positions where performance cannot be easily measured.

After objectives are established, other plans can be developed throughout the organization. Standing, or repeat-use, plans are used to direct action that deals with recurring situations. They include policies, rules, and procedures. A policy is a guide to individual decision making. While policies allow some flexibility, rules are final and definite as to what action must be taken. A procedure outlines the steps that should be taken to complete a given action, such as taking a vacation leave, processing a grievance, and so on. Single-use plans are one-time plans that are discarded upon their completion. Examples of these are programs, projects, and budgets.

QUESTIONS FOR REVIEW AND DISCUSSION

1. What is meant by planning?
2. Why is planning called the primary management function?
3. How is planning closely related to the controlling function?
4. A supervisor says, "How can I ever get ahead of the game when I can't find time to plan? It seems every minute of my day is already taken up with putting out a fire of one kind or another." How would you answer this supervisor?
5. What is meant by a hierarchy of objectives? Explain.
6. What are some guidelines for setting performance objectives?
7. What is MBO, and what steps are involved?
8. What are the advantages and disadvantages of MBO?
9. What is the difference between a policy, a rule, and a procedure?
10. What is a budget, and what function does it perform?

LEARNING EXERCISE 2–1
SETTING PERFORMANCE OBJECTIVES

Jane Persons supervised the typing pool at Computronix, which consisted of seven clerk-typists. Work done by this section consisted of typing various reports and correspondence as required by other departments and handling all photocopying for the plant. Jane had just attended a meeting with the other section heads and heard Edna Strong, Administration Department head, talk briefly about the new planning system that was in store for the Dixon Plant. As Edna heard it from Marshall, the plant manager, every department head and supervisor would be required to identify three to five key performance areas in their departments. These were supposed to be areas that had a significant impact on performance.

It was the meeting with Edna that puzzled Jane. Edna had asked her to come up with the three to five key performance areas for her clerk-typist section. Jane said: "I can understand how our sales group or production groups can have specific objectives. But I can't see how a typing pool can have anything like that. What am I supposed to come up with? Number of pages typed? Number of pages without an error? This whole thing seems like a lot of 'wheel spinning' to me. My people know their objectives without this planning stuff. Their objective is to do a good job at getting the required typing work done for these other departments as quickly as possible."

Answer the following questions:

1. Do you agree with Persons' view that the new planning system is "wheel spinning"? Why or why not?
2. Are there some key performance areas that Persons can identify for her section? What are they?
3. To what extent does Persons' statement of an objective for her section meet the criteria mentioned under the "Guidelines for Setting Performance Objectives" discussed in the text?

LEARNING EXERCISE 2–2
DIFFERING PERCEPTIONS OF PRIORITIES

Juanita Perez, vice-president of manufacturing for Design Fabricators, had just examined the results of a survey in the six plants under her jurisdiction. Since taking over the job two weeks ago, Perez, who was hired from the outside, had spent time getting a feel for the job. In previous discussions with the president of Design Fabricators, Perez had zeroed in on "quality" as the president's primary concern. This was echoed in her discussions with the vice-president of sales, and also in discussions with two key former clients who had recently switched to a competing firm. Armed with this "feel," Perez began by surveying the six plant managers who reported directly to her. No formal, written statement of objectives had ever been set within the manufacturing function, although each plant operated as a separate profit center.

In the survey of the plant managers, each was asked to rank seven areas of performance in order of importance. The results are shown on the following page.

THE SIX PLANT MANAGERS' RANKINGS

	PM #1	PM #2	PM #3	PM #4	PM #5	PM #6
Quality	2	3	5	1	4	3
Safety	4	4	1	5	3	6
Cost control	3	2	2	3	1	4
Employee relations	6	5	6	6	6	5
Housekeeping	7	7	7	7	7	7
Production output	1	1	3	2	2	1
Equipment maintenance	5	6	4	4	5	2

Answer the following questions:

1. What do you feel accounts for the different rankings given by the six plant managers?
2. How might the differences in plant managers' priorities affect the operations at lower management levels of the six plants? Give some examples.
3. Put yourself in Perez's role. What will you do with this information?

LEARNING EXERCISE 2–3
MBO ROLE PLAY

"This MBO goal-setting attempt is an absolute joke," said Susan Myrick, teller supervisor of Citizens Bank. "I knew this was going to happen; so why not just grin and bear it." What Susan was referring to was the five-minute meeting she had just had with Stanley Rayborn, branch manager of the bank. The bank had just implemented a costly MBO approach called "Performance Management" and had employed a nationally known consulting firm to help it implement the new system. According to Step E of this system, "The supervisor and the subordinate should meet and jointly agree upon the key performance objectives established for the subordinate's position. These will be forwarded, in writing, to the level immediately above the supervisor."

"What happened?" asked Norma Bain, a friend of Susan's who worked in the bank's loan office.

"Oh, you'll get yours," Susan replied. "It went like this. I walked in and had my list of objectives, written in longhand. He looked at them, then handed me the list he'd made out. His list was all typed up, ready for me to sign, with the carbons all inserted. You know how he is—perfect in every detail. He says, 'Mrs. Myrick, these are the objectives we're going to set in your department.' And he handed me the list to sign."

"Did you sign it?" asked Norma.

"You bet I did, just like you'd better sign yours when he calls you in," Susan responded.

Answer the following questions:

1. Why would Rayborn use the approach that he did with Susan?
2. Suppose that Susan came in with much lower objectives than Rayborn for areas such as teller end-of-day balances, training time for new tellers, teller absences, and scores for courtesy and efficiency as rated by a customer survey. How should these differences be handled?
3. Role play the meeting suggested in question (2).

SUGGESTIONS FOR FURTHER READING

Baker, H. Kent, and Steven H. Holmberg. "Stepping Up to Supervision: Planning for Success." *Supervisory Management* 26 (November 1981): 12–18.

Bologna, Jack. "Why Managers Resist Planning." *Managerial Planning* 28 (January-February 1980): 23–25.

Himes, Gary K. "Better Planning, Fewer Crises." *Supervision* 43 (July 1981): 5–7.

Megginson, Leon C., Donald C. Mosley, and Paul H. Pietri, Jr. *Management: Concepts and Applications.* 2d ed. New York: Harper & Row, 1986. See especially Chapter 5, "The Planning Process,' pp. 117–51, and Chapter 6, "Setting Organizational Objectives and Goals," pp. 173–79.

Pollack, Ted. "How to Be a Planner." *Supervision* 46 (April 1984): 25–26.

Treese, Matthew A. "Supervision by Objectives—A Workable Approach." *Supervision* 44 (August 1982): 12–15.

3
DECISION MAKING AND PROBLEM SOLVING

OBJECTIVES

After reading and studying the material in this chapter, you should be able to:

- Show how decision making is the heart of management.
- Explain why supervisors need to make so many decisions.
- Define decision making and identify at least four elements involved.
- Explain how to make decisions.
- Name some factors to keep in mind when making decisions.
- Decide when to use the individual approach or the group approach to decision making.
- Discuss some ways of improving decision making.

IMPORTANT TERMS

span of management *or*
   span of control
decision making
programmed decisions
unprogrammed decisions

opportunity
problem
alternatives
risk
intuition

CHAPTER OUTLINE
CASE 3-1. ABLE OR BAKER?

I. ROLE OF DECISION MAKING IN SUPERVISORY MANAGEMENT
   A. Decision making: The heart of management
   B. Why supervisors need to make decisions
II. WHAT IS DECISION MAKING?
   A. Decision making defined
   B. Elements involved in decision making
      1. Is a decision needed?
      2. Decisions involve the future only
      3. Decision making is a conscious process
      4. Decision making involves more than one alternative
   C. Types of decisions to be made
   D. Decision making versus problem solving
III. HOW TO MAKE DECISIONS
   A. Step 1. Defining the idea or problem
   B. Step 2. Developing alternatives
   C. Step 3. Collecting, interpreting, and evaluating information about alternatives
   D. Step 4. Selecting the preferred alternative
      1. Cost/benefit analysis
      2. Risk analysis
   E. Step 5. Implementing the decision
   F. Step 6. Following up, evaluating, and changing—if needed
IV. FACTORS TO KEEP IN MIND WHEN MAKING DECISIONS
   A. The right person should make the decision
   B. Decisions should contribute to objectives
   C. There's seldom only one acceptable choice
   D. People's feelings should be considered
   E. Effective decision making takes time and effort
   F. Decision making improves with practice
   G. A decision may not please everyone
   H. A decision starts a chain reaction
V. INDIVIDUAL AND GROUP DECISION MAKING
   A. Approaches to decision making
   B. Advantages and disadvantages of individual and group decision making
VI. IMPROVING DECISION MAKING
   A. Bases of decision making
      1. Authority of position
      2. Experience
      3. Facts
      4. Intuition
      5. "Follow-the-leader" attitude
   B. Some guides to less stressful decision making
Chapter Review
Questions for Review and Discussion
Learning Exercise 3–1. The Overworked Maintenance People
Learning Exercise 3–2. Whom Do You Promote?
Suggestions for Further Reading

He who makes no mistakes makes no progress.
Theodore Roosevelt

There are few things as useless—if not as dangerous—as the right answer to the wrong question.
Peter F. Drucker

CASE 3–1
ABLE OR BAKER?

Several years ago, Ken Parker was sent to Operating Department B of Petrochem Corporation to replace Dave Mann, who was retiring after 15 years as supervisor of the department.[1] Ken, 38 years old, with a B.S. in Chemical Engineering, had been with Petrochem 12 years and had been a supervisor for four years. On the basis of his excellent record, he was asked to see if he could improve the performance in Department B, which had around 15 operators. Because of improved facilities, the company had been able to reduce its work force through attrition until about three years before. Consequently, no one had been involuntarily terminated in the past 20 years. Three years earlier, Petrochem had started hiring again, and had hired people with much higher qualifications than those required of the older employees. Consequently, a third of Department B's employees were younger and more qualified than the rest.

Because of a severe recession, Parker received a call three months later from the plant manager telling him that all departments were being asked to terminate at least one person. The choice of who was to go was left up to each supervisor, but the terminations were to be permanent.

There were two men who were the most likely candidates for discharge in Department B: Mr. Able and Mr. Baker. Able, 53 years old, with 25 years' service, was a high-school graduate. His performance ratings for the past 11 years had varied from "poor" to "fair." His wife was an invalid; an only son was overseas in the U.S. Army; his divorced daughter and her young child, with no income of their own, lived with him. Baker, age 25 and unmarried, had three years' service and a B.S. in engineering. His performance ratings had consistently been "very good" to "excellent."

Parker knew that morale would suffer if he fired Able. Yet, if he kept him and let Baker go, it would appear that good performance was considered to be of little value to the company. These events occurred before the passage of the Age Discrimination in Employment Act and the many entitlement programs we now have. Moreover, there was no union at Petrochem. The person whom Parker terminated would get only one week's severance pay for each year of service.

Ken Parker is certainly in a difficult position here, isn't he? This chapter deals with his problem—decision making and problem solving. As the case shows, supervisors must make effective, but often difficult, decisions if they are to be successful.

Chapter 2 covered the overall topic of the fundamentals of planning. Throughout this discussion, it was implied that decision making was involved. We now look at that subject in detail. Decisions must be made about people, about processes, and about priorities, to name just a few! Keep Parker's problem in mind, as we shall return to his situation throughout the chapter.

ROLE OF DECISION MAKING IN SUPERVISORY MANAGEMENT

Managers must make decisions whenever they perform any of the management functions discussed in Chapter 1. Without decision making, those functions couldn't be performed, and the entire management system would cease to exist. For example, in planning, the supervisor must choose which objectives to seek, which policies to establish, and what rules and regulations to institute. In organizing, choices must be made as to who gets what authority and how duties and responsibilities are to be grouped. The function of leading entails how best to communicate with and motivate employees. In staffing, decisions must be made concerning matters such as selection, placement, training and development, performance appraisal, compensation, and health and safety. In controlling, if actual performance does not conform to planned performance, decisions about how best to bring them together must be made.

Which of the five management functions is most closely related to the decision Ken Parker faces in our opening case?

The decisions managers make must also be made quickly—often with little information or perhaps even conflicting information. Then those decisions must be carried out in order to achieve the department's objectives!

Decision Making: The Heart of Management

Decision making is central to the supervisor's job. Supervisors must continuously decide *what* is to be done, *who* is to do it, *how* it is to be done, and *when* and *where* are the best time and place to do it (see Figure 3–1). As we will show throughout the chapter, these decisions are interrelated and interacting, although they may be discussed separately. One decision builds upon previous ones. For

FIGURE 3–1 DECISION MAKING IS THE HEART OF MANAGEMENT

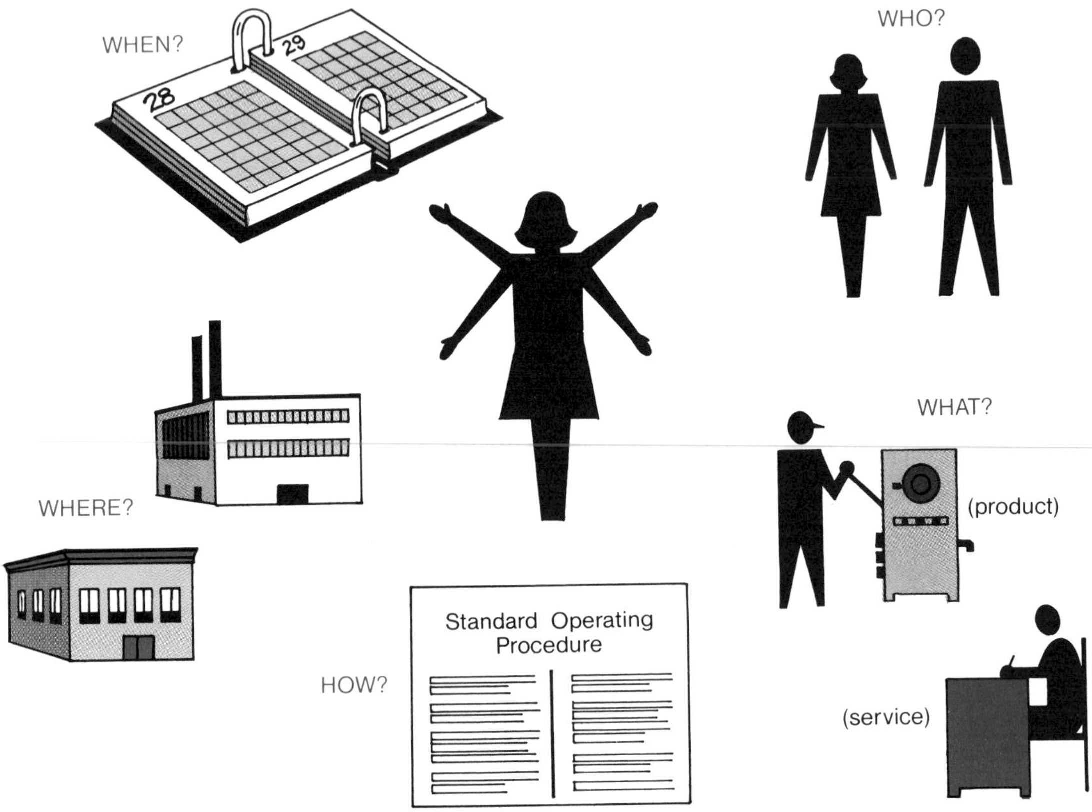

WHEN?

WHO?

WHERE?

WHAT?

(product)

HOW?

Standard Operating
Procedure

(service)

example, what your department produces determines what type of production facilities are needed. These decisions, in turn, influence the type of employees needed and the training and compensation they should receive. All these decisions affect the amount of money budgeted for the department.

Why Supervisors Need to Make Decisions

Supervisory managers—even more than managers at other levels—are involved in directing employees' behavior toward achieving the organization's goals, as well as those of the employees themselves. Therefore, supervisors must make more decisions more frequently—and often more quickly—than other managers since they're operating on a day-by-day, person-to-person basis.

Wilma Malone, nursing supervisor at Alquippa Medical Center, had been at work for only three hours, but she had already made seven major decisions. These were:

1. To attend a one-day course on time management offered the following week.

2. *To fill out the performance appraisal forms on five of her new nurses.*
3. *To approve vacation schedules for two nurses in her department.*
4. *To refer to the floor physician a patient's request to be taken off a prescribed medication.*
5. *To resolve a dispute between one of the nurses and a floor orderly.*
6. *To name Jane Moore as her replacement when she took her vacation in three weeks.*
7. *To fill out a purchase requisition for needed supplies.*

In addition, she made five other minor decisions. The young trainee assigned to Wilma said, "Are you always this busy or is it just because it's Monday morning?" Wilma replied, "It's all a normal part of a supervisor's job."

Employees look to their supervisor for more direction, assistance, advice, guidance, counsel, and protection than subordinates of managers at higher levels. Also, in general supervisors are more involved in socializing since they have more employees than other managers. The lower the level of management, the greater the **span of management** or **span of control**, which is the number of immediate subordinates a manager can supervise effectively. All these activities require decision making. Therefore, supervisors make decisions that affect not only their own behavior, but also that of many other people.

WHAT IS DECISION MAKING?

Let us now define decision making, discuss the elements involved in decision making, look at some selected types of decisions, and see some differences between decision making and problem solving.

Decision Making Defined

Have you known people who just couldn't ever make up their minds? They might say, "I really don't know what to do. If I do this, such and such will happen. If I do that, then another thing might happen." They just can't make decisions. The word *decide* comes from a Latin word meaning "to cut off." When you make a decision, you first consider a matter causing you some uncertainty, debate, or dispute and then make a choice or judgment that more or less results in a definite conclusion. You cut off further deliberation on the matter. Thus, **decision making** is the conscious consideration and selection of a course of action from among available alternatives to produce a desired result.

Elements Involved in Decision Making

There are several elements involved in decision making and problem solving. The most important ones are realizing that (1) a decision may not be needed, (2) decisions involve the future, (3) the process is a conscious one, and (4) there must be more than one alternative solution.

IS A DECISION NEEDED? It may seem strange to include this question in a discussion of decision making, but it's important. In many supervisory situations, no decision is needed, or making a decision may be in vain. For example, if a given event is inevitable, or if higher management is going to act in a certain way regardless of the supervisor's wishes, then a decision is a waste of time. Also, some things cannot be changed regardless of the supervisor's wishes or actions.

"You really have guts, Will," said Carol Sheffield to Will Hauser, office supervisor for Gridtronics, Inc. "You didn't waste a lot of time with competing bids or even looking at what different word processors can do. Don't you feel uncomfortable getting the vice-president to approve the purchase of a $10,000 piece of equipment? What if he wants some evidence that you really shopped around?"

"Well," said Will, "that's a good question, I suppose. But there's one thing you don't know. Getting competing bids and spending a lot of time evaluating different systems would have been a waste of my time. There really wasn't a 'decision' needed. The guy I bought that piece of equipment from is the vice-president's son!"

Do you agree with Will that there was no decision to be made in the example given above? Why or why not?

DECISIONS INVOLVE THE FUTURE. The second element of decision making is its orientation toward the future. Surely you have often heard others say, "If only I had done this, then that wouldn't have happened." They assume that if they had made a different decision, it would have resulted in a happy marriage, a rapid promotion, or a killing in the stock market. It is said that hindsight has 20–20 vision, but the supervisor's world is no place for Monday-morning quarterbacking. Rather it's one of preparing for today or tomorrow. Because a supervisor's decision making is future-oriented, it always contains an element of uncertainty.

Referring to Case 3–1, what are some of the uncertainties involved in Parker's decision to terminate either Able or Baker?

DECISION MAKING IS A CONSCIOUS PROCESS. The third element of decision making is that it involves a conscious process of selection. No decisions are needed about breathing or sleeping because these are unconscious, reflex bodily actions. In making a true decision, the individual consciously (1) becomes aware of a want that needs to be satisfied, (2) seeks relevant behavior alternatives, and (3) evaluates them as a basis of choice, as shown in Figure 3–2.

FIGURE 3–2   THE DECISION-MAKING PROCESS

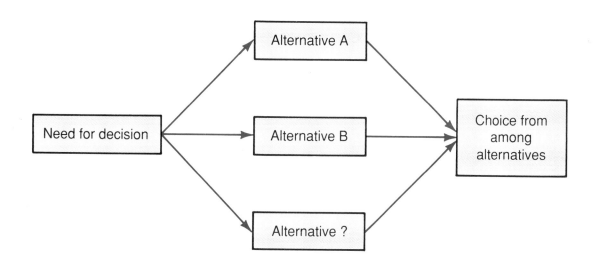

DECISION MAKING INVOLVES MORE THAN ONE ALTERNATIVE.   As indicated above, for a true decision to be made there must be two or more available alternatives to choose from, including the possibility of doing nothing. Frequently, these alternatives involve only two choices, as in a "yes or no" or "to do or not to do" situation. The decision to do nothing is sometimes the worst decision.

As shown in Figure 3–3, most decision situations involve several alternatives with varying expected outcomes. Notice that you may not be aware of some of the alternatives and may not have decision authority over others (see A–5 in Figure 3–3). For other alternatives (see A–1, A–2, and A–3) you must estimate their expected outcomes. You then evaluate each outcome in terms of its desirability. Figure 3–3 shows that A–3 is expected to have an undesirable outcome, so you would reject it. While A–1 is more desirable than A-3, Figure 3-3 shows that A–2 is the *most desirable*, so it's the one you'd choose. Sometimes there are no desirable alternatives. As a result, you might have to decide between two undesirable ones.

FIGURE 3–3 HOW ALTERNATIVES AND THEIR EXPECTED OUTCOMES AFFECT DECISIONS

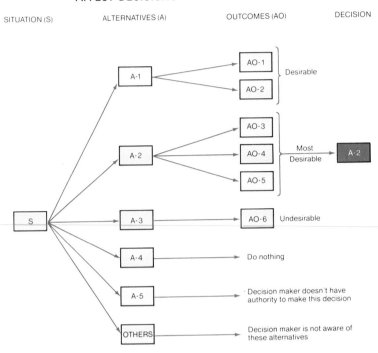

SITUATION (S)   ALTERNATIVES (A)   OUTCOMES (AO)   DECISION

> *Did you notice that in Case 3–1, Ken Parker narrowed his choice for permanent discharge to only two people? Since he had "around 15" operators, we must assume that he has used some mental process, such as that shown in Figure 3–3, to narrow his decision down to Able and Baker. Notice also that there is no apparently desirable alternative in Parker's case.*

Types of Decisions to Be Made

Although there are many ways of classifying decisions, we will discuss only one at this point, namely, how routine and repetitive they are, or how unusual they are and how infrequently they occur. Decisions can thus be classified as *programmed* or *unprogrammed*.

Programmed decisions are those that are routine and repetitive. Since they tend to be similar and must be made frequently, supervisors usually devise an established, systematic way of handling these decision situations. Some examples of this type of decision are

1. How to handle a worker who reports to work late or is absent without permission.
2. How to schedule work, shifts, vacations, and other time variations.
3. Which employees need training, and what type of training should be given them.
4. How frequently to do maintenance servicing of machinery and equipment.

The supervisor handles these decisions in a systematic way and may even set up a decision framework, including guidelines such as policies, procedures, or rules to follow.

Unprogrammed decisions are those that occur infrequently and, because different variables are involved, require a separate and different response each time, making it difficult to establish a systematic way of dealing with them. Some examples of unprogrammed supervisory decisions are

1. Whether to buy an important piece of machinery or equipment, especially an expensive, complex one.
2. How to react to a union representative who tries to organize your employees or calls a strike.
3. How to handle a severe accident or explosion.
4. Whom to promote to a supervisory position.

Decision Making Versus Problem Solving

In one of his educational films, Joe Batten, a well-known management consultant, has a manager say, "We have no problems here, just opportunities. Each problem should be considered an opportunity." While we don't necessarily agree with that conclusion, it does give us a chance to show how decision making and problem solving are related. An **opportunity** is a chance for development, progress, or advancement. A **problem** is a source of anxiety or distress.

Effective supervisors must be able to identify problems, analyze complex and involved situations, and "solve" the problem by removing its cause. But placing too much emphasis on problems can prevent one from identifying opportunities. After all, solving a problem only eliminates or neutralizes a negative situation. On the other hand, progress or advancement comes from seeking and identifying opportunities; recognizing the emotions, needs, and motivations of the people involved; and analyzing ways of satisfying them. Here are some examples of "opportunity" decision making at the supervisory level:

1. Replacing a piece of equipment that, while it is still functioning well, can be upgraded to increase efficiency.
2. Improving an already effective preventive maintenance system.
3. Cross-training employees to broaden their skills and raise morale.
4. Creating a new position for a highly skilled technician who has recently left the employ of a competitor.
5. Instituting the most innovative new processes and techniques.

What other examples of "opportunity" decision making can you think of?

HOW TO MAKE DECISIONS

Figure 3–4 shows that the decision-making process involves six basic steps. We have already been discussing most of them. We'll use Case 3–1 involving Ken Parker to illustrate each step of this process.

Step 1. Defining the Idea or Problem

As Peter Drucker stated in the opening quotation, a decision is only as good as the correct definition of the problem. In other words, the right cure for the wrong problem is just as bad as the wrong cure for the right problem. But it is not always easy to know what the problem is, or what is the best opportunity to seek. For example, when you have a fever, it is only a symptom of the true problem—an infection or other disorder. As a supervisor, you should likewise know that low morale, high turnover, many complaints or grievances, waste, and declining sales are not the *real* problem. Instead, they are only symptoms of the real problem.

FIGURE 3–4   STEPS IN DECISION MAKING

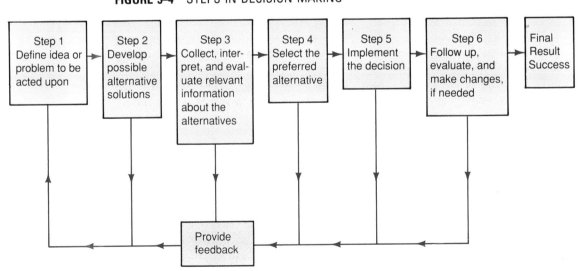

What do you see as the real problem facing Ken Parker?

Step 2. Developing Alternatives

The next step is to develop alternative ways of solving the problem or taking advantage of the opportunity. **Alternatives** are possible courses of action that can satisfy a need or solve a problem. Usually several choices are available to the decision maker if he or she is able to identify or develop them. It is also easier to choose from a few alternatives rather than many; so reduce the number to as few as is feasible. Also, be aware that if choices are limited, they may include only undesirable ones.

Notice in Case 3–1 that Ken Parker narrowed the number of alternatives to two, neither of which was desirable.

As indicated earlier, one choice is to do nothing, hoping that the problem will go away or solve itself in time. You must be careful, though, that this doesn't become an excuse for not making a difficult choice. If it does, you may get a reputation for being indecisive—the "kiss of death" to many promising supervisory careers.

Finally, this is the stage where you decide whether you should make the choice or channel it to the person who has the authority or expertise to make it.

Notice in Case 3–1 that Ken Parker was specifically given the authority to make the decision within limits set by the plant manager. The manager agreed, in advance, to back him up.

Step 3. Collecting, Interpreting, and Evaluating Information about Alternatives

Usually there are many sources from which to gather information affecting a decision. Sometimes standing orders, policies, procedures, rules, and regulations provide relevant information. In fact, these documents may have already made the decision for you or at least can indicate how you should decide. Other sources of information include your own experience, company records and reports, discussion with the people directly and indirectly involved, and personal observations.

Where do you think Ken Parker got the information he needed to make his decision? What additional information beyond that given in the case would be helpful to him in reaching a decision that would be fair to everyone concerned?

Perhaps you've heard the saying, "Tell me what you want to prove, and I'll get you the data to prove it." The effective evaluation of alternatives, though, involves looking *objectively* at the pros and cons of each one. Choices can be evaluated in many ways. The information can be written down as a simple "balance sheet," as shown in Figure 3–5, with the reasons for each alternative on one side and the reasons against it on the other. Or a process of elimination can be used, dropping the undesirable (or less desirable) choices.

What do you see as the pros and cons of terminating Able? Baker?

Step 4. Selecting the Preferred Alternative

Finally, you reach the point where you must make a choice. You look at your conclusions from Step 3 and then logically and rationally pick the alternative you think is most desirable for all concerned from an objective, ethical, and practical point of view. Selecting the preferred alternative involves cost/benefit analysis and risk analysis.

FIGURE 3–5   EVALUATING ALTERNATIVES

COST/BENEFIT ANALYSIS.   Using the technique of cost/benefit analysis, you will estimate what each alternative will cost in terms of human, physical, and financial resources. Then you estimate the expected benefits. Finally, you compare the two estimates. You choose the one with the greatest "payoff," where the ratio of benefits to cost is more favorable.

RISK ANALYSIS.   **Risk**, which is the possibility of defeat, disadvantage, injury, or loss, is inherent in decision making. But prudent decision makers will try to minimize the risks involved by effectively forecasting outcomes and considering all variables involved.

What is the worst possible thing that could happen if Parker decided to terminate Able? Baker? Why? Whom do you recommend he terminate? Explain.

Step 5. Implementing the Decision

Effective decision making doesn't stop when you choose from among alternatives. Instead, the decision must be put into operation. This is another difficult part of decision making, because you must face and deal with people who may not like your choice. For example, you might need to obtain and allocate some equipment and supplies. Or you might need to develop methods and procedures. Or you might have to select, train, or even terminate some employees. In fact, many "good" supervisory decisions may be ineffective because of the way they're implemented.

> *Ken Parker in Case 3–1 chose to terminate Baker because Baker could get another job, while Able probably could not. Also, since this was the first discharge at the company in 20 years, morale might suffer too greatly if 25 years of service were ignored. Yet outstanding performance had to be rewarded and poor performance punished.*
>
> *Parker handled the situation as follows: He (1) told Baker the reasons for his decision, (2) had the Personnel Department prepare an up-to-date résumé for Baker, (3) gave him time off to look for another job, (4) called other companies himself on Baker's behalf, and (5) ultimately helped him get a better job with better pay at another plant in Houston. Parker then told Able his decision. While granting that 25 years of service deserved consideration, he also told Able that he would be the next to go if he didn't "straighten up and fly right." Able replied that this was the first time in 25 years that anyone had told him his work was unsatisfactory.*

Step 6. Following Up, Evaluating, and Changing—If Needed

This last step in the decision-making process involves exercising the control function of management. It also determines whether the implementation of the decision is proceeding smoothly and achieving the desired results. If not, and if the decision can be changed or modified, it should be. If it can't be changed, then you "live with it" and try to make it succeed.

> *Able in Case 3–1 performed "satisfactorily" until retiring at age 60. Baker had progressed into the second level of management at his new company when this case was written. Parker was satisfied with the outcome of his decision, and so was top management. Parker ultimately became the plant manager at Petrochem.*

FACTORS TO KEEP IN MIND WHEN MAKING DECISIONS

It is relatively easy to describe the steps in decision making in general, but supervisory decision making is much more difficult because of several factors. The number and variety of such factors is quite extensive, but we'll discuss only the more important ones.

The Right Person Should Make the Decision

While there is no hard-and-fast rule as to who should make a given decision, in general decisions are best made by the person in authority closest to the point of action. The key consideration is that the decision maker should have adequate knowledge of local conditions as well as the authority needed to implement the decision.

Decisions Should Contribute to Objectives

Relating each decision to the organization's objectives facilitates decision making and helps the organization carry out its mission. It also helps in getting decisions accepted and carried out. If a given decision doesn't help achieve objectives, it should be questioned. For example, the manager of an agricultural cooperative decides to buy fertilizer from a company owned by him, his wife, and his son to sell to farmers. While the manager and his family are making a nice profit on their operations, the farmers are paying higher prices for their fertilizer.

There's Seldom Only One Acceptable Choice

Most organizational problems can be solved, or resolved, in a variety of ways. Therefore, the best choice depends on what factors you consider important, what weight you give to each, and what you do about them. Even when a "wrong" decision is made, people tend to try to make it come out "right." For example, if a supervisor hires a computer programmer over the objections of the personnel manager, the supervisor will do everything possible to see that the new employee succeeds, regardless of any weaknesses exhibited on the job.

People's Feelings Should Be Considered

All of us tend to resist change. But what we resist is not so much the technical aspects of change as the sociocultural changes such as modification of our status, position, or interpersonal relationships. Employees will more likely accept decisions that introduce new equipment or processes if their own income, position, or status is improved—or at least not changed adversely. Also, the secret to implementing any change is communicating the rationale for the change, assuring the understanding of employees' reactions, and in other ways allaying their fears.

Effective Decision Making Takes Time and Effort

There is no such thing as the button-pushing, finger-snapping supervisor spitting out decisions with machine-gun rapidity. Instead, it takes quality time and effort—mental and often physical—to make effective decisions. Unfortunately, many choices are made simply on the basis of fatigue. After spending many hours evaluating various alternatives, the exhausted supervisor will subconsciously say, "I'll choose the next one, regardless of what it is, just to get it over with." Or, to save time, a supervisor will say, "That's not a bad choice. I can live with it if you can." These rarely turn out to be successful choices.

Decision Making Improves with Practice

People can't really be taught to make effective decisions. Instead, they must learn to do so by actually going through the process and "living with" the consequences. Thus, as with any learned skill, your decision making improves the more you exercise it, assuming that you use it effectively.

A Decision May Not Please Everyone

Seldom does a decision make everyone concerned happy. The challenge facing the supervisor after the decision is made is to explain the decision and to attempt to win the individual or group's cooperation.

> *For example, an office manager was authorized to phase out 12 old typewriters over a period of a year, replacing three every four months. She assigned the first three new ones to the most efficient typists, only to hear complaints from those with the most seniority. She told them that, if their performance improved, they would get the next new ones.*

A Decision Starts a Chain Reaction

All parts of an organization are interrelated. Don't be surprised, therefore, when a decision made in another department affects yours, or vice versa. Hence the decision maker should be prepared to defend, change, or drop the decision in view of the chain of events it starts.

> *Julie Acree was perplexed. She had recently made a decision to allow Maria Montano, one of her top technicians, to attend a two-day seminar on some of the new developments in her field. The superintendent had agreed and approved payment of the $150 tab for tuition. Now, Julie had just come from the superintendent's office where she'd been told that supervisors in a number of other departments had also recommended their people for seminars. The decision to pay Maria's way was temporarily on hold until a policy could be worked out. "I can't afford to have 20 people attend seminars all of a sudden," the superintendent said.*

INDIVIDUAL AND GROUP DECISION MAKING

As a supervisor, should you make decisions by yourself, or should you involve your work group in the decision? In this section, we will provide some ideas to help you answer this question.

Approaches to Decision Making

Figure 3–6 shows that there are three basic decision-making approaches. In the first approach (A), the individual supervisor runs the show. As a supervisor using

FIGURE 3–6   ROLE OF SUPERVISOR AND WORK GROUP
IN DECISION MAKING

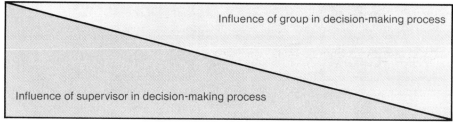

Approach A	Approach B	Approach C
<u>Supervisor</u> defines problem, develops and evaluates alternatives, and makes decision.	Supervisor solicits <u>group</u> input and advice about the problem, alternatives, and possibly even the recommended decision. <u>Supervisor</u> makes the decision.	Supervisor allows <u>group</u> to define the problem, develop and evaluate alternatives, and make the decision.

this approach, *you* would define the problem, *you* would determine and evaluate alternatives, and *you* would choose the most appropriate alternative. If you use the opposite approach (C), your work group would call the shots. That is, the group would define the problem, develop and evaluate alternatives, and make the decision as *they* think best. If you use the middle approach (B), you would get your group's help in defining the problem and in identifying and evaluating the alternatives. Perhaps you would even ask them for a recommendation. But as supervisor *you* would make the final decision.

Advantages and Disadvantages of Individual and Group Decision Making

Table 3–1 shows the advantages and disadvantages of involving your work group in decisions. A major advantage of doing this is that, ideally, improved decisions will result from doing so. An old adage says that "two heads are better than one." The involvement of your employees in the decision-making process can also result in better communication, improved morale, and a stronger group commitment to the decision once it is made.

The major disadvantages, though, may outweigh the advantages in certain circumstances. The time it takes, the presence of strong personalities in the work unit, and the fact that as a supervisor you're still accountable for group decisions must all be considered. In some situations, group decision making may be a case of too many cooks spoiling the broth! However, you don't have to be "locked into" just one of the approaches mentioned earlier. As one supervisor put it,

My decision approach depends on the situation. Sometimes things are pretty routine, and I make the decision myself. At other times, I get input from just

TABLE 3–1   ADVANTAGES AND DISADVANTAGES OF
GROUP DECISION MAKING

Advantages	Disadvantages
• Provides the supervisor with a broader range of information on the problem, alternatives, and recommended solution.	• Holds the supervisor accountable for the group's decisions.
• Lends a more "creative" approach to solving problems since ideas may be "piggy-backed."	• Takes the work group's time away from other aspects of their jobs.
• Improves communication in the department because the work group becomes aware of issues facing the supervisor.	• May result in "choosing sides" and causing morale problems over differing opinions.
• Creates a higher morale in the work group.	• Allows for strong personalities to dominate the work group, and the decision may not reflect the entire group's opinion.
• Stresses a stronger commitment to the decision once it is made since the work group helped to make it.	• Requires more supervisory skill in communicating and clarifying the group's role in a given decision.
	• Is difficult to use if the decision must be made quickly.

one or two people, or I might even hold a meeting to get the views of the entire group. Just recently, I pretty much let them make the decision about which of three new pieces of equipment we needed most. I said, "Whatever you guys decide on, I'll put it at the top of my list." I went with the majority vote, which was to rank a certain microcomputer Number One.

Which of the three approaches mentioned in this section would you have recommended that Ken Parker in Case 3–1 use? Why?

Whenever it is possible to do so, involving your staff in decision making is one way of attempting to overcome employee alienation by encouraging the free exchange of information.

IMPROVING DECISION MAKING

In order to improve decision making, a supervisor should understand the basis on which the decision is made and the techniques used to make it. The *basis* of the decision is the frame of reference in which it is made. The *technique* is the method used in the decision process.

Bases of Decision Making

Some of the most frequent bases used in making decisions are authority of position, education, experience, facts, intuition, and a "follow-the-leader" attitude. From a practical point of view, there is no one best basis upon which to choose among alternatives. Instead, supervisors should use the bases that best suit them under the existing circumstances.

AUTHORITY OF POSITION. Many decisions are based on the authority vested in the decision maker's position. In fact, it is probably the most frequently used basis. Decisions made on this basis tend to conform to the organization's strategies, policies, and procedures. They also tend to provide continuity and permanence since they are generally "official," to be readily accepted, and to be considered authentic and "legitimate." Yet these decisions may also reflect an unpopular "company position," may be too routine, and may be made without due regard to the situation.

EXPERIENCE. We see and understand things in terms of concepts and ideas with which we are familiar. Experience provides us with meaningful guides for selecting alternatives. Therefore, this basis provides practical knowledge of what has been done in the past and what was the outcome of those decisions. It also provides "tried and true" knowledge that tends to be accepted by those who've shared the experience. Yet a decision maker's experience may be limited or unique, and the choice made may be based on outmoded or obsolete experience.

FACTS. Most discussions of decision making state that a decision should be based on "all the pertinent facts." If that ideal can be reached, well and good, for it gives the impression that the resulting choice is logical, sound, and proper. Yet, if one waits to get all the pertinent facts, these may not be readily available and no decision can be made. Also, it may be too costly or take too much time to get the facts. Furthermore, "facts" may sometimes be misleading—or even wrong (see Figure 3–7)—and may be merely someone's opinion or belief. Thus, facts must be carefully classified, diagnosed, and interpreted. However, a supervisor must use the facts available, even though they are inadequate or flawed.

> *Recognizing that quick access to information is essential to decision making, Hewlett-Packard Company has provided its supervisors and managers with computer terminals. These people can now study cause-and-effect relationships between parts failure, process schedules, and reworking of production. So they make consistently better decisions.*[2]

INTUITION. Decisions may be unconsciously based on a person's cultural background, education, and training, as well as knowledge of the situation. This

FIGURE 3–7   "FACTS" CAN BE WRONG

"Miss, I don't care what my check says. This is not my hat."

Source: 1963 © Saturday Review Magazine Co. Reprinted by permission.

basis is called **intuition**. Conclusions reached on this basis may conflict with those resulting from other methods, as shown in Figure 3–8.

Choices based on intuition may be quite satisfactory, as they're based on the decision maker's total background. Also, these choices use the person's emotions as well as the mind, and a decision can be reached quickly. Finally, intuition seems to work. For example, Jack Chamberlin of General Electric decided to "go by gut" and select the cassette tape over eight-track cartridges in the early days of their development. His hunch was proved correct. Charles Revson, the founder of Revlon, has an uncanny knack for determining what customers want. And Albert Einstein attributed his theory of relativity to a "flash of insight."[3]

> *"Why'd I choose Able?" repeated Ken Parker. "Well, I had the facts and consulted with a couple of close friends. Most of the facts—and advice—said for me to keep Baker. He was younger, a better performer, and had a lot of potential. But from the start, I had a feeling that Able would be the one I'd keep. It was just a 'gut feeling' that made me decide."*

But intuition may not lead to optimal choices or solutions, and if your intuition is wrong, the decision will probably be wrong. Also, relying on intuition

FIGURE 3–8 INTUITION OR FACTS?

may lead you to minimize the use of other bases. Finally, it is practically impossible to defend this type of decision to your colleagues, higher management, or others.

"FOLLOW-THE-LEADER" ATTITUDE. Some decisions are based on doing what others are doing. This is sometimes called the "herd instinct" and is based on the assumption that other people know more about the subject than you do. If you use this method, you'll be "in the swing of things," but you may suffer if the "leader" is wrong.

Some Guides to Less Stressful Decision Making

In addition to the concepts discussed in this chapter, the following practical suggestions should help supervisors make better decisions with less stress:

1. *Try to avoid having to make crisis decisions.* With careful and adequate planning, fewer decisions will need to be made on a crisis basis. In fact, you usually have more time than you realize to make a sound decision. Therefore, a few minutes of careful thinking can have a significant impact on the quality of a decision.
2. *Use established policies, procedures, rules, and regulations when applicable.* Most decisions on work situations are programmed decisions or are similar to those that have been made before, and guidelines are set up for supervisors to follow. Use them and reserve your energy—and emotions—for the unusual problems.

3. *Give the decision the attention it warrants—and no more.* A small decision doesn't require going through an elaborate decision-making process. Perhaps you can even delegate some of these. On the other hand, a major decision (such as Parker's choice of terminating either Able or Baker, or a major change in operating method) can have a significant impact on the functioning of your unit—and on your career. In other words, don't get involved in counting the paper clips in the office or the toothpicks in the cafeteria.

4. *Seek help, if needed, from specialists and other managers.* Recognize (and accept) that some decisions are beyond your competence or knowledge. If it is an involved problem, such as a question of environmental control, health and safety, or affirmative action, call in the experts.

5. *Don't dwell on your decisions, once made.* Few of us make the "right" decisions all the time. In other words, while you should follow up on the outcome of a decision, don't wallow in nonproductive worry about whether it was a "good" or "bad" decision. Instead, follow the example of effective leaders: Do the best you can and then "leave it in the lap of the gods."

CHAPTER REVIEW

Decision making is the heart of management, as it is involved in performing all the managerial functions. It is the conscious consideration and selection of a course of action from among available alternatives to produce a desired result. Decision making is taking advantage of an opportunity for progress, development, or advancement. Problem solving is removing a source of anxiety or distress. To be successful, supervisors must make effective, but often difficult, decisions. And these decisions must be carried out in order to achieve the organization's objectives.

Decisions may be programmed if they are routine and repetitive and hence can be made using an established, systematic process. Or they may be unprogrammed if they occur infrequently and must be made without an established system. The elements involved in decision making are that (1) the supervisor must determine that a decision is needed, (2) decision making involves the future only, (3) it is a conscious process, and (4) it involves more than one alternative.

Decision making involves six steps: (1) defining the problem, (2) developing possible alternative solutions, (3) collecting, interpreting, and evaluating information about the alternatives, (4) selecting the preferred alternative, (5) implementing the decision, and (6) following up, evaluating results, and making changes, if needed.

Some of the factors to keep in mind when making decisions are that (1) the right person should make the decision, (2) decisions should contribute to objectives, (3) there's seldom only one acceptable choice, (4) people's feelings should be considered, (5) effective decision making takes time and effort, (6) decision making improves with practice, (7) a decision may not please everyone, and (8) a decision starts a chain reaction.

The three basic decision-making approaches are these: (1) the individual supervisor runs the show, making all the decisions; (2) the work group calls the shots, making the decisions; and (3) the supervisor gets the group's help in defining the problem, evaluating the alternatives, and suggesting solutions, but the supervisor actually decides. Group decision making improves communication and morale, broadens options, and increases commitment. However, the individual approach is quicker, provides for better accountability, and improves supervisory skills.

Decisions are made on several bases. The most popular bases are (1) authority of position, (2) education, (3) experience, (4) facts, (5) intuition, and (6) a "follow-the-leader" attitude. Effective decisions result from using a combination of these bases so that both facts and feelings are used.

Some practical guides to less stressful decision making are (1) try to avoid having to make crisis decisions; (2) use established policies, procedures, rules, and regulations where applicable; (3) give the decision only the attention it warrants; (4) seek help, if needed, from specialists and other managers; and (5) don't dwell on decisions after they are made.

QUESTIONS FOR REVIEW AND DISCUSSION

1. How is decision making involved in performing the five management functions? Explain.
2. Explain programmed and unprogrammed decisions and give examples of each.
3. Define decision making and explain the elements involved.
4. What is meant by the statement, "Decision making is the heart of management"?
5. Is there really a distinction between decision making and problem solving? Explain.
6. Name and give a *short* explanation of each of the six steps in the decision-making process.
7. Name and explain the factors to keep in mind when making decisions.
8. What are the advantages and disadvantages of group decision making? With which approach would you personally feel more comfortable? Why, and under what circumstances?
9. What is your feeling about the use of facts versus feelings in decision making?
10. Can you think of other guides to less stressful decision making? If so, what are they? Explain.

LEARNING EXERCISE 3–1
THE OVERWORKED MAINTENANCE PEOPLE

The maintenance department of a midwestern manufacturing plant had seven maintenance employees. Two of them, Jay and Ricky, did much better work and were more dependable, cooperative, and obliging than the rest. For this reason, some of the other maintenance workers, and even the supervisor of the department, would take advantage of them. For example, when the supervisor made his rounds and found that there was a paint job or some repair work that hadn't been done properly, instead of mentioning this to the workers involved, he would send Jay and Ricky to do the job over. Other personnel, seeing this, began to do their work only halfway, knowing that Jay and Ricky would be sent to bail them out.

The supervisor hadn't realized that this wasn't being fair to Jay and Ricky and other conscientious workers. However, at a meeting with the plant manager to discuss the "poor maintenance problem," this was brought to his attention. The plant manager indicated that something had to be done about it, and in a hurry.

Answer the following questions:

1. If you were the supervisor, what would you do after the meeting was over?
2. How would you define the problem?
3. How would you solve the problem? Explain.
4. What type of follow-up would you maintain?

LEARNING EXERCISE 3–2
WHOM DO YOU PROMOTE?*

Your company recently developed a plan to identify and train top hourly employees for promotion to first-line supervision. As a part of this program, your boss has requested a ranking of the six hourly workers who report to you with respect to their promotion potential. Given their biographical data, rank them in the order in which you would select them for promotion to first-line supervisor; that is, the person ranked Number One would be first in line for promotion.

Biographical Data

1. **Sam Nelson**—White male, age 45, married, with four children. Sam has been with the company for five years and his performance evaluations have been average to above average. He is well-liked by the other employees in the department. He devotes his spare time to farming and plans to farm after retirement.
2. **Ruth Hornsby**—White female, age 32, married, with no children; husband has a management-level job with the power company. Ruth has been with the company for two years and has received above-average performance evaluations. She is very quiet and keeps to herself at work. She says she is working to save for a down payment on a new house.
3. **Joe Washington**—Black male, age 26, single. Joe has been with the company for three years and has received high performance evaluations. He is always willing to take on new assignments and to work overtime. He is attending college in the evenings and someday wants to start his own business. He is well liked by the other employees in the department.
4. **Ronald Smith**—White male, age 35, recently divorced, with one child, age four. Ronald has received excellent performance evaluations during his two years with the company. He seems to like his present job but has removed himself from

*This exercise was prepared for this book by Carl C. Moore, University of South Alabama.

the line of progression. He seems to have personality conflicts with some of the employees.

5. **Betty Norris**—Black female, age 44, married, with one grown child. Betty has been with the company for ten years and is well liked by fellow employees. Her performance evaluations have been average to below-average, and her advancement has been limited by a lack of formal education. She has participated in a number of technical training programs conducted by the company.

6. **Roy Davis**—White male, age 36, married, with two teenage children. Roy has been with the company for ten years and received excellent performance evaluations until last year. His most recent evaluation was average. He is friendly and well liked by his fellow employees. One of his children has had a serious illness for over a year, resulting in a number of large medical expenses. Roy is working a second job on weekends to help with these expenses. He has expressed a serious interest in promotion to first-line supervisor.

Answer the following questions:

1. What factors did you consider in developing your rankings?
2. What was the most important factor you considered?
3. What information in the biographical data, if any, should not be considered in developing the rankings?

ENDNOTES

1. The name of this large energy company has been disguised.
2. John A. Young, "One Company's Quest for Improved Quality," *The Wall Street Journal*, July 25, 1983, p. 20.
3. See Mortimer R. Feinberg and Aaron L. Wenstein, "How Do You Know When to Rely on Your Intuition?" *The Wall Street Journal*, June 21, 1982, p. 16.

SUGGESTIONS FOR FURTHER READING

George, Claude S., Jr. *Supervision in Action.* 3d ed. Reston, VA: Reston Publishing Co., 1982.

Murnighan, Keith H. "Group Decision Making: What Strategies Should You Use?" *Management Review* 70 (February 1981): 55-58.

COMPREHENSIVE CASE FOR PART I
"BUT I DON'T WANT TO BE A MANAGER"*

"I can't figure you out, Sandy," said Paula Burton. Paula was the manager of the data-processing department, and she was talking to her head operator. "Why on earth did you bid for the head operator position in the first place if you weren't interested in moving beyond that to manager when the position became vacant?"

*Source: Reprinted, by permission of the publisher, from *Supervisory Management*, September 1985. © 1985 by American Management Association, New York. All rights reserved.

"Well, for one thing, Paula, as head operator I have set hours, and I get more overtime. If I were a manager, I'd have to put in more time, handle more headaches, deal with more paperwork, and I wouldn't get any extra pay to compensate for the aggravation I'd have to endure."

"True enough. However, the main thing about the job is that it puts you in line for the manager's job. You knew that."

"Not necessarily. Anyway, I figured I'd have a choice. Don't I?"

"Well, sure you do. I mean, no one can *force* you to be manager. But I will say that no one had to spend any time talking *me* into it." She looked at Sandy curiously. "Why don't you want it?"

Sandy put down the computer sheet she had been working on and smiled. "For one thing, I work well with computers, but not with people. I just don't think that I'd make a good manager."

"Oh, I don't know," Paula said. "You seem to handle yourself all right."

"Yeah, but I've been getting a better look at what I'd have to do as a manager since I took this job."

"So?"

"So, it's a headache. There's always something irritating going on. I see what you have to go through, for instance. You catch it from the union, and you catch it from the company, too. The manager is the first person everyone leans on. You have to handle problems in the department, problems between departments, and you even help out with personal problems. And what do you get for all your trouble? Ulcers!"

Paula grinned. "You're making it sound a little worse than it is, Sandy. Anyway, how else are you going to get ahead?"

"Maybe I'm not interested in getting ahead, Paula."

"Yes, you are. You're the kind of person who is interested. You've demonstrated that you like a challenge and can deal with pressure."

"All right, maybe I am. But the point is, I'm doing okay right now. I made a lot of money in this place last year. And I want to keep on making it. When I come in on a Saturday, I want it to be for time-and-a-half. If I were a manager, I'd get only straight time, right?"

Paula nodded.

"And while everybody else got double time on Sundays and triple time on holidays, I'd only be getting time-and-a-half, right?"

Paula nodded again.

Sandy picked up the computer sheet again. "Of course, if a manager gets sick," she continued, "she gets full pay. But I just don't get sick that much. And even if I did, with the insurance we get, I'd still get most of my pay anyway. So tell me— what's the big advantage?"

Consider these questions and ask your own:

1. What might Paula have answered?
2. Do you think Paula should try harder to get Sandy to accept the position of manager?
3. What should a manager do about an employee who is happy where he or she is, and not interested in advancement?

PART II

ORGANIZING

4
FUNDAMENTALS
OF ORGANIZING

OBJECTIVES

After reading and studying the material in this chapter, you should be able to:

- Understand the stages of organization growth.
- Explain the principles of unity of command and span of control.
- Describe the difference between line and staff.
- Understand how to avoid excessive conflict between line and staff.
- Explain the three types of authority found in organizations.
- Recognize the distinction between centralization and decentralization.
- Understand the concept of project or matrix organization.

IMPORTANT TERMS

line organization
unity-of-command principle
span-of-control principle
line personnel
staff personnel
advisory authority

line authority
functional authority
decentralization
centralized organization
project *or* matrix organization

CHAPTER OUTLINE

> The only things that evolve by themselves in an organization are disorder, friction, and malperformance.
> *Peter Drucker*

In Chapter 1, we defined the term *organizing* and noted that it is one of the five functions of any manager or supervisor. In this chapter, we present concepts, principles, and a frame of reference for understanding this function. You will note that we are not beginning this chapter with a short case as we did in previous chapters. This is because we will use a long, continuing case—presented in brief parts—to illustrate the stages of growth in most organizations.

Many first-level managers understand organization only from a narrow vantage point—their immediate department or perhaps one or two levels above them. We feel that it is equally important to be able to see and understand the organization from a much broader standpoint. The better supervisors understand "the big picture," the better equipped they are to work effectively as key members of the management team. Consequently, organizing is presented from a broad, overall perspective in this chapter. In Chapter 5, we will focus on organizing concepts that are directly applicable to the supervisory management level.

Failure to understand the organizing function from a broader viewpoint can lead to the following problems:

1. Excessive violation of the unity-of-command principle.
2. Failure to develop additional departments when needed.
3. Unclear and misassigned duties and responsibilities for new employees.
4. Ineffective use of organizational units and inadequate development of human resources because of improper decentralization of authority.
5. Excessive and unhealthy conflicts between departments and between line supervisors and staff personnel.

THE FOUR-STAGE GROWTH OF AN ORGANIZATION

To see the organizing function of management in operation, let us study the growth and development of a hypothetical manufacturing business in terms of the number of people required to run it. Usually a business organization grows in four stages: Stage 1—the one-person organization; Stage 2—the hiring of assistants; Stage 3—the line organization; and Stage 4—the line-and-staff organization. Not all organizations go through all these stages. In fact, many skip the first stage and go directly to Stage 2. For clarity's sake, however, we'll discuss each stage.

Stage 1: The One-Person Organization

JOHN MOODY (a)—Continuing Case

Our story begins in 1970 in a small Midwest city of 75,000. Our main character is John Moody, 29, a high-school graduate and Vietnam veteran, who has been working in a large paper mill on the outskirts of the city since his discharge from the service in 1965. John still holds the same semiskilled job at the operative level that he started with. His wife's relatives believe he is a lazy person with a low IQ who will never amount to much. Actually, John is quite an intelligent person, but his basic satisfaction in life comes from the challenge of building and creating things in his garage workshop. Although he assumes that he will never get rich, he feels his take-home pay is sufficient to take care of the necessities of life and to support his hobbies. Even though his job at the mill is not very challenging, he gets all the challenge he needs from tinkering around in his workshop.

Unfortunately, in early 1970 the country begins to slide into an economic recession, which has an adverse effect on the paper industry. Several mill employees, including John, are laid off because of excessive inventory buildup. John signs up for unemployment compensation and decides to spend time building a new boat trailer in his garage. He puts a lot of thought and effort into the task. The result is an excellent boat trailer—such a fine one that several of his friends talk him into building boat trailers for them for 20 percent more than his expenses. Even at this price, his boat trailer sells for less than those sold in local stores. Before long, so many requests are coming in that John finds himself spending all his time in his garage.

At this point, John decides to work full time building boat trailers as long as he can make a living doing so.

Figure 4–1 shows that John Moody's business is in the first stage of organizational growth, that is, a one-person operation. This means that he and he

FIGURE 4–1   JOHN MOODY'S ONE-PERSON ORGANIZATION

JOHN MOODY
Owner and Operator

Finance
Production
Sales

alone performs the three basic activities common to all manufacturing operations: financing, producing, and selling.

Stage 2: The Hiring of Assistants

JOHN MOODY (b)—Continuing Case

After three months, John Moody finds so many orders are coming in that he cannot fill them. In the past few years, the federal government has built a number of dams near John's town, creating four new lakes in the region. Fishing has been good, and there has been a large demand for boats and boat trailers. John is now making more money per day than he did when he was with the mill. To keep pace with the orders, he hires Ray Martin, a former army buddy, to help build the trailers. For a small monthly salary, John also hires his wife, Nancy, to keep books and handle the financial details. Before the month is out, Ray has mastered his job so well that he and John are producing more boat trailers than they have orders for.

At this point, John and Ray start thinking about someone they can hire as a salesperson. Ray's brother, Paul, has just graduated from college with a major in marketing. After being approached by John and Ray, Paul decides that John's business has possibilities. With the assurance of an opportunity to buy into the business in the future, Paul starts to work as a salesperson for John.

Figure 4–2 shows that John Moody has had to hire three assistants to help carry out the three primary activities of his business. This stage is a critical time because over 50 percent of new businesses fail in their first year of operation from lack of capital, ineffective management, or both.

FIGURE 4–2   JOHN MOODY HIRES ASSISTANTS

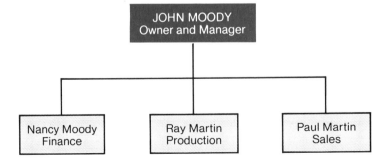

JOHN MOODY (c)—Continuing Case

Paul Martin proves to be an excellent salesperson, and the business continues to grow. To keep up with the increasing volume of orders, John hires additional people. Also, the business moves to a larger building. As Figure 4–3 shows, after two years the business has grown so that John has 19 people working for him. His net income is such that Nancy has quit working, but John finds himself so busy that he cannot enjoy his higher income. More important, he feels he is losing control of the business; the increased costs per trailer support this belief.

FIGURE 4–3   JOHN MOODY'S ORGANIZATION AFTER TWO YEARS

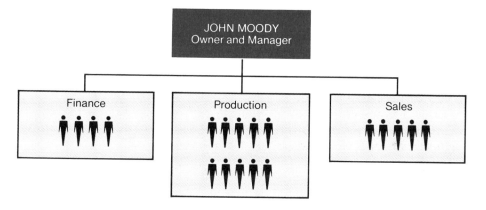

Before reading further, look at the organization chart in Figure 4–3. Can you explain why John Moody is losing control of his business?

JOHN MOODY (d)—Continuing Case

In desperation, John Moody calls the Martin brothers to ask advice about his problem. Paul Martin recalls that in one of his college courses, the instructor talked about the management principle of *span of control*. This principle holds that there is a limit to the number of people a manager can supervise effectively. In Paul's opinion, the solution is to select managers for the areas of finance, production, and sales.

Paul's solution seems so simple that John Moody wonders why he didn't think of it himself. Accordingly, he places Beth Fields —his best accountant—in charge of finance, Ray Martin in charge of production, and Paul Martin in charge of sales.

Stage 3: The Line Organization

Figure 4–4 shows that John Moody has selected a manager for each of the three major departments, and his span of control has been reduced from 19 to 3 employees. Beth Fields is responsible for three employees, Ray Martin for nine employees, and Paul Martin for four employees. In effect, John Moody's business is now structured as a **line organization**. This means that each person in the organization has clearly defined responsibilities and reports to an immediate supervisor.

There are two advantages to having a line organization at an early stage of a business organization's growth:

1. Quick, decisive action on problems is possible because authority is so centralized— it is in the hands of John Moody and his three managers.
2. Lines of responsibility and authority are clearly defined. Everyone knows what his or her job and obligations are. As a result, there is a minimum of evasion of responsibility and accountability.

FIGURE 4–4 THE SPAN OF CONTROL IN JOHN MOODY'S
LINE ORGANIZATION

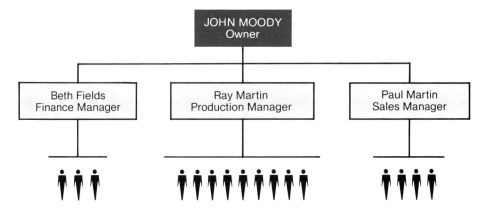

JOHN MOODY (e)—Continuing Case

As a result of the line organization and the capabilities of each manager, the unit cost of making each boat trailer is lowered. Under the leadership of sales manager Paul Martin, the business expands its sales territory to cover most of the states in the Midwest. As sales increase, production also increases. New people are added in both sales and production. Thus, the line organization develops to accompany the increased growth.

Keeping in mind the principles of span of control, John Moody adds new sections in production and sales whenever the volume of business justifies the new additions. He now also finds time to concentrate more on such things as developing plans for the future, coordinating the work of the three departments, and supervising his managers.

JOHN MOODY (f)—Continuing Case

After ten years, John Moody's business is employing over 700 people. During this period, John has promoted Ray Martin to be in charge of five production department heads. Figure 4–5 shows that this move creates an additional level of management in the production department. The department heads, in turn, are each responsible for four production supervisors. Each production supervisor is responsible for ten production workers. Similarly, John has made Paul Martin sales manager in charge of three regional sales managers, each of whom is supervising eight salespersons.

FIGURE 4–5   JOHN MOODY'S LINE ORGANIZATION AFTER TEN YEARS

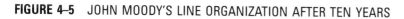
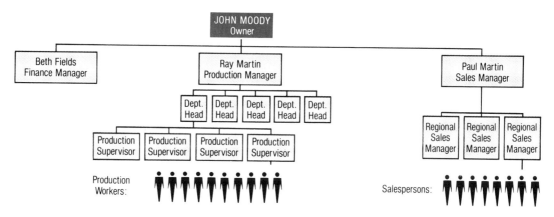

Stage 4: The Line-and-Staff Organization

JOHN MOODY (g)—Continuing Case

Unfortunately, increasing sales require John Moody's business to add more people in order to meet production quotas. So the profit on each unit produced declines. Finally, Beth Fields, the head of finance, reports to John that each $1.00 in sales is costing $1.10. In other words, a boat trailer that the business sells for $200 is costing $220 to manufacture. Although the business is now sound financially, John is aware that, with the way things are going, it will not take long for the business to go bankrupt. He therefore decides to call in a reputable management consultant.

Before reading the consultant's recommendations, what would you think is the primary problem or problems causing manufacturing costs to increase in John Moody's business?

JOHN MOODY (h)—Continuing Case

The management consultant interviews managers from different levels in the company. After several days of investigation, the consultant makes the following report to John Moody:

My investigation reveals that you have made a mistake that many companies make: You are operating purely as a line organization, whereas at your stage of growth, you need to adopt a **line-and-staff organization.** This means that you will need to hire several staff experts to perform some of the activities your line managers presently do. As it now stands, your organizational structure and way of operating tend to overload your managers. They are, in effect, wearing too many hats. More specifically, I have found evidence of the following three kinds of inefficiency:

1. Your supervisors are doing their own hiring, firing, and disciplining. Consequently, you have no uniform way of screening, selecting, promoting, and disciplining employees. Moreover, a number of the super-

visors are hiring friends and relatives for their departments, and other employees believe favoritism is rampant throughout the company.

2. The several department heads independently purchase materials and supplies for their departments. This duplication of effort has resulted in excessive space and dollars tied up in raw materials inventory. In addition, this practice has opened the door for waste and pilferage of supplies and materials.

3. Your department heads and supervisors are involved in method and layout studies, maintenance and repair work, scheduling and dispatching, and, to cap it off, quality control—all of these activities on top of their primary jobs of supervising the work and motivating their employees. The old proverb that "a jack of all trades is master of none" is certainly borne out by the situation I find in your plant.

My primary recommendation, therefore, is that you hire a personnel manager to screen and select new employees, a production-control manager to do all the purchasing and inventory control, and an industrial engineering manager to do method and layout studies and the like. [Their relationship to the organization is shown in Figure 4–6.] By adding these three staff specialists, you will give your department heads and supervisors a chance to really do their primary job of overseeing production and motivating their employees. Equally important, you should receive immediate benefits and cost savings by eliminating inefficiencies and installing improved ways of operating.

FIGURE 4–6   JOHN MOODY'S LINE-AND-STAFF ORGANIZATION

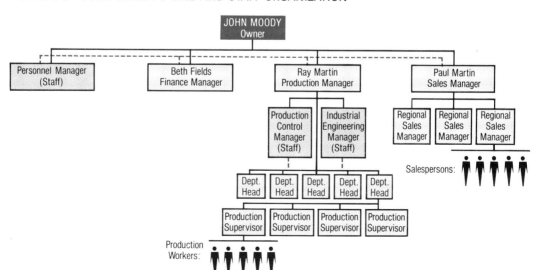

What adjustments will the supervisors need to make to accommodate the consultant's recommended changes? Do you think these changes will help or hinder the supervisor in the job of motivating and managing his or her crew?

JOHN MOODY (i)—Continuing Case

The consultant went on to report that, in the future, additional staff people would be needed if the company continued its rate of growth. He also stated that, in the future, the company might want to consider diversification by adding additional product lines that would require similar skills.

John Moody accepted the consultant's recommendations to become a line-and-staff organization and went on to achieve not only record sales, but also record profits and growth. Ultimately, any growing business needs to pass into this fourth stage. Unfortunately, some do not and may suffer the consequences of possible decline and bankruptcy.

TWO IMPORTANT ORGANIZING PRINCIPLES

Two important principles involved in the organizing function were hinted at in the case of John Moody's organization. These are unity of command (found in line organizations) and span of control (or span of management). Let us now discuss these principles in detail.

Unity of Command

The **unity of command principle** states: Everyone in an organization should report to and be accountable to only one boss for performing a given activity. This superior is responsible for evaluating performance, passing down orders and information, and developing subordinates to become better employees in the organization. It is to this person that subordinates should turn for help in carrying out their duties and for communicating any deviations, either positive or negative, in implementing their duties. In sum, the superior is the one responsible for motivating his or her employees to achieve effective results and for taking action when subordinates deviate from planned performance.

Adherence to the unity-of-command principle is important for five reasons:

1. It prevents duplication and conflict when orders and instructions are passed down.
2. It decreases confusion and buck passing because everyone—including managers—is accountable to only one person for a given assignment.
3. It provides a basis whereby a supervisor and his or her employees can develop a knowledge of each other's strengths and weaknesses.
4. It provides an opportunity for a supervisor and employees to develop supportive relationships and to realize their individual and group potential in achieving organizational objectives.
5. It promotes higher morale than is generally found in organizations that do not follow it.

Unfortunately some managers only give lip service to this principle, although their organization chart may seem to reflect it.

Recently, one of the authors of this book was working with a branch plant of a large company to tailor a management development program. Among other things, this author was examining the leadership styles practiced by key managers and their effect on subordinates. To determine these leadership styles, managers at all levels were interviewed. The results showed that the plant manager, though unusually capable and generally effective, made one mistake with his subordinate managers: he violated the unity-of-command principle by periodically conducting inspections throughout the plant and making on-the-spot suggestions to operative employees. Oftentimes, he made these suggestions when the employees' supervisor was not present. As a result, operative employees were following instructions their immediate supervisors were unaware of. Moreover, the employees would stop working on their assigned duties in order to carry out the instructions of the plant manager. Figure 4–7 illustrates the problem this practice caused the supervisors.

As a result of this one error, a serious morale problem had developed. Many of the plant manager's otherwise effective managerial practices were being undermined. When this situation was called to his attention, he was quite surprised. It seems that he had slipped into this habit without being fully aware of its long-range consequences. This manager thereupon began passing his suggestions and instructions through lower-level managers. As a result, morale improved.

Although employees should have only one superior, they may, of course, have relationships with many people. For example, in a line-and-staff organization, line supervisors and department heads will have many contacts with staff personnel. These contacts are necessary so that both line and staff personnel can accomplish their duties. Later in this chapter, we will explain how these relationships can be developed without violating the unity-of-command principle. The important thing to remember is this: If there should be a conflict between a staff request and a line manager's command, the employee should have a single manager to turn to for clarification or a final decision.

FIGURE 4-7 VIOLATING THE UNITY-OF-COMMAND PRINCIPLES

Span of Control

Before World War II, experts maintained that the span of control should be three to eight people, depending on the level of management. In those days, therefore, one of the first things an organizational consultant examined when a company was having problems was the span of control at various levels. Today the three-to-eight-people limit does not hold as true. This is why we have defined the **span-of-control principle** simply as this: There is a limit to the number of people a person can manage effectively. Just as you can span only a limited number of feet and inches with your arms, your mental reach can span only a limited number of problems, situations, and relationships that make up the activities of management.

NARROWER SPAN OF CONTROL AT THE TOP. One thing we can say without qualification: The higher managers are in an organization, the fewer people they should have reporting directly to them, and vice versa. There are at least three reasons for this practice:

1. Top-level managers should have the ability to solve a variety of different, non-recurring problems. Much mental concentration is required to solve these problems.
2. Middle managers must spend much of their time in long-range planning, working with outside interest groups, and coordinating the various activities of the organization. They cannot afford to be tied down by the excessive burden of supervision when a large number of people report directly to them.

3. First-level managers, by contrast, tend to be concerned with more clearly defined areas of operation. Although they will be responsible for a certain amount of coordination with other departments, most of their contacts are directly with their immediate subordinates. Hence, they are able to supervise more people than higher-level managers.

DIFFERENT APPROACHES TO A SUPERVISOR'S SPAN OF CONTROL. Figure 4–8 shows that there are three different approaches to a supervisor's span of control. As you examine Figure 4–8, you will notice that the jobs of the supervisors must be quite different. Can we say that one of these approaches is the best? No, because the correct size of a supervisor's span of control depends on a number of circumstances, as shown in Table 4–1.

Companies that follow a policy of a narrow span of control are often hampered in achieving effective results. A large organization of, say, a thousand people, that rigidly adheres to a span of between three and seven will have a tall, narrow organizational structure (with many, many management levels), which will cause some disadvantages. More supervisory managers will be required, resulting in higher payroll costs. Communication must pass up and down through many levels, causing greater possibility of distortion. The danger of oversupervision may restrict decision making by employees and limit their opportunity to develop their potential. On the other hand, the advantage of tight control is that the work can be closely directed. So the company can hire relatively lower-skilled people.

FIGURE 4–8   NARROW, WIDE, AND VERY WIDE SPANS OF CONTROL

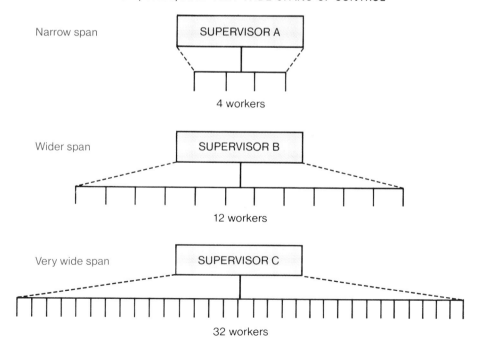

TABLE 4–1   FACTORS CONTRIBUTING TO A NARROW OR WIDE SPAN OF CONTROL

Factor	Narrow Span Indicated	Wide Span Indicated
How physically close are people in performing the work?	Dispersed, perhaps even in different geographical locations.	Very close, perhaps all in one physical work area or location in a building.
How complex is the work?	Very complex, such as development of a manned space station that would orbit the earth.	Rather routine and simple, such as an assembly-line operation.
How much supervision is required?	A great deal. So many problems arise that supervisor needs to exercise close control.	Little. Workers are well-trained, able to make normal job decisions easily.
How much "nonsupervisory" work is required of the supervisor?	Much. Supervisor may spend much time planning, coordinating, and performing nonsupervisory tasks.	Little planning and coordination time is required of the supervisor. Spends most of time "supervising" employees.
How much organizational assistance is furnished to the supervisor?	Little. Supervisor may do own recruiting, training and controlling.	Much. Supervisor may be aided by a training department, quality control department, etc.

TENDENCY TOWARD WIDER SPANS OF CONTROL. Over the years, many companies have tended to broaden their span of control at all levels. There are at least three reasons for this trend:

1. Higher educational attainment, management and supervisory development programs, vocational and technical training, and generally increased knowledge on the part of the labor force have increased the abilities and capacities of both managers and employees. The greater the supervisor's capacity, the greater his or her ability to supervise more people.
2. Research indicates that in many situations, *general* supervision is more effective than *close* supervision.
3. New developments in management permit us to broaden the span of control and supervise by results without losing control. For example, by using a computer an organization can process information more quickly and develop more efficient information-reporting systems.

RELATIONSHIPS BETWEEN LINE AND STAFF

Line personnel carry out the primary activities of a business such as producing or selling products and/or services. **Staff personnel**, on the other hand, have the expertise to assist the line people and aid top management in various areas of business activities. Line departments, therefore, are like a main stream. Staff departments are like the tributaries serving and assisting the main stream, although they should not be thought of as being secondary to the line departments. Both line and staff people are important.

Of the various jobs you've held, which were "line" and which were "staff"?

Once a business has reached the fourth stage of growth and is no longer a small organization, it becomes more complex and difficult to coordinate. A line-and-staff structure that places competent specialists in certain positions, such as in human-resources management, legal and governmental departments, research and development, and public relations, will help eliminate confusion, duplication, and inefficiency. But it will not solve all problems for all time. A growing organization must be continually alert to pitfalls and potential trouble spots.

Conflicts Between Line and Staff

One common problem area in most large organizations is excessive conflict between line and staff personnel and between different departments. Differences in viewpoint between people and departments are, of course, natural, inevitable, and healthy; but excessive conflict can disrupt an entire organization. As shown in Figure 4–9, many line and staff contacts are normal.

There are many reasons why excessive conflict between line and staff personnel can develop within an organization. Figure 4–10 summarizes some reasons for conflict between line and staff personnel.

Before reading further, what do you think might be done to decrease or eliminate the reasons for conflict between line and staff personnel?

FIGURE 4–9   LINE-AND-STAFF CONTACTS

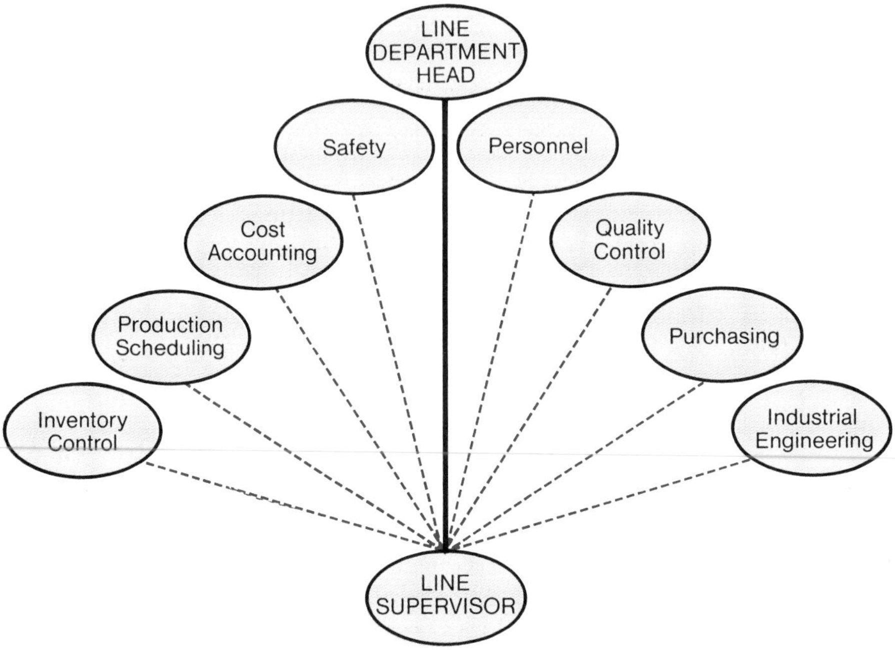

How to Avoid Excessive Line-Staff Conflict: Delineating Authority

While conflict between line and staff people may not be completely eliminated, a major way to avoid it is to have people clearly understand the authority/responsibility relationships between individuals and departments. To show this, let us examine the three types of authority: advisory, line, and functional.

FIGURE 4–10   SOME REASONS FOR CONFLICT BETWEEN LINE AND STAFF PERSONNEL

- Staff personnel give direct orders to line personnel.
- Good human relations are not practiced in dealings between line and staff.
- Overlapping authority and responsibility confuse both line and staff.
- Line people feel that staff people are not knowledgeable about conditions at the operating level.
- Staff people, because of their expertise, may attempt to influence line decisions against line managers' wishes.
- Top management misuses staff personnel or fails to use them properly.
- Each department views the organization from a narrow viewpoint instead of looking at the organization as a whole.

ADVISORY AUTHORITY. The primary responsibility of most staff departments is to serve and advise the line departments. This type of authority is called **advisory authority** or the *authority of ideas*. However, some staff people may be so zealous in trying to sell their ideas to line personnel that they, in effect, hand out orders. When this happens, and if the line supervisor permits it to occur frequently, the unity of command begins to break down.

LINE AUTHORITY. The second type of authority, **line authority,** is concerned with the power to directly command or exact performance from others. This power to command does not mean that effective performance results simply from giving out orders. It means that when you have line authority, you are directly responsible for the results of a certain department or group of workers. As you can see, line authority is not restricted to line personnel. The head of a staff department also has line authority over the employees in his or her department.

FUNCTIONAL AUTHORITY. The third type of authority, **functional authority,** is usually a restricted kind of line authority. It gives a staff person a narrow type of limited line authority over a given *function,* such as safety or quality, regardless of where that function is found in the organization.

For example, a staff safety specialist may have functional authority to insist that line managers follow standard safety procedures in their departments. The staff safety specialist may have top management's blessing to dictate to lower-level line managers exactly what they must and must not do concerning any matter that falls within the safety picture. A quality-control inspector may tell a line worker that certain parts need to be reworked. A human-resources specialist may say to a line supervisor that the latter cannot fire a certain employee. A cost accountant may notify line departments that certain cost information must be furnished weekly, and so on.

Can you think of some other common examples of functional authority?

Are you perhaps thinking that functional authority violates the unity-of-command principle? It does! For this reason, it is important that all individuals clearly understand what functional authority is. Top line managers have the major responsibility for this. Moreover, it is important for line personnel to exercise their right to appeal to higher management levels when there are disagreements between them and staff personnel. Functional authority is necessary, but it can be dangerous if it is passed around indiscriminately. Normally, it is given only to a staff area where there is a great deal of expertise and the staff expert's advice would be followed anyway.

Another way to avoid excessive conflict between line and staff people is to have effective communication between people and between departments. Key managers overseeing both line and staff people can improve the communication process by periodically bringing line and staff people together to discuss problems that cut across departmental lines. This example may also inspire lower-level managers to do the same thing with their key employees. Thus, the danger of seeing only part of the picture will be minimized.

DECENTRALIZATION VERSUS CENTRALIZATION

The concept of decentralization is closely related to the concept of delegation, which is examined in the next chapter. Both concepts are concerned with the giving of authority to someone at a lower level. **Decentralization** is the broader concept, as it refers to the extent to which authority is delegated from one level or one unit of the organization to another. In a *decentralized* organization, middle and lower levels of management make broader, more important decisions about their units. In a **centralized organization**, a strong central staff makes most of the important decisions that concern all levels or units within the organization.

Factors Affecting Decentralization

No organization is completely centralized or decentralized. Decentralization is a relative concept and depends on a number of factors. These are listed below:

1. *Top management philosophy.* Some top managers have a need for tight control. They put together a strong central staff and will want to make the most important decisions themselves. Others believe in strong delegation and push decisions to the lowest levels of their organization.
2. *History of the organization's growth.* Organizations that have grown by merging with other companies or acquiring them tend to be decentralized. Those that have grown on their own tend to be centralized.
3. *Geographic location(s).* Organizations that are spread out, with many units in different cities or regions, tend to be decentralized so that lower-level managers can make decisions that fit their territory or circumstances.
4. *Quality of managers.* If an organization has many well-qualified, well-trained managers, it will more likely be decentralized. If it has few, top management will centralize and make the most important decisions.
5. *Availability of controls.* If top management has an effective control system — good, timely information about performance at lower levels — the organization will tend more toward decentralization. Without a good control-information flow to monitor end results, it will tend to be more centralized.[1]

Select one of your past employers. Would you say that the organization was centralized or decentralized? Why?

Decentralization Affects Organizational Structure

The degree to which an organization is decentralized will have a direct effect on the number of levels within the organization's structure. As shown in Figure 4–11, Ford Motor Company, which is relatively centralized, has 12 layers of managers and supervisors between the operative employees and the chairman. Toyota, which is relatively decentralized, has only seven levels of management. There appears to be a trend in the United States toward reducing the number of levels of management and shifting toward more decentralization. Both the Japanese success in the automobile industry and the recession of the early 1980s, during which time many United States companies trimmed organizational "fat," have had an impact on this trend. Marvin Runyon, who retired as vice-president of Ford Motor Company, accepted the position of chief executive officer with the Nissan Motor Manufacturing Corporation, U.S.A. When Runyon was asked how the Nissan plant in Tennessee would be operated, he replied that the

FIGURE 4–11   LAYERS OF MANAGEMENT REFLECTING A CENTRALIZED VERSUS A DECENTRALIZED STRUCTURE

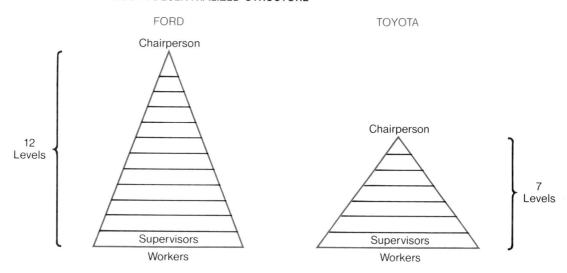

plant would take the best of both American and Japanese management concepts and methods. He went on to state:

> We are reducing the management levels that are customarily found in United States auto manufacturing companies. A lot of companies are very tiered. We're going to have five levels of management—president, vice-president, plant manager, operations manager, and supervisor. And then we have technicians. The reason we are doing that is to foster good communications, which I think is the key to running any business.
>
> We're going to have a very participative management style. What I mean is, everybody participates in what is done in this company. It will be more of a bottom-up management than top-down. Usually the top fellow decides everything that's going to happen, tells everybody, then expects everybody to march to that drummer. Japanese don't work that way. They work from a bottom-up technique. And that's what we plan to do.
>
> Now the reason for that is very simple. You go into a company and ask even a third-level person—say, the level of plant manager—"What are the problems in your operation?" He can give you about 4 percent of the real problems. Then you go to the operations-manager level, and they can give you, say, 40 percent. You go to the supervisor level and maybe they can give you 70 percent. If you go to the technicians and ask them, they'll give you 100 percent of the problems. So, who better to participate in running the company than the people who actually know what's going on?[2]

PROJECT OR MATRIX ORGANIZATION

Most organizations today are still structured as either a line or a line-and-staff organization along functional or product lines. Line organizations and line-and-staff organizations have served their purposes well for many years. They place considerable emphasis on basic organizational principles such as unity of command. However, many other organizational structures have developed. One of these structures is a hybrid type of organization called the **project** or **matrix organization**, where both functional departments and project teams exist.[3] The functional departments, such as production, purchasing, and engineering, are permanent parts of the organization. The project teams are created as the need arises, and they are disbanded when the projects are completed. Let's look at an example.

> *Stan Douglas is plant manager for the XYZ Company. For some time, Stan has been concerned with increasing costs, which are reducing the profit margin for the products his plant produces. The functional departments in his plant are shown in Figure 4–12. Under this arrangement, Stan Douglas has line authority over his functional managers, and they, in turn, have line authority over the people who report to them. The unity-of-command principle is adhered to throughout the company. However, Stan decides to form three*

FIGURE 4–12   THE TRADITIONAL ORGANIZATION

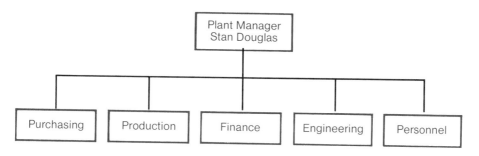

project teams composed of personnel from various departments charged with developing cost-reduction recommendations.

With this new assignment, the organizational changes are reflected in Figure 4–13. The broken lines in Figure 4–13 show that the project supervisors have functional authority over project team members drawn from the different functional departments. Nevertheless, Stan Douglas retains line authority over the functional departments.

FIGURE 4–13   THE PROJECT OR MATRIX ORGANIZATION

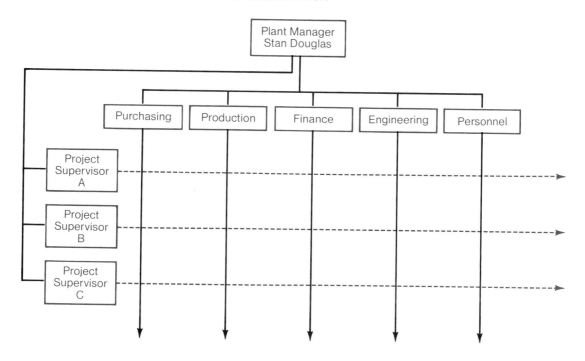

The recommendations from members of the three project teams are excellent. As a result, costs are reduced. After one year, the project teams are disbanded.

Under the project or matrix organization form, is the unity-of-command principle followed? Explain.

If your answer to the above question was "no," then you are correct. People from the functional departments are working for two bosses: the line manager in the functional department and the project supervisor. If the matrix form violates this important principle, why would Stan Douglas use this approach? The answer, of course, is to increase his plant's *flexibility* in dealing with an important problem—cost reduction. The matrix form allows the plant to use expertise from several functional areas to focus on the problem. You should think of "principles" as guidelines and not as rigid rules.

Another type of organizational structure that is related to the matrix organization concerns the increasing use of "quality circles" at lower levels, which we will examine in Chapter 16.

CHAPTER REVIEW

In this chapter we focused on concepts that should give supervisory managers a better understanding of their organization. We presented several phases of organizational growth and emphasized that it is important for a growing company to evolve from a line organization to a line-and-staff organization. This evolution allows the company to take advantage of specialization in such areas as human resources, quality control, purchasing, maintenance, scheduling, and safety. It also allows line managers and supervisors to concentrate more on supervising and motivating their employees.

The importance of following the principles of unity of command and span of control as guiding concepts was stressed. Following the unity-of-command principle is important because it prevents duplication and conflict when orders and instructions are passed down. It also decreases confusion and buck passing and provides a basis for managers and their employees to develop a better understanding of what they expect of each other. Finally, it promotes higher morale than is found in organizations that excessively violate the unity of command.

The span-of-control principle emphasizes that there is a limit to the number of people a person can effectively manage. As one moves down the organization chart from top management to supervisory management levels, the span of control should increase. The reasons for this are that (1) top management requires the freedom to solve a variety of different, non-recurring problems; (2) higher-level managers must spend much of their time in long-range planning, working with outside interest groups, and coordinating the various activities of the business; and (3) supervisory managers tend to be concerned with more clearly defined areas of operation.

Having a line-and-staff organization sometimes leads to excessive conflict between line and staff departments. To avoid this, it is crucial to have people understand the authority/responsibility relationships between individuals and departments. Another way to avoid excessive conflict is to have effective communications between people and between departments.

We examined the concept of centralization versus decentralization and noted the factors that influence the extent of centralization and decentralization. We also noted that computer technology increases the ability of higher management to shift in either direction. The trend, however, seems to be in the direction of decentralization.

Finally, we discussed the concept of the project or matrix organization and indicated that, although this form violates the unity-of-command principle, sometimes it is necessary to increase flexibility and problem-solving effectiveness.

QUESTIONS FOR REVIEW AND DISCUSSION

1. Outline the four stages of organizational growth and relate them to an organization with which you are familiar.
2. What two important management principles affect the successful operation of a growing organization? Do you think John Moody's difficulties could have been avoided if he had understood these principles?
3. What is the relationship between levels of management and span of control? Explain the advantages and disadvantages.
4. Distinguish between line and staff functions. Are they always easily identified in various types of business enterprise? Justify the existence of both line and staff departments.
5. What conflicts may arise between line and staff personnel? What reasons can you give for these problems? How does effective communication ease the conflict?
6. What are the three types of authority? Do they all exist in all four stages of functional growth?
7. What are some factors that favor centralization or decentralization?
8. Briefly give some primary reasons why managers might move to a project or matrix organization.

LEARNING EXERCISE 4–1
THE SUPERVISOR'S VIEWPOINT
OF CENTRALIZATION VERSUS DECENTRALIZATION

Assume that two cousins, Sandra and Bob, graduate from the community technical school. Bob accepts a job with Ford Motor Company, a relatively centralized organization, as a first-line supervisor. Sandra accepts a job with Nissan Motor Manufacturing Corporation, U.S.A., a relatively decentralized company, also as a first-line supervisor.

Six months later, they meet and have a debate regarding who has the better job and the greater opportunity for growth and development.

1. Make a list of the debate points supporting Bob's position with Ford.
2. Make a list of the debate points supporting Sandra's position with Nissan.
3. On the basis of your two lists, who do you think will win the debate? Why?

LEARNING EXERCISE 4–2
CONFLICTING VIEWS

Imagine that you are a management trainee in a company. You spend time talking with people from various departments to get a good feel for how things work. Here are excerpts from what two supervisors told you recently.

Production Supervisor: What a job! Top management is breathing down my neck to get the work out. My people do a real good job, considering our equipment and how crowded we are. But what a problem I have with that crowd from maintenance! You'd think they owned the whole company the way they carry on. They act like they're doing you a big favor to do a repair job—letting you know how important they are and how they have to schedule their jobs. And they hate for you to tell them what's wrong with the equipment, like they have to be the ones to do a "complete diagnosis." They always seem to drag their feet for me, and yet other production departments get things done right away. I've told the superintendent about their favoritism and cockiness, but it doesn't help.

Maintenance Supervisor: What a job! I've got production people running around here all day telling me what they've *got* to have done. I've got six mechanics, and sometimes we'll have 20 calls a day, not to mention our *scheduled* maintenance. So I try to assign priorities—that's the only way to survive. And then one of those @#$%¢&* production supervisors takes his or her problem to the superintendent! What really burns me up is the abuse my people get from them. You try to do what's right, and some say you play favorites. I'd like to straighten that whole bunch of production yo-yos out!

Answer the following questions:

1. What concepts presented in the chapter are involved here?
2. What do you recommend to resolve the problem between the two supervisors?

3. Present a role in which a third party works with the two supervisors to attempt to resolve this problem.

ENDNOTES

1. James A. F. Stoner, *Management* (Englewood Cliffs, NJ: Prentice-Hall, 1978), p. 284.
2. "Theme and Variation," *The Owen Manager* (Owen Graduate School of Management, Vanderbilt University) 4 (Spring 1983): 2.
3. James L. Mercer, "Organizing for the '80s—What about Matrix Management?" *Business* 31 (July-August 1981): 25–33.

SUGGESTIONS FOR FURTHER READING

Boyle, R. J. "Designing the Energetic Organization." Management Review (March 1983): 21-15.

Davis, S. M., and P. R. Lawrence. *Matrix*. Reading, MA: Addison-Wesley Publishing Co., 1977.

Obert, S. L. "Development Patterns of Organizational Task Groups: A Preliminary Study." *Human Relations* 36 (January 1983): 37–51.

Van Fleet, D. D., and A. G. Bedeian. "A History of the Span of Management." *Academy of Management Review* 2 (July 1977): 356–67.

5
DELEGATING AUTHORITY

OBJECTIVES

After reading and studying the material in this chapter, you should be able to:

- Recognize the importance of delegation.
- Explain what is involved in the delegation process, including authority, responsibility, and accountability.
- Indicate what negative consequences occur when supervisors fail to delegate effectively.
- Discuss some principles that are relevant to effective delegation.
- Understand why some supervisors are reluctant to delegate.

IMPORTANT TERMS

experiential learning
delegation of authority
job descriptions

accountability
parity principle
reframing

CHAPTER OUTLINE
CASE 5–1. JANE OSBORN'S PROBLEM

I. WHY DELEGATE?
- A. Delegating develops people
- B. Delegating allows the supervisor to do other things
- C. Delegating allows more work to be accomplished
- D. Delegating improves control

II. PROCESS OF DELEGATION
- A. Granting authority
- B. Assigning responsibility
- C. Requiring accountability

III. EFFECTIVE DELEGATION
- A. Knowing when to delegate
- B. How the delegation process operates
- C. The principle of parity of authority and responsibility
- D. Effective delegation takes time

IV. ROLES INVOLVED IN EFFECTIVE DELEGATION
- A. The role of higher management
- B. The role of the supervisor
- C. The role of employees to whom authority is delegated

V. WHY SUPERVISORS FAIL TO DELEGATE

VI. RELATING DELEGATION TO SUCCESS OR FAILURE

VII. INEFFECTIVE DELEGATION: A SOLUTION

Chapter Review

Questions for Review and Discussion

Learning Exercise 5–1. Solving Jane Osborn's Problem

Learning Exercise 5–2. The New Employee at Happy Valley

Learning Exercise 5–3. A Quiz on Delegation

Suggestions for Further Reading

The best executive is the one who has sense enough to pick good people to do what he wants done and self-restraint enough to keep from meddling with them while they do it.
Theodore Roosevelt

CASE 5–1
JANE OSBORN'S PROBLEM

Jane Osborn was quite pleased when she graduated from the community college with an associate degree in industrial technology. While pursuing her degree, she had been employed as an assembler in a high-technology plant. She was a very efficient worker and had been promised an opportunity to be a supervisor upon completion of the technology program. Two months later, the company named her supervisor of one of the assembly groups. As an achievement-oriented person, Osborn saw this as the first step toward her long-range goal of becoming plant manager of one of the company's five plants.

In her position as supervisor, things went well. Osborn was familiar with all operations and spent considerable time in trouble-shooting, training and directing employees, and, in general, monitoring results. She knew from past experience that supervisors considered for department manager positions were usually elevated from high-producing sections.

Since Osborn was accountable for results, she practiced close supervision, stayed on top of things, and really stressed high production. This approach paid off in dividends. After two years as a supervisor, she was promoted to department manager. In this capacity, Osborn was responsible for overseeing and coordinating the work of three assembly supervisors, two production supervisors, and one shipping and receiving supervisor. An overview of the reporting relationships involving Osborn would look like Figure 5–1.

At this stage in her career, Osborn was well ahead of schedule in her long-range program of becoming a plant manager. She had anticipated spending a minimum of four years as supervisor before having an opportunity to advance to department manager. Her next career objective of becoming a production manager in one of the company's plants seemed well within reach since the industry and company were growing at a rapid rate.

What had worked for her as a supervisor would also work for her as a department manager, Osborn thought. She was not really concerned that five of the six supervisors who would be reporting to her were older and more experienced in the plant than she was. After all, results were what counted and her department's results had been higher than those of any other department.

Osborn's job was to insure that the six units she was responsible for showed improved end results and that they maintained a high performance

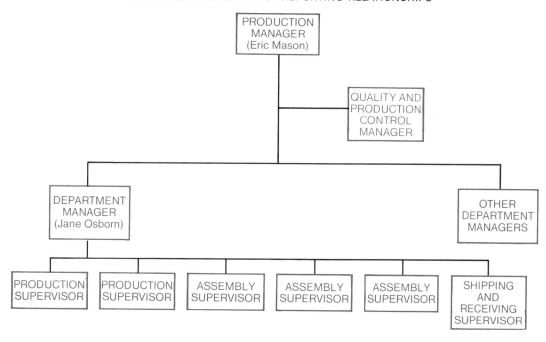

FIGURE 5–1 PARTIAL ORGANIZATION CHART OF REPORTING RELATIONSHIPS

level. At her first meeting with the supervisors, she stressed her high expectations and set as an objective "to increase production by 10 percent within three months." The yearly objective was to be a 20 percent increase. She indicated that she believed strongly in the management principle of "follow-up." Not only would she be closely following up on their work, but also she would expect them to do the same thing with their people.

Two months later, the overall production in her department was down by 7 percent, and Osborn was beginning to worry. It seemed that the more she stressed production and tried to follow delegated assignments closely, the more resistance she encountered from her six supervisors. Although the resistance was not open, it was nevertheless definitely present. In fact, when she went to the assembly and production areas, she sensed hostility even from the operative people, a group she had previously been close to.

At the end of three months, production had decreased by 10 percent. The quality control manager reported to Osborn and her boss that the reject rate was at its highest level ever, and something had to be done to correct the problem.

At this point, Eric Mason, the production manager, called Osborn in for a conference. He began by expressing his confidence in her as a manager and said that she had been his choice for department manager. Among other things, he indicated that she was bright, capable, and achievement-oriented, and that he valued those qualities in his managers. He then suggested that he would like for her to read several basic books on supervision and to attempt to diagnose for herself what was causing the drop in production. He further suggested that they meet in two weeks to discuss her findings and jointly develop a plan of action to solve the problem. After completing her reading, Osborn concluded that her problem revolved around ineffective delegation of authority.

This case illustrates a common problem for new managers. The ideas in this chapter correspond closely with what Jane Osborn discovered. Many potentially able first-line managers fail to reach their true capabilities as supervisory managers because of their inability to delegate authority effectively. As you probably noted, Jane Osborn was quite effective as a first-line manager but began to fail in her department-manager position.

As a supervisor, Osborn relied on her technical skills and strong desire for high production. She knew the work, and she more than met high performance goals relying on her own skills. In the higher position, however, she had to rely more on the skills of other people—people older and more experienced than she. Her close, nondelegative style of management caused considerable resentment and resulted in a negative response to her high production goals.

The previous chapter covered the fundamentals of organizing—one of the management functions discussed in Chapter 1. Delegation is at the heart of organizing. Yet it is one of the concepts least understood and most underutilized by managers, especially middle managers. Research indicates that when people are elevated to middle-level management positions, they will either remain there for the rest of their careers or be demoted unless they learn to delegate authority effectively. The best time to learn to do this is at the first managerial level—the supervisor's level.

WHY DELEGATE?

The opening case hinted at some of the reasons why it is important for supervisory managers to delegate effectively. Let's highlight these reasons and see if you can add others.

Delegating Develops People

People cannot grow and develop if they are oversupervised or not trusted to handle their normal duties and responsibilities. It is a well-known principle that we learn not only from books, but also by doing things. In learning through doing, we will make mistakes. But the wise supervisor realizes this truth and uses mistakes as an opportunity for discussing with employees what happened and how it can be prevented in the future. The employees, in turn, learn from the experience. This procedure is called **experiential learning**. Figure 5–2 shows the steps the supervisor and employee would follow in order to learn from successes or mistakes.

FIGURE 5–2 LEARNING FROM SUCCESSES AND MISTAKES

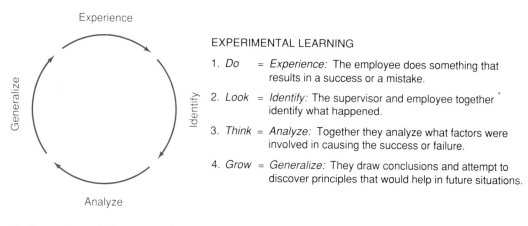

EXPERIMENTAL LEARNING

1. *Do*   = *Experience:* The employee does something that results in a success or a mistake.

2. *Look* = *Identify:* The supervisor and employee together identify what happened.

3. *Think* = *Analyze:* Together they analyze what factors were involved in causing the success or failure.

4. *Grow* = *Generalize:* They draw conclusions and attempt to discover principles that would help in future situations.

Delegating Allows a Supervisor to Do Other Things

A supervisor's job, as we have seen, involves more than just direct supervision. Effective delegation allows the supervisor to spend more time planning the work and coordinating with other departments. It allows more time for trouble-shooting—dealing with problems before they get out of hand and taking advantage of opportunities in a timely manner.

Delegating Allows More Work to Be Accomplished

Instead of taking power away from supervisors, effective delegation expands the basis of their power. More people become knowledgeable about what the priorities are and are given meaningful assignments toward getting the job done. A climate of trust is established. In this environment, when the supervisor leaves the work area, employees continue to work effectively. They do so because of commitment and a sense of ownership in the work of the department.

Delegating Improves Control

In the effective delegation process, the emphasis is on results, not activities. Thus, the supervisor focuses on how well standards and objectives are being met, not on the specific details of how they are being met. In many cases, delegation also serves as a basis for evaluating people and compensating them according to the results achieved.

Can you identify other reasons why effective delegation is so important? What are they?

PROCESS OF DELEGATION

Delegation of authority refers to the process by which managers grant authority downward to the people who report to them. The three key principles in the process of delegation are granting authority, assigning responsibility, and requiring accountability. As shown in Figure 5–3 (and later in Figure 5–6 on page 121), they are like the three legs of a stool, all equally necessary. Let us examine each principle and their interrelationships.

Granting Authority

In the previous chapter, we defined line authority as the right and power to command others and to exact performance from them. Moreover, it could also encompass the right to determine a course of action or judge the quality of work performed.

> *James Walker, supervisor of Department A, is concerned because four new workers have recently been assigned to his department. Although normally he has the responsibility for indoctrinating and training new workers, his schedule is so loaded for the next month that he cannot properly carry out the training assignments. He calls his two most senior workers and, after expressing his confidence in their abilities, assigns them the task of indoctrinating and training the four new workers.*

In this example, Walker has just delegated authority. The example illustrates that delegation to lower levels can occur above and beyond the normal assignment of duties and responsibilities. It also illustrates why it is important for supervisors to know both the weak and the strong points of their employees. James Walker

FIGURE 5–3   THREE PRINCIPLES OF THE DELEGATION PROCESS

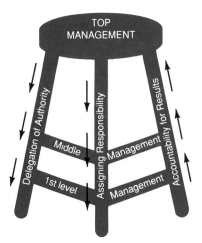

WORKERS

knew his crew and chose the two people who could most effectively carry out the training function.

Can you think of other activities beyond the normal duties and responsibilities that a supervisor might delegate to lower levels? What are they?

Assigning Responsibility

The second principle of delegation is the assignment of duties and responsibilities. Most jobs, whether that of a nurse in a hospital, a bank teller, or an assembly worker in a manufacturing plant, have certain duties and responsibilities that usually go with the job. For example, a bank teller not only is responsible for providing service to bank customers, but also is expected to be friendly, to identify prospective customers who do not have proper identification in cashing out-of-town checks, and to maintain the correct cash balances.

In addition, the unique nature of the banking industry or special priorities of the employing organization may require the assignment of duties and responsibilities beyond the traditional requirements. An aggressive bank might add the extra responsibility of selling services. For example, a teller might present a form describing the bank's new money market account to the customer. If the customer shows interest, the teller can then engage in direct selling.

Many jobs in medium-sized or large organizations have been provided with job descriptions, which are usually written by a human-resources specialist after interviews with the jobholder and the jobholder's immediate supervisor(s). These **job descriptions**, which spell out the primary job duties and responsibilities, as well as other job-related activities, should assist in the process of delegation. Figure 5–4 provides an example of a job description for a production supervisor in a paper mill. It identifies 13 key duties and responsibilities, such as crew leadership (#1), crew work assignments (#5), and safety and health (#11). For the purpose of illustration, we have spelled out the tasks for the coaching and counseling responsibility (#8).

Requiring Accountability

The third principle of delegation is holding those people to whom you have delegated and assigned duties and responsibilities accountable for results. Thus, **accountability** simply means that an obligation is created when a person accepts duties and responsibilities from higher management. Moreover, the person is accountable to the next higher level to carry them out effectively. Accountability

FIGURE 5–4   JOB DESCRIPTION FOR A PRODUCTION SUPERVISOR

Title: Production Supervisor, Finished Products
Purpose of job: To plan, organize, control, and exercise leadership of the efficient and effective utilization of assigned crew personnel, equipment, and material resources for timely achievement of the crew's production performance objectives and standards.

1. Crew leadership responsibility
2. Crew performance standards
3. Crew performance improvement
4. Daily shift-change management
5. Crew work assignments
6. Crew performance supervision
7. Crew education, training and development
8. Individual coaching and counseling
9. Production-relationships management
10. Maintenance-relationships management
11. Safety and health management
12. Labor contract administration
13. Work-environment improvement

a. Routinely observes and carries on conversation with individual crew members at their work stations on a daily basis to determine if there are any special problems that require attention.
b. Provides on-the-job coaching in job skills at operator stations to reinforce classroom training and develop specific job skills.
c. Provides counseling to crew members on job relationship attitudes to improve their performance.
d. Refers crew members to company employee-assistance resources on personnel problems that require special help.

flows *upward* in an organization. It is in this aspect of the delegation process where the controlling function plays an important role.

Suppose that a department manager delegated a special assignment to a supervisor. The supervisor made a mistake in carrying out the assignment, which cost the firm $5,000. Who would you say should be held accountable for the mistake? Why?

If you answered that both the department manager and the supervisor should be held accountable, you are correct. The supervisor is, of course, accountable to the department manager, but the department manager is also accountable to her or his own superior.

In Case 5–1, Jane Osborn discovered in her reading assignment that one reason she was not delegating effectively was that she knew she was being held accountable for results. So she was reluctant to trust others because they might make mistakes.

An important fact to remember is that *accountability cannot be delegated!* Accountability is essential to maintain effective control over results. Therefore, a person who delegates an assignment should not be able to escape accountability for poor results. However, this aspect of the delegation process is one of the primary reasons why some supervisors are reluctant to delegate effectively. Sometimes higher management mistakenly reinforces this reluctance of supervisors to delegate. Figure 5–5 shows how this can happen.

FIGURE 5–5   HOW HIGHER MANAGEMENT REINFORCES THE RELUCTANCE TO DELEGATE

What is another way the $5,000 mistake mentioned above might have been handled so that it would be a learning experience and not reinforce a manager's reluctance to delegate?

EFFECTIVE DELEGATION

In one of the classic books on the delegation process, Donald and Eleanor Laird point out that there is a big difference between making really meaningful assignments to those below you and asking them to do the dirty jobs and meaningless activities you don't want to do yourself.[1] They emphasize that true delegation involves granting to the delegatee the authority needed to get the job done. Also, the decision making involved in the assignment is either shared or delegated entirely, and the delegatee is given freedom to handle details on his or her own initiative.

In order to ensure accountability, controls are set up to check the effectiveness of the delegation. These controls can take many forms, such as personal observation by the delegator, periodic reports by the delegatee, or statistical reports concerning output, costs, grievances, and so forth. When mistakes occur, the supervisor can use these as a basis for coaching and developing employees.

Knowing When to Delegate

It's not always easy to know when to delegate authority—and what authority to delegate—to those working for you. While there are no absolute guidelines to go by, there are at least a lot of red flags that will signal that you need to delegate. Consider the following:

1. Do you do work that an employee could do just as well?
2. Do you think that you are the only one who actually knows how the job should be done?
3. Do you leave the job each day loaded down with details to take care of at home?
4. Do you frequently stay after hours catching up with work even though your peers don't?
5. Do you seem never to get through with your work?
6. Are you a perfectionist?
7. Do you tell your employees how to solve problems?[2]

If you answered "yes" to many of the questions above, you probably need to learn to delegate more effectively.

How the Delegation Process Operates

Figure 5–6 illustrates how an effective delegation process should operate. Notice that authority, such as for performing assigned duties, carrying out special assignments, achieving objectives, and meeting standards, is granted down the line from higher management to supervisory managers, then to workers. In turn, responsibility for using that authority is created, and accountability controls are established to insure that the authority is properly used.

FIGURE 5–6   PROCESS OF EFFECTIVE DELEGATION

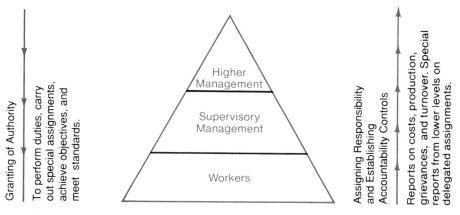

When there are differences between actual performance and planned performance, corrective action takes place by coaching, counseling, or correcting mistakes.

The practical steps needed to delegate authority effectively using this process are shown in Figure 5–7. Notice that the process begins with creating an organizational climate in which delegation can effectively occur and ends only when other managers, as well as the employee, know about the delegation.

FIGURE 5–7   STEPS IN EFFECTIVE DELEGATION

- Management establishes an organizational climate in which delegation can effectively occur.
- Higher management makes sure that one manager's responsibility and authority do not overlap or duplicate those of other managers in the organization.
- Management establishes controls (feedback mechanisms) to measure the progress of an employee from start to finish of the assignment.
- The supervisor grants specific duties and responsibilities to an employee, who accepts them.
- The supervisor and the employee agree on the specific results expected and how the results will be measured.
- The supervisor grants enough authority to the employee to allow the latter to carry out the assignment.
- The supervisor clearly communicates the delegated responsibility to all other managers so that the employee can carry out the assignment with a minimum of confusion and disagreement with other managers.

The Principle of Parity of Authority and Responsibility

When responsibilities and duties are assigned, adequate authority should be delegated to meet the responsibilities and carry out the assignments. This is known as the **parity principle**. Some management experts go so far as to say that authority should be equal to responsibility. Quite candidly, first-line managers rarely have all the authority they would like to have to meet their responsibilities. Actually, this is also true of many other positions, including staff positions.

> *Win Cagle, a supervisor with Toole Gasket Company, was responsible for 25 employees who worked in the processing department. He had just walked out of a meeting where the same old line had been handed down—how supervisors were being given more authority and whether they should be accountable for results. "I've heard it all before—many times," he said. He continued: "The personnel department will send me the same losers they always do, just to give me warm bodies. The training department will turn them loose before they're ready, and the pay is so low we don't keep them very long. I can't discipline the way I'd like to without running into opposition. The maintenance department is stretched thin. Last week I had some machinery shut down for four hours before they even got to it. We ran out of raw materials last week because of the shippers' strike. And yet they talk about how I'm responsible for results. That's a laugh! We have all the responsibility, but no authority."*

Is the example given above true in most organizations? Do supervisors really have the authority to match their responsibility? Explain.

As we indicated in Chapter 1, many of the duties held by supervisors a number of years ago have now been shifted to staff departments such as the human-resources department. Consequently, some of the authority that went with the supervisor's position years ago, such as the right to hire and fire, no longer remains with the position or has been greatly modified. As a result, supervisors are required to be very effective and wise in the use of what little authority is assigned to the position. This situation also places a premium on the supervisor's being an effective leader and skilled in communicating with, motivating, counseling, coaching, and developing employees. We will explore these areas in depth in later chapters.

Effective Delegation Takes Time

The process of effective delegation does not occur quickly or easily. As we shall examine in depth when we get into the chapter on leadership, how much a supervisor can delegate depends on the ability and willingness of employees to handle delegation. Sometimes a supervisor is faced with untrained and relatively new employees. In such situations, effective delegation is contingent on the training and development of the employees. Thus, the process requires planning and should be done gradually. On the other hand, if a supervisor has a group of capable and well-trained employees, the process can occur more rapidly.

ROLES INVOLVED IN EFFECTIVE DELEGATION

If a delegation system is to be effective, three important parties must have a role in it. These are higher management, the supervisor, and the employees to whom authority is delegated.

The Role of Higher Management

As we have already observed, higher management can have a major impact on whether effective delegation takes place. A fault-finding atmosphere—where higher management is quick to criticize and fails to offer positive feedback for good results—will negate the process of effective delegation.

> *In Case 5–1, Eric Mason's response to Jane Osborn's problem is an example of higher management playing a facilitative role in the process of effective delegation. Mason has a good idea of what is causing Osborn's problem, but he has elected to take a counseling and coaching posture and to assist her in discovering the problem herself.*

One reason delegation is so difficult is that either overcontrol or undercontrol by higher management can hinder the delegation process. Other factors controlled by higher management that could hinder the process would be a lack of objectives, a lack of policies, not sharing information with lower levels, and slow decision making.

The Role of the Supervisor

In his practical book, *No-Nonsense Delegation*, Dale McConkey has developed quite well the role of both delegator and delegatee.[3] The points that apply to the role of the supervisor are these:

1. Communicate clearly.
2. Specify authority.
3. Encourage employee participation.
4. Review results, not methods.
5. Show trust.
6. Seek recommendations.
7. Share credit, not blame.
8. Give support.
9. Be consistent.
10. Know your people.
11. Develop your people.

Points 3, 5, and 11 in the above list are especially important. No one has highlighted this idea better than Tom Peters, coauthor of the best-selling book *In Search of Excellence.* After this book was published, Peters discussed what is involved in achieving supervisory excellence. He indicated that the biggest mistake managers make is forgetting that excellence does not come from a good reporting system or other system of control but from people who care. He concluded that "managers have to be willing to give up enough control to allow the average person who works for them to honest-to-God own his or her job and feel responsible for it. A supervisor isn't going to win unless he or she does that."[4]

Most important for the supervisor is that employees be trained to ensure that they do their jobs without the supervisor stepping in to do them. Although it may be ego-satisfying to have employees frequently asking your advice and help regarding their duties, it does not develop them nor assist you in effectively carrying out your responsibilities.

The Role of Employees to Whom Authority Is Delegated

McConkey's ideas regarding the employees to whom authority is delegated include the following points. Employees should:

1. Take the initiative.
2. Relate to the supervisor.
3. Be sure the delegation is realistic.
4. Determine and give feedback regarding results.
5. Report periodically to the supervisor.
6. Carry out the delegated assignments effectively.
7. Develop themselves to be able to handle more involved assignments.

It is important for the employees not to run to the supervisor each time a minor problem arises. Figure 5–8 illustrates how a wise supervisor might handle a situation of this sort. Rather than take on a task that is the nurse's responsibility (the monkey), the supervisor refuses to accept the responsibility and tosses the monkey back to the nurse. In summary, only when major problems arise should an employee solicit the supervisor's advice.

WHY SUPERVISORS FAIL TO DELEGATE

Industrialist Andrew Carnegie once said: "When a man realizes he can call others in to help him do a job better than he can do alone, he has taken a big step in his life." In the formative years of your life, most of your success in school work and in summer jobs depends primarily on your individual efforts. Achievement and success usually do not come from how well you can inspire and work with and through people. Then, all of a sudden, you leave school. After working

FIGURE 5–8   THE SUPERVISOR "PLACING THE MONKEY BACK" ON
THE EMPLOYEE WITH THE PRIMARY RESPONSIBILITY

awhile, you are placed in a leadership position. Now, instead of having two or three assignments to be responsible for, you are responsible for working with and through people to accomplish numerous assignments.

Perhaps, as a new supervisor, you can do several things better than anyone you supervise, but can you possibly do all things as well? Unfortunately, many supervisors apparently think they can because they fail to delegate. Or, like Jane Osborn in Case 5–1, they don't trust people and they destroy the effects of delegation by oversupervising.

Why do some supervisors have so much difficulty in delegating authority? As we have already indicated, their previous experience in nonleadership positions sometimes gives them a mistaken notion of how a supervisor should function. In addition, since supervisors are accountable for what their employees do or do not accomplish, it is natural to want to stay on top of everything that happens. However, this usually causes resentment in the people supervised.

Some head football coaches delegate the actual calling of offensive plays to assistant coaches. Some coaches for the offensive team delegate it to their quarterback. But other head coaches, like Dallas Cowboys coach Tom Landry, call most of the plays themselves. What factors should influence the extent to which a head coach delegates this task?

As shown in Figure 5–9, supervisors who do not delegate must carry the entire burden of both their jobs and their subordinates' jobs. The following are some of the reasons why supervisors have difficulty delegating:

1. Since supervisors are being held accountable for results, some of them hesitate to delegate because they are afraid their employees will make mistakes.
2. Some supervisors feel that when they delegate, they surrender some of their power, thus decreasing their authority.
3. Some supervisors have a personality that makes them want to dominate things completely. We see this in some parents in raising their children.

FIGURE 5–9   CARRYING THE ENTIRE BURDEN

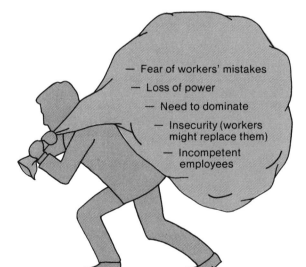

— Fear of workers' mistakes

— Loss of power

— Need to dominate

— Insecurity (workers might replace them)

— Incompetent employees

"If you don't share the burden as a supervisor,
then you've got to carry it alone."

4. Some supervisors do not delegate because they are insecure and afraid their subordinates will do so well that they will be recognized and promoted ahead of the supervisors.

5. In some cases, some supervisors realize that employees do not have the ability or maturity to handle things without close supervision.

Can you identify other reasons why some supervisors have difficulty delegating? What are they?

RELATING DELEGATION TO SUCCESS OR FAILURE

Some of us are better delegators than others. In many cases, we resort to delegation only as a last-ditch effort. Perhaps we have no technical expertise in the area to which we have been assigned. Or perhaps we are stretched so thin that, against our better judgment, we call on others to help because we have no choice! This is how one manager puts it:

> Our company has an interesting approach to training high-potential supervisors in becoming delegators. We assign the supervisor who is disinclined toward delegation to head up a work unit of 30 or more people. The supervisor either learns to delegate, or he fails.

Undoubtedly, your ability to delegate becomes more crucial the greater your responsibility on the job. This ability becomes vital to your success or failure. Dr. Van Oliphant, a Memphis State University vice-president and management consultant, has examined jobs from the standpoint of *failure*. His eight ways to guarantee failure on the job include several delegation-related items, as shown in Figure 5–10. These eight points are particularly applicable to the supervisor's job.

FIGURE 5–10   EIGHT WAYS TO GUARANTEE FAILURE ON THE JOB

- Develop a "know-it-all" attitude.
- Do most things yourself since you do them better.
- Submerge yourself in details and trivia.
- Disregard the need to cultivate peer relationships.
- Procrastinate in making decisions.
- Forget to balance the emphases on production and people.
- Refuse to share the credit for success.
- Place the blame for failure on subordinates.

Which of the items listed above seem most related to delegation? Explain. Are you guilty of practicing any of these? If so, which one(s)?

INEFFECTIVE DELEGATION: A SOLUTION

Through her work with thousands of supervisors, management consultant Suzanne Savory has gained insight into the problem of ineffective delegation.[5] While the supervisor's primary job is working with and through people, she says, unfortunately the people selected for that position throughout corporate America are often the best technicians, not the best managers of people. She goes on to say that these individuals get their "high" by developing their technical skills in order to become top achievers. Then, when they are promoted to the position of supervisor, they continue to try to get their high by being good technicians; consequently, they oversupervise or do the important technical work themselves.

The solution is what Savory calls **reframing**, or emphasizing management training and development programs. She states that this reframing is the goal of most management education today. "Generally," she concludes, "supervisory and management training is designed to teach Joe how to be a coach rather than a player. If Joe is to be an effective supervisor, he must learn to get his high not from playing but from coaching."

The authors of this text agree with Savory. In fact, this book has been based on our experience in working with thousands of supervisors and managers in development programs. These programs have encompassed both experienced and inexperienced supervisors and managers. Almost without exception, evaluations from those receiving management training for the first time rated the programs exceptional in helping them to do a better job of managing. They usually add, "I wish I had received this type of training earlier."

Organizations throughout this country are realizing that they have neglected the training of managers and are beginning to spend more energy and money on correcting that situation. For example, a large hospital designed a series of management development programs around the contents of this book.

CHAPTER REVIEW

Many potentially effective managers have failed primarily because of their inability to delegate. We saw an example of that possibility in the case of Jane Osborn.

In this chapter, we discussed some reasons why effective delegation is essential to performing the supervisory management job successfully. For example, delegating (1) develops people, (2) allows the supervisor to do other things, (3) allows more work to be accomplished, and (4) improves control.

We also examined the process of delegation, which involves three principles: delegating authority, assigning responsibility, and holding people accountable for results. Although supervisors rarely receive all the authority they desire, it is important that they be granted enough authority to carry out their responsibilities. In the process of effective delegation, controls are established to measure progress of the work and end results.

The roles of higher management, the supervisor, and the employee to whom authority is delegated were examined. It was concluded that only when there is a major problem should an employee run to the supervisor for help.

We also looked at how important it is for supervisors to delegate effectively and gave some reasons why some supervisors fail to do so. Since a supervisor is accountable to a superior, it is a natural tendency for the supervisor to want to provide close supervision or do the employees' work. When this happens, the employees' development suffers, and the supervisor does not have adequate time for planning and coordinating with other departments. On the other hand, when effective delegation takes place, more work is accomplished and the supervisor's controlling function is improved.

Finally, we examined concepts central to effective delegation and looked at eight ways to guarantee failure on the job. Two of the ways to guarantee failure on the supervisor's part are directly related to the delegation process: (1) doing most things yourself since you do them better, and (2) submerging yourself in details and trivia. The other ways to guarantee failure are indirectly related to the delegation process.

One of the solutions to ineffective delegation is to emphasize management training and development.

QUESTIONS FOR REVIEW AND DISCUSSION

1. Discuss four reasons why delegation is important.

2. Describe the process of delegation.

3. Explain the interrelationships among authority, responsibility, and accountability.

4. What is the principle of parity of authority and responsibility? How does it operate in actual practice?

5. Why do some supervisors fail to delegate effectively? If this situation was a common problem in an organization, what could be done to increase a supervisor's knowledge and skills in delegating effectively?

6. What are the roles played in effective delegation?

7. In what way or ways may higher management affect the delegation process?

8. In what way or ways may employees affect the delegation process?

LEARNING EXERCISE 5–1
SOLVING JANE OSBORN'S PROBLEM

Referring to Jane Osborn in Case 5–1, we find that after completing her reading assignment, she was convinced that her problem involved ineffective delegation.

Assume that you are Osborn. Develop a proposed action plan for solving the problem to discuss with your superior. Would your action plan include a meeting with your supervisors in which you share with them your diagnosis of the problem? Why or why not?

LEARNING EXERCISE 5–2
THE NEW EMPLOYEE AT HAPPY VALLEY

Alex Simpson was very frustrated. He had been on the job for three days and wondered when Dennis Cholak, the manager of the Grain and Seed Department of Happy Valley, would finally get off his back. First, the job wasn't hard at all. Simpson just sat around in the warehouse, filling the orders that farmers had brought to the front and for which they had obtained receipts. He could read the orders and, while it took a little time to learn where all the different items were stored, he knew it pretty well now. But it seemed that about every half hour or so, Cholak would come into the warehouse and check up on things. In fact, whenever a farmer would pull his truck up to the warehouse entrance to have a big order filled, Cholak would come in and start giving Simpson all sorts of directions about filling the order: "Be careful, don't rip that bag of seeds," or "Put the grass over here in this corner of the truck and the beans on the other side," and so on. Moreover, Cholak would come in and watch Simpson weigh the merchandise and even correct him for having an ounce or two too much grass seed on a 40-pound order. "He sure as hell is a nitpicker. I thought he'd lay off after a couple of days, but he's that way with the older workers, too," said Simpson.

Answer the following questions:

1. If you were Simpson, would you try to do anything about this situation?
2. Assume that you want to try to improve the situation. Consider the following alternatives and rank them in order of preference. Be prepared to defend your rankings.

    _____ a. Quit.

    _____ b. Work for a month and, if the situation continues, talk with Cholak about the problem.

    _____ c. Photostat a copy of this chapter and mail it to Cholak anonymously.

    _____ d. Talk with the older workers and see if one of them would discuss the matter with Cholak.

    _____ e. Do the best you can and forget the problem since Cholak is the boss.

    _____ f. Other (develop your own alternative approach).

LEARNING EXERCISE 5–3
A QUIZ ON DELEGATION*

	Yes	No
1. Do you take work home regularly?	____	____
2. Do you work longer hours than the people who work for you?	____	____
3. When you return to work after an absence (a trip), do you find your "in basket" too full?	____	____
4. Are you still handling activities and problems you had before you were promoted to your present job?	____	____
5. Are you often interrupted with questions or requests from others regarding their assignments or projects?	____	____
6. Do you have to rush to meet deadlines?	____	____
7. Do you spend more time than you should doing detail work that others could do?	____	____
8. Can you answer any questions your boss asks you about any operation in your work section?	____	____
9. When you're away at a meeting and someone enters with a message, do you automatically assume it's for you?	____	____
10. Do you require your subordinates to get your approval before making contacts with other personnel in job-related matters?	____	____

Scoring: How many "yes" answers did you have?

    0–1   Excellent delegator.
    2–4   Good delegator, but could improve.
    5–10 Poor delegator; you have a problem!

ENDNOTES

1. Donald A. Laird and Eleanor C. Laird, *The Techniques of Delegating: How to Get Things Done through Others* (New York: McGraw-Hill Book Company, 1957), pp. 107–8.
2. Claude S. George, *Supervision in Action: The Art of Managing Others*, 4th ed. (Englewood Cliffs, NJ: Prentice-Hall, 1985), p. 283. Reprinted by permission.
3. Dale D. McConkey, *No-Nonsense Delegation* (New York: AMACOM, 1974), pp. 90–100.
4. "Tom Peters' Formula for Supervisory Excellence," *Supervisory Management* 30 (February 1985): 2–3.
5. Suzanne Savory, "Ineffective Delegation—Symptom or Problem?" *Supervisory Management* 24 (June 1979): 28.

*Adapted, by permission of the publisher, from *The Time Trap* by R. Alec Mackenzie, pp. 141–142. © 1972 by AMACOM, a division of American Management Association, New York. All rights reserved.

SUGGESTIONS FOR FURTHER READING

Arthur, D. "Guidelines for Effective Delegation." *Supervisory Management* 24 (October 1979): 9–13.

Bevardo, D. G. "Positive Delegation Techniques Reduce Anxiety, Tension." *Data Management* 23 (December 1985): 10–12.

Feinkerg, M. R. "Delegating the Details." *Restaurant Business* 84 (September 20 1985): 86.

Muir, J. "Effective Management Through Delegation." *Management World* 15 (June 1985): 30–31.

Treeze, L. "Combating Reverse Delegation." *Supervision* 48 (July 1986): 6–8.

COMPREHENSIVE CASE FOR PART II
REORGANIZATION AT TONAWANDA

The Tonawanda Plant of Bickel, Inc., a large international manufacturer of paper cups and towels, was one of the least efficient within Bickel's 16-plant manufacturing system. Built in 1928, the Tonawanda plant had costs about 13 percent higher than those of other plants in the Bickel system. As one of the oldest sites in Bickel's history, Tonawanda had antiquated facilities and a system considered to be top-heavy with layers of management. About 900 operative-level employees were included among the 1,200 employees at the plant. Figure II–1 shows the chain of command within the production side of the organization.

As shown in Figure II–1, five levels of management intervened between operative-level employees and the plant manager. Consequently, communications from top to bottom at Tonawanda were notoriously slow, with a great deal of "filtering." Moreover, the numerous levels of management resulted in very steep payroll and benefit costs at Tonawanda in comparison with other Bickel plants.

The company could not afford the capital spending needed to upgrade the plant. Moreover, the union was militant and had stiffly rejected pay and benefit concessions

FIGURE II–1 CHAIN OF COMMAND, TONAWANDA PLANT
MANUFACTURING ORGANIZATION

○ Plant Manager

○ Assistant Plant Manager

○ Manager of Manufacturing

○ Department heads

○ Supervisors

○ First-line foremen

○ Operative-level employees

as a condition for guaranteeing the plant's continued operation. So rumors were circulating that Tonawanda would be closed within two years.

Six months ago, in an attempt to trim costs throughout the corporation, all salaried personnel at Bickel were offered very attractive "sweeteners" to elect early retirement. A surprisingly large number of senior-level people and management personnel at Tonawanda accepted the offer, apparently because they didn't feel the Tonawanda operation could survive much longer anyway.

An opportunity was thus presented to Chuck Bayers, the Tonawanda plant manager. Bayers, acknowledged to be a "comer" in the company, had been at the Tonawanda site for a little over a year and had received high marks for his leadership, despite the gloomy outlook at the plant. Since the long-term survival of the plant was relatively hopeless, the company's top management went along with Bayers' plan to dramatically alter the organization structure within the manufacturing function at Tonawanda. What was there to lose, since the plant was likely to be closed anyway? After the reorganization, which was preceded by numerous meetings at all levels of the Tonawanda plant, the organization structure within manufacturing was as shown in Figure II–2.

As shown in Figure II–2, the reorganized plant had only two levels of management intervening between operators and the plant manager, in contrast to five levels under the old system. The span of management for a shift supervisor was as high as 200. The 8-to-5 shift, for example, used four shift supervisors for about 600 total operators. This contrasts with over 40 first-line foremen who had previously occupied the level above operating employees.

Central to the reorganization were the key operators. The key operator was a senior worker in each designated work group who now assumed some quasi-management duties, including (1) assigning jobs to the work group, (2) monitoring work, (3) making decisions regarding routine problems, such as maintenance or materials needed, (4) training, and (5) communications with the shift supervisor. Thus the key operators, in addition to their operator duties, now performed some of the functions formerly handled under the old organization by the first-line foremen.

FIGURE II–2   REVISED CHAIN OF COMMAND, TONAWANDA PLANT
MANUFACTURING ORGANIZATION

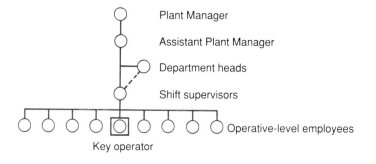

After the system had been in effect for a month, the following comments reflected varying views about how smoothly it was functioning.

Chuck Bayers, Plant Manager: This is the wave of the future. There's no way we could survive as top-heavy as we were. What we've done is turn the plant over to the operators, try to stay out of their way, and help them when they need it. It's not easy to introduce a change like this. I know we've got some problems, especially in the new relationships. Some of the department heads have had their noses bent out of joint in the adjustment and still won't let go of the old system. I'm convinced that we've got people who can make this new concept work. We were overmanaged before—we seemed to be saying that we didn't have confidence in our operators' ability to run the plant. Well, now we're going to find out whether they can.

Department Head: We all know why Bayers did it—he had no choice but to try something like this. The problem, though, is that the shift supervisors are spread so thin that they aren't there when key operators need them. I'm always getting calls from key operators about what to do—in some cases it's so trivial I tell them to handle it themselves. I don't think our key operators were ready. They will still consider themselves operators rather than leaders. They're really working foremen, but they won't accept that fact. Some of them hate the added responsibility. Under the old system, the foremen made all their decisions. But that's changed now, and we'll see what happens.

Shift Supervisor: I'm learning what management is all about. This is a tremendous learning experience for me. Before, I supervised seven people. Now I have over 200. I used to try to keep pretty close tabs on my people—now I have to depend on them, and that's been very scary, especially these first few weeks. If I don't hear from a key operator, my assumption is that things are okay in his group. Sometimes I don't even get to tour certain areas of the plant because I'm putting out fires somewhere else.

My biggest problem? It's the department heads. They still communicaate directly with operators and don't keep me informed. Sometimes they contradict my instructions or a decision I've made, and when I check out an operating area, I get upset to find out that they [department heads] have contradicted me. Some of the key operators prefer going to a department head rather than me, even though, technically, they're accountable to me.

Key Operator: It's okay, I guess. For 25 cents an hour more, I have to sorta be what the old foreman was. They really didn't prepare us too well for this, though. I think I'm supposed to report to the shift supervisor, but the department heads like to think they're the ones who call the shots. So I've gotten caught in the middle a few times. It's hard to get hold of your shift supervisor since he's stretched so thin. So they expect us to make the decisions now. I know this: I used to come to this job pretty relaxed; now I wake up to come to work, and I've got a knot in my stomach. There is definitely more pressure. I haven't had to chew on anybody in the crew yet, and I don't know if I'll be able to. It's tough to do this job, and I know several key operators who want to step down and turn it over to somebody else.

Operator 1: I think we pretty much favor the change because it gets the foremen off our backs. They could be a royal pain. Most of 'em didn't have that much to do; so they'd spend their time nitpicking. Now we may go sometimes all day long and not even see the shift supervisor. Our top operator pretty much leaves us alone, too.

Operator 2: I don't like it. Before, when you needed something, the foreman was right there to handle things that came up. It seems like we can't get answers to things now. The key operator tells me to make the decision because he doesn't want to get involved, and he can't locate the shift supervisor. I preferred the old way when the foreman was right there all the time.

All eyes in the Bickel system are carefully watching what happens at the Tonawanda plant as a result of the reorganization. If it turns out to be successful, you can be assured that other plants will introduce elements of the new system.

Answer the following questions:

1. Identify the pros and cons of the new organization structure at the Tonawanda plant.
2. Explain how the changes made in the organization structure at Tonawanda affect each of the following concepts:
   a. span of management
   b. delegation
   c. levels of hierarchy
   d. unity of command
   e. authority and responsibility
3. Why might key operators be reluctant to accept the greater authority given to them under the reorganization?

PART III

LEADING

6
COMMUNICATION

OBJECTIVES

After reading and studying the material in this chapter, you should be able to:

- Explain what communication is.
- Describe the five components of the communication process model.
- Explain the different ways in which nonverbal communications influence supervisory communication.
- Identify the three basic flows of formal communication in an organization.
- Identify and explain how organizational, interpersonal, and language barriers affect supervisory communication.
- Give an example of how planning can aid communication effectiveness.
- Show how a supervisor can use feedback to improve communication.
- Define and illustrate "active listening" skills.

IMPORTANT TERMS

communication process model
sender
message
channel
receiver
feedback
vocal signals
body signals
object signals
space signals
time signals

downward communication
upward communication
lateral-diagonal communication
informal communication
grapevine
perception
stereotyping
active listening
reflective statement
probe

CHAPTER OUTLINE
CASE 6–1. A SNAG IN COMMUNICATION

I. WHAT IS COMMUNICATION?
- A. Communication process model
  1. The sender
  2. The message
  3. The channel
  4. The receiver
  5. Feedback
- B. Meaning lies in people
- C. Importance of nonverbal messages

II. FLOWS OF COMMUNICATION
- A. Downward communication
- B. Upward communication
- C. Lateral-diagonal communication
- D. Informal communication
  1. The grapevine
  2. Purposes served by informal communication
  3. Living with informal communication

III. BARRIERS TO EFFECTIVE SUPERVISORY COMMUNICATION
- A. Organizational barriers
  1. Levels of hierarchy
  2. Authority and status
  3. Specialization and related jargon
- B. Interpersonal and language barriers
  1. Differing perceptions
  2. Imprecise language

IV. IMPROVING SUPERVISORY COMMUNICATIONS
- A. Setting the proper climate
  1. Mutual trust between supervisor and employees
  2. A minimum of status barriers
- B. Planning your communication
  1. Anticipating situations in advance
  2. Examples of planned communications
- C. Considering your receiver's frame of reference
- D. Using repetition to reinforce key ideas
- E. Encouraging the use of feedback
  1. Creating a relaxed environment
  2. Taking the initiative
- F. Becoming a better listener
  1. Active listening techniques
  2. Other listening fundamentals

Chapter Review
Questions for Review and Discussion
Learning Exercise 6–1. Called to the Office
Learning Exercise 6–2. The Active Listener
Learning Exercise 6–3. Rate Your Listening Habits
Suggestions for Further Reading

CASE 6–1
A SNAG IN COMMUNICATION

Pete Platt, senior project forest supervisor with Wisconsin Timberlands, was instructing one of his three work crews on their day's first project:

Pete: Folks, we need to plant these five acres of winter wheat for use as a game food plot. We've gotta get it before the rough weather moves in this weekend; so I'd like to wrap this one up today. Here's what I'd like you to do. First, sow the area with fertilizer; then disk it twice with the heavy disk. Then sow the winter wheat seed evenly over the disked area. Finally, pull a log over the area twice to cover the seed. The equipment and supplies will be here any minute—ah, here they come now. I'll be back around 3 o'clock to check things out. Harold, you run the show on this job, okay? [Harold Deak was the senior employee.]

About 3:10 p.m., Pete returned to the area to check on the job's progress. He found Harold and the other three workers huddled around the equipment near the road.

Pete: Well, it looks like you've wrapped the job up.

Harold: Yeah, we were just untying the log, Pete.

Pete: (*Observing that the log was hitched to the back of the disk*) Good grief! Don't tell me that's how you pulled the log—behind that disk!

Harold: Like you said, we sowed the fertilizer, disked it twice, then sowed the wheat and put the disk back on with a log behind it and dragged the area twice to cover up the seed.

Pete: Man, you all didn't listen to me! Those seeds are probably buried a foot deep. You don't disk *after* putting seed out—nobody said anything about putting the log behind the disk. We'll never get a stand of wheat out of this. You've ruined the day and wasted 150 pounds of seed; and, with that front moving in, I don't know when we'll be able to get to this again!

The opening quotation certainly applies to Case 6–1, doesn't it? Obviously, there was a lack of effective communication between Pete and his work group. Each day, organizations pay a very high price for miscommunication, including money, time, lack of cooperation between people and departments, poor attitudes among personnel, and even physical injury.

In Chapter 1 you learned how important human relations skills are in performing the supervisor's job. Communication plays a critical role in human relations, as well as in task-related areas of supervision. In a typical workday, supervisors assign jobs, discuss coordination efforts with people from other departments, have discussions with their own bosses, attend meetings, listen to and counsel employees— the list could go on and on. In fact, studies of managers and supervisors have shown that they spend 60 to 80 percent of their time involved in some form of communication.[1]

WHAT IS COMMUNICATION?

Many supervisors think that communication is just a matter of "telling it like it is." They fail to recognize the difficulties involved in such a simple approach. When communication breakdowns occur, they are more interested in placing blame than in finding out what went wrong. For you to really understand a supervisor's role in communication, it is important that you learn about the basic communication process.

Communication Process Model

Rather than define communication in words, we will use an illustration of the **communication process model** (see Figure 6–1). The components of the model are (1) the sender, (2) the message, (3) the channel, (4) the receiver, and (5) feedback.

THE SENDER. The **sender** is the person who originates and sends a message. Sometimes an inner need triggers the urge to communicate. When you say, "Pass the salt, please," you are reacting to a physical need. When you say, "I love you," you are reflecting a need for affection. When, as a supervisor, you say, "You'll have to do this report over," you may be reflecting a need for esteem (you want to be proud of work done in your department) or a need for security (you may fear that your own boss will reprimand you).

FIGURE 6–1   COMMUNICATION PROCESS MODEL

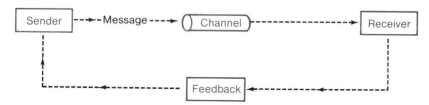

THE MESSAGE. The **message** consists of words or nonverbal expressions that are capable of transmitting meaning. The examples given above are examples of verbal messages. But nonverbal messages, such as a smile or a frown, are equally—if not more—important.

THE CHANNEL. The **channel** is the means used to pass the message. Channels may be face-to-face, the telephone, written forms (such as memos, reports, or newsletters), group meetings, or others.

One supervisor related how his crew was working on an important machine breakdown when the plant manager chewed him out, by name, for taking too long to complete the job. "I didn't mind getting chewed out as much as I minded the way he did it," said the supervisor. "It was over the intercom, and the whole plant heard it."

Do you think the intercom is an appropriate channel by which to convey a reprimand? Why or why not?

THE RECEIVER. The **receiver** is the ultimate destination of the sender's message. In fact, the receiver is the one who assigns meaning to the message. Each day, a supervisor frequently acts in the dual role of sender and receiver, as Figure 6–2 shows.

FEEDBACK. Frequently we also send messages *in response to* someone else's message. The response is called **feedback**. For example, your employee may ask, "Why do I have to do the report over?" When you answer this question, you will be "sending" feedback as a response to someone else's message.

The communication process model makes communication appear very simple, doesn't it? But in reality, the communication process is quite complicated and involves many variables.

Test yourself! How would you answer the following questions?

1. Meaning lies in words. True or false?

2. Words are the most important means of communication. True or false?

In the next section, you'll find the correct answers to these two questions.

FIGURE 6–2   THE SUPERVISOR AS A SENDER AND A RECEIVER

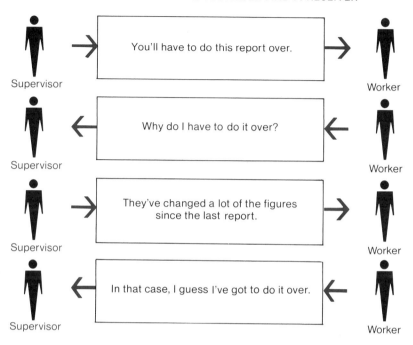

Meaning Lies in People

Do words have meaning? The answer is no; words themselves do not have meaning! A supervisor must constantly be aware that meanings lie in *people*, not in the words they use.

> *Shop supervisor Betty Ruhl was mad, mad, mad! She'd just checked on an important project she had given one of her best workers, Chuck Duke. The project should have been finished an hour ago. To Betty's dismay, the project not only wasn't finished, it hadn't even been started!*
>
> *The reason for the communication breakdown lay in the way Betty had assigned the job to Chuck. She'd said, "Get on this as soon as you can," but in her mind she'd meant "in four or five minutes." To Chuck, it meant "after I finish the job I'm presently working on." And he still hadn't completed that job!*

Whom would you blame for the communication breakdown, Betty or Chuck? Blaming Chuck would help protect the supervisor's ego, but it represents a poor approach to her communication responsibilities. The meaning did not lie in the words "as soon as you can" but in the people saying and hearing them—Betty and Chuck. Unless you realize that the meaning of words used depends on your receiver's interpretation and not your own understanding of them, you will live in a glass bubble and see all communication breakdowns as the other person's fault. Perhaps another example will drive home the point.

"I certainly don't mean anything negative by it," said Max Jones, office supervisor for Hunter Supply Co. "But if you say so, I'm sure that's the way they must take it. I'll be careful not to do it again."

What Max was talking about was something Linda Carson had just told him. Linda was older than the other women employees. It seems that they were quite turned off by Max's referring to them as "the gals." To them this word had a very negative and unprofessional meaning. It especially turned off the younger women in the department!

Importance of Nonverbal Messages

Nonverbal messages play a big role in communication. One expert, Albert Mehrabian, finds that only about 7 percent of emotional meaning is communicated verbally; the other 93 percent is communicated nonverbally.[2] In other words, your impression of someone's emotions, such as anger, happiness, or fear, comes through more loudly from that person's tone of voice, facial expression, or other nonverbal means than through the words the person uses.

Supervisors have to be careful that their verbal and nonverbal signals are consistent and do not give the wrong impression. Moreover, supervisors can obtain much information from the nonverbal signals of others. Consider the following two examples in which nonverbal messages strongly influence the communication situation.

Harold Lee is tour supervisor at a local food processing plant. While listening to one of his new crew members talk about a job problem, Harold continues to fill out a report.

Becky Lewis, technical supervisor for a chemical company, glances at her watch several times while telling one of her technicians, "Sure, Jill, what is it you wanted to discuss?"

Basically, nonverbal signals, which can send positive or negative information, fall into five categories:

1. **Voice signals**—emphasis on certain words, pauses, or tone of voice. For example, can you say, "Nice job, Evans," in such a way that it's actually a put-down?
2. **Body signals**—slumped posture, clenched fist, raised eyebrows, or the act of kicking a piece of equipment.
3. **Object signals**—office furniture, protective helmet, plush carpet, or plaques and awards on the wall.
4. **Space signals**—huddling close, being distant, or sitting beside someone.
5. **Time signals**—being on time, being available, or saving time.

FLOWS OF COMMUNICATION

In order to put the supervisor's communication role in perspective, we need to examine the flows of communication in an entire organization. Here we will look at communication *within* the organization, rather than with outside groups such as customers, suppliers, or government agencies. Figure 6–3 shows that there are several directions in which formal communication flows: (1) downward, (2) upward, and (3) lateral-diagonal. A fourth flow is the flow of informal communications, commonly known as the *grapevine*.

Downward Communication

Downward communication originates with managers and supervisors and passes down to employees. Tremendous amounts of communication constantly flow in this direction. Examples of downward communication include announcements of goals and objectives, policies, decisions, procedures, job assignments, and general information.

In Case 6–1, Pete Platt's communications to his crew were examples of downward communication. Note that Pete passed the following specific verbal messages:

1. That a five-acre plot was to be planted with winter wheat.
2. That the job needed to be completed that day.
3. That he would return later in the day to evaluate the job's progress.
4. That Deak was in charge of the task.

   Can you identify any other downward communication that Pete sent?

FIGURE 6–3   FLOW OF FORMAL COMMUNICATION IN AN ORGANIZATION

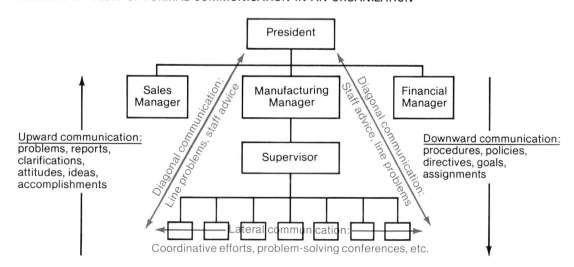

The channels for downward communication are (1) face-to-face contacts, (2) group meetings, (3) memos, (4) bulletin boards, and (5) a variety of other means such as newsletters and letters mailed to employees' homes.

Of the examples listed above, which do you think is generally the most effective way for a supervisor to pass information to his or her work group? Why?

Figure 6–4 lists communications that employees *like* to hear from their supervisor. Take a few seconds to examine carefully the list before reading further. Do any items on this list strike you as being more crucial than others?

FIGURE 6–4 COMMUNICATIONS EMPLOYEES LIKE TO HEAR

Role clarifications: what's expected of the employee, how much authority and responsibility the employee has, and the employee's job assignments.

Praise and recognition: A supervisor's compliments on a job well done, compliments in the presence of third parties, and demonstrations of appreciation.

Constructive criticism and feedback: properly given by a supervisor, this demonstrates interest and implies a personal and professional concern.

Demonstrations of interest by the supervisor: communications reflecting interest in the employee's professional growth and development, working with the employee to help her or him do a better job, and full attention during conversation (as opposed to lack of eye contact or doing something else).

Requests for information or assistance: a supervisor asking an employee's opinion or advice, or consulting about relevant matters on the job.

Information from a supervisor:
a. That makes an employee feel important by being "in the know" or being let in on things.
b. That pertains to departmental progress, to other work team members, to future plans for the department, and to contemplated changes.
c. That pertains to the overall organization in terms of sales, forecasts, objectives, future outlook, and general internal changes of which the supervisor is aware.
d. That pertains to promotions, merit increases, desirable job assignments, and favors that can be granted by the supervisor.

"Knowing where you stand" is listed by many employees as their single most important need. As one supervisor said to us in a workshop:

I think there's nothing worse than not knowing where you stand with your boss. I like knowing when I'm doing well, but I also need to know when I've goofed up. Having praise and compliments is nice; but when I screw up, I usually know it. So when my boss doesn't let me have some constructive criticism, he's really saying my work's not important enough to bother with or, even worse, that that's all he expects out of me. Performance feedback, good and bad, is my most important information need on the job.

Upward Communication

Upward communication is initiated by employees with their immediate supervisors, as shown in Figure 6–5. It may consist of progress reports on a job; requests for help or clarification; communication about their concerns, attitudes, and feelings; and ideas and suggestions for improvements on the job.

Unfortunately, many supervisors seldom solicit these forms of upward communication, especially the progress reports, from their employees. Neither do they obtain information about their employees' true attitudes, feelings, and suggestions for improvements. Japanese managers have a much better reputation than American managers for really being receptive to their workers' needs and opinions.

In addition to oral or written progress reports, other forms of upward communication from employees include requests for the establishment of a formal suggestion system, an open-door policy, a completion of attitude and morale surveys, and group or individual meetings where employees are encouraged to speak up.

FIGURE 6–5   UPWARD COMMUNICATION FROM WORKERS TO SUPERVISOR

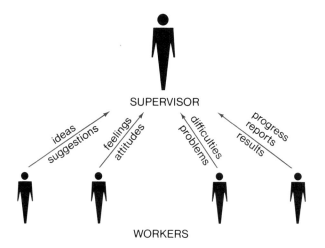

Lateral-Diagonal Communication

Lateral-diagonal communication takes place between individuals in the same department or in different departments. This form of communication has become more important than ever in the past 20 years because organizations continue to become more specialized. Do you recall the line-and-staff form of organization discussed in Chapter 4? Today, members of staff departments interact regularly with line supervisors and managers to coordinate, recommend or advise, perform a service, and sometimes actually give orders (recall our definition of functional authority in Chapter 4). Today's managers depend greatly on their relationships with individuals from departments other than their own. As Figure 6–6 shows, frequently these communications lend themselves to great misinterpretation!

Informal Communication

The upward, downward, and lateral-diagonal communication flows that we have just presented are examples of formal communication. **Informal communication** is that which exists separately from the formal, established communication system. Some examples of informal communication are given below. Each example represents a communication channel that you will not find listed in the com-

FIGURE 6–6 LATERAL COMMUNICATION RUNS AMOK

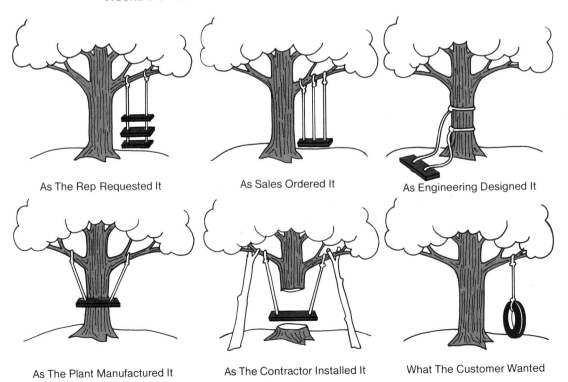

As The Rep Requested It   As Sales Ordered It   As Engineering Designed It

As The Plant Manufactured It   As The Contractor Installed It   What The Customer Wanted

pany's formal organization chart. Yet, informal communications such as these are a way of life!

Lisa, Diane, Fred, and Bob carpool since they all work for the same company and live about 35 miles away. Their driving time is usually spent talking about their departments, people who work at the company, and other job-related matters. Since they all work in different departments, they are very much "in the know" about a number of company matters long before the formal company communications channels carry them.

Before seeing her boss about an important request, Mildred O'Neil dropped by to get Kathie Troy's opinion. Kathie was a close friend of Mildred's boss and would probably have some excellent advice for Mildred as to how best to present her request.

THE GRAPEVINE. The best-known informal communication is the grapevine, also called *the rumor mill*. It is called a **grapevine** because, like the plant it is named after, it is tangled, twisted, and seemingly grows without direction. Yet some surveys have found the grapevine to be employees' major source of information about their company, and it has also been found to be surprisingly accurate. In fact, the research of Keith Davis, an authority on human relations, has found that in normal work situations over 75 percent of grapevine information is correct.[3]

PURPOSES SERVED BY INFORMAL COMMUNICATION. Informal communication accomplishes a number of purposes. Among these are (1) it provides a source of information not ordinarily available, (2) it reduces the effects of monotony, and (3) it satisfies personal needs such as the need for relationships or status. Some persons, in fact, take great pride in their "unofficial" knowledge of company matters.

LIVING WITH INFORMAL COMMUNICATION. Effective supervisors realize that informal communication serves important purposes. A supervisor must realize that, unless employees are informed through formal channels, the informal channels will take up the slack. Keeping employees well informed is the best way to manage the grapevine, although it can never be eliminated. It will tend to be much more active when employees are concerned for their security or status.

BARRIERS TO EFFECTIVE SUPERVISORY COMMUNICATION

Given your understanding of the communication process, let's explore some typical communication barriers that a supervisor faces on the job. The nature of these barriers may be organizational, interpersonal, or language-related.

Organizational Barriers

Three types of organizational barriers to communication are (1) levels of hierarchy, (2) authority and status, and (3) specialization and its related jargon.

LEVELS OF HIERARCHY. Have you ever asked another person to give a message to a third person and found that the third person received a totally different message from the one you sent? The same thing occurs in organizations. When a message goes up or down the organization, it passes through a number of "substations" at each level (recall the example given in Figure 6–6). Each level can add to, take from, qualify, or change the original message completely!

At higher levels of management, messages are usually broad and general. At lower levels, these same "broad" messages must be put into specific use. That's frequently the fly in the ointment, especially when lower and top levels have a "gap" of understanding between them.

AUTHORITY AND STATUS. The very fact that one person is a boss over others creates a barrier to free and open communication.

Do you recall how you, as a student in elementary or high school, felt when you were told to report to the principal's office? Even if you had done nothing wrong, you were probably still very anxious and defensive about the visit.

Perhaps you have witnessed situations such as this:

The conference room patter before the superintendent walked in was loose and jovial. Some verbal horseplay occurred among the members, and there was kidding and joking. Some made very negative remarks about the major item on the agenda, which was a discussion of proposed changes in the company's system of performance evaluation. One person joked about another being the one to tell the boss about the flaws in the new system, even though the boss strongly favored it. But when the boss walked in, the entire mood shifted dramatically. He did most of the talking; those in attendance listened attentively. Even when he asked for their opinions, he received only favorable comments about the proposal.

Since, as a supervisor, you must fill out employees' performance evaluations and determine rewards and penalties, employees will tend to give you the information that you are most likely to welcome. Frustrations, disagreements with your policies, job problems, below-standard work, and other unfavorable information tend to be withheld or changed to look more favorable.

SPECIALIZATION AND RELATED JARGON. The *principle of specialization* states that employees are more efficient when each performs just one task or only certain aspects of the task. For example, accountants do accounting work;

salespersons sell; industrial engineers prepare efficiency studies; safety specialists see to it that working conditions are safe; and so on.

Today's increased specialization, however, also creates problems. Specialists have their own technical language or jargon, interests, and narrow view of the organization. Many special terms used by maintenance technicians, electronic data processing specialists, and other groups are completely foreign to people in other departments. This can severely hamper effective communication.

What are some technical words that you're familiar with that your class-mates probably wouldn't understand?

Interpersonal and Language Barriers

Even though the three organizational barriers just discussed might not exist, a supervisor's communication can still be distorted by interpersonal as well as language-related problems. Figure 6–7 lists a number of these problems, some of which we will discuss.

FIGURE 6–7   INTERPERSONAL BARRIERS TO EFFECTIVE
SUPERVISORY COMMUNICATION

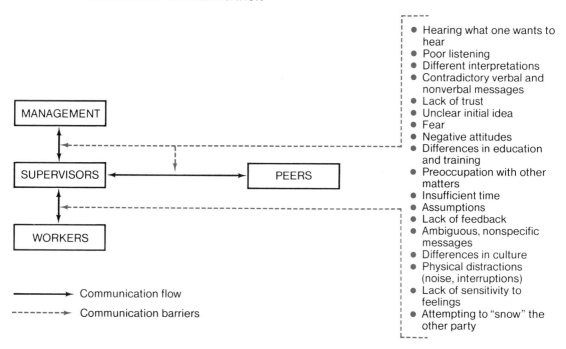

DIFFERING PERCEPTIONS. The term **perception** may be defined as the process by which one selects, organizes, and gives meaning to the world around oneself. All of us have a special way of "filtering" things around us based on our needs, moods, biases, expectations, culture, experiences, and so on.

One limiting factor in our perception is that we can't grasp the whole of a situation at a given instant of time. Some matters receive greater attention than others, while some matters receive none at all. Those matters we do focus on usually serve some immediate purpose. Your needs, moods, cultural and social influences, and attitudes all come together to determine which things are important to you.

In a factory accident, for example, the following persons might "see" the accident differently: the supervisor (who may have lost a valuable worker); the safety engineer (whose safety record may have been blemished); the fellow worker (who is the injured worker's best friend); the company physician (who attends to the injured worker); and the human-resources manager (who is concerned with workers' compensation and finding a replacement for the injured worker). If each of these persons were to communicate about the accident, there would be different versions, depending on how each "saw" it.

When we do go about interpreting things around us, we have a tendency to put similar things in the same categories. This makes it easier to deal with them. This tendency is called **stereotyping**. There are strong stereotypes for various nationalities, races, religions, sexes, occupations, and other groups in our society. For example, a production manager may label all women as "misfits," all union people as "agitators," and all staff employees as "a bunch of meddlers." Obviously this stereotyping will have a strong influence on this manager's communications to and from these people.

On the other hand, stereotypes may also be favorable. As a supervisor, you must be aware that your attitudes, biases, and prejudices—both positive and negative—strongly influence your communications with others.

IMPRECISE LANGUAGE. We have already indicated how important language is in the process of communication. The fact that people interpret words differently may be traced to lack of precision in the use of language. True, you can say that a drill press weighs 270 pounds, or that Sam Eggers is 5'11" tall, or that Judy Snead has completed 10 years of service with the hospital. Language is precise in that regard, and we can verify it.

However, compare this to a salesperson selling drill presses who tells a production superintendent that the drill press is "the finest on the market." Or one supervisor telling another that "Sam is a loyal employee." Or a supervisor saying that "Judy Snead is a good nurse." What is "loyal" or "good"? What means "loyal" to you (e.g., Sam has turned down several job offers from competing firms) may be "complacent" or "unambitious" to someone else. A "good nurse" to you may be one who is a sympathetic listener and spends a lot of time talking with patients and being cheerful and friendly; to someone else, a "good nurse" may mean one who is knowledgeable and competent and goes about her or his work without trying to make conversation.

Sometimes a supervisor uses imprecise language when more precise language is necessary. Suppose a supervisor tells an employee, "You must improve on your absenteeism, as it has been excessive. Otherwise, you'll be disciplined." What does the supervisor mean by "improve on your absenteeism" or "excessive"? What "discipline" does the supervisor have in mind?

Another language barrier is that not all people have the same level of language skill. Many terms familiar to a veteran employee, for example, may be quite over the heads of a new crop of employees going through an orientation program. In some cases, people even try to "snow" others by using terms they know the others will not understand!

Examine Figure 6–7 on page 151. Which barriers do you feel were responsible for the communication breakdown between Pete Platt and his work group in Case 6–1?

IMPROVING SUPERVISORY COMMUNICATIONS

As we've indicated, communication is too critical to your success as a supervisor to be left to chance. In order to be effective in accomplishing your "task" and "people" goals, you can do much to be a more effective communicator. Some specific things you can do are (1) set the proper climate with your employees, (2) plan your communication, (3) consider your receiver's frame of reference, (4) use repetition to reinforce key ideas, (5) encourage the use of feedback, and (6) become a better listener.

Setting the Proper Climate

A supervisor doesn't communicate in a vacuum. Communications take place within the entire superior-subordinate or superior-group relationship. A supervisor and his or her work group each bring a store of experiences, expectations, and attitudes into the communication event. These mental pictures strongly influence the meaning each person assigns to the message sent and received. Thus, the "setting" is very important for good communication.

What type of setting best contributes to effective communication? We feel that two important factors are (1) mutual trust between the supervisor and subordinates, and (2) a minimum of status barriers.

MUTUAL TRUST BETWEEN SUPERVISOR AND EMPLOYEES. Trust helps communication in two ways. For one thing, if an employee trusts you, he or she is more willing to communicate frankly about job problems. Second, if employees trust you, they are less likely to distort your motives and make negative assumptions about your communications. If you fight for your employees' interests by bargaining with higher management, if you discipline fairly and consistently, and if you respect your employees' abilities, you are more likely to be trusted by them. You'll be looked upon as a positive source in helping them to reach their goals.

A MINIMUM OF STATUS BARRIERS. Generally the best communication occurs in a setting where people are relaxed and comfortable rather than "uptight." Also, the way a supervisor arranges his or her office furniture has much to do with establishing a relaxed setting, as shown in Figure 6–8.

One supervisor says he likes to discuss certain sensitive matters away from his own turf so as to make an employee feel more comfortable and less nervous. By design, supervisors may communicate in the employee's work area or in a neutral situation such as over a cup of coffee or lunch.

At Honda of America, Honda President Shochiro Iramafiri wears no tie and eats in the company cafeteria. On the front of his white overalls, which are just like those everyone else in the plant wears, is his first name, "IRI." He has no private office but works at a desk in the same work area as 100 of his other white-collar work group. This represents a distinct effort to diminish the status differences between himself and all other employees.[4]

Planning Your Communication

How many times have you completely blown a communication situation by not being prepared for it? After it's over, you think, "Now why didn't I say this?" or "I never should have said such and such."

ANTICIPATING SITUATIONS IN ADVANCE. If you are a supervisor, many of your contacts will occur without much warning and may not allow much planning. Yet you can anticipate many situations and give thought to them before they occur. For example, you can anticipate the following situations:

FIGURE 6–8 DESK-CHAIR ARRANGEMENTS THAT AFFECT FORMALITY OF COMMUNICATING

1. When you must give employees their performance evaluation.
2. When you discipline employees and make work corrections.
3. When you delegate authority for a job and communicate job assignments and instructions.
4. When you persuade employees to accept changes in the job or work environment.
5. When you have to sell an idea to your boss or to other staff members.

If you understand how complex good communications are, you'll be more aware of the existing barriers and try to minimize their effects. Moreover, to be understood by your subordinates, you must put yourself in *their* shoes and try to see things from *their* viewpoint. An old Indian prayer expresses the thought this way: "Lord, grant that I may not criticize my neighbor until I've walked a mile in his moccasins."

EXAMPLES OF PLANNED COMMUNICATIONS. Once you establish an objective for a communication, make a plan to achieve it. Let's look at two examples.

Suppose an excellent employee has asked in advance to speak to you about a transfer to another department. Assuming that you don't know all the facts, one objective of your meeting would be to gain insight into the request for transfer, including the reasons for it, timing, and so on. This will help you make a decision or make readjustments in your department. Your plan could be to take a listening role and use active listening techniques which will be explained shortly. This strategy prevents you from commanding the interaction, monopolizing the communication, and preventing the achievement of your objective.

Suppose you are going to ask a promising employee to participate in a voluntary training program. Your objective in this case is to gain the employee's acceptance of the program and to develop enthusiasm for it. Your plan, then, is to focus on what's in it for the employee if she or he participates in the program. How will training aid the employee's development, future in the company, and so on? You would try to uncover any objections by using listening skills. And you would attempt to anticipate possible objections and determine how they can be overcome.

These two examples show the advantage of planning your communication. If you fail to plan when you can do so, you may depend too much on your spontaneous, off-the-cuff ability to communicate. The planning stage, therefore, spills over into the act of communication itself. The nature of your communication role, the message(s), and the strategy in message content and sequence can, to some extent, all be predetermined. Thus, the four major concepts presented in the rest of this chapter relate clearly to planning.

Considering Your Receiver's Frame of Reference

Earlier we discussed how each of us has unique "filters" that influence the way we interpret the world around us. Obviously the better attuned you are to your subordinates' and others' patterns of evaluation, the more effective your communications to and from them will be. Effective communication, then, requires you to step into the shoes of others and visualize situations from their perspective.

Have you ever been in a class where the instructor was talking so far over the heads of the students that no one was even capable of asking an intelligent question? If so, what was your reaction? Why is it that some people overshoot their audience and don't even realize it?

A supervisor must frequently ask questions like these:

1. How is this person *like* me?
2. How is this person *different* from me?
3. How is this person *similar* to other employees?
4. How is this person *different* from other employees?
5. How will this person react if I say such and such?

A supervisor doesn't find out the answers to these questions by reading employees' biographical data from their personal files. He or she must interact with them. That is the only real opportunity to recognize employees' different motives, needs, attitudes, and the *probable* way they'll interpret things. The use of effective feedback and listening techniques are important ways to accomplish this.

Using Repetition to Reinforce Key Ideas

Repeating a message plays an important part in communicating effectively. This is especially true when you have to communicate technical information or a direct order. Repetition, or redundancy, reduces the chance that incorrect assumptions will be made by the receiver. For example, you can state a complicated message in several ways. You can clarify your meaning by the use of examples, illustrations, or comparisons. You can also say the same thing several times, but in different words. Here, for instance, is how a supervisor might communicate an instruction to a subordinate.

Danny, we just got a telephone order for a 42-by-36-inch fireplace screen in our KL-17 series. I know you haven't done one up like it since last year when a customer gave us so much trouble about the screen not fitting his fireplace opening. That's the same style this guy wants, with black and gold trim as shown in this catalog clipping. And you heard me right: He wants it 42 inches high by 36 inches wide—higher than it is wide. That's a new one for me, and I'm sure it's a new one for you too. Can you get it out in the next two weeks?

Note how the supervisor used a past example and a catalog to clarify the style of the fireplace screen, and how the supervisor repeated the required measurements!

Encouraging the Use of Feedback

As mentioned earlier, feedback is the response that a communicator receives from the receiver of the message. Two ways in which a supervisor can encourage the use of feedback to communicate better with employees are (1) by creating a relaxed environment, and (2) by taking the initiative.

CREATING A RELAXED ENVIRONMENT. Earlier in this section, we discussed the importance of establishing a favorable setting for communication. A relaxed setting is also required when the supervisor wants to obtain feedback from his or her employees. As a supervisor, you certainly should not look down on subordinates for asking questions or for openly stating their opinions, suggestions, or feelings toward a subject. A defensive attitude on your part discourages feedback from employees. *How* you communicate also determines, to a large extent, the amount of feedback you will receive. For example, written instructions or memos don't allow for the immediate feedback that can be gained from face-to-face communication.

In ancient times, there was an Oriental king who hated to hear bad news. Whenever a courier reported bad news or an unfortunate event to the king, the king became furious and had him beheaded. After three couriers bit the dust, the king soon began hearing only good news! The moral here for supervisors is that they must be open and receptive to all information, both good and bad, from their employees, or they too will have a smokescreen surround them.

TAKING THE INITIATIVE. Although the type of communication used and the setting for the communication are important in determining what feedback is obtained, the supervisor must also take the initiative in getting responses from the work group. For example, after giving a job assignment, you might ask, "Do you have any questions?" or "Did I leave anything out?" A better approach would be to say, "To make sure I've gotten my message across, how about repeating it to me?" Frequently this approach produces a number of clarifications that someone might otherwise be unwilling to ask for fear of looking stupid, as Figure 6–9 shows. Finally, you can set the stage for further feedback with comments such as "If anything comes up later or if you have some questions, just let me know."

The participative leadership style (discussed in Chapter 9) relies heavily on good two-way communication—which is a form of feedback. When a supervisor allows subordinates to make decisions or to express opinions, their responses are a form of feedback. This style helps the supervisor better understand the subordinates' thinking.

FIGURE 6–9 ENCOURAGING FEEDBACK TO INSURE COMMUNICATION

Feedback can also help you learn how to better send messages in the future. When you discover that your initial message wasn't clear, or that your "persuasion" was not effective, you can refine your future messages. A summary of tips about feedback is given in Figure 6–10.

Becoming a Better Listener

It has been said that Mother Nature blessed human beings with two ears and only one mouth as a not-so-subtle hint which, unfortunately, we often ignore. "How to Be a Good Listener" has become a popular subject and is being taught today in many elementary and high schools throughout our country.

Our own research reveals that of the four communication skills (writing, speaking, reading, and listening) which managers and supervisors most frequently use, listening is the skill in which they have had the least training. Why do you think this is so?

ACTIVE LISTENING TECHNIQUES. A particular listening technique that places the supervisor in a receiver's role and encourages feedback from others is called **active listening** (also known as *feeling listening, reflective listening,* and *nondi-*

FIGURE 6–10   TIPS ABOUT FEEDBACK

■ Generally, feedback is likely to be better where there is a trusting relationship between people. If a person doesn't trust you, she or he is not likely to "level" with you or share feelings very readily. As a result, you are told what you want to hear, instead of what you *should* hear. For example, the person may say, "Yes, sir, things are going okay on the Anders job" (when in reality there may be a real lack of progress or some severe hangups). Or the person may say, "I certainly agree with you, boss" (when in reality the person doesn't agree with you at all but doesn't want to upset you or risk being chewed out).

■ Some people give feedback readily, but others need some encouragement. Examples of the latter type are people who are timid, quiet, or insecure, or have learned that "it's best to keep your mouth shut around here." *Asking* such people for their ideas, suggestions, or feelings often helps give them a green light. For example, you can say, "Dale, how will this new policy affect your group?" or "What do you think about . . . ?"

■ Complimenting people for providing feedback reinforces their willingness to *continue* providing feedback. When you say, "I appreciate your honesty in discussing this," or "Thanks, Joan, for raising some questions that needed to be clarified," you are encouraging the other party to give feedback in the future.

■ When giving instructions, it is a good habit to ask the listener if he or she has any questions. For example, you can ask, "Is this clear, Dick? Have you any questions?" Some supervisors end their instructions with, "Now, Dick, let's see if we're together on this. In your own words run by me what it seems I've just said." If the instructions are given over the telephone, you can say, "Okay, Dick, read back to me those seven dates I just gave you so we can make sure we're together on this."

■ When you have potentially negative feedback to give, it is helpful to begin by saying, "Sarah, may I offer a suggestion about . . . ?" or "May I give you my impression of . . . ?" or "Can I share my feelings about . . . ?" This approach is less pushy, and the message will be received with less defensiveness than when you bluntly blurt out the negative information.

■ Nonverbal signals and body language offer a wide variety of feedback. Frowns, nervous fidgeting, nods of the head, and other facial expressions and body movements give us a lot of information. Frequently, however, we overlook these signals completely because we are not looking at the other person or because we are absorbed in our own thoughts and messages.

rective listening). Basically, active listening requires the listener to make a response that tosses the ball back to the sender and says, "Yes, I understand; tell me more." It is used by psychologists, psychiatrists, counselors, and others when it is necessary to understand how someone feels and thinks. We think that active listening is of great value to supervisors as a philosophy for encouraging more open feedback.

The **reflective statement** is a form of active listening in which you repeat what you think the speaker has just told you. For example:

Suppose the speaker is Jim Atkins, one of your employees. He tells you: "Say, I've got a little problem I'd like to discuss. It's about Klaric, the new guy in our department. He doesn't seem to fit in at all. Some of the guys have even kidded me about it, saying 'Where did we dig this guy up? He's a real nerd!' He won't even try to fit in, and the others seem to resent him for that. I've tried to help him work into the group because you know the pride we have in our work and in getting along so well together. Klaric's a good worker, but he's causing us more trouble than he's worth."

What is Jim telling you? How would you respond? One way is to respond with a summary in your own words of what Jim has just told you. For example, you can say, "What you seem to be saying, Jim, is that while Klaric is a good worker, you're concerned because he doesn't fit in well." This statement *reflects* back to Jim what he has just said and allows him to continue talking about the subject.

Frequently, the speaker will elaborate on certain aspects of an earlier statement which seem to be more critical to that person. Using the above example, Jim might elaborate by saying: "Well, the thing that gets me most, I guess, is that I really messed up in my evaluation of Klaric. When you asked my opinion, I honestly thought he would fit in. I just don't see how I could have been so wrong in evaluating him." Thus, in going into detail, you can see that Atkins is mainly concerned about making a poor evaluation of Klaric's ability to fit into the department.

The **probe** is more specific than the reflective statement. It directs attention to a particular aspect of the speaker's message. For example, in the Klaric case, your response to Atkins could be any of the following:

1. "He doesn't seem to fit in at all?"
2. "You say the other guys seem to resent him?"
3. "He's a real nerd, eh?"

Note that these probes are more specific than the reflective statement, and they allow you to pursue what you feel may be important. The probe may provide additional insight into the problem by encouraging Atkins to discuss it more deeply. In addition, a probe is less likely to cause a speaker to become defensive than direct questions. When you ask, "Who's been kidding you about it?" or "Why do you call him a nerd?", Atkins may feel that you're putting him on the spot. You would do better to delay such questions until later stages of this communication situation.

OTHER LISTENING FUNDAMENTALS. A number of other important techniques can help your listening effectiveness. These are presented in Figure 6–11.

FIGURE 6–11 TIPS FOR BETTER LISTENING

- Try to avoid doing most of the talking yourself. Give the other person an opportunity to speak.
- Avoid distractions. Close your office door or move to a quieter area.
- Act interested in what the other person says. Don't doodle, write, or work on something else. Give the employee your full attention.
- Ask questions. As long as the questions aren't considered nosy or brash, this will help keep you interested and encourage the employee to give more details.
- Summarize what you think someone has said. "What you're saying is . . . ." This will reinforce what you have heard and also enable the other person to correct your possible misunderstanding.
- Be empathetic. Try to put yourself in the speaker's shoes.
- Don't lose your temper or show signs of being upset by what the speaker is saying. Try to listen with an open mind.
- Don't interrupt. Let the person continue his or her statement before you respond.
- After an important conversation or meeting, jot down notes to yourself about the main points discussed.
- Use active listening techniques—reflective statements and probes—to assure your understanding of key points, to help the speaker talk, or to steer the conversation in certain directions.

As you can see, good listening is hard work. But it is an essential tool for the supervisor!

CHAPTER REVIEW

The communication process was shown to consist of five parts: a sender, a message, a channel, a receiver, and feedback. In reviewing this process, we stressed that "meaning" lies in people rather than in words, and that nonverbal messages communicate our emotions more strongly than words.

Supervisors spend anywhere from 60 to 80 percent of their time involved in some form of communication. In any organization there is a tremendous volume of formal communication that flows in three directions: downward, upward, and lateral-diagonal. Downward communication includes announcements of goals, objectives, policies, decisions, procedures, job assignments, and general information. Upward communication consists of progress reports from employees; their requests for assistance; communication about their attitudes, feelings, and concerns; and ideas and suggestions for job improvement. Lateral-diagonal communication occurs between persons within a department or in different departments. It typically involves contacts between line and staff members. Informal communication, commonly called the *grapevine*, also plays an important role in the organization.

A number of organizational, interpersonal, and language barriers hamper a supervisor's effectiveness in communication. Organizational barriers include the levels of hierarchy a message must pass through, the authority and status of managers, and the jargon of specialized departments. Interpersonal and language barriers include people's differing perceptions and the general impreciseness of language.

Several ways to improve supervisory communication were discussed. First, a supervisor should establish the proper setting when communicating with employees. The proper setting is a climate with a high trust level, where the supervisor is viewed as a source of help and where status barriers are minimized. Second, a supervisor should plan his or her communication. This involves determining in advance a communication strategy that will enable the supervisor to reach an objective. Third, a supervisor must consider the receiver's frame of reference. This requires a look at things from the receiver's view, which can be very difficult. Fourth, a supervisor should use repetition to reinforce key ideas. Finally, a supervisor should encourage and induce feedback and become a better listener.

QUESTIONS FOR REVIEW AND DISCUSSION

1. What are the five components of the basic communication process model? Define each.
2. Explain the different ways in which nonverbal signals influence supervisory communication.
3. Identify the three major flows of communication in an organization. Give an example of each direction.
4. What are three organizational barriers to supervisory communication?
5. Do you think the grapevine is as important and accurate as we stress? Why?
6. In what ways is feedback important in the communication process?
7. Define *active listening*.
8. A supervisor says, "I like to put as many of my communications as I can in writing. That way I have a record of what I've said, and my employees can't get off the hook so easily." What is your reaction to this supervisor's practice and attitude?
9. A common problem faced by many supervisors who have an open-door policy is that some employees are long-winded and never seem to want to stop talking. What are some nonverbal signals that a supervisor can send that will help terminate the conversation?
10. Why do you suppose so many supervisors, when orienting or training a new employee, tend to speak above the new employee's level of understanding? Explain.

LEARNING EXERCISE 6–1
CALLED TO THE OFFICE

George Bullard waited in the office of his supervisor, Bill Henly. He felt again like a grade-school kid who'd been called to the principal's office, and he wondered what he'd done wrong this time. Bill Henly opened the door of the office from behind George, walked past him, sat down behind his desk, and began to leaf through some papers. The following brief conversation took place.

> **Henly:** I'll get right to the point, George. The reason I called you in is that I just received this report from Quality. You've messed up badly on the last batch—13 percent defective. What's the story?
>
> **George** (*fidgeting in his chair*): I think you know the answer to that.
>
> **Henly:** Now just what is that supposed to mean?
>
> **George:** I told Industrial Engineering that that machine wouldn't pull the load they're putting on it during all three shifts, but they wouldn't believe me. Nobody can get the kind of production you want without something giving, and in this case it's quality. You let me slow down and I'll get you quality.
>
> **Henly:** Just one second, George! (*Rises, raises voice while pointing finger*). Don't go shifting the blame to your machine! For the last three or four weeks, even before this latest incident, you've been slacking off. I don't know what your problem is, and I don't really care as long as you get the work back up to what it should be. Consider this an oral warning. I know you can do better than this and, if you can't, we'll find someone who can! Any questions? (*Rises and walks toward door.*)
>
> **George:** No. (*Under his breath as he leaves*) There's no way I'm going to be the scapegoat in this. Riley [the shop steward] will see to that when I slap a grievance on Henly. You can be sure of that!

Answer the following questions:

1. Do you feel that Henly accomplished his objective in his discussion with George?
2. What would you have recommended that Henly say or do differently? That George do or say differently?

LEARNING EXERCISE 6–2
THE ACTIVE LISTENER

In each of the following situations, which response best demonstrates the use of active listening?

1. A worker who has recently been bypassed for promotion says, "That's the reward I get for putting in 15 years around here. If you're not a brown-nose, you don't get ahead here. I'm much better qualified than the last two people who've gotten Supervisor I jobs. It's not fair."
   a. Maybe you ought to discuss your career with the personnel manager.
   b. Have you thought about filing a formal grievance?

c. You don't feel the promotion system is fair.

d. Have you let them know you'd really like a supervisory job?

e. Maybe your attitude has something to do with it. Sounds like sour grapes to me.

2. One of your subordinates tells you, "I don't know—maybe it's time for me to change jobs. I seem to be bored. I don't find the work challenging, and I've lost interest in my job. I really need some advice."

a. You seem to need a few days off. Why not take some vacation time?

b. A job change would do some good. There's a new project I could assign you to.

c. Are you having any personal problems?

d. You're concerned because you've lost interest in your job.

e. Tell me how you think I might be able to help.

3. When you ask about his progress, a new employee says, "I really like it around here. My work group has been really good about helping me learn the ins and outs and where different materials are located. Everybody seems very helpful, and I feel good about my work."

a. The work group has been a big help to you.

b. I told you they'd be very helpful to you.

c. What do you like best about your work?

d. Have they told you about the new flextime system we'll be putting in next month?

LEARNING EXERCISE 6–3
RATE YOUR LISTENING HABITS*

The subject of listening has become most popular in management and supervisory training seminars. Several years ago, Sperry Corporation undertook a large scale "listening" skills workshop for personnel throughout their organization; "At Sperry We Listen" became the theme of a most successful promotional campaign in newsprint and television advertising. Figure 6–12, "Rate Your Listening Habits," has been used by the authors in seminars with several thousand managers and supervisors.

Instructions

1. Complete the Listening Profile and tally your score.

2. Meet with a group of three to five of your class members. Compare your ratings. On which items did the group as a whole rate themselves *most favorably? Most unfavorably?*

*Used with permission of Sperry Univac Corporation.

FIGURE 6–12   RATE YOUR LISTENING HABITS

As a listener, how frequently do you engage in the following listening behaviors? Place a check in the appropriate column and complete your score based on the scale at the bottom of the page.

Listening Habit	Very Seldom 10	8	6	4	Almost Always 2
1. Faking attention, pretending to be interested when you're really not	___	___	___	___	___
2. Being passive—not asking questions or trying to obtain clarifications, even when you don't understand	___	___	___	___	___
3. Listening mainly to what a speaker *says* rather than his/her feelings	___	___	___	___	___
4. Allowing yourself to be distracted easily	___	___	___	___	___
5. Not being aware of the speaker's facial expressions, non-verbal behavior	___	___	___	___	___
6. Tuning out material that is complex or contrary to your own opinion	___	___	___	___	___
7. Drawing conclusions, having your mind made up before hearing the speaker's full line of reasoning	___	___	___	___	___
8. Allowing yourself to daydream or wander mentally	___	___	___	___	___
9. Feeling restless, impatient, eager to end the conversation	___	___	___	___	___
10. Interrupting the speaker, taking over the conversation to get in your own side of things	___	___	___	___	___

Your total score: _____
                   100

90–100 — Superior
80–89 — Very Good
70–79 — Good
60–69 — Average
50–59 — Below Average
0–49 — Far Below Average

ENDNOTES

1. E. E. Lawler, L. W. Porter, and S. Tannenbaum, "Managers' Attitudes Toward Interaction Episodes," *Journal of Applied Psychology* 52 (1968): 432–39.
2. Albert Mehrabian, "Communication without Words," *Psychology Today* 2 (September 1968): 53–55.
3. For further details, see Keith Davis, *Human Behavior at Work*, 5th ed. (New York: McGraw-Hill Book Co., 1978), p. 280.
4. "The Difference Japanese Management Makes," *Business Week*, July 14, 1986, p. 47.

SUGGESTIONS FOR FURTHER READING

Barnard, Janet C. "The Principal Players in Your Communication Network." *Supervisory Management* 28 (June 1983): 20–24.

Gordon, Thomas. *Leadership Effectiveness Training*. Ridgefield, CT: Wyden Books, 1987. See Chapter 5, "Making Everyday Use of Your Listening Skills," pp. 75–92.

Kikoski, John F. "Communication: Understanding It, Improving It." *Personnel Journal* 59 (February 1980): 126–31.

St. John, Walter D. "Successful Communication Between Supervisors and Employees." *Personnel Journal* 62 (January 1983): 71–77.

Sunderlin, Reed. "Information Is Not Communication." *Business Horizons* 25 (March-April 1982): 40–42.

Timm, Paul R. "Driving Out the Devils of Communication." *Management World* 13 (July 1984): 27–29.

7
GROUP DYNAMICS AND MEETINGS

OBJECTIVES

After reading and studying the material in this chapter, you should be able to:

- Identify the processes in group dynamics.
- Differentiate between the leader-controlled approach and the group-centered approach used in meetings.
- Identify the advantages and disadvantages of meetings.
- Describe the actions that a supervisor can take before, during, and after a meeting to make it effective.
- Discuss the important principles to remember in making presentations at meetings.

IMPORTANT TERMS

group dynamics
status
roles
formal roles
informal roles
norms of behavior
cohesiveness
information-giving meeting

information-exchange meeting
fact-finding meeting
problem-solving meeting
leader-controlled approach
group-centered approach
closure
minutes
KISS principle

CHAPTER OUTLINE
CASE 7–1. THE QUIET MEETING

III. PURPOSES OF MEETINGS
    A. The information-giving meeting
    B. The information-exchange meeting
    C. The fact-finding meeting
    D. The problem-solving meeting
IV. APPROACHES USED AT MEETINGS
    A. Leader-controlled approach
        1. Advantages of the leader-controlled approach
        2. Disadvantages of the leader-controlled approach
    B. Group-centered approach
        1. Advantages of the group-centered approach
        2. Disadvantages of the group-centered approach
    C. Which approach is better?
V. ADVANTAGES AND DISADVANTAGES OF MEETINGS
    A. Advantages of meetings
        1. Save time
        2. Assure consistency of information
        3. Permit formal exchange of information
    B. Disadvantages of meetings
        1. May not be cost-effective
        2. May become too impersonal
VI. MAKING MEETINGS EFFECTIVE
    A. Factors to consider before the meeting
        1. Have a clear purpose
        2. Preplan the meeting
    B. Factors to consider during the meeting
        1. Clarify your expectations
        2. Provide leadership
        3. Encourage two-way communication
        4. Get "closure" on items discussed
    C. Factors to consider after the meeting
        1. Distribute copies of the minutes
        2. Follow up on decisions made
VII. MAKING PRESENTATIONS AT MEETINGS
    A. Determine the objective of your presentation
    B. Plan your presentation
    C. Employ visuals for effect
    D. Keep your presentation simple and organize it
    E. Use a conversational delivery
    F. Practice in advance
Chapter Review
Questions for Review and Discussion
Learning Exercise 7–1. The Required Weekly Meeting
Learning Exercise 7–2. Evaluating a Leader's Effectiveness in Meetings
Learning Exercise 7–3. The Quiet Meeting: Advice to Debra
Suggestions for Further Reading

> A meeting is a place where you take minutes and waste hours.
> *Author Unknown*

> A meeting still performs functions that will never be taken over by telephones, teleprinters, Xerox copiers, tape recorders, television monitors, or any other technological instruments of the information revolution.
> *Antony Jay*

CASE 7-1
THE QUIET MEETING

Debra Ronson, sales supervisor of the Western Telephone Company, was just opening a meeting she had called for members of her department. Debra did most of the talking for the first five minutes, recounting her group's performance of the past week. Then she asked, "Are there any questions?" No one responded.

Debra then changed subjects. "As you know, in two weeks we'll be going to a new format for scheduling our sales calls. This was outlined in the memo from the vice-president, copies of which I sent to each of you. This is going to alter your calling schedules and significantly change the way we've been doing things. I have some ideas on how we can best work into this new system. But before getting into that, I'd like to see if anyone here has any ideas. . . . (pause) Anyone care to contribute anything?" No one in the group responded.

Debra continued, "Well, here's what I think we should do . . . . " Debra then spent eight minutes outlining her plan. After the meeting was over, Debra discussed it with one of her fellow supervisors. "I don't know what it is," she said, "but I can never get my people to say much at meetings. I try to give them a chance, but I always end up doing most of the talking. It seems they're either shy or disinterested, but I really don't know if that's the reason or not. I just wish they'd contribute their ideas."

What is going on in this meeting? Why is it that Debra does all of the talking? Why didn't anyone answer her questions? Why won't the members contribute their ideas?

The two important topics discussed in this chapter are small-group dynamics and meetings. As shown in Case 7–1, Debra doesn't appear pleased with the way that the meeting has gone, does she? Moreover, she appears puzzled by her group's failure to respond during the meeting.

Being able to conduct effective meetings requires that a supervisor understand something about the behavior of small work groups. In this chapter, we will begin with a broad discussion of some key elements of small-group behavior, then discuss the supervisor's role in conducting and participating in meetings.

THE SUPERVISOR AND GROUP DYNAMICS

An organization consists of various groups of individuals working together to achieve common goals. The fact that members must work together leads to their relationships with one another. **Group dynamics**, then, refers to the social process by which people interact face to face in small groups. Understanding the dynamics of groups is very important for supervisors because their job performance is linked directly with several key groups, including (1) the supervisor's immediate work group, in which the supervisor acts as the formal leader of the group (as Debra did in Case 7–1); and (2) those groups, including committees, task forces, and other supervisors, of which the supervisor is a member.

To what small groups do you belong? Think in terms of more than just work groups; include school, social, religious, and professional groups as well. With what small groups do you interact?

GROUP DYNAMICS

When we talk about the dynamics of a group, we normally refer to certain processes that take place among its members. In this section, we will examine some of these processes, including leadership, status, roles, norms of behavior, pressures to conform, and cohesiveness.

Leadership

One of the most important small-group processes is leadership. The leaders of a small group are awarded leadership status by members for any of a number of reasons, including influence with management, seniority, experience, personality, and so on. While the group leader may have no formally designated authority to act as group leader, he or she guides the group or influences it in a similar manner.

> *John Mason is a large man (6'4", 230 pounds) who was a professional athlete in his younger days. He has trained and mentored many of the other technicians in his department, and everyone respects his ability. Recently, upper management issued a memo indicating that all technicians would be required to wear standard uniforms while on the job. Yesterday, during lunch break, John told his co-workers he'd quit rather than wear a grade-school uniform. All his fellow department workers heard of John's position and pledged to go along with him. A petition was drawn up stating that if they were required to wear uniforms, they would walk off the job. John agreed to serve as the group spokesperson, just as he had done on other occasions.* [1]

While Mason has no formal authority over his fellow workers, he demonstrates leadership through his influence over the group. Had Mason gone along with the uniform edict, it is probable that he would have influenced group members to follow suit, too.

Status

Another important characteristic of small groups is **status**. This refers to the group's "pecking order" and varies according to factors such as seniority, expertise, job classification, job location, and so on. Higher-status individuals generally have stronger privileges among members than do those of lower status, such as preferred seating at meetings, having their ideas solicited by other members, being the first members to receive grapevine information, and so on. Lower-status members may refrain from disagreeing or conflicting with higher-status members, in hopes of gradually gaining increased group status and maintaining or improving their place in the pecking order.

Roles

Roles are the expected behaviors among group members. While **formal roles** are written out in job descriptions, the **informal roles** for group members are not stated in writing but develop as a result of the dynamics within the group. Some of the various group roles that may be played are leader, elder statesman, and those accorded to higher- and lower-status group members.

Norms of Behavior

Small groups have **norms of behavior**, which define what is and is not acceptable behavior within the group. Some examples of group norms are listed in Figure 7–1. Note that, from management's point of view, some of the norms are favorable and some are unfavorable.

FIGURE 7–1   EXAMPLES OF GROUP-BEHAVIOR NORMS

- Members dress neatly at work.
- Members do not tattle to management about fellow members.
- Members voluntarily help or assist other members.
- Members don't engage in horseplay on the job.
- Members adhere to time limits for lunch and breaks.
- Members don't exceed specified performance levels.
- Members call in sick only when it is absolutely unavoidable.
- Members don't volunteer suggestions or ideas to management.
- Members don't put in more than a few minutes past quitting time.
- Members don't badmouth their work group.
- Members cooperate with people from other departments.
- Members don't use profanity or curse.

In Case 7–1, what was evidently the group norm regarding member participation in meetings?

Why do such norms or codes of conduct exist? The reason is that group members stand to benefit from them in several ways. Observing the norms may assure group members job protection, an orderly flow of work, or enhancement of status or ego.

Pressures to Conform

Another important characteristic of small groups is their ability to pressure their members to conform to established group norms. Individuals who violate group norms or drift from them too badly may be subjected to a form of group "discipline," as shown by the following example.

Recently, one of the authors of this text observed a meeting of a large firm's 10 department managers. In the early stages of the meeting, one manager was observed to be carrying on in a seemingly uncooperative manner. He was joking, laughing, and talking loudly to those seated next to him. It became apparent that his colleagues were uncomfortable with his behavior. Finally, while one team member was making a comment to the group, the disruptive member began talking loudly to the person on his right. Obviously distracted, the person who had the floor turned and said, "Dammit, Bill, we've had enough of you. Will you quit acting like a child or get out of here so everybody else can learn something?" There was absolute silence. Bill looked around, noted from his colleagues' expressions that this behavior had been out of line, and apologized. For the duration of the meeting, he paid attention and participated on a level equal to that of other group members.

Since group members' needs are satisfied by their inclusion in the group, there can be strong pressure to conform to other members' expectations. Possible punitive actions by a group may include subtle verbal or nonverbal reprimands, a temporary cold shoulder from other members, or even permanent ostracism. Extreme cases include possible pressure through physical threats or bodily harm.

Cohesiveness

Cohesiveness is the degree to which group members pull in the same direction and have unity. When group membership is attractive to members and meets their needs, there is a greater likelihood that the group will be cohesive. Like glue, cohesive groups stick together. The more cohesive a group, the more likely its members will accept the group's behavior norms, go along with group decisions, and defend group goals and individual members. Cohesive groups have a higher level of friendly, open communication, higher levels of trust among members, and generally less friction among themselves than less-cohesive groups.

In addition to group norms, in what ways are the small-group processes discussed above reflected in Case 7–1?

As you can see, then, it is very important for a supervisor to be aware of these key processes within small groups. In order to achieve departmental goals, the supervisor must continually work to develop harmony within the work group and attempt to integrate the goals of the department with those of the work group. Since much of the behavior of individual workers is influenced by the groups to which they belong, effective management requires continual attention to the small-group processes that we have discussed. Keep these important small-group concepts in mind while we examine the supervisor's role in conducting and participating in meetings.

PURPOSES OF MEETINGS

Supervisors normally spend a great deal of time in meetings. In some meetings a supervisor functions as the meeting leader, or perhaps as a project or committee leader. In others, the supervisor functions as a participant rather than as a leader. But the fact of the matter is that meetings are a part of every supervisor's life. The more effectively a supervisor functions as a meeting leader, the more effectively he or she will perform the total job.

Figure 7–2 shows that meetings generally are called to achieve any of the following purposes: (1) to give information, (2) to exchange information, (3) to obtain facts about a particular situation, and (4) to solve a problem.

FIGURE 7–2   PURPOSES OF MEETINGS

The Information-Giving Meeting

The **information-giving meeting** is held to make announcements of new programs and policies or to update the present ones. It is generally controlled closely by the leader or those who might be called upon to provide information to the group, as is frequently done in committee reports. There tends to be little feedback from group members unless they have questions to ask or points to clarify about the information presented. Normally this is the easiest type of meeting to conduct since its format is highly structured and lends itself well to large groups.

The Information-Exchange Meeting

The **information-exchange meeting** is called to obtain information from group members and to allow them to provide information to one another.

At Southeast Paper Manufacturing Co. of Dublin, Georgia, a meeting of the plant manager and seven or eight of his key department heads is conducted each morning. Each of these department heads presents a status report on the previous day's activities and on any carry-over information from the previous day. Thus, these key department heads are "in the know" about the major activities in the plant as a result of the daily exchange of information.

The Fact-Finding Meeting

Only relevant facts about a problem or situation should be sought out in a **fact-finding meeting**. The meeting leader does not focus on solutions but rather on an understanding of the problem or situation. A supervisor might begin this meeting as follows: "The reason I called this meeting is to discuss the high cost overruns we've been experiencing during the past month. I want to find out as much as I can about your perspective on the causes of this situation. Later we can consider some steps we can take to reduce these costs." Once the facts are understood, the supervisor will have a better understanding of the situation.

The Problem-Solving Meeting

Typically the **problem-solving meeting** combines the other purposes of information giving, information exchange, and fact finding. This type of meeting is held to identify the major elements of a problem, to discuss alternative solutions and evaluate them, and ultimately to make a decision as to the proper action to take. Topics of problem-solving meetings might include any of the following:

1. Improving plant safety.
2. Reducing machine downtime.
3. Determining production schedules or job assignments.
4. Implementing a new company policy in the best way.

The problem-solving meeting involves much group interaction. To lead this meeting effectively, a supervisor should have considerable skill. Unfortunately, many supervisors would rather obtain the facts from their subordinates and then make the decision themselves, instead of having the entire group work toward a decision. As we mentioned in Chapter 3 on decision making, under the proper circumstances group decisions can be very effective.

In your opinion, in which of the four types of meetings does group dynamics play the strongest role? Why?

APPROACHES USED AT MEETINGS

The interactions that take place at meetings can vary greatly. Much depends upon the purpose of the meeting and the meeting leader's personal style. Two approaches are generally used in conducting meetings: (1) a leader-controlled approach, and (2) a group-centered approach.

Leader-Controlled Approach

The **leader-controlled approach** is often used at information-giving meetings or when large groups prohibit an open flow of information among members. The leader clearly runs the show. He or she opens the meeting, makes announcements, or calls on those who have information to present. If anyone in the group has questions to ask or comments to make, he or she addresses them to the leader. The leader may answer the questions or bounce them to someone else. Figure 7–3 illustrates this approach. Should a stranger walk in after the meeting has begun, she or he would have no difficulty identifying who was clearly in charge.

ADVANTAGES OF THE LEADER-CONTROLLED APPROACH.   One advantage of this approach is that the meeting is generally easier on the leader because its fairly rigid structure means that few surprises occur. Another advantage is that, when a large amount of material must be covered in a short period of time, the leader is apt to accomplish the purpose of the meeting.

DISADVANTAGES OF THE LEADER-CONTROLLED APPROACH.   An obvious disadvantage is that the leader-controlled approach discourages a free flow of information. The fact that comments from the group must go through the leader means that spontaneous, direct remarks may go unmade. The creativity that results from the "piggybacking" of ideas is stifled. Another disadvantage is that, for sensitive and emotional issues, members have no real opportunity to get things off their chest and blow off some emotional steam.

FIGURE 7–3   INTERACTION IN A LEADER-CONTROLLED APPROACH

LEADER

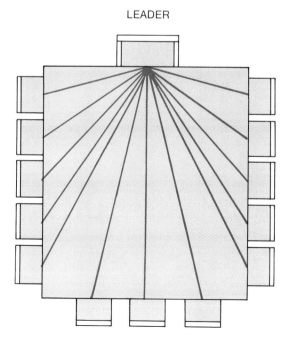

Group-Centered Approach

In the **group-centered approach** the group members interact more freely and address and raise questions to one another. Figure 7–4 illustrates this approach. The meeting leader does not dominate the discussions. Rather, the leader's job becomes one of keeping the meeting moving along and redirecting the focus of comments.

ADVANTAGES OF THE GROUP-CENTERED APPROACH. The advantages of the group-centered approach stem from the greater interaction that occurs at the meeting. First, it results in a better understanding or clarification of the members' viewpoints. Second, if the purpose of the meeting is to solve a problem, the free flow of information may contribute to a better-quality decision. Third, when people can express their emotions or disagreements, they feel better.

DISADVANTAGES OF THE GROUP-CENTERED APPROACH. One disadvantage of the group-centered approach is that the meeting takes up a great deal more time than with the leader-controlled approach. Another disadvantage is that the increased interaction among members means that the leader's skills will be tested more severely (see Figure 7–5). The leader must be sensitive as to when to move

FIGURE 7–4 INTERACTION IN A GROUP-CENTERED APPROACH

LEADER

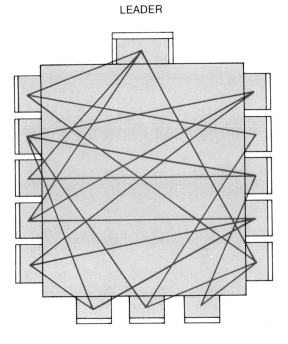

FIGURE 7–5   WHO'S IN CHARGE?

a topic along. He or she must make sure that everyone gets a chance to speak up and that discussions stay close to the subject. Also, since the leader must deal with diverse personalities, he or she must know how to handle emotions that may arise. A third disadvantage is that this approach is not well suited to large groups because of its interpersonal nature.

Do you think Carl has lost control of the meeting in Figure 7–5? If so, what are some possible reasons?

WHICH APPROACH IS BETTER?

Which approach would be better for you as a supervisor to use? The answer to this question depends upon a number of factors, such as the size of the group, the ability of the group members, the amount of time allowed for the meeting, your skills, and the subjects to be discussed. Remember that you can shift from one approach to the other at a single meeting, depending upon the nature of the items on your agenda.

Yoshi Tanabe's approach at meetings suits his purposes. Take Wednesday's meeting, for instance. The first item on his agenda was the new vacation-scheduling procedure. At this point Yoshi was the "expert" in the room. He made a three-to-four-minute presentation on the new procedure and then fielded questions from the group.

The next topic on the agenda was the need to develop and submit to higher management a plan for the department's participation in the company's 10-year anniversary open house for members of the community. Yoshi used a more open approach for the discussion of this topic. It took up about 20 minutes, with much interaction among the group. Within this time Yoshi and the group came up with a plan for the department's role during the open house.[2]

ADVANTAGES AND DISADVANTAGES OF MEETINGS

Some supervisors despise attending and conducting meetings. They prefer to communicate on a one-to-one basis. But because meetings are a fact of life for supervisors, it might be appropriate at this point to give the advantages and disadvantages of meetings. Then, in the remainder of the chapter, we will give pointers on how to make meetings effective and how to give presentations at meetings.

Advantages of Meetings

Meetings save time, allow the supervisor's communications to be consistent, and permit a formal exchange of important information and ideas. Let's explore how these advantages work.

SAVE TIME. Suppose you as a supervisor have a group of employees whose jobs are *not* performed in the same work area (as is the case with outside sales, delivery services, maintenance, or patient care). If you prefer to communicate on a one-on-one basis, you would have to move from one location to another during the work period. By having a meeting, you can save a great deal of your personal time that would otherwise be spent tracking down each of your subordinates.

ASSURE CONSISTENCY OF INFORMATION. Meetings provide an opportunity for all present to hear the same message. If you were to communicate separately to each of your workers, you might present the information to some more effectively than to others. Also, some of your workers might ask questions or make comments that help clarify the communication or add a slightly different flavor to it. In one-on-one contacts, the grapevine goes to work, especially if there is a long lapse of time before you talk with each worker individually.

Because all members present at a meeting hear and see the same thing, will they all interpret it the same way? Explain.

PERMIT FORMAL EXCHANGE OF INFORMATION. Sometimes individual members of a work group have information which *must* be shared with all the other group members. This is particularly true when a problem confronts the work group. In a meeting, a comment made by one member frequently triggers an important idea by another member. This can lead to solutions which might not have been thought of by any one member.

The degree of formality inherent in a meeting can be used advantageously by a supervisor. For example, suppose that you, a supervisor, have been told by the plant manager that production must be increased by 15 percent over the next year; otherwise the plant will be closed. Presenting this information to your work group in a meeting would convey the seriousness of the situation and dramatize the impact of the message.

Disadvantages of Meetings

Meetings may not be cost-effective and may be too impersonal. Let's see how these disadvantages arise.

MAY NOT BE COST-EFFECTIVE. Meetings are more expensive than most people realize. When employees are attending meetings, they are not performing their normal jobs. Suppose 10 persons attend a one-hour meeting, and their average salary is $40,000. The cost of the meeting includes not only their salaries, but also other costs such as vacations, holidays, sick leave, medical insurance, social security, time taken to travel to and from the meeting, and so on. As shown in Table 7–1, the cost of the meeting would be $365. The meeting must therefore provide information important enough to justify the costs associated with it. Table 7–1 does not include the costs associated with time spent planning for the meeting. As we will point out shortly, the meeting leader has a number of planning steps to take that may involve considerable time.

MAY BECOME TOO IMPERSONAL. Meetings may not allow the personal kinds of interaction required for many sensitive issues. On a one-on-one basis, employees may communicate readily with their supervisor. But because a meeting involves a more formal setting with many persons present, often some employees will be reluctant to speak up.

TABLE 7–1 MEETINGS COST!

Have you ever thought about the cost of a meeting? The following table is a rough approximation of hourly costs of managers at four salary levels. The hourly rates are illustrative and include loading for benefits, overhead, travel time, and the like.

Salary	Number of Participants in Meeting							
	10	**9**	**8**	**7**	**6**	**5**	**4**	**3**
$70,000	$700	$630	$560	$490	$420	$350	$280	$210
$50,000	$466	$419	$372	$326	$280	$233	$186	$140
$40,000	$365	$329	$292	$256	$219	$183	$146	$110
$20,000	$208	$187	$166	$146	$125	$104	$ 83	$ 62

Source: Adapted from Edward F. Konczai, "Making the Most of Meetings," *Supervisory Management* 7 (March 1982), 4.

MAKING MEETINGS EFFECTIVE

This section will present some ideas that should prove helpful to you in having more effective meetings. Some of these ideas should be acted upon *before* the meeting, some *during* the meeting, and some *after* the meeting.

Factors to Consider before the Meeting

Before calling a meeting, you should first determine whether or not the meeting is necessary. For example, can you convey the information you intend to give through other means, such as in a memo or over the telephone? Do all members of your group need the information, or just a few? Will the format of the meeting help accomplish your purpose?

Many supervisors claim that too much time is wasted in meetings called by their bosses, while they themselves hold too many unnecessary meetings with their own subordinates. So, when thinking about the next meeting you plan to hold, ask yourself, "Do I really need this meeting?"

HAVE A CLEAR PURPOSE. Assuming that a meeting is necessary, you should have a clear purpose for it. Otherwise you will waste everyone's time, including your own.

"Why are we having the meeting this afternoon, Rhoda?" asked Margaret Parker, one of the lab technicians in the plant. "I'm a little behind in some of our tests from the last shift."

Rhoda, her supervisor, responded, "Well, Margaret, we always have a meeting the first Friday of the month, and today is the first Friday. But there's nothing important on my agenda; so don't worry about making it. Go ahead and run your tests."[3]

What are the pros and cons of having regular weekly meetings at an established time?

PREPLAN THE MEETING. Many meetings are doomed from the start because of poor initial planning. Two groups may have a time conflict involving the use of a conference room, for example. Or the bulbs in the overhead projector are burned out. Or the people present at the meeting weren't notified that they should have certain needed information with them. Or perhaps the leader simply hasn't done his or her homework! Proper planning requires you to do some work before the meeting actually begins. Such work might include the following:

1. Make sure that the people who are to attend the meeting have adequate advance notice (unless it's an emergency meeting).
2. Make sure that key people will be able to attend.
3. Let people know in advance if they will be counted on to provide information.
4. Distribute copies of the meeting agenda in advance. This will enable people to bring essential documents with them or to gather information that may prove helpful.
5. Check to see that the meeting room is arranged as you desire and that the visual aids you intend to use are functioning properly.
6. Have a general idea of how long the meeting should last. You may want to indicate this to those who will attend. It is easier to predict the length of information-giving and information-exchange meetings, however, than meetings held for fact finding or problem solving.

Factors to Consider During the Meeting

There may be occasions when one or two employees do not arrive in time for the meeting. To avoid unnecessary delays, however, the supervisor should begin the meeting as scheduled.

CLARIFY YOUR EXPECTATIONS. Earlier in this chapter we stated that a meeting could serve the following purposes: to inform, to exchange information, to obtain facts, or to solve a problem and make a decision. As the leader of the meeting, make sure that you introduce each item on the agenda by stating your purpose for including that item. For example:

1. I'd like to *give you some information* about . . . . (information giving)
2. Attached to the agenda that I sent each of you was the memo from Human-Resources Department regarding the new benefits. I'd like to *get your reactions* to these new benefits. (information exchange)

3. The purpose of this meeting is to review the recent changes in our billing policy and their impact upon collections. Your input will help give me an idea of the success or failure of our new billing policy. What has been *the effect from your experience* with it? (fact finding)
4. I'd like to get your ideas on what we can do to show our department in its best light during our open house. After hearing your ideas, I'll *put together our plan.* (decision making)
5. The plant manager wants to know what our department's position is on the ten-hour day, four-day week that we discussed in our meeting last week. I can go any way you want to on this. *What do we want to do?* (decision making)

In each example, the supervisor spells out and clarifies his or her expectations regarding each item on the agenda. Take special notice of Examples 4 and 5, in which the supervisor carefully outlines the role of the group in the decision-making process.

PROVIDE LEADERSHIP.   Ineffective leadership ruins many well-prepared meetings. The supervisor must be prepared to demonstrate leadership in a variety of ways. This can be done by

1. Keeping the meeting moving. Don't allow it to drag on and on, and don't stray too far from the topic being discussed. If people stray from the topic, you might say, "We seem to have drifted from our major issue. Let's go back . . . . "
2. Seeing to it that most or all members contribute to the discussion. Don't allow one or two people to dominate the meeting. If this happens, call on others first for their comments or reactions.
3. Summarizing the apparent position of the group from time to time. You might say, "Do I read the group properly? You seem to be saying that . . . . "

ENCOURAGE TWO-WAY COMMUNICATION.   In most meetings the leader's job is to encourage and facilitate openness and interaction among group members. This is even more important when the leader uses the group-centered approach. The leader must be an alert listener and be skilled in ways to help individuals in the group express themselves. A key skill is the ability to use questions as a major way to involve individual members or the entire group in the communication process. Figure 7–6 shows some questioning techniques that can be used by the meeting leader.

GET "CLOSURE" ON ITEMS DISCUSSED.   Make sure there is a *closure* on each item on the agenda. At many meetings that we've observed, an item will be discussed; then everyone looks around wondering what has been concluded because the leader has gone on to the next item on the agenda. **Closure** means successfully accomplishing the objective for a given item on the agenda which has been discussed. In the following example, notice how a department head accomplished closure for the particular agenda item.

FIGURE 7–6   QUESTIONING TECHNIQUES FOR LEADERS OF MEETINGS

■ *Clarifying or elaborating on a point made by someone.*
Example: "Are you saying that . . . ." or "Fred, would you mind giving us a little more detail about the situation? When did it happen?"

■ *Calling on someone who's reluctant to talk.*
Example: "Pete, you've been through more maintenance shutdowns than most of us. What do you think about all of this?"

■ *Getting at specific facts.*
Example: "Exactly what were our production figures last month? Can someone give us that figure?"

■ *Examining possible alternatives.*
Example: "What are the pros and cons of converting to the new system?" or "Would we be able to keep up our quality under the new system?" or "What would happen if . . . ?"

■ *Initiating group discussion.*
Example: "What is your reaction to this new vacation policy?" or "Does this new policy affect anyone in here?"

■ *Obtaining more participation from the group.*
Example: "We've heard two alternatives. Are there any more?"

■ *Guiding the meeting tactfully in certain directions.*
Example: "We seem to have already discussed this issue pretty thoroughly and agreed on a course of action. Is everyone ready to move on?"

■ *"Testing the water" as to the group's feeling.*
Example: "What would be your reaction if we went to the system we've been discussing? Would you support it?"

Martha Briem, a department head, presented comparative information which showed that her department had a quality-rejection rate that was 10 percent higher than that of other departments in the company. She asked for her supervisors' input about possible actions. The discussion lasted about 25 minutes. Then she asked each supervisor to come up with a plan for improving product quality in his or her area and to make a five-minute presentation at a meeting to be scheduled in two weeks.[4]

Factors to Consider after the Meeting

If someone has been designated to record important points discussed and agreed upon at the meeting, those points will be outlined in what is called the **minutes** of the meeting. If not, members attending the meeting are advised to take notes on their own.

   DISTRIBUTE COPIES OF THE MINUTES.   Distributing copies of the minutes of the meeting is important for the following reasons:

1. The minutes serve as a permanent record of what has been agreed upon and committed to at the meeting.
2. The minutes identify topics on the agenda that may not have been dealt with completely or that may have been suggested for a future meeting.
3. The minutes permit a smooth transition for taking up where you left off in the next meeting.

FOLLOW UP ON DECISIONS MADE. It is crucial that the supervisor follow up on agreed-upon actions or decisions made during the meeting. The follow-up may consist of personal observations or visits. It may also involve reports that keep the supervisor informed on the progress being made regarding the agreed-upon commitments at the meeting.

"Oh, I make it a point to follow up on my meetings," stated Luis Santos. "We have a pretty active crowd who say what they think. If I feel that someone has really gotten ticked off or hurt by what was brought up at the meeting, I'll make it a point to try to smooth things out on a one-on-one basis. I can also go one-on-one with somebody who might have said something I wanted to follow up on but didn't feel the meeting was the place to do it." [5]

MAKING PRESENTATIONS AT MEETINGS

Many persons dread having to give a formal stand-up-in-front-of-a-group presentation. In fact, in a survey of 3,000 Americans, 41 percent named "giving a speech" as their single greatest fear—greater than death, snakes, or heights![6] Yet supervisors frequently find themselves having to give formal presentations. This may come about in conducting safety meetings, quality improvement meetings, or informational meetings with their employees, but also includes those occasions when they are required to make a presentation to higher management.

The oral presentation is a function which many supervisors perform poorly. However, you don't need the skills of a professional speaker to be effective in front of groups. Trying to observe the principles discussed below will prove helpful.

Determine the Objective of Your Presentation

How many presentations have you attended where you kept asking yourself, "Why am I being told this?" or "I wonder what the speaker is getting at?" Perhaps you walked away scratching your head. Don't let this happen during *your* presentations. Know exactly what purpose you want to accomplish and specifically build your presentation around this goal.

You must ask yourself: Just what is it that I want my audience to do after they receive my information? Do I want them to understand something better? Do I want to change or influence their behavior? If you want your audience to take some action, then you must be very persuasive in your presentation. You must present data, logic, and facts to build your case. If your purpose is simply to present information, then you will want to make sure that your talk is organized clearly and logically.

"There's no question about what Riley was telling us in the meeting," said Jim Warden, operating machinist at Barton Iron Works. "It came through loud and clear. We've got to keep our work areas cleaner or all hell is going to break loose. I never realized before how important it was to have clean areas."

Plan Your Presentation

You must think carefully about what you want to say, how long you have to say it, and how it can best be put across to your audience. Examine the room where you will make your presentation. Will it allow for the use of visual aids? What information will you present and where will you obtain it? Will you use handouts that must be prepared in advance? If so, make sure that your handouts are clear and neatly done.

Employ Visuals for Effect

A visual aid is very effective in aiding your presentation (see Figure 7–7). This is especially true if you have to communicate many numbers, a series of steps, or a diagram of relationships.

When preparing your visual aid, keep in mind the following points:

1. Make sure the visual is simple. It should be easy to follow and should simplify the point you are making, not complicate it. A visual should be an *aid*, not a handicap.
2. The visual should be large enough for all to see. You have probably attended meetings where the visual presented was not clear to you. Perhaps the writing was too small or too light, or perhaps the visual itself was just too small considering the size of the group.
3. If possible, make the visual look professional. Watch for misspelled words, use different colors, and draw lines and charts neatly. This will show your audience that you think enough of your subject and your audience to have prepared well for it.

Finally, when making the presentation, be sure to position the visual so that everybody can see it. Be careful not to block it with your body when you are referring to it.

Keep Your Presentation Simple and Organize It

Ask yourself the following questions: What should I include, and what is the best sequence for presenting my material? Many speakers try to cram too much into a presentation. As a result, they lose or turn off their audience. So, don't try to become too technical or to include all aspects of a situation. Remember, you

FIGURE 7–7 COMMUNICATING WITH VISUAL AIDS

may be quite familiar with your topic, but the audience may not be. A popular general guide to public speaking in this regard is the **KISS principle**. It stands for

Keep
It
Short and
Simple

The best sequence of presenting materials consists of three steps:

1. *Tell them first what you are going to tell them.* This means that you explain the purpose of your talk and give an overview of what you're including in your talk.
2. *Tell them.* Present your main ideas and support them with information or examples. This will be the longest part of your presentation.
3. *Tell them what you have told them.* Reinforce and review by summarizing your key points and conclusions.

Use a Conversational Delivery

Try to sound like yourself during your presentation. Your eye contact with your audience is important in that it provides you with feedback as to how they are taking your message. It also helps to establish rapport with them.

For an especially long presentation, don't be afraid to use notes. You may read important parts of your presentation for emphasis, but avoid the temptation to rely totally on your notes. There is no quicker way to put a group to sleep than to read your entire presentation with your head down!

Practice in Advance

Many persons never can get rid of the butterflies that invade the stomach when they have to speak before a group. But practicing in advance can be very helpful. In a dry run, listen to yourself say the words aloud. This will tend to make it easier and smoother for you when the real event takes place. So, don't be afraid to go into the meeting room, stand where you'll be in just a few hours (or days, if you wish to be even *more* prepared), turn on the tape recorder, and let fly!

CHAPTER REVIEW

Group dynamics is the social process by which people interact face-to-face in small groups. Among the important characteristics of small groups are leadership, status, roles, norms of behavior, pressures to conform, and cohesiveness. All supervisors must be aware of these important processes, especially as they occur within the context of group meetings.

Meetings can serve four general purposes: (1) to give information, (2) to exchange information, (3) to find out facts, and (4) to solve problems. With a leader-controlled approach, the leader clearly runs the show and conducts a very structured meeting. The advantages of this approach are that it lends itself better to established time frames, has more predictable outcomes, and is more appropriate for large groups. With a group-centered approach, there is more interaction among members. It allows greater understanding and enables people to speak up, and the exchange of ideas is more apt to generate creativity.

The typical supervisor is called upon frequently to conduct meetings with his or her work group. Meetings have the following advantages over one-on-one contacts: (1) they save time, (2) they allow all present to hear exactly the same message, and (3) they lend a degree of formality. The disadvantages of meetings are that (1) they may not be cost-effective, and (2) they may become too impersonal.

A number of factors can help to make meetings more effective. First of all, the supervisor should determine whether a meeting is necessary. *Before* the meeting, the supervisor should establish a clear purpose for the meeting and plan it. *During* the meeting, the supervisor should clarify his or her expectations, provide leadership, encourage two-way communication, and see to it that closure occurs on items discussed. *After* the meeting, minutes of the meeting should be distributed, and a follow-up on agreed-upon commitments should take place.

Frequently the supervisor is placed in the position of having to make a formal stand-up presentation during a meeting. For best results, the supervisor should carefully plan the presentation in advance, determine the presentation objective, use visuals, try to speak in a conversational manner to the audience rather than read from notes, and organize the presentation in a simple, logical manner. Practicing the presentation is also a most helpful step.

QUESTIONS FOR REVIEW AND DISCUSSION

1. Name five processes of group dynamics and briefly explain each.
2. Presumably you are reading this book as part of a course that you are taking with other students. What are some "norms of behavior" for your class group?
3. Name the four basic purposes of meetings. Of these, which generally requires the most skill on the part of the leader?
4. Suppose that your work group consists of 35 persons, all of whom directly report to you. What are the pros and cons, when conducting meetings, of using (a) the leader-controlled approach, and (b) the group-centered approach?
5. What are the advantages and disadvantages of meetings?
6. List at least five questioning techniques that a leader can use during a group meeting. Consider the class in which you're studying this course. Which techniques, if any, are used more frequently by your instructor?
7. What is meant by "closure"? Give an example.
8. In what ways are minutes helpful as a follow-up step after a group meeting? Discuss.

LEARNING EXERCISE 7-1
THE REQUIRED WEEKLY MEETING

Charlie Simon, who supervised 18 employees at Damon Warehousing, looked at the following memo which had been placed on his desk.

TO: All Supervisors

FROM: Ramon Garcia, Plant Manager

SUBJECT: Weekly Meeting

Beginning on October 1, all supervisory personnel will conduct a meeting with their employees each Friday afternoon at 4:40 p. m. The purposes of these meetings will be to make announcements of interest, to use the occasion to update your work group on departmental and company progress, and to address problems, issues, and concerns that your work group may have. This action is being taken to improve communications in the plant. I appreciate your effort in making these meetings effective.

Shutting down 20 minutes early didn't bother Charlie at all. Neither did the fact that a weekly meeting would probably waste everyone's time. What did concern him was that he had little experience running meetings and addressing large groups. How would he kill the time if there was nothing to say? What if his employees asked questions that he couldn't answer? Would these meetings end up being gripe sessions? "This might be just what Hank Fellows, the union steward, needs as a platform to mouth off and stir up trouble," thought Charlie. "It seems like we've done pretty well around here without meetings in the past," he said to himself. Then he went to talk to Virgil Robinson, his good friend and supervisor of the maintenance department. He wondered what Virgil would say about this required weekly meeting.

Answer the following questions:

1. What are the pros and cons of the required meetings on Fridays?
2. To what extent are Charlie Simon's concerns justified?
3. Assume that Charlie came to you for advice on how to handle such meetings. What suggestions could you offer?

LEARNING EXERCISE 7–2
EVALUATING A LEADER'S EFFECTIVENESS IN MEETINGS

In this exercise, a group of students will be asked to role-play a meeting before the entire class to address one of the two topics suggested below. One student should be selected by the group to play the role of the leader. The rest of the class should be designated as "observers" and be prepared to evaluate the leader's effectiveness in conducting the meeting. The "Leader Assessment Scale" shown in Figure 7–8 may be helpful to the "observers" in evaluating the leader's performance.

1. A group of experienced supervisors at a manufacturing plant, who had been promoted from the operating level, are to develop—*in order of priority*—a list

FIGURE 7–8 LEADER-ASSESSMENT SCALE

	Good	Fair	Weak
1. Established clear objective of the meeting.	___	___	___
2. Kept discussion relevant.	___	___	___
3. Made sure everyone participated.	___	___	___
4. Used questioning techniques effectively.	___	___	___
5. Kept meeting moving along.	___	___	___
6. Helped group fully examine issues.	___	___	___
7. Summarized key points thoroughly.	___	___	___
8. Made a "closure" for each item on the agenda.	___	___	___

of the five most important criteria for promoting employees at the operating level to supervisory positions.

2. A group of employees at AJAY, a large insurance company, have been appointed to a task force by the manager of the claims-processing department. The goal of the task force is to collect $8,000—or an average of $20 per employee for the total work force of 400 people—for the United Fund drive. In past years, AJAY has not done much for the UF drive. This year, however, the manager of the claims-processing department has assured the United Fund people that AJAY will contribute more than any other small business in the community. The task force is to hold a meeting to develop a plan of action for reaching the goal of $8,000. This plan of action is to be submitted to the claims-processing manager in three weeks.

LEARNING EXERCISE 7–3
THE QUIET MEETING: ADVICE TO DEBRA

Instructions: Refer to Case 7–1 at the opening of the chapter. Assume that you are the fellow supervisor that Debra has just confided in about her inability to get her group to contribute their ideas at meetings.

1. What do you feel may be some plausible reasons for the group's failure to speak up?
2. Before you could advise Debra on a strategy for overcoming this problem, what additional information from Debra would be helpful? Why?
3. Finally, recommend a course of action to Debra.

ENDNOTES

1. Name has been disguised.
2. Name has been disguised.
3. Names have been disguised.
4. Name has been disguised.
5. Name has been disguised.
6. David Wallechinsky and Irving Wallace, *The Book of Lists* (New York: William Morrow Co. , 1977), p. 469.

SUGGESTIONS FOR FURTHER READING

Alcorn, Seth. "What Makes Groups Tick." *Personnel* 62 (September 1985): 52–58.

Bradford, Leland. *Making Meetings Work: A Guide for Leaders and Group Members.* La Jolla, CA: University Associates, 1981.

Feldman, Daniel C. "The Development and Enforcement of Group Norms." *Academy of Management Review* 9 (January 1984): 47–53.

Howell, William S., and Ernest G. Bormann. *Presentational Speaking for Business and the Professions.* New York: Harper & Row, 1971.

Konczai, Edward F. "Making the Most of Meetings." *Supervisory Management* 27 (March 1982): 2–6.

O'Connell, Sandra E. *The Manager as Communicator*. New York: Harper & Row, 1980. See especially Chapter 3, "Getting Work Done at Meetings," pp. 28–63.

Timm, Paul R. "Let's Not Have a Meeting!" *Supervisory Management* 27 (August 1982): 2–7.

Van Raalte, Susan D. "Preparing the Task Force to Get Good Results." *S. A. M. Advanced Management Journal* 47 (Winter 1982): 11–16.

8
MOTIVATION

OBJECTIVES

After reading and studying the material in this chapter, you should be able to:

- Understand and explain Maslow's hierarchy of needs theory.
- Explain the supervisor's role in helping employees achieve satisfaction of their needs, especially needs of the lower level.
- Understand and explain Herzberg's theory of motivation.
- State the relationship among money, motivation, and the expectancy theory.
- Define and explain other theories of motivation, such as the equity theory and the positive-reinforcement theory.

IMPORTANT TERMS

motivation
hierarchy of needs
physiological *or* biological needs
safety *or* security needs
social *or* belonging needs
ego *or* esteem needs
self-fulfillment *or*
   self-actualization needs

motivators
hygiene factors
expectancy theory
equity theory
positive-reinforcement theory
law of effect

CHAPTER OUTLINE
CASE 8-1. THE DEMOTIVATING ENVIRONMENT

CASE 8–1
THE DEMOTIVATING ENVIRONMENT

Charles Washington and John Thorpe grew up in a small town and were teammates on the high-school football team.[1] After graduating from high school, Charles joined the Army and John joined the Navy. Charles progressed rapidly and, at the time of his discharge three years later, he had attained the rank of corporal. Upon resigning after four years, John had become a skilled technician with special expertise in electronics.

Both Charles and John eventually accepted jobs with the largest employer—a nonunion textile mill—in their home county. The mill paid exceptionally high wages and employed over 600 workers. In addition, both men started off in the maintenance department as trainees and eventually were elevated to maintenance supervisors.

The mill manager had the reputation of being tough and excessively authoritarian in dealing with people. Although this authoritarian leadership style had influenced other departments in the plant, it had not had a great deal of impact in the maintenance department.

Charles and John's boss, the maintenance superintendent, was a man they had known all their lives. They had played high-school football with the superintendent's younger brother and had gone on hunting trips with both of them. Charles and John liked and respected their boss.

One day, the maintenance superintendent was discussing a major cost-improvement work assignment with Charles and John. About that time, a call from the mill manager to the maintenance superintendent came in over the intercom system. All the supervisors in maintenance, production, and the power plant could hear the conversation. The mill manager proceeded to chew out the maintenance superintendent, up one side and down the other. Charles and John noticed an almost complete transformation in their boss. In responding to the mill manager, his voice trembled, and it was obvious that he was a shaken man. Upon ending the conversation with the mill manager, he could not remember what he had been discussing with Charles and John.

Two weeks later, Charles was leaning against a piece of equipment talking to his crew about work assignments. The mill manager happened to come by and reprimanded Charles in a loud voice for leaning on the equipment.

196

As a result of these and other incidents, Charles began to look into other job opportunities. A month later, he accepted a position as supervisor with a mill in a neighboring state, taking a 10 percent pay cut to make the change. Two months later John joined him, also at a lower salary.

This case illustrates the need for another critical management skill—that of motivating employees. It shows how certain managerial behavior can have a *demotivating* effect. We will refer to this case as we explore various theories of motivation in the chapter.

What would you do if you were in a similar situation as Charles's?

MOTIVATION: UNDERSTANDING THE "WHY" OF HUMAN BEHAVIOR

Perhaps you've heard people say that no one can motivate someone else. What they mean by this is that motivation comes from *within*. It is the result of a person's individual perceptions, needs, and desires. Using that theme, in this chapter we will focus on how supervisors can understand human behavior and establish conditions so that their employees *will* be motivated to improve performance at individual, group, and organizational levels. From this standpoint, we define **motivation** as the act of inducing a person or a group, each with his or her own distinctive needs and personality, to work to achieve the organization's objectives, while also working to achieve individual objectives.

Some people believe that management can never become a science because managers have to deal with human behavior, which is often unpredictable and irrational, and with human beings, who often act out of emotion rather than reason. Probably few social scientists would deny that people often act emotionally, but many would dispute whether most people behave irrationally and unpredictably. However, they would argue that, if more people understood the *why* of human behavior, other people's behavior would seem more rational and predictable.

Since the 1960s, there has been much research on the behavior of people at work. Some significant theories have been developed which are important to anyone in a position of leadership who wants to avoid unnecessary friction arising from human relationships in the organization. We will discuss some of these theories of motivation and see how they relate to supervision.

Some students do not enjoy studying theory because they feel it is abstract and unrelated to the real world. Actually, whatever the discipline, a sound theory provides a basis for understanding, explaining, and predicting what will happen in the real world. Kurt Lewin, famous for his work in the study of groups, once said that nothing is more *practical* than good theory.[2] For a person of action, such as a supervisor who has to work with and through people, an understanding of motivation theory is essential.

MASLOW'S HIERARCHY OF NEEDS THEORY

One theory that is particularly significant and practical has been developed by psychologist Abraham H. Maslow.[3] This particular theory is known as the **hierarchy of needs** concept and is probably the best known of all motivation theories among managers.

Principles Underlying the Theory

The two principles underlying Maslow's theory are that (1) people's needs may be arranged in a hierarchy, or ranking of importance, and (2) once a need is satisfied, it no longer serves as a primary motivator of behavior. To understand the significance of these principles to Maslow's theory, let us examine the hierarchy of needs as shown in Figure 8–1.

PHYSIOLOGICAL OR BIOLOGICAL NEEDS. At the lowest level, but of primary importance when they are not met, are our **physiological** or **biological needs.**

FIGURE 8–1   MASLOW'S HIERARCHY OF NEEDS

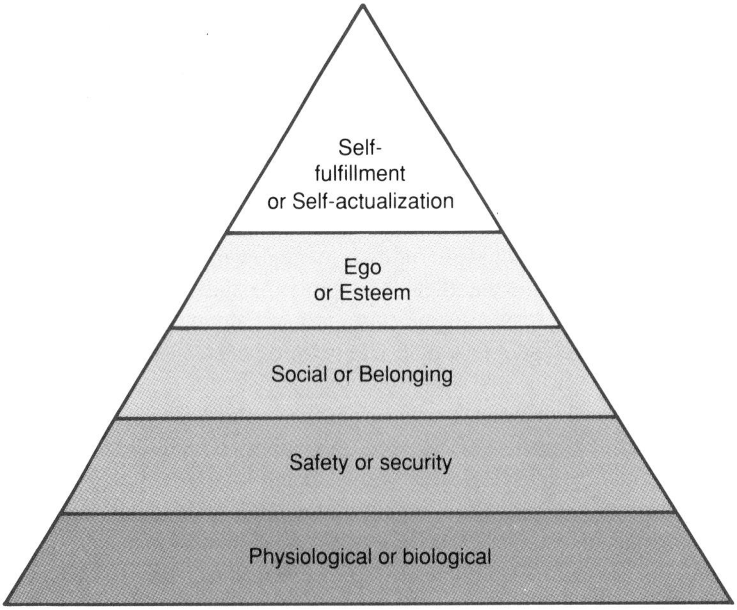

"Man does not live by bread alone," says the Bible, but anything else is less important when there is no bread. Unless the circumstances are unusual, the need we have for love, status, or recognition is inoperative when our stomach has been empty for a while. But when we eat regularly and adequately, we cease to regard hunger as an important motivator. The same is true of other physiological needs, such as air, water, sex, rest, exercise, shelter, and protection from the elements.

SAFETY OR SECURITY NEEDS. When the physiological needs are reasonably well-satisfied, **safety** or **security needs** become important. We want to be protected from danger, threat, or deprivation. When we feel threatened or dependent, our greatest need is for protection or security.

Most employees are in a dependent relationship at work, so they may regard their safety needs as being very important. Arbitrary management actions such as favoritism, discrimination, or the unpredictable application of policies can be powerful threats to the safety needs of any employee at any level.

SOCIAL OR BELONGING NEEDS. **Social** or **belonging needs** include the need for belonging, for association, for acceptance by colleagues, and for friendship and love. Most supervisors probably know that these needs exist but may assume—quite wrongly—that they represent a threat to the organization. Therefore, fearing group hostility to its own objectives, management may go to considerable lengths to control and direct human efforts in ways that are detrimental to cohesive work groups. When the employees' social needs, as well as their safety needs, are not met, they may behave in ways that tend to defeat organizational objectives. They become resistant, antagonistic, and uncooperative. But this behavior is a consequence of their frustration, not the cause.

EGO OR ESTEEM NEEDS. Above the social needs are the **ego** or **esteem needs.** These needs are of two kinds: (1) those that relate to one's self-esteem, such as needs for self-confidence, independence, achievement, competence, and knowledge, and (2) those that relate to one's reputation, such as the need for status, recognition, appreciation, and respect from one's colleagues.

Unlike the lower-level needs, ego needs are rarely fully satisfied because people seek more satisfaction of these needs once they have become important to them. The typical organization offers few opportunities for satisfaction of the ego needs of lower-level employees. The conventional method of organizing work, particularly in mass-production industries, gives little consideration to these aspects of motivation.

SELF-FULFILLMENT OR SELF-ACTUALIZATION NEEDS. At the top of Maslow's hierarchy are the **self-fulfillment** or **self-actualization needs**. These are needs for realizing one's own potentialities, for self-development, and for being creative. It seems clear that the quality of work life in most organizations gives only limited opportunity for fulfilling these needs. When higher-level needs are not satisfied, employees compensate by trying to satisfy lower-level needs. So the needs for self-fulfillment may remain dormant.

Referring to Case 8–1, how can you explain why Charles and John left their supervisory positions for lower-paying positions in another state? Which level(s) of needs in Maslow's hierarchy were involved?

Making Maslow's Theory Come to Life

If your answer to the above question is that security and ego needs were involved, you are right on target. Recall that when we discussed security needs, we emphasized that employees react negatively to arbitrary and excessively autocratic leadership because they are in a dependent position. Charles and John were grown men. They had had successful experiences in the military and simply would not tolerate being treated in an arbitrary, capricious manner.

The ego need was also involved in this situation. Although Charles and John felt sorry for their boss when he was chewed out by the mill manager, they may also have lost respect for their boss because of his reactions. Moreover, when Charles was reprimanded in front of his crew for leaning against a piece of equipment, it adversely affected his ego and esteem needs.

Another example to emphasize some points in Maslow's theory is illustrated below. Recall that when the lower-level needs are relatively well-satisfied, they cease to be important motivators of behavior. However, those needs can come back in a rush when a person is threatened with the loss of a job.

During the 1982 recession, a **Wall Street Journal** *article noted that what had once been rare was happening with greater frequency. Many middle-aged, middle-level managers with long service at their companies and comfortable in their careers, with good salaries and nice suburban homes, were getting the shock of their lives—they were being forced out! Most of them, in their 40s or early 50s, were too young to retire and too old to easily start anew. They posed a painful problem for U. S. business.*[4]

Assume that you are a 50-year-old supervisor earning $40,000 annually, with a house mortgage, two automobiles, and three high-school-aged children. What needs are important to you if you find yourself out of work?

Qualifying the Theory

Maslow's theory is a relative rather than absolute explanation of human behavior. You should be aware of the following four important qualifiers to his theory:

1. Each level of needs in the hierarchy does *not* have to be completely satisfied before needs on the next level become important.
2. The theory does not pretend to explain the behavior of the neurotic or the mentally disturbed.
3. Some people's priorities are different. For example, an artist may practically starve while trying to achieve self-actualization through the creation of a great work of art. Also, some people are much less security-oriented or achievement-oriented than others.
4. The theory states that a satisfied need is not a motivator of behavior. Yet the two highest levels of needs (unlike the lower levels) can hardly ever be fully satisfied. There are always new challenges and opportunities for growth, recognition, and achievement. Or a person may remain in the same job position for years and still find a great deal of challenge and motivation through his or her work.

Bob Buschka, a computer programmer for a large bank in a midwestern state, has held his position for 20 years and would like to remain in that position. He enjoys programming and is looked upon as one of the top programmers in banking in the area. The bank sends him to various schools to keep him growing and developing on the job.

"Bob's a remarkable person," says his boss. "He's passed up promotions into management to keep his present job, he's so into it. We know what a gem he is, and we do everything we can to give him lots of room to operate— special key projects, training and developing new programmers, and keeping up with new applications to our industry."

Supervisor's Help in Satisfying Employees' Lower-Level Needs

Earlier in the chapter, we stated that the higher-level needs are blocked most often. So it is in the area of satisfying the lower-level needs of their employees that supervisors can be most helpful. Maslow's theory should be used by the supervisor as a general guide to motivating employees, not as a formula for routine motivation. But Table 8–1 shows how some of the needs at the various levels can be met with the supervisor's help.

Refer to Table 8–1 and determine which needs a supervisor could help employees reach and which would be beyond her or his control.

TABLE 8-1 HOW THE JOB SATISFIES EMPLOYEE NEEDS

Need	Ways of Satisfying the Need on the Job
Self-actualization	Learning new skills, growing and developing, feeling a sense of accomplishment, exercising responsibility.
Esteem	Praise, recognition, promotion, getting one's name in the company paper as "employee of the month," being given more responsibility, being asked for help or advice.
Social	Work groups, group meetings, company-sponsored events.
Safety	Safe working conditions, pensions and benefits, good job security, knowing that one will be treated fairly, fair grievance system.
Physiological	Pay, rest breaks, clean air.

How can a supervisor help employees achieve satisfaction of their lower-level needs? The answer to this question centers around what employees expect of their supervisor, namely, (1) knowledge provided by the supervisor, (2) an atmosphere of approval, and (3) consistent discipline.[5]

KNOWLEDGE PROVIDED BY THE SUPERVISOR. Most employees expect their employer to provide them with information on organizational policies, rules and regulations, and their duties and responsibilities. As a rule, most companies and supervisors do a fair job of providing this type of information. However, employees today have the right to *expect* more, and this is where many supervisors fall down on the job. For example, new employees need to know what the probationary period is before they are accepted as full-fledged members of the organization. They also need to know

1. What assistance they can count on to help them become proficient in their work.
2. On what basis they will receive promotions and pay increases.
3. How management determines who will be laid off first in slack times.
4. How much advance notice they will be given on changes that may affect them.
5. Probably most important, feedback on how they are performing. Employees not only need this knowledge, but also expect it as part of their employment agreement.

ATMOSPHERE OF APPROVAL. An atmosphere of approval is an atmosphere free of fault-finding. This atmosphere is less dependent on a supervisor's standards of performance or the strictness of his or her discipline (see Figure 8–2) than on his or her attitudes toward employees when correcting errors on their part. Does the supervisor use this situation to help employees do a better job in the future or to make them feel like "dummies" who made stupid mistakes?

FIGURE 8–2

"GOOD MORNING, YOU LUCKY STIFF!"

Source: Cartoon by Fred Maes. Reproduced with permission.

Recall in Case 8–1 how the mill manager dealt with the superintendent and Charles. He made them feel like children being scolded by a parent rather than like mature adults. Think about how your parents or professors treat you. How does it affect your morale?

By helping employees overcome learning mistakes in a positive manner, a supervisor is not necessarily being slack or easy. And if new employees simply cannot master the work during their probationary period, the supervisor should let them know whether they will be transferred or dismissed.

CONSISTENT DISCIPLINE. Most subordinates expect and want consistent discipline. One of the worst mistakes you can make as a supervisor is to try to be a "nice guy" and look the other way when subordinates violate rules and policies, because sooner or later you will have to crack down. Then your subordinates will feel you are playing favorites because earlier you let other employees get by with rule-breaking.

Discipline should be consistent not only in its application to wrong actions, but also in support of right actions. In other words, employees should have positive support when they do things beyond the normal expectations of their jobs. If you look for ways to compliment subordinates sincerely—to consistently give praise and acknowledgment to different people for similar types of achievement— you will be amazed at the *esprit de corps* this practice creates in your department.

HERZBERG'S FINDINGS ABOUT HIGHER-LEVEL NEEDS

After an environment has been provided to satisfy employees' lower-level needs, supervisors may try to motivate them to fulfill higher-level needs. It is by tapping these needs that real achievements in efficiency, productivity, and creativity can be gained in working with and through people.

Herzberg's Original Study on Job Satisfaction

Several research studies have demonstrated the importance of higher-level needs as motivators. The originator of these experiments is Frederick Herzberg, an American psychologist whose findings have had considerable impact on American management.

In the initial study, Herzberg and his associates conducted in-depth interviews with 200 engineers and accountants from 11 different firms in the Pittsburgh, Pennsylvania, area.[6] Those interviewed were asked to recall an event or series of related events from the past year that had made them feel *unusually good* about their work. They were also asked to speculate on how much the event(s) affected their performance and morale. Conversely, they were asked to recall an event or series of related events that had made them feel *unusually bad* and to speculate on how the event(s) affected their performance and morale.

Try to answer Herzberg's survey questions yourself. Think about a job you've held in the past or presently hold. If you haven't had a job, think of your school work.

1. What specific incident or event (singular or recurring) in that situation gave you the most satisfaction?

2. What caused the most dissatisfaction?

From this study, Herzberg and his associates found that the top-ranking factors that caused job satisfaction and the top-ranking factors that caused job dissatisfaction were those shown in Table 8–2. Most important, the study revealed that in almost all cases the factors causing job satisfaction had a *stimulating* effect on performance and morale. On the other hand, the factors causing job dissatisfaction had a *negative* effect.

TABLE 8–2   RESULTS OF HERZBERG'S ORIGINAL STUDY ON
JOB SATISFACTION

Factors That Caused Job Satisfaction	Factors That Caused Job Dissatisfaction
Achievement	Company policy and administration
Recognition	Supervision
The work itself	Relationship with supervisor
Responsibility	Working conditions
Advancement	Salary

MOTIVATORS AND HYGIENE FACTORS. Another important finding of Herzberg's study was that the factors that caused job satisfaction were *intrinsic* to the job, while those that caused job dissatisfaction were *extrinsic* to the job. That is, when these people felt good about their job, it was usually because something had happened that showed that they were doing their work particularly well or that they were becoming more expert in their professions. In other words, good feelings were keyed to the specific tasks that they performed rather than to extrinsic factors such as money, security, or working conditions. Conversely, when they felt badly, it was usually because something had happened to make them feel that they were being treated unfairly.

Herzberg and his associates therefore made a distinction between what they called motivators and hygiene factors. **Motivators** are those factors that have an uplifting effect on attitudes or performance. **Hygiene factors** are those factors that can prevent serious dissatisfaction or a drop in productivity, thereby preventing loss of morale or efficiency, but cannot motivate by themselves. In other words, hygiene factors do *not* increase a worker's desire to do the job well.

SIGNIFICANCE OF HERZBERG'S ORIGINAL STUDY. This study tended to support Maslow's concept of a hierarchy of needs. The motivators relate to the two highest levels of that hierarchy (self-fulfillment and esteem); hygiene factors relate to the lower-level needs, primarily the need for security.

What all this means is that employees today *expect* to be treated fairly by their supervisors. They *expect* decent working conditions and pay comparable to that of people doing similar work in other firms. They *expect* company policies to be consistently and equitably applied to all employees. When these expectations are not realized, employees are demotivated. This condition is usually reflected by inefficiency and a high turnover rate. But fulfilling these expectations does *not* motivate employees. As Maslow's theory maintains, it is only when the lower-level needs are satisfied that the higher-level needs can be used most effectively in motivating employees. Figure 8–3 indicates ways in which a supervisor can use higher-level needs to create a motivating environment.

FIGURE 8–3   WAYS TO USE MOTIVATORS ON THE JOB

- Delegate more authority to workers.
- When you have an important project to complete or are facing difficult problems, call your workers in and get their ideas.
- Cross-train your employees so that they become more broadly experienced.
- Compliment and recognize employees for good work.
- Assign workers to special projects.
- Ask the more experienced workers to assist in training new employees.
- Send employees to training courses for skill upgrading.

Additional Studies on Job Satisfaction

After the original Herzberg study of engineers and accountants, critics were quick to point out that, while the findings might apply to professionals who sought creativity in their work, they would not apply to other groups of employees. But similar studies, conducted by different investigators in different countries, have shown surprisingly similar results, except for minor deviations. Figure 8–4 summarizes the results of 12 studies involving people from all walks of life — accountants, agricultural administrators, assemblers, engineers, food handlers, hospital maintenance personnel, housekeepers, manufacturing supervisors, military officers, nurses, retired managers, scientists, teachers, and technicians.

Although supervision is characterized as a hygiene factor, you shouldn't conclude that supervision is not important in motivating employees. In the summary of the 12 studies cited above, ineffective supervision was ranked as the second most important factor in causing job dissatisfaction. Moreover, one of the authors of this textbook who conducted a study in New Zealand discovered that ineffective supervision ranked as the *number one factor* in causing job dissatisfaction. The following quotation from a New Zealander illustrates how poor supervision can reduce motivation:

> *I was once given a job to do that involved a bit of responsibility. The job, I was told, was to take several days, and I was to be completely responsible for the job. I was told to report back at a later date and tell the boss how I was getting on. I didn't particularly worry when, a couple of hours later, the boss came down and asked me how I was doing; in fact, I was quite glad that he was taking an interest.*
>
> *However, when he repeated the process at intervals of every two or three hours, I got decidedly annoyed. In fact, I was fed up, and I was look-*

FIGURE 8–4   FACTORS AFFECTING JOB ATTITUDES, AS REPORTED IN 12 STUDIES

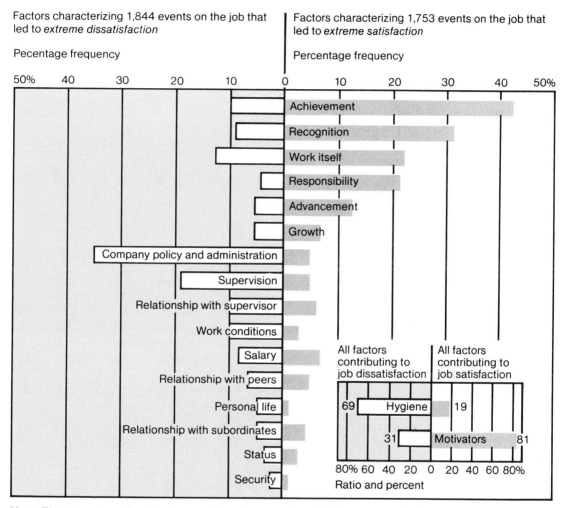

Factors characterizing 1,844 events on the job that led to *extreme dissatisfaction*

Factors characterizing 1,753 events on the job that led to *extreme satisfaction*

Note: The percentage of satisfaction was based on a study of 1,753 events on the job; the percentage of dissatisfaction was based on a study of 1,844 events on the job.
Source: Reprinted by permission of the *Harvard Business Review*. An exhibit from "One More Time: How Do You Motivate Employees?" by Frederick Herzberg (January/February 1968). Copyright © 1968 by the President and Fellows of Harvard College; all rights reserved.

ing for ways of palming the job off onto someone else. I felt that the boss thought I was incapable of doing the job properly, and I wondered why he gave it to me in the first place. The more I thought about this, the more unhappy I got. Consequently, I began to take longer on the job than I should have done, and couldn't have cared less if it was right or wrong. After all, the boss was constantly checking it; so he would pick up my mistakes.[7]

As you can see, supervision is one of the major influences on whether such motivators as achievement, recognition, creative and challenging work, and responsibility are operating in the work environment. In short, supervision helps determine whether the satisfaction of higher-level needs can be realized by employees in their work.

Is money a motivator for you? Explain.

Is Money a Hygiene Factor?

At a recent management development program conducted by the authors of this textbook, several first-level supervisors challenged Herzberg's finding that money is not a motivator. They argued that money was a motivator not only for them, but also for the employees in their departments. They cited as evidence a recently instituted plant bonus system tied to production quotas. After the bonus system was introduced, production was increased, resulting in more money for employees.

We maintain that money is a powerful force in motivation, especially when related to achievement and performance as shown in the example on the bottom of this page. Alan Mode supports this thesis in his article "Making Money the Motivator?" He maintains that desired performance should be rewarded through an effective merit salary performance-evaluation program.[8] The explanation of the employees' behavior lies in the expectancy theory of motivation, which is discussed in the next section of this chapter.

Although money is a powerful motivator, especially when used as a reward for outstanding performance, there are cases where it is *not* a motivator, as Herzberg indicates. This situation usually occurs when people are so financially well off that their lower-level needs are taken care of and they don't have any worries about security in the future. For example:

Bill Daley, earning $85,000 a year, was the top salesperson for XYZ Corporation in the state of California. Higher management at the New York home office was impressed with him and offered him a sales manager's position in the New York office. They were quite surprised when he turned down a proposed salary of $140,000 along with a bonus of $20,000 for making the move. Bill preferred to remain in San Diego with his wife and two teen-aged daughters.[9]

What are some of the probable reasons why Bill Daley turned down an additional $55,000 in annual salary and a healthy bonus?

Qualifying Herzberg's Theory

We believe that Herzberg's theory is valuable as a general guide to understanding motivation at work. However, here are some qualifications you should bear in mind:

1. Money *can* sometimes be a motivating factor.
2. For some people, especially professionals, the motivating factors can be dissatisfiers if these are not present in their job.
3. Research studies that use Herzberg's research method support his findings; however, studies that use a different method arrive at different conclusions. This fact has led some researchers to conclude that Herzberg's theory is "method bound."[10] On the other hand, in a study made by Charles and Donna Hanson, they conclude that Herzberg's theory has considerable validity, especially in comparison with other theories of motivation.[11]

THE EXPECTANCY THEORY OF MOTIVATION

The **expectancy theory** of motivation (Figure 8–5) is concerned with the belief that workers expect that a good effort, resulting in effective performance, will be followed by a reward. This theory was developed by Victor H. Vroom. Using the previous example of employees' behavior after the plant bonus system was instituted, this theory can be illustrated as follows:

FIGURE 8–5   EXPECTANCY THEORY

| Motivation | = | Expectancy that increased effort will lead to increased rewards | × | Increased effort leading to higher production | = | Year-end bonus for employees |

Figure 8–5 is a graphic illustration of the expectancy theory. It shows that rewards based on current performance cause subsequent performance to be more effective.

What happens to worker expectancies and effort when an employer follows a policy of across-the-board pay increases for all employees over a period of years?

THE EQUITY THEORY OF MOTIVATION

Another concept that has received research support is called the **equity theory** of motivation. This theory is concerned with motivating employees by reducing feelings of inequity when such feelings exist. The concept is especially relevant for companies that are sensitive to having a fair wage and salary system. It is as basic as comparing your own wage or salary with that of other people who logically should be making the same money as you, if not less. When you find out that they are making more, then you become dissatisfied and possibly demotivated. In a case like this, salary is a hygiene factor, as revealed by Herzberg's findings.

Have you ever received a lower grade than you thought you deserved, only to find that others you considered to be poorer students had gotten better grades? How did it make you feel?

Here is an example of the equity theory in action.

Sue Smith started to work as an accountant at a local hospital after graduating from college. During her two years on the job, she had received excellent annual appraisals and salary increases. She was pleased with her progress and with the job until she discovered that two new college graduates without experience had been hired in the accounting department at slightly more than she was making. She immediately started looking for employment elsewhere. [12]

As far as you can tell, is Sue Smith's situation a widespread problem in today's working world? Why or why not?

THE POSITIVE-REINFORCEMENT THEORY OF MOTIVATION

One of the best ways to influence and modify employee behavior in a favorable direction is explained by the **positive-reinforcement theory** of motivation. We have talked about this concept *indirectly* throughout this chapter. It is based on the **law of effect**, which holds that those activities that meet with pleasurable consequences tend to be repeated, whereas those activities that meet with unpleasurable consequences tend not to be repeated.

Since the supervisor in most companies has control of the reward-and-discipline system for subordinates, he or she controls the reins of the *law of effect*. The immediate supervisor, more than any other person, is responsible for whether employees develop into an excellent, a fair, or a poor work team. This situation will in turn determine to a large degree the employees' satisfaction with their jobs.

MOTIVATIONAL PRACTICES AT AMERICA'S BEST-MANAGED COMPANIES

Many companies and supervisors are quite adept at penalizing employees for mistakes or poor performance. A recent best-selling book, drawing lessons from America's best-run companies, states that "the dominant culture in most big companies demands punishment for a mistake no matter how useful, small, invisible."[13] The book goes on to say that the dominant culture in the *best-managed companies* is just the opposite. These companies develop "winners" by constantly reinforcing the idea that employees *are* winners. The performance targets are set so that they provide a challenge but are attainable. Recall in the Herzberg studies that recognition was one of the primary motivators. The effective supervisor continually provides recognition for good performance on the part of employees.

In a presentation to the 1985 American Psychological Association meeting, Barry Stow notes that organization psychologists have been advocating for years certain company actions to increase motivation of individuals. Many of America's best-managed companies have implemented these actions, which include

1. Tying extrinsic rewards (such as pay) to performance.
2. Setting realistic and challenging goals.
3. Evaluating employee performance accurately and providing feedback on performance.
4. Promoting on the basis of skill and performance rather than personal characteristics, power, or connections.
5. Building the skill level of the work force through training and development.
6. Enlarging and enriching jobs through increases in responsibility, variety, and significance.[14]

The above actions demonstrate the practicality of the theories presented in this chapter.

On a more all-encompassing basis, James O'Toole has published a book on employee practices at the best-managed companies. He shows that these companies place a lot of emphasis not only on the rights and responsibilities of employees, but also on the value of employee contribution through participative management. Specifically, these companies provide stakeholders' status for unions, employee stock ownership, a fair measure of job security, lifelong training, benefits tailored to individual needs, participation in decision making, freedom of expression, and incentive pay.[15]

CHAPTER REVIEW

In this chapter, we have pointed out the importance of understanding the *why* of motivation. We discussed concepts of motivation developed by Maslow, Herzberg, Vroom, and others that are especially relevant to supervisors. In addition, we demonstrated that supervisors are, in effect, need controllers and have considerable impact on the satisfaction and performance of employees.

Herzberg's findings support Maslow's concept of a hierarchy of needs. Herzberg's motivators relate to the higher-level needs (esteem and self-fulfillment), and his hygiene factors relate to the lower-level needs, primarily the security needs. We also presented criticism of Herzberg's finding that money is a hygiene factor, noting that money *can* be either a motivator or a demotivator. For employees who are not wealthy, money is primarily a motivator, especially when it is tied in with a reward system for good performance.

We examined the relationship among motivation, money, and the expectancy theory. The equity theory has a similar relationship, in that feelings of inequity trigger feelings of insecurity which can cause demotivation, whereas feelings of equity cause one to strive even more diligently to better one's performance. We also pointed out that the positive-reinforcement theory of motivation was a concept that was implied throughout the chapter. Finally, we examined the employee practices at America's best-managed companies.

QUESTIONS FOR REVIEW AND DISCUSSION

1. Briefly outline Maslow's theory of the hierarchy of needs. What are the two basic principles underlying this theory? Can you relate the theory to a real situation?
2. What kinds of knowledge should a leader furnish his or her subordinates? How does this information satisfy their needs?
3. What findings resulted from Frederick Herzberg's research concerning employee motivation? Can these findings be correlated with Maslow's hierarchy of needs?
4. Is security the most important job need of blue-collar workers?
5. What is being done to improve motivation in United States companies?

LEARNING EXERCISE 8–1
EXCESSIVE COFFEE BREAKS

An office manager for the Hawthorne Company has a staff with high morale and generally good productivity. However, several employees have been extending their coffee breaks by five to eight minutes. The manager feels that the more conscientious employees resent this, yet wonders whether these extended coffee breaks should be stopped at the risk of alienating the employees guilty of this practice. How should the manager handle this situation?

LEARNING EXERCISE 8–2
UNNEEDED OVERTIME

Irwin Bates is 53 years old and works as an installer for Midland Telephone Co. His three children are married, and his modest 1,000-square-foot home is almost paid for. His wife, Edna, enjoys working part-time in a small fabric shop. Irwin is an avid outdoorsman. He and his group of five or six of "the boys" spend many weekend mornings at a nearby recreation area hunting or fishing. In fact, this coming Saturday is the opening day of the deer season.

    Do you think Irwin's supervisor will have much luck getting Irwin to work overtime this Saturday morning at time-and-a-half pay? Such overtime work is strictly voluntary and not required of Irwin. Assume that you are his supervisor. What motivational appeals would you use in trying to persuade him to work on Saturday?

LEARNING EXERCISE 8–3
DISTINGUISHING MOTIVATORS FROM HYGIENE FACTORS

The items listed on page 214 represent ways in which organizations attempt to meet employees' needs and increase organizational effectiveness. Using Herzberg's theory, identify which factors are motivators and which are hygiene factors.

	Motivators	Hygiene Factors
1. Raises based on performance.	———	———
2. Company-sponsored supervisors' club.	———	———
3. Suggestion system with monetary rewards for cost-saving ideas.	———	———
4. Pensions.	———	———
5. Health insurance.	———	———
6. Promotions.	———	———
7. Company newsletter.	———	———

ENDNOTES

1. Names have been disguised.
2. Quoted in Alfred J. Marrow, *Behind the Executive Mask: Greater Managerial Competence Through Deeper Self-Understanding*, Report No. 79 (New York: AMACOM, 1964), 7.
3. Abraham H. Maslow, *Motivation and Personality* (New York: Harper & Row, 1954).
4. "Middle-Aged Officials Find New Group Hit by Slump: Themselves," *The Wall Street Journal*, September 1, 1982.
5. The material in this section is adapted and updated from Douglas McGregor's article, "Conditions of Effective Leadership in the Industrial Organization," which first appeared in the *Journal of Consulting Psychology*, (March-April 1944), 55–63.
6. Frederick Herzberg, Bernard Mausner, and Barbara Snyderman, *The Motivation to Work*, 2d ed. (New York: John Wiley & Sons, 1959).
7. Donald Mosley, "What Motivates New Zealanders?" *Management* (Journal of the New Zealand Institute of Management), (October 1969), 37.
8. Alan Mode, "Making Money the Motivator," *Supervisory Management* 24 (August 1979), 16–20.
9. Names are disguised.
10. See, for example, C. L. Hulin and M. R. Blood, "Job Enlargement, Individual Differences, and Worker Responses," *Psychological Bulletin* 69 (1975), 41–55.
11. Charles A. Hanson and Donna K. Hanson, "Motivation: Are the Old Theories Still True?" *Supervisory Management* 23 (June 1978), 14.
12. Name is disguised.
13. Thomas J. Peters and Robert H. Waterman, Jr., *In Search of Excellence: Lessons from America's Best-Run Companies* (New York: Harper & Row, 1982), 48.
14. Barry M. Stow, "Organizational Psychology and the Pursuit of the Happy/Productive Worker," *California Management Review* Vol. XXVIII, No. 4 (Summer 1986), 48.
15. James O'Toole, "Employee Practices at the Best-Managed Companies," *California Management Review* Volume XXVIII, No. 1 (Fall 1985), 35–66.

SUGGESTIONS FOR FURTHER READING

Holmes, K. R., and P. A. Brook. "Maslow's Hierarchy Revisited." *Supervisory Management* 30 (April 1985), 29–32.

King, D. "Rewarding Can Be Rewarding." *Supervisory Management* 30 (January 1985), 32–33.

Peters, R., and N. Austin. "Management by Walking Around." *California Management Review* (Fall 1985), 9–34.

Strong, T. S. "Positive Reinforcement: How Often and How Much?" *Supervisory Management* 30 (January 1985): 10–13.

Walton, R. E. "From Control to Commitment in the Workplace." *Harvard Business Review* 2 (March-April 1985), 77–84.

9
LEADERSHIP

OBJECTIVES

After reading and studying the material in this chapter, you should be able to:

Describe the factors affecting the leadership style used.

Discuss and explain two frequently used leadership models.

Develop insight as to which leadership style is most appropriate in different situations.

Discuss how to inspire self-confidence, develop people, and increase productivity.

IMPORTANT TERMS

leadership
Theory X
Theory Y
maturity level
Managerial Grid®
authority-obedience *or*
  task management
country-club management
middle-of-the-road management
impoverished management

team management
life-cycle theory of leadership
task behaviors
relationship behaviors
situational leadership
structuring and telling style
coaching and selling style
participating and supporting style
delegating style
continuum of leadership behaviors

CHAPTER OUTLINE
CASE 9–1. KENNY: AN EFFECTIVE SUPERVISOR

I. LEADERSHIP: WHAT IS IT ALL ABOUT?
- A. Factors affecting leadership style
    1. The supervisor's management philosophy
    2. The followers' maturity level
    3. The situation faced by the supervisor
- B. Two leadership models
    1. Blake and Mouton's Managerial Grid®
    2. Hersey and Blanchard's situational leadership
- C. Is one leadership style best?
- D. Tannenbaum and Schmidt's leadership continuum

II. HOW LEADERS CAN INSPIRE SELF-CONFIDENCE, DEVELOP PEOPLE, AND INCREASE PRODUCTIVITY
- A. Try saying "thank you"
- B. Expect the best from your people
- C. Maintain a positive self-regard
- D. Develop the entire team

Chapter Review

Questions for Review and Discussion

Learning Exercise 9–1. Developing a List of Leadership Skills

Learning Exercise 9–2. A Debate on What Causes Productivity

Suggestions for Further Reading

CASE 9–1
KENNY: AN EFFECTIVE SUPERVISOR

The most effective supervisor whom one of the authors of this textbook has met was encountered in an organization development and change effort where the author served as consultant.[1] His name was Kenny, and he was maintenance supervisor in a chemical plant of an international corporation.[2] The author was called in as a consultant because the plant was suffering from the results of the ineffective, autocratic leadership of a former plant manager. Such leadership at the top had adversely affected all levels, resulting in low morale and losses from plant operations.

In gathering data about the plant through interviews, questionnaires, and observations, the consultant discovered that one maintenance crew was completely at odds with other departments in the plant. Unlike the rest of the plant, this crew—under Kenny's supervision—had very high morale and productivity.

In the interview with Kenny, the consultant discovered that Kenny was a young man in his early thirties who had a two-year associate degree from a community college. The consultant was impressed with his positive attitude, especially in light of the overall low plant morale and productivity. Kenny said the plant was one of the finest places he'd ever worked, and the maintenance people had more know-how than any other group with which he had been associated. Kenny's perception of his crew was that they did twice as much work as other crews, that everyone worked together, and that participative management did work with his crew.

Kenny's boss reported that Kenny was wrong about his crew doing twice as much work as other crews; actually, they did *more* than twice as much. He also maintained that Kenny was the best supervisor he had seen in 22 years in the industry.

One thing the consultant was curious about was why pressure and criticism from the old, autocratic manager seemed not to have had any effect on Kenny's crew. The crew gave the consultant the answer. They explained that Kenny had the ability to act as an intermediary and buffer between upper management and the crew. He would get higher management's primary objectives and points across without upsetting his people. As one crew member described it:

The maintenance supervisors will come back from a "donkey barbe-cue" session with higher management where they are raising hell about shoddy work, taking too long at coffee breaks, etc. Other supervisors are shook up for a week and give their men hell. But Kenny is cool, calm, and collected. He will call us together and report that nine items were discussed at the meeting, including shoddy work, but that doesn't apply to our crew. Then he will cover the two or four items that are relevant to our getting the job done.

Unfortunately, Kenny did have a real concern at the time of the consul-tant's interview. He was being transferred from the highest-producing crew to the lowest-producing one. In fact, the latter was known as "the Hell's Angels crew." The crew members were considered to be a renegade group who were constantly fighting with production people as well as with one another. The previous supervisor had been terminated because he could not cope with them. In the course of this chapter, we will return to Kenny and what happened with the renegade crew.

Do you think Kenny can turn things around in a year with the renegade crew? Why or why not?

Motivation, which we have just examined in the previous chapter, cannot take place in a vacuum. For things to happen, effective leadership or direction must be exhibited. This chapter focuses on effective leadership.

We don't want the opening case to give you the idea that being an effective leader is easy. Today there are many supervisors and managers who are using a less effective leadership style than they could be using, often because they don't have the skills or perhaps don't even realize the benefits of using other styles. Moreover, they don't realize that the most effective style in one situation may not be the most effective in another. Hence this chapter addresses such questions as:

1. Why do some leaders use one style and other leaders use another?
2. What effects do different styles have on employee productivity and morale?
3. What style is most appropriate in a particular situation?
4. Should a particular style be used consistently, or should the style be changed as circumstances change?

Such questions are vital for an organization, since supervisory leadership is one of the primary determinants of organizational performance and productivity.

LEADERSHIP: WHAT IS IT ALL ABOUT?

Leadership is defined as a process of influencing individual and group activities toward goal setting and goal achievement. In our opening case, Kenny successfully influenced his group in the achievement of effective results, whereas the former supervisor of the "Hell's Angels" had not. This chapter provides insight and concepts that will assist supervisors in successfully leading their work groups.

Factors Affecting Leadership Style

Three factors, or variables, have a major impact on the choice of a leadership style. These are (1) the supervisor's management philosophy, (2) the followers' maturity level, and (3) the situation faced by the supervisor. Figure 9–1 shows that these factors are interrelated.

FIGURE 9–1 FACTORS AFFECTING CHOICE OF LEADERSHIP STYLE

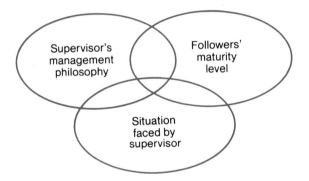

THE SUPERVISOR'S MANAGEMENT PHILOSOPHY. A supervisor's management philosophy is basically determined by his or her assumptions about the nature of people. Whether they are aware of it or not, most supervisors have a philosophy that influences their style in working with and through people. This philosophy is affected by several factors. Three of the critical factors are given below. These factors interact to influence a supervisor's view of the nature of people and consequently shape his or her philosophy:

1. The supervisor's family and early school environment.
2. The supervisor's experience and training in the area of leadership.
3. The supervisor's present work environment, including the type of work and the general management system.

Kenny had a very supportive and happy home environment. His father was a big influence and served as a role model. He always stressed to Kenny that he should treat people as he would want to be treated.

Two of the most widely publicized views of the nature of people are Douglas McGregor's Theory X and Theory Y assumptions.[3] On the basis of his consulting and research work in industry, McGregor highlighted two different and contrasting sets of assumptions that influenced a manager's leadership style. The most significant assumptions of **Theory X** are given below. Supervisors who accept Theory X assumptions will be more inclined to prefer a structured, autocratic leadership style.

1. The average human being has an inherent dislike of work and will avoid it if possible.
2. Because of this human characteristic—dislike of work—most people must be coerced, controlled, directed, or threatened with punishment to get them to put forth adequate effort toward the achievement of organizational objectives.
3. The average human being prefers to be directed, wishes to avoid responsibility, has relatively little ambition and, above all, seeks security.

The basic assumptions of **Theory Y** are given below. Supervisors who hold Theory Y assumptions will be more inclined to prefer a supportive, participative leadership style.

1. The expenditure of physical and mental effort in work is as natural as play or rest.
2. External control and the threat of punishment are not the only means of bringing about effort toward organizational objectives. People will exercise self-direction and self-control in the service of objectives to which they are committed.
3. Commitment to objectives is a function of the rewards associated with their achievement.
4. The average human being learns, under proper conditions, not only to accept but also to actively seek greater responsibility.
5. The capacity to exercise a relatively high degree of imagination, ingenuity, and creativity in the solution of organizational problems is widely, not narrowly, distributed in the population.
6. Under the conditions of modern industrial life, the intellectual potentialities of the average human being are only partially utilized.

Which of these assumptions did Kenny hold concerning his people? Also, what views did he hold regarding his boss and the new plant manager?

What if the renegade crew decides not to cooperate with Kenny, and its members continue to be poor performers? Should Kenny continue to be supportive and use Theory Y assumptions? Why or why not?

THE FOLLOWERS' MATURITY LEVEL.   A person's **maturity level** is based on a drive and a need for achievement as a result of his or her experience, education, attitudes, and willingness and ability to accept responsibility. These maturity variables should be considered only in relation to a specific task to be performed. The maturity concept is expressed by the following formula:

$$\text{Maturity} = \text{Ability} \times \text{Willingness}$$

If followers are low on maturity, the leader should certainly use a different style than if followers were high on maturity. Unfortunately, some supervisors fail to take into consideration the maturity level of their subordinates.

After Kenny was assigned to the new crew, he had to make a decision on the leadership strategies he would use in dealing with them. His initial diagnosis was that the crew had the ability to do the work but lacked the willingness because of a poor attitude.

In a meeting with members of the "Hell's Angels" crew, the consultant learned that the first day on the job Kenny called a meeting, shut the door, and conducted a "bull session" that lasted over two hours. Among other things, he told them about his philosophy and the way he liked to operate. He especially stressed that he was going to be fair and treat everyone equally. The crew members were allowed to gripe and complain as long as they talked about matters in the plant, while Kenny played a listening role without arguing with them. In the course of the session, Kenny expressed his expectations of the crew. They, in turn, told him they would do it his way for two weeks to see if he "practiced what he preached."

As you may have surmised by now, Kenny's leadership made the difference. Before the year was out, his new crew was the most productive in the plant.

THE SITUATION FACED BY THE SUPERVISOR. Common sense dictates that the situation faced by a supervisor should have a major influence on his or her leadership style. A platoon leader directing troops in combat, an airline pilot who suddenly has engine trouble, or a supervisor such as Bill Morrow in Case 1–1 (Chapter 1) would certainly not call for a group meeting and get people "involved" to deal with the emergency.

The nature of the work and the types of assignments must be considered in assessing a situation. Research scientists who are involved in creative and complex jobs, for example, would require more freedom to operate than those in jobs involving repetitive, assembly-line work. Finally, a leader's choice of style is influenced by how her or his unit is progressing. For example, a football team with outstanding potential that loses the first three games would get a different leadership response from the coach than a team that had won its first three games.

Two Leadership Models

There are a number of theories and theoretical models regarding leadership. We have selected two that are especially applicable for supervisors. These are (1) Robert Blake and Jane Mouton's well-known Managerial Grid®, and (2) Paul Hersey and Kenneth Blanchard's situational leadership model. Probably more supervisors have been trained using these models than any others. For example, well over a million people have been trained in situational leadership alone. [4] Thus, the reason we have selected these two models is that businesses see them as more practical than the more theoretical models.

BLAKE AND MOUTON'S MANAGERIAL GRID®. The **Managerial Grid**® in Figure 9–2 shows that a leadership style has two concerns: production and people. [5] "Concern for Production" is plotted on the horizontal axis of the Grid, while "Concern for People" is plotted on the vertical axis. Although the Grid identifies five basic leadership styles, theoretically there are 81 combinations of "concerns" that could be plotted by using the nine-point system in the Grid.

If a supervisor is primarily concerned with production and shows little concern for people, he or she would be a *9,1* leader (9 in concern for production and 1 in concern for people). The *9,1* leader is one who structures the work, delegates as little as possible, and usually is an autocrat in getting work accomplished. This style is called **authority-obedience**, or **task management**.

Conversely, if a supervisor shows primary concern for people and little concern for production, he or she would be a *1,9* leader. The *1,9* leader is supportive and somewhat permissive, emphasizing the need to keep employees happy and satisfied. Leaders of this type tend to avoid pressure in getting the work done. This style is called **country-club management**.

The *5,5* leader represents a **middle-of-the-road management** style by placing some emphasis on production and some emphasis on people. Usually the unstated agreement in this style is "If you give me reasonable production, I will be reasonable in my demands on you."

FIGURE 9–2   THE MANAGERIAL GRID®

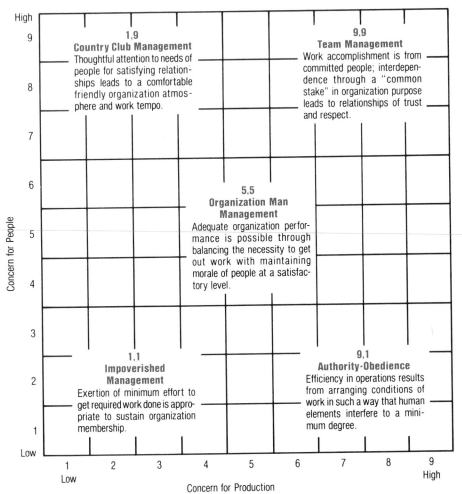

Source: The Managerial Grid® figure from *The Managerial Grid III: The Key to Leadership Excellence*, by Robert R. Blake and Jane S. Mouton. Houston: Gulf Publishing Company, Copyright © 1985, page 12. Reproduced by permission.

The *1,1* leader reflects the poorest of all styles on the grid, which is called **impoverished management**. Supervisors using this type of leadership have completely abdicated the leadership role. If any significant work gets done, it is due to the initiative of people working for this leader. In actuality, the leader has retired on the job!

The *9,9* leader believes that the heart of work direction lies in mutual understanding and agreement about what organizational and unit objectives are and in the means of attaining them. This type of leader has a high concern for both people and production and uses a participative approach called **team management** in getting the work done.

Which style do Blake and Mouton advocate as the style that works best?

If your answer was the *9,9* style, then you were correct. Blake and Mouton strongly believe that the *9,9* style is the way to manage in leadership situations. They cite the many managers and supervisors in organizations they have worked with who conclude that a *9,9* (team-participative) leader is using the ideal style.

HERSEY AND BLANCHARD'S SITUATIONAL LEADERSHIP.   It sounds as if we have leadership licked, doesn't it? You may conclude that the best approach is a high concern for both production and people. But not so fast—a number of people disagree, saying that there is *no one best approach for every situation*, but only a best approach for a given situation.

One of the most popular "situational" approaches is called the **life-cycle theory of leadership**. It draws heavily on leadership research conducted at Ohio State University. In these studies, leadership behaviors and strategies in a number of different organizations were examined. The researchers concluded that many leadership behaviors fall into either one of two areas—task behaviors or relationship behaviors. **Task behaviors** involve clarifying the job; telling people what to do, how to do it, and when to do it; providing follow-up; and taking corrective action. **Relationship behaviors** involve providing people with support, giving them positive feedback, and asking for their opinions and ideas.

These two concepts, along with the concept of the maturity level of followers, are central to understanding the Hersey-Blanchard model.[6] Recall our earlier indication that the maturity level of followers is focused on their ability to do a specific job or task. It encompasses their desire for achievement, experience, education, attitudes, and a willingness to accept responsibility. Now that we have a few building blocks, let's examine Hersey and Blanchard's **situational leadership** as illustrated in the model shown in Figure 9–3.[7]

The Hersey-Blanchard model shows the relationship between the maturity of followers and the leadership style based on task and relationship behaviors of leaders. The model consists of four labeled blocks, or quadrants, with a curved line running through each quadrant. At the bottom of the model is a scale showing various ranges of maturity: high, moderate, and low. The direction of the arrow on the maturity scale and the direction of the arrow on the task-behavior axis indicate that the higher the degree of maturity, the lower the degree of task behavior.

FIGURE 9-3 THE HERSEY-BLANCHARD LEADERSHIP MODEL

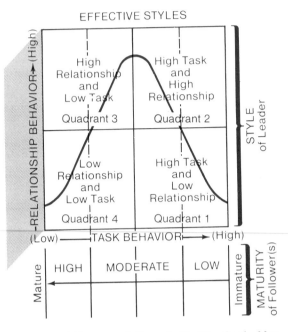

Source: Paul Hersey and Kenneth H. Blanchard, *Management of Organizational Behavior: Utilizing Human Resources,* 4th ed., © 1982, p. 200. Reprinted by permission of Prentice-Hall, Inc., Englewood Cliffs, N.J.

To use this model, first identify the maturity level of the members of your work group at some point (high, moderate, or low) on the maturity scale. Keep in mind that this point represents your assessment only in regard to their ability to carry out a specific task or assignment. Then draw a vertical line. The point of intersection will fall within one of the four quadrants, and the label on the quadrant gives the most effective leadership style for the particular situation.

Hersey and Blanchard use the model to explain not only leadership in dealing with adults, but also parents' leadership in raising children. Let's first illustrate the model using a family situation.

STOP AND THINK

Assume that a four-year-old boy is going to a birthday party. Although the party is in the neighborhood, it is two blocks away and there are two busy streets to cross. Since a car is not available, diagnose the leadership style the child's mother would use to get her son to the party.

If you responded that a high-task and low-relationship style is appropriate, then you were correct. The task involves some danger (crossing busy streets), and the follower is immature. Hence the mother should use a structured, high-task approach, perhaps even holding the child's hand as they cross the streets.

The four quadrants in Figure 9–3 can be translated into four basic leadership styles: (1) structuring and telling, (2) coaching and selling, (3) participating and supporting, and (4) delegating. The structuring and telling style usually works best with new or immature employees and in dealing with individuals or groups whose performance is slipping. For example, if a department's costs have increased considerably beyond the standard, then a highly structured, close leadership style would be called for to correct the situation. Thus, the **structuring and telling style** (Q1: high task and low relationship) would be used with an individual or group that is relatively low in maturity for a given task.

The **coaching and selling style** (Q2: high task and high relationship) is usually best used with individuals or groups who have potential but haven't completely mastered their assignments. For example, a high-school football coach with young but talented players should probably use this approach. The coach would have a high concern for both task accomplishment (coaching) and convincing the players through positive reinforcement that they have the ability to win (selling).

An appropriate style to use as individuals or groups mature is the **participating and supporting style** (Q3: high relationship and low task). The leader should use more participative management in getting ideas and involving the followers in setting objectives and solving problems. Think of Maslow's hierarchy of needs theory: As employees gain in experience and competence, they have a need for more support and involvement regarding their work.

The **delegating style** (Q4: low relationship and low task) is one of the more difficult styles for a supervisor to use even when individuals or groups working under the supervisor are exceptionally mature and capable. A primary reason is that the supervisor is being held accountable for results and therefore is reluctant to involve subordinates in her or his work. The expression, "If it ain't broke, don't fix it," illustrates why the wise supervisor needs to delegate in certain situations.

Suppose you are a supervisor and have a skilled, capable worker who has never caused you any difficulties. In fact, for three years she has been a productive person in your department. Since she has proved to be a capable person, you would probably be using a delegating style in regard to her work. However, in the past two weeks her work has steadily deteriorated. Projects are late and the work, when completed, is of poor quality. As her supervisor, what leadership style will you use in this situation?

You certainly would not continue to delegate, would you? Most supervisors would shift all the way to either a coaching and selling style or even a structuring and telling style. Depending on what the problem is, either style could be appropriate. This situation shows how a leader might use a different style with an individual or group depending on the situation.

Is One Leadership Style Best?

As we indicated, research supports the Hersey and Blanchard thesis that there is no one best style for all situations. However, Hersey and Blanchard and others recognize that, in most situations, the appropriate style would be either coaching and selling or participating and supporting. So, we can learn a lot from the Blake and Mouton thesis regarding the payoffs from utilizing a participative, team approach to managing.

The long-run trend in American industry is for supervisory managers to use more participative styles, although they initially resist the move toward more participation.[8] An explanation for this trend is that employees are becoming better educated and have their lower-level needs relatively well satisfied. It is only through tapping the higher-level needs, then, that significant motivation will occur. In Chapters 18 and 19 we examine in more depth how a supervisor can receive a big payoff from a participative, team approach to managing.

Tannenbaum and Schmidt's Leadership Continuum

Robert Tannenbaum and Warren Schmidt are two other writers who take a situational viewpoint toward leadership. Their **continuum of leadership behaviors**, shown in Figure 9–4, is especially useful when a supervisor is considering to what degree employees should be involved in decision making. The figure is a rectangular block representing a continuum of power which is divided by a diagonal line into two distinct parts: (1) use of authority by supervisor, and (2) area of freedom for subordinates. The greater the authority the supervisor uses, the smaller the area of freedom for subordinates. Conversely, the more freedom subordinates have, the less authority the supervisor has. The continuum also indicates the range of available behaviors from which the supervisor can draw.

Tannenbaum and Schmidt maintain that each situation calling for a decision requires a different approach. The path the leader chooses to follow should be based on a consideration of the following three forces:

1. *Forces in the leader.* These include the leader's value system, confidence in subordinates, leadership inclinations, and feelings of security or insecurity.
2. *Forces in the subordinates.* These include the subordinates' need for independence, need for increased responsibility, knowledge of the problem, attitudes about their interest in tackling the problem, and expectations with respect to sharing in decision making.
3. *Forces in the situation.* These include the type of organization, the group's effectiveness, the pressure of time, and the nature of the problem itself.

FIGURE 9–4   CONTINUUM OF LEADERSHIP BEHAVIORS

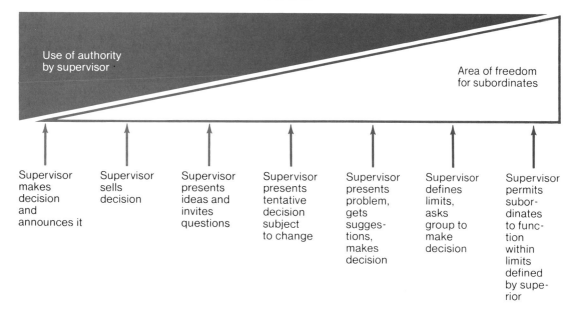

Use of authority by supervisor ·

Area of freedom for subordinates

| Supervisor makes decision and announces it | Supervisor sells decision | Supervisor presents ideas and invites questions | Supervisor presents tentative decision subject to change | Supervisor presents problem, gets suggestions, makes decision | Supervisor defines limits, asks group to make decision | Supervisor permits subordinates to function within limits defined by superior |

Source: Reprinted by permission of the *Harvard Business Review*. An exhibit from "How to Choose a Leadership Pattern" by Robert Tannenbaum and Warren Schmidt (May-June 1973). Copyright © 1973 by the President and Fellows of Harvard College; all rights reserved.

The key point to remember is that the successful supervisor is one who has a high batting average in assessing the appropriate behavior to use in a given situation.

As the result of a dramatic upward shift in sales, the XYZ firm will have to rearrange vacation schedules. The previous supervisor consulted individually with employees and, when possible, gave them their first or second choice of vacation time. Because of time pressure, this approach would take too long now. Donna Douglas, the supervisor, has a lot of confidence in her group of employees. They have a good work record. Drawing from the continuum of leadership behavior, what approach would you recommend that she use in rearranging vacation schedules?

HOW SUPERVISORS CAN INSPIRE SELF-CONFIDENCE, DEVELOP PEOPLE, AND INCREASE PRODUCTIVITY

The concept of the "power of positive thinking" is not a fictional viewpoint developed by Dr. Norman Vincent Peale. Research supports the thesis that a supervisor's attitude, outlook, and communication have a major impact on his or her employees. This section highlights the importance of such an impact.

Try Saying "Thank You"

Jack Falvey states that most people at work use only 20 to 25 percent of their brain capacity, and that productivity can be drastically increased simply by saying "thank you." These "thank you's" can run the gamut from financial bonuses for good work to simply writing letters of commendation, as IBM does.[9] One of the best ways is to continually search for positive contributions and to give people feedback right on the spot. This is an approach popularized in the best-selling book *The One Minute Manager*. The authors, Blanchard and Johnson, maintain that in most organizations managers spend most of their time catching people doing things wrong, whereas the emphasis should be just the reverse. Their suggested one-minute praising works well when you:

1. Tell people *up front* that you are going to let them know how they are doing.
2. Praise people immediately.
3. Tell people what they did right—be specific.
4. Tell people how good you feel about what they did right, and how it helps the organization and the other people who work there.
5. Stop for a moment of silence to let them "feel" how good you feel.
6. Encourage them to do more of the same.
7. Shake hands or touch people in a way that makes it clear that you support their success in the organization.[10]

Expect the Best from Your People

A major insight into effective leadership is the realization that bringing out the best in people involves assuming the best about them. If you expect the best from your people and develop realistic yet difficult performance objectives, your expectations will often become a self-fulfilling prophecy. The key ingredient is to have trust between yourself and your work team, and the essence of trust is to do what you say you will do. A study of school teachers has revealed that having high expectations of students can increase their IQ scores up to 25 points.[11]

As indicated in the text, Kenny gained the trust of his renegade work team. They gave him two weeks to see if he would do what he said he would do in regard to supervising them, and he did.

Maintain a Positive Self-Regard

Interviews with nearly 100 outstanding leaders in different fields revealed that having a good feeling about yourself is a key to effective leadership.[12] In this area we are not talking about cockiness or self-worship but a sincere self-respect, such as Kenny revealed in our opening case. In maintaining this self-respect, it is important to be aware of your strengths and weaknesses and to keep working on improving your talents. If you have a weakness that is difficult to overcome, you can compensate by bringing someone on your team who can offset that weakness. The end result of a good self-image is to induce the same good feelings in others.

Develop the Entire Team

Kenny of our opening case makes a conscious effort to sit down once a month to talk with each member of his crew. However, he goes beyond, focusing on developing the entire team. He holds regular crew meetings and emphasizes the importance of working together. As a result, the crew thinks and acts as a team— they help one another. For example, one team member is afraid of heights; so, other members cover for this person when an assignment involves heights. This activity is so important that a later chapter is devoted to concepts involved in team building.

CHAPTER REVIEW

Leading is a process of influencing individual and group activities toward goal setting and goal achievement. How well this process is carried out has a major impact on both performance and morale.

There are three interrelated variables that have an impact on the choice of leadership style. These are (1) the supervisor's management philosophy, (2) the followers' maturity level, and (3) the situation faced by the supervisor. The maturity level must be evaluated only with regard to carrying out a specific task or assignment.

Two leadership models that are widely used in leadership training programs were examined: Blake and Mouton's Managerial Grid® and Hersey and Blanchard's situational leadership. The Managerial Grid plots five basic leadership styles, and Blake and Mouton recommend the team management style as the ideal leadership style.

Hersey and Blanchard highlight four basic leadership styles: structuring and telling, coaching and selling, participating and supporting, and delegating. They make a strong case that the ideal style to use depends on the maturity level of employees and the situation faced by the supervisor. Research tends to support the Hersey and Blanchard position that there is no one best style for all situations. However, with the increasing maturity and education of employees today, there is a trend in American industry to utilize both the coaching and selling style and the participating and supporting style in influencing individual employees and groups.

Finally, supervisors can greatly increase their employees' productivity by expressing appreciation, expecting the best from their people, maintaining a positive self-image, helping others to build their own self-respect, and developing a team feeling among employees.

QUESTIONS FOR REVIEW AND DISCUSSION

1. What is meant by leadership?
2. Briefly discuss the major factors that may influence the choice of an individual's leadership style. Correlate these factors with different leadership styles.
3. Discuss how a supervisor would determine the maturity level of a subordinate.
4. What leadership actions would fall under the category of task behaviors, and what actions would fall under the category of relationship behaviors?
5. Do you agree or disagree with Blake and Mouton that there is one best leadership style? Support your position.
6. Why do you think praise and appreciation is so effective in boosting productivity? Can you think of an instance when a pat on the back made you want to work harder or do better? Did someone else's expectations influence your ambition?
7. Why do you think self-respect or self-confidence is important in a leader? Can a leader be effective without self-confidence?
8. Do you agree with the authors about the importance of team building? Are there some circumstances in which a team approach would not work and individual competition might be more effective?

LEARNING EXERCISE 9–1
DEVELOPING A LIST OF LEADERSHIP SKILLS

Have each member of the class rank-order the eight leadership skills most important in carrying out a supervisor's job. Then divide the class into teams of five and have each team rank-order the eight leadership skills. Have all teams post their rank-order lists to allow for comparison and discussion.

LEARNING EXERCISE 9–2
A DEBATE ON WHAT CAUSES PRODUCTIVITY

Select two teams from the class and have them debate the issue presented below. The rest of the class will act as observers and decide who wins the debate.

AFFIRMATIVE SIDE: Leadership styles are the primary determinant of productivity.

NEGATIVE SIDE: Productivity is the primary determinant of what leadership styles should be.

ENDNOTES

1. Donald C. Mosley, "System Four Revisited: Some New Insights," *Organization Development Journal* 5 (Spring 1987).
2. The company would not permit use of its name.
3. Douglas McGregor, *The Human Side of Enterprise* (New York: McGraw-Hill Book Co., 1960), 33–42.
4. *Trainer's Bookshelf*, Interview with Dr. Paul Hersey (San Diego, CA: Learning Resources Corporation, 1982).
5. Robert R. Blake and Jane S. Mouton, *The Managerial Grid III: The Key to Leadership Excellence* (Houston: Gulf Publishing, 1985).
6. Paul Hersey and Kenneth H. Blanchard, *Management of Organizational Behavior: Utilizing Human Resources*, 3d ed. (Englewood Cliffs, NJ: Prentice-Hall, 1977), 161–62.
7. Hersey and Blanchard acknowledge that they were strongly influenced by William J. Reddins, "3-D Management Style Theory" found in William J. Reddins *Managerial Effectiveness* (New York: McGraw-Hill, 1970). We use Hersey and Blanchard's model because it is better known.
8. Leonard M. Apcar, "Middle Managers and Supervisors Resist Moves to More Participatory Management," *The Wall Street Journal*, September 16, 1985, 25.
9. Jack Falvey, "Manager's Journal," *The Wall Street Journal*, December 6, 1982, 7.
10. Kenneth Blanchard and Spencer Johnson, *The One Minute Manager* (New York: William Morrow & Co., 1982), 44.
11. Warren Bennis, *The Unconscious Conspiracy: Why Leaders Can't Lead* (New York: AMACOM, 1976), 174.
12. Warren Bennis and Burt Nanus, "The Leading Edge," *Ideas* (publication of Ernst & Whinney), (Fall-Winter, 1985–86.)

SUGGESTIONS FOR FURTHER READING

Bennis, Warren, and Burt Nanus. *Leaders: The Strategies for Taking Charge.* New York: Harper & Row, 1985.

Blanchard, Kenneth, and Spencer Johnson. *The One Minute Manager.* New York: William Morrow & Co., 1982.

Hamlin, R., and J. Garrison. "Choosing Between Directive and Participative Management." *Supervisory Management* 31 (January 1986), 14–16.

Klein, J. H., and P. A. Posey. "Good Supervisors Are Good Supervisors –Anywhere." *Harvard Business Review* 44 (November-December 1986), 125–28.

Micolo, A. M. "Gaining Acceptance as a New Supervisor." *Supervisory Management* 30 (June 1985), 5–7.

COMPREHENSIVE CASE FOR PART III
KENNY'S LEADERSHIP—A FURTHER ANALYSIS

In Case 9–1, we presented Kenny, an effective leader. We now offer additional information derived from the comments of Kenny's old crew, his new crew (the former "Hell's Angels" group), the plant's production manager, and Kenny's boss, the plant's maintenance mananger.* It should be noted that both the production manager

*With the exception of minor editing, the comments are presented exactly as made to Donald C. Mosley.

and the maintenance manager are relatively new in their positions and are not part of the former "autocratic management systems." As you read these comments, review what you have learned in Chapters 6 through 9 and summarize the principles, points, and concepts from the text material that Kenny puts into practice as a leader.

Maintenance Manager, Kenny's Boss:

- He's very knowledgeable in the maintenance area.
- He has considerable self-confidence.
- He interacts with people in the plant more than other supervisors do and works well with people from other departments.
- He has the ability to motivate his crew and gets along well with them.
- He functions well as a leader in one-on-one situations and in conducting crew meetings. For example, in both cases he lets people know how they stand and provides them with feedback, and together they discuss ways of improving performance.
- He's better organized than most supervisors, and there's less confusion in his department than elsewhere in the company.

Production Manager:

- He doesn't give the production people any hassle. He doesn't give you a lot of questions about why production wants it done. Instead, he tells them what needs to be done—and why.
- He's a team player—and he wants to get the job done.
- He's good with people—a great leader—and his crew works well together.
- He's conscientious—he does his job, does it right, and wants others to do the same.
- He goes out into the plant with his people, and he's there with them when they need help and advice.
- His crew doesn't give planners and coordinators a lot of static about what they put into a memo.

Kenny's Old Crew:

- He's fair.
- He has a good attitude and a positive outlook.
- He's concerned about, and looks out for, the welfare of his people.
- He keeps crew problems within the crew and doesn't run to upper management with every little detail.
- He has a broad-based knowledge of our work; people feel confident about his decisions.
- He's a good intermediary between upper management and the crew. He gets points across without getting the crew upset.
- When things are tight, he doesn't mind helping his men with the actual work.
- He has a level personality—he doesn't show much emotion.
- He's very supportive of his crew.

Kenny's New Crew (the former "Hell's Angels"):

- He treats us fairly and equally.
- He takes up for the crew and his men.

He doesn't threaten you and doesn't come back after a bad job and nitpick and tell you what you did wrong. He takes a positive approach to solving problems.

He can be trusted.

He helps you with your personal problems.

He's competent at what he does and relates that competence to us.

He places his men real well. We're not all like oranges—some are like apples—but he places us where we can do our best.

He lets us work at our own pace—actually makes us want to work harder.

He never appears to get angry; he's always the same—cool, calm, and collected.

He's helpful on the job. He's there, but he's not there—doesn't hang over you, telling you what to do and how to do it. Instead, he wants results but lets us get them our own way.

He seems to enjoy work and being around us.

He listens to anything we have to say.

Answer the following questions:

1. How do you explain Kenny's acceptance by so many other people and the respect they have for him?
2. Can all supervisors operate the way Kenny does—and be effective? Explain your answer.
3. Given Kenny's effectiveness in his present job, would you recommend promoting him into high levels of management? Explain.
4. What concepts and practices of supervisory management have you learned from this case?

PART IV
MANAGING HUMAN RESOURCES

10
SELECTING AND
TRAINING EMPLOYEES

OBJECTIVES

After reading and studying the material in this chapter, you should be able to:

- Know and explain who is responsible for selecting, training, and appraising employees.
- Describe how to plan personnel needs and how to find employees for specific jobs.
- State the laws providing equal employment opportunity for protected groups of employees.
- Describe the steps in the employee selection procedure, including the proper orientation of new employees.
- Give five or six reasons why training is necessary.
- Name four methods used to train employees, and tell when these methods may be most effective.

IMPORTANT TERMS

job analysis
job specification
technological unemployment
upgrading
transferring
promoting
seniority
merit
job posting
affirmative-action programs (AAPs)
protected groups
IQ tests
proficiency and skill tests
aptitude tests
vocational interest tests

personality tests
achievement *or* proficiency test
work sampling *or* work preview
polygraph (lie detector)
structured interviews
unstructured interviews
preliminary interview
training needs survey
on-the-job training
apprenticeship training
internship training
vocational-technical education
   programs
vocational rehabilitation programs
private-industry councils (PICs)

CHAPTER OUTLINE
CASE 10–1. JOHN WOLF: THE BYPASSED EMPLOYEE

CASE 10–1
JOHN WOLF:
THE BYPASSED EMPLOYEE

The Ames Manufacturing Company was a medium-sized company that produced various pumps and gauges for vehicles such as automobiles, buses, and trucks. Human-resources needs of one department in the plant were usually filled by transfers from other departments within the company.

John Wolf came to the production department of the firm from a human-resources pool with the verbal recommendation of his former supervisor. Wolf served a mandatory three-month probationary period; his progress was reviewed at the end of that time. He was a borderline employee and a little slow in learning the work. This type of work and the absence of close supervision were completely new to him. But, by mutual consent, he was retained past the probationary period. Wolf was cautioned, however, to keep improving his performance.

Each year for three years, Wolf's progress was reviewed. While his work "improved somewhat," he was not up to the caliber of the rest of the work force. During this time, several new employees were added. They had been given tests on general knowledge, mechanical aptitude, and personality traits, and had been selected from among many applicants.

When a supervisor from another part of the department transferred out, Wolf called his department head. Wolf informed the department head that he felt he was capable of assuming the vacated position, that he was the most knowledgeable person in his group, and that he expected to receive the promotion. After advising Wolf that he would be considered along with other eligible people, the department head held a meeting to review those employees available to fill the opening. The department head then explained to Wolf that, while Wolf could get by in his own day-to-day work with occasional help on unusual problems, there were other employees—hired more recently—who were more capable of being advanced.

Wolf was bypassed. Management believed and told him that he was not ready to be promoted and might be better suited for work that was less mechanically involved and that had closer supervision.

We have discussed the functions of planning, organizing, and leading employees. Now we look at the process of staffing the organization. The case of John Wolf: The Bypassed Employee, illustrates some of the problems involved in selecting, training, and developing employees. It shows that potential employees for a given job can be obtained from inside or outside the firm. Also, there must be some form or forms of selection used to find capable people. Finally, the case points out the need to improve employees' performance through training and developing their abilities. These and other aspects of selecting and training employees will be covered in this chapter.

We feel that supervisors need to understand the "big picture" of the staffing process. Certainly not all supervisors are involved in the concepts presented in this chapter, such as human-resources planning, testing, checking references, or planning and conducting training activities. But if supervisors understand the big picture of staffing, they will be in a better position to perform this function in their own work setting. They need to understand their responsibility for selecting and training employees, how to plan for employee needs and find capable workers to satisfy those needs, and how to train them to be better workers.

RESPONSIBILITY FOR SELECTING AND TRAINING EMPLOYEES

A business can be successful only if it has the right kind and number of people to do the required work. Therefore, a primary duty of all supervisors is the proper selection, placement, training and development, and utilization of competent employees. How well—or poorly—they perform these functions is a major factor in their success or failure.

A Shared Responsibility

Like almost all aspects of supervision, selecting and training employees are shared responsibilities. In general, the responsibilities are divided as follows:

1. *Top management* sets human-resources objectives and does long-range planning and organizing.
2. *Middle managers* control the operating procedures needed to achieve these objectives and carry out personnel policies.
3. *Supervisors* interpret policies to employees and carry out higher management's wishes as to selecting and training employees. Also, they interpret and transmit workers' interests to higher management.

The Role of Supervisors

Operative employees usually have little contact with high-level managers. Therefore, they tend to think of their supervisor as being "the management" or "the organization." As a result, these employees interpret their supervisor's actions, attitudes, and methods as those of all managers. This is why supervisors are probably the most important people in achieving an organization's human-resources objectives. Supervisors usually have the final word in selecting employees. They supervise and control the employees' daily activities. Then they appraise the employees' performance, and this often becomes the basis for further rewards and promotions for employees.

In the Johnson Company, a large department store, sales positions are filled directly by the personnel office. When a selection decision is made, the sales department supervisor is notified and the new employee reports to the supervisor for assignment. Typically, the new employee first meets his or her supervisor on the first day of work. What are the pros and cons of this system?

PLANNING PERSONNEL NEEDS AND FINDING EMPLOYEES TO FILL THE JOBS

Most organizations can't afford the luxury of having more workers than they need. Yet neither can they afford to do without the needed number of employees. Therefore, the beginning of the staffing function is planning personnel needs. There are two aspects to this: (1) deciding what jobs need to be filled and what they involve, and (2) setting the personal characteristics needed by employees to handle these jobs successfully. The first aspect involves the preparation of a job description, while the second aspect calls for a job specification.

Types and Number of Employees Needed

In Chapter 5 we described a *job description* as a written statement covering the duties, authority, responsibilities, and working conditions of a particular job. The supervisor can obtain information about the job from experience in performing it, by observing other people perform it, or by having a personnel expert do a job analysis. **Job analysis** is the process of gathering information and determining the elements of a job by observation and study.

The job description also shows the relationship of that job to others. Thus it becomes the basis not only for selecting someone for the job, but also for further training of the worker and appraising his or her performance of the job. The first two main factors in Figure 10–1 are typically included in a job description.

The personal characteristics required of a person to perform a job as described are set forth in a **job specification**, which can be used to select the proper person for the job. Some of the categories of qualifications are education and training,

FIGURE 10–1   FACTORS INCLUDED IN A TYPICAL JOB DESCRIPTION
AND JOB SPECIFICATION

■ *Descriptive job data:* Job title, department, code, salary range, supervisor, etc.

■ *Job duties and working conditions:*

 a. Physical demands of the job and the minimum physical requirements needed to fill it.

 b. Working conditions, including psychological conditions such as relationships with others and responsibilities for other people, money, and equipment.

 c. A summary of the duties and responsibilities of the job.

 d. Days and hours of work.

 e. Machines, tools, formulas, and equipment used.

■ *Job specifications:*

 a. Educational background and knowledge, skills and techniques, and training and experience required to perform the job, as well as special training and development needed.

 b. Personal characteristics such as sociableness, articulateness, aggressiveness, etc.

aptitudes, temperament, interests, physical capabilities, experience, and attitudes. The job specification should provide a statement of the *minimum* acceptable standards the person should meet in order to perform the job satisfactorily. One major reason for this is to satisfy the Equal Employment Opportunity Commission (EEOC) and to be in compliance with its guidelines. The last main factor in Figure 10–1 pertains to a job specification.

Finally, the number of people to be selected to fill each of the job and skill categories must be estimated. This is done by determining the total number of workers needed and subtracting the number already employed; the difference is the number to be found and selected.

Once the number and type(s) of employees needed for given jobs have been determined, the next step is to decide where to seek them. There are only two basic sources: from within and from outside the organization. A balanced program of using people from both sources is better than using either source exclusively. A balanced policy of promoting from within and recruiting from outside when the need arises provides for both continuity and new ideas.

If the type of personal qualifications being sought has been decided, then the sources most likely to produce people with such qualifications must be consulted. Some of these sources are more costly in terms of time and money than others. While these factors should be taken into consideration, the choice of source should be based on which source provides the best results from the standpoint of employee performance.

Filling Jobs from Within

The *ultimate source* of all employees is some educational institution outside the firm. Yet there are many other specific outside sources, as you will soon see. Most managers try to fill jobs from within, if possible.

In Case 10–1, where did the production department obtain John Wolf? Why was he accepted in the production department?

REASONS FOR AND AGAINST USING INTERNAL SOURCES. The *advantages* of using internal sources include (1) lower cost, and (2) knowledge of the person's capabilities, strengths, and weaknesses. Promotion from within will probably provide continuity and also build the morale of all employees (except, perhaps, the bypassed individual who is jealous). The *disadvantages* of internal sources may be (1) the lack of anyone capable of filling a vacancy or willing to take it, (2) the possible inbreeding produced by excessive reliance on internal sources, and (3) the possible development of complacency among current employees.

How did the recruitment of John Wolf from within work out? Why was this source used?

METHODS OF OBTAINING EMPLOYEES FROM WITHIN. There are three methods of securing employees internally: (1) upgrading the employee currently holding the position, (2) transferring an employee from a similar position elsewhere in the organization, and (3) promoting an employee from a lower-level job.

Increasing skill requirements in various areas have led to **technological unemployment**, a situation in which employees can no longer perform their jobs because educational or skill demands have increased beyond their capacity. Such virtually vacant positions can be filled by **upgrading** present employees, that is, retraining unskilled or semiskilled workers in their present positions. This method was very effective during World War II. For this method to work effectively, employees must be willing to make the sacrifice of time and effort to take the training.

An organization that had always used conventional ledgers, journals, and office machines to keep its books decided to computerize its accounting processes. The woman who kept the books was not qualified to perform the new job, but she was not replaced. Instead, she was given a leave of absence to take courses at the local university to prepare herself to learn the new system. When the change was made, she successfully made the transition.[1]

Positions can also be filled by **transferring** employees from the same organizational level elsewhere in the organization. This is usually done when a person has greater capabilities than those required by the position held, or when the transfer provides for greater potential advancement. Essentially, a transfer involves a change in responsibilities and duties, either with or without a change in pay. In fact, transfers are often requested for other reasons.

Van Ludwig was the purchasing clerk at Tri-State Company. In this capacity he served other departments of the company, especially city sales. He was a good worker—rapid, efficient, and reliable. But even though his pay increased steadily during the five years in the position, he became dissatisfied with the working hours, which required him to remain at the office until 6:00 or 7:00 p.m.

When a position opened up at city sales, Van applied for it. But his transfer was rejected because he hadn't cleared it with his supervisor. Furthermore, he had done nothing to prepare himself for a sales career.

A few months later Van applied for the next opening in city sales. This time the city sales supervisor pointed out to Van his lack of experience and training in sales. This supervisor suggested that Van would have to accept a considerable reduction in pay, and it would take Van two years in city sales to reach the pay level he was currently receiving in purchasing. Finally, there was Van's worth to the company to be considered. In purchasing he was a trained, efficient clerk; in city sales he would be just a trainee.

Would you have accepted Van as a transferee if you had been the city sales supervisor?

Promoting is moving a person from a lower- to a higher-level job. Thus, a position is filled, but another one is vacated. The person who is promoted will need more skill and/or have more responsibility but may also gain more status, prestige, and money. There are three bases for promotion: (1) **seniority**, or the person's length of service; (2) **merit**, which refers to the employee's ability to perform the job better than others; and (3) a combination of the two. In theory, promotions based on merit are more desirable from a motivational standpoint because these encourage employees to produce more in order to demonstrate their merit. For lower-level jobs, however, particularly where unions are involved, seniority is usually the more common basis for promotion. But there is considerable virtue in using a combination of length of service (seniority), which provides a good understanding of the job and the company, and merit, or the mental and physical ability to do the job effectively.

In Case 10–1, which method of obtaining employees internally was used to get John Wolf? Were the employees who were advanced over him promoted on the basis of seniority or merit?

If a union represents the employees, the firm will probably be required to post available job openings on a bulletin board to give present employees a chance to bid on them. This procedure, called **job posting**, has also been found to be a good method of complying with equal employment opportunity laws if there are no evidences of discrimination. Many nonunion firms are using it to foster employee growth and to prevent unionization.

Filling Jobs from Outside

Even if a policy of hiring from within is used, outside sources must often be used as well. As individual positions are filled through upgrading, transferring, or promoting employees, the vacated positions must be filled externally. Some of the specific external sources of new employees are

1. Former employees.
2. Friends and relatives of employees.
3. Personal applications received in person or through the mail.
4. Competing firms.
5. Labor organizations.
6. Employment agencies, either public or private.
7. Educational institutions, including high schools, business schools, vocational-technical schools, junior colleges, colleges, and manufacturers' training schools.
8. Retired military personnel, minority agencies, churches, job fairs, professional associations, and others.

REASONS FOR USING EXTERNAL SOURCES. A growing organization must go outside to obtain employees for at least its lowest-level job. But there are also reasons for going outside for high-level personnel, many of which are associated with problems caused by computers and automation. New skills that are needed in a hurry must often be found in people from outside the organization who have the required education, training, and experience. Moreover, even when an internal promotion policy is followed, mistakes are inevitably made. It is almost impossible to anticipate the skills that will be needed in the future and to hire someone with those skills who will join the firm at an entry-level position, and then to expect that person to progress all the way through the organization.

METHODS OF RECRUITING FROM OUTSIDE. Some of the methods used to recruit new employees include

1. Scouting at schools or colleges.
2. Advertising through newpapers, trade journals, radio, billboards, and window displays.
3. Using the services of private and public employment agencies.
4. Acting on employee referrals.

The choice of the proper method to use is not an easy one, but it can be very important, as the following example shows.

A store manager put a "Help Wanted" sign in the window. She found this practice time-consuming because many unqualified applicants inquired about the job. Furthermore, when she rejected an applicant, she stood the risk of losing the applicant as a customer, and possibly that person's family and friends as well. The manager found that newspaper advertising also reached large groups of job seekers but brought in many unqualified people. If the store's telephone number was given in the ad, calls tied up the line and customers couldn't reach the store.[2]

COMPLYING WITH EQUAL EMPLOYMENT OPPORTUNITY LAWS

All aspects of selecting and appraising employees are affected by laws and regulations. Some of these laws and their effects on recruiting and selection are now explained.

Equal Employment Opportunity (EEO) Laws

The Civil Rights Act of 1964, as amended by the Equal Employment Opportunity Act of 1972, prohibits discrimination based on race, color, religion, sex, or national origin in all employment practices. There are also laws protecting the handicapped, older workers, and Vietnam veterans. Table 10–1 shows who is covered by these laws and regulations. It also shows their basic requirements and the agencies that enforce them.

TABLE 10-1   EQUAL EMPLOYMENT OPPORTUNITY (EEO) LAWS

Laws	Coverage	Basic Requirements	Agencies Involved
Title VII of Civil Rights Act, as amended by Equal Employment Opportunity Act and others	Employers with 15 or more employees, engaged in interstate commerce; federal service workers and state and local government workers	Prohibits employment decisions based on race, color, religion, sex, or national origin	Equal Employment Opportunity Commission (EEOC)
Executive Order 11246 as amended by Executive Order 11375 and others	Employers with federal contracts and subcontracts	Requires contractors to develop affirmative action programs (AAPs), including setting goals and timetables, to recruit, select, train, utilize, and promote minorities and women	Office of Federal Contract Compliance Programs (OFCCP) in the U.S. Labor Department
Age Discrimination in Employment Act, as amended	Employers with 20 or more employees	Prohibits employment discrimination against employees aged 40 and above, including mandatory retirement	EEOC

(continued)

Enforcement of EEO Laws

The Equal Employment Opportunity Commission (EEOC) is the primary agency that enforces the EEO laws. It receives and investigates charges of discrimination, issues orders to stop violations, and may even go to a U.S. District Court. The Commission encourages **affirmative action programs (AAPs)** to put the principle of equal employment opportunity into practice. These programs are required by the Office of Federal Contract Compliance Programs (OFCCP) in the Labor Department, which enforces Executive Order 11246, by the Vocational Rehabilitation Act, and by the Veterans Readjustment Act.

TABLE 10–1   (continued)

Laws	Coverage	Basic Requirements	Agencies Involved
Vocational Rehabilitation Act	Employers with federal contracts or subcontracts	Prohibits discrimination and requires contractor to develop AAPs to recruit and employ handicapped persons	OFCCP
Vietnam Era Veterans Readjustment Act	Employers with federal contracts or subcontracts	Requires contractors to develop AAPs to recruit and employ Vietnam-era veterans and to list job openings with state employment services, for priority in referrals	OFCCP

Source: Leon C. Megginson, *Personnel Management: A Human Resources Approach*, 5th ed. (Homewood, IL: Richard D. Irwin, 1985), 97. Extracted from BNA's Policy and Practice Series, Fair Employment Practices (Washington, D.C.: The Bureau of National Affairs, Inc.).

In essence, AAPs promise to do the following:

1. Make good-faith efforts to recruit the **protected groups** (the groups mentioned under "Basic Requirements" in Table 10–1) through state employment services.
2. Limit the questions that are asked of applicants during interviews (see Table 10–2).
3. Set goals and timetables for hiring the protected groups.
4. Avoid testing applicants unless the test meets established guidelines.

TABLE 10–2   GUIDELINES ON LAWFUL OR UNLAWFUL QUESTIONS TO ASK OF JOB APPLICANTS

Subject of Inquiry:	It Is Not Discriminatory to Inquire About:	It May Be Discriminatory to Inquire About:
1. Name	Whether applicant has worked under a different name	a. The original name of an applicant whose name has been legally changed b. The ethnic association of applicant's name

TABLE 10–2 (continued)

Subject of Inquiry:	It Is Not Discriminatory to Inquire About:	It May Be Discriminatory to Inquire About:
2. Birthplace and residence	Applicant's place of residence, length of applicant's residence in the state and/or city where employer is located	a. Applicant's birthplace b. Birthplace of applicant's parents c. Birth certificate, naturalization or baptismal certificate
3. Race or color	General distinguishing characteristics such as scars, etc.	a. Applicant's race or color of skin
4. National origin or ancestry		a. Applicant's lineage, ancestry, national origin, descendants, parentage, or nationality b. Nationality of applicant's parents or spouse
5. Sex and family composition		a. Applicant's sex b. Applicant's dependents c. Marital status
6. Creed or religion		a. Applicant's religious affiliation b. Church, parish, or religious holidays observed
7. Citizenship	Whether the applicant is in the country on a visa which permits him or her to work, or is a citizen	a. Whether applicant is a citizen of a country other than the United States
8. Language	Language applicant speaks and/or writes fluently	a. Applicant's native tongue, language commonly used by applicant at home
9. References	Names of persons willing to provide professional and/or character references for applicant	a. Name of applicant's pastor or religious leader
10. Relatives	Names of relatives already employed by the organization Name and address of person or relative to be notified in an emergency	a. Name and/or address of any relative of applicant

TABLE 10–2 (continued)

Subject of Inquiry:	It Is Not Discriminatory to Inquire About:	It May Be Discriminatory to Inquire About:
11. Organizations	Applicant's membership in any union, professional service, or trade organizations	a. All clubs, social fraternities, societies, lodges, or organizations to which the applicant belongs where the name or character of organization indicates the race, creed, color, or religion, national origin, sex, or ancestry of its members
12. Arrest record and convictions		a. Number and kinds of arrests and convictions unless related to job performance
13. Photographs		a. Photographs with application or before hiring b. Résumé with photo of applicant
14. Height and weight		a. Any inquiry into height and weight of applicant, except where it is a bona fide occupational requirement
15. Physical limitations	Whether applicant has the ability to perform job-related functions	a. Whether applicant is handicapped, or the nature or severity of a handicap
16. Education	Training an applicant has received if related to the job applied for	a. Educational attainment of an applicant unless there is validation that having certain educational backgrounds (i.e., high-school diploma or college degree) is necessary to perform the functions of the job or position applied for
17. Financial status		a. An applicant's debts or assets b. Garnishments

Source: Used with permission of Omaha, Nebraska, Human Relations Department.

SELECTING EMPLOYEES FOR SPECIFIC JOBS

A suggested procedure for selecting employees is shown in Figure 10–2. But conditions may cause individual companies to modify this procedure—or depart from it when desirable. In this section, each of the steps listed in Figure 10–2 is explained briefly.

Requisition

Notice that selection really begins with a requisition from the supervisor to the personnel department. This requisition (see Figure 10–3), which is based on the

FIGURE 10–2   FLOWCHART OF A SUGGESTED SELECTION PROCEDURE

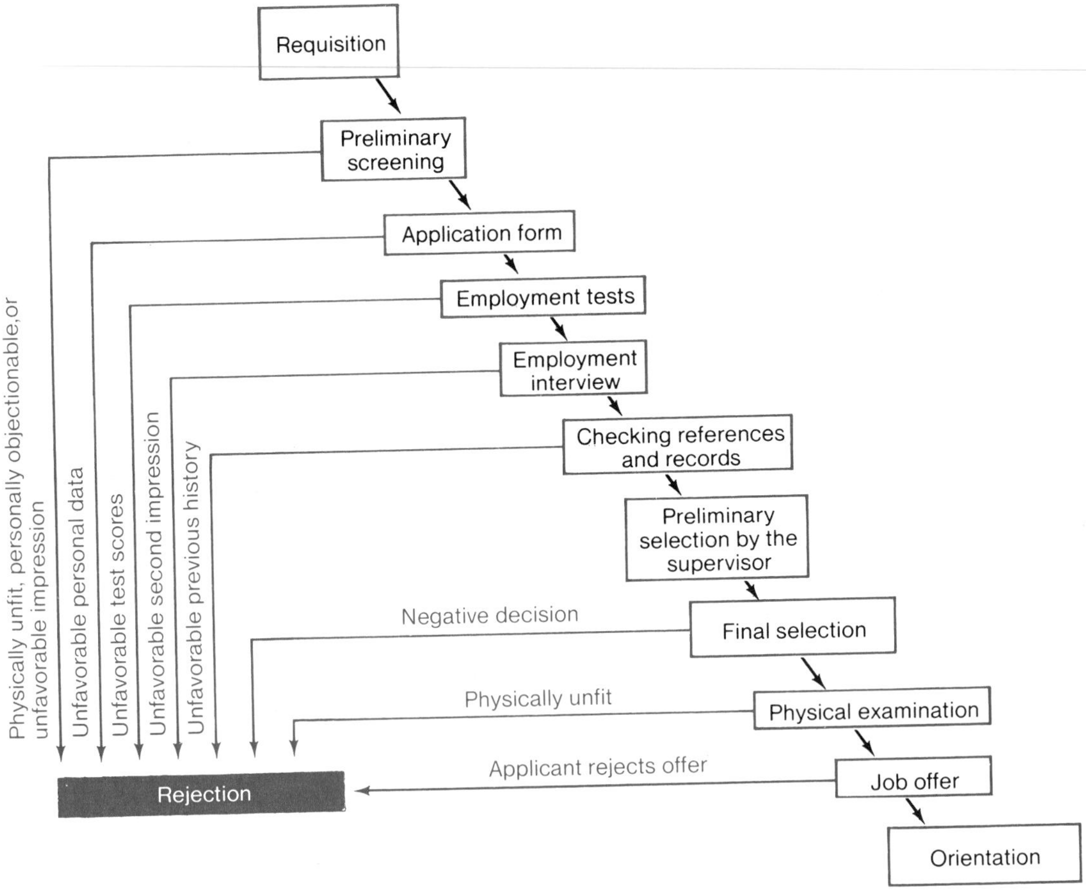

Source: Based on Leon C. Megginson, *Personnel Management: A Human Resources Approach,* 5th ed. (Homewood, IL: Richard D. Irwin, 1985), pp. 195 and 203. © 1985 by Richard D. Irwin, Inc.

FIGURE 10–3 SAMPLE PERSONNEL REQUISITION

PERSONNEL REQUISITION

Job Title: ___Warehouse worker___   Job Code Number: ___7-103___

Number of employees needed _____2_____   Date needed ___16 July 198-___

    Full-time ☐   Part-time ☐   Temporary ☑
                                                  approx. 2 weeks
Whom to report to: ___Norma Mills, Supervisor___

Where to report: ___#1 warehouse, main office___

Time to report: ___8 AM___

Requesting supervisor: ___Norma Mills___   Date ___5 July 198-___

(For use by Personnel Department)

	Applicant's Name	Soc. Sec. No.	Date Available	Hire?
1.	Mike A. Johnson	344-62-9307	16 July	
2.	Carmen Carreon	433-54-3470	16 July	OK
3.	William S. Lloyd	460-65-0719	16 July	OK
4.	Laura Y. McGhee	478-60-3181	16 July	
5.				

previously prepared job description and specifications, is the authorization the personnel department needs to recruit applicants for the position(s) available. In many small and medium-sized firms, the supervisor makes an informal visit or phone call to the personnel officer or senior officer who is authorized to make the final job offer.

A reminder is needed at this point. If you as a supervisor are involved in selecting job applicants, your procedure must conform to EEO guidelines. You should also conform to your affirmative-action program of hiring people from various groups. The personnel officer, in particular, should be certain that the selection procedure conforms to national and local laws and customs. Since laws and administrative interpretations in the area of employee selection are constantly changing, you should keep current on the present status of those regulations that apply to you and your business.

Preliminary Screening

Whether formal or informal, some form of preliminary screening usually helps weed out the obvious misfits, saving their time and yours. This step deals with such factors as educational background, training, experience, physical appearance, grooming, and speech—if these are relevant to job performance.

The tough new Immigration Reform and Control Act of 1986 is causing employers many headaches. From 1952 to 1987, federal law allowed employers to hire illegal aliens (or illegal immigrants) with impunity—even though the workers themselves were subject to deportation if caught. Since June 1, 1987, employers have been required to validate all newly hired employees' citizenship documents. The new law is intended to remove the possibility of employers hiring illegal aliens. Now employers are subject to a fine if they hire such workers.

Although enforcement of the new law relies largely on self-policing by employers, anyone wanting a job in this country must show proof of citizenship or legal residency or attest to their plans to file for legal residency. Thus, the new law places an enormous responsibility on employers to do the arduous documentation process required. They must complete a new form—the I-9 form—for each new hire, showing what evidence was used (whether a passport, a certificate of U.S. naturalization, or a resident alien card with photograph). An employer must sign a statement that he or she believes—under penalty of perjury—that each worker's documents are genuine.[3]

Application Form

The job applicant completes an application form after passing the preliminary screening. (Some applications are received by mail or in person before that time.) The applicant lists employers for whom he or she has worked, titles of jobs held, and the length of employment with each company. Background, education, military status, and other useful data are listed. The form should be carefully designed to provide information that you need about the applicant's potential performance, but it should not be a hodgepodge of irrelevant data. The completion of the form in longhand will provide you with a sample of the applicant's neatness, thoroughness, and ability to answer questions. Since many states have restrictions concerning the kinds of questions that may be included on an application form, you should check any laws that your state may have on such practices.

Employment Tests

By means of various employment tests, you can determine such factors as intelligence quotient (IQ), skills, aptitudes, vocational interests, personality, and performance.

TYPES OF TESTS. IQ tests are designed to measure the applicant's capacity to learn and solve problems and to understand relationships. They are particularly useful in selecting employees for supervisory and managerial positions.

Proficiency and skill tests are tests of ability to perform a particular trade, craft, or skill, and are useful in selecting operative employees. **Aptitude tests** are used to predict how a person might perform on a given job and are most useful for operative jobs. **Vocational interest tests** are designed to determine the applicant's areas of major interest as far as work is concerned. Interest does not guarantee competence, but it can result in the employee's working and trying harder. **Personality tests** are supposed to measure the applicant's emotional adjustment and attitudes. These tests are often used to evaluate interpersonal relationships and to see how the person might fit into your organization.

Probably the most effective test the supervisor can use in selecting operative employees is an **achievement** or **proficiency test**. This test measures fairly accurately the applicant's knowledge of and ability to do a given job. It is also used to spot "trade bluffers"—people who claim job knowledge, skills, and experience they don't really have. **Work sampling** or **work preview** is one form of such a test. It consists of having the prospective employee do a task that is representative of the work usually done on the job. In addition to showing whether the person can actually do the job, it also gives her or him a more realistic expectation of the job.

VALIDITY OF TESTS. If tests are used in making the selection decision, they must be valid. That is, there must be a high positive correlation between the applicant's test scores and some identifiable, objective measures of performance on the job. Furthermore, the tests must be designed, administered, and interpreted by a professional (usually a licensed psychologist); be culturally unbiased so that they don't discriminate against any ethnic group; and be in complete conformity with EEOC guidelines.[4] This will help assure that the tests are reliable in that the results will be the same if given to the same person by two or more individuals. Care should be exercised in interpreting tests, as some persons are adept at faking answers. Because of these and other problems, many firms are now dropping tests in favor of other selection techniques.

USE OF THE POLYGRAPH. The **polygraph (lie detector)** is now used extensively to meet the surge of employee thefts (see Figure 10–4). It can be used for this purpose on three occasions: (1) during the preemployment security clearance exam, (2) when there is a specific loss, and (3) when a periodic spot check is made. To be legal, however, the lie detector test must be given greatest use in culling out potentially bad employee risks before they get in.[5] Because the polygraph hasn't been proven beyond a shadow of a doubt to be reliable, many states either prohibit it or control its use.

Employment Interview

In preparing for the employment interview, which is the only two-way part of the selection procedure, you should use the information in the application form and the test "scores" to learn about the applicant. A list of questions prepared

FIGURE 10-4   USING THE LIE DETECTOR

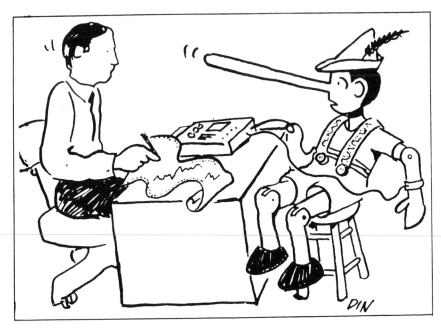

Source: *Baton Rouge Sunday Advocate*, DIN.

beforehand can help you avoid missing significant information with which to judge the applicant. Compare your list of questions with the job specification to see that you are matching the individual's personal qualifications with the job requirements. Some specific questions might be

1. What did you do on your last job?
2. How did you do it?
3. Why did you do it?
4. What job did you like best? Least?
5. Why did you leave?
6. What are your strong and weak points?
7. Why do you want to work for us?

If you are observant and perceptive during the interview, you can obtain some impressions about the candidate's abilities, personality, appearance, speech, and attitudes toward work. You should also provide information about the company and the job. Remember, the applicant needs facts to decide whether to accept or reject the job, just as you need information to decide whether or not to offer the job.

The interview may be done individually by the supervisor or in cooperation with someone else—the personnel officer or some other senior manager. Also, it may be structured or unstructured, directive or nondirective. **Structured inter-**

views are standardized and controlled with regard to questions asked, sequence of questions, interpretation of replies, and weight given to factors considered in making the value judgment as to whether or not to hire the person. In **unstructured interviews**, the pattern of questions asked, the conditions under which they are asked, and the bases for evaluating results are not standardized.

The interview may occur in one or two stages. Some firms have a **preliminary interview**, during which the application form is completed and general observations of the applicant are made by someone in the personnel office. A more penetrating, in-depth interview may be held later to probe the applicant's attitudes, belief system, and willingness and desire to work. The method used will depend on the time available and the importance of the position to be filled.

Checking References and Records

The importance of carefully checking applicants' references cannot be overemphasized. Reference checks provide answers to questions concerning a candidate's performance on previous jobs. They are helpful in verifying information on the application form and statements made during interviews. They are also useful in checking on possible omissions of information and in clarifying specific points. Three sources of references are (1) personal, such as friends, religious leaders, banker, and so forth; (2) academic, such as former teachers and principals; and (3) former employers. The last source is the most useful in predicting future job performance.

Reference checks made in person or by telephone are preferred to written ones. Past employers are sometimes reluctant to write uncomplimentary letters of reference. Be sure to ask specific questions about the candidate's performance. The type of information you are allowed to seek is restricted by laws such as the Fair Credit Reporting Act and the Privacy Act. But you can check on dates and terms of employment, salary, whether termination was voluntary, and whether this employer would reemploy the candidate.

Preliminary Selection by the Supervisor

By this time, you—the supervisor—have narrowed the number of potential employees to one or a very few. If there is only one, the applicant can be hired on a trial basis. If more than one are qualified, a review of the information collected should reveal who is the best choice. This person should be hired, but those not hired should be made aware of any possible future openings. This preliminary selection may be subject to approval by the personnel department or some higher authority.

Final Selection

Personnel officers are usually brought in on the final hiring decision because of their expertise. They ensure that all laws and regulations, as well as company policies, are adhered to. Also, they have a voice in such questions as salary and employee benefits to be offered to the applicant.

Physical Examination

The applicant's health and physical condition should be matched to the physical requirements of the job. Therefore, for some jobs it is wise to have each job candidate examined by a physician before being hired. The examination should reveal any physical limitations that would limit job performance. Also, it will help you comply with your state's workers' compensation laws by providing a record of the employee's health at the time of hiring. Furthermore, compensation claims for an injury that occurred prior to employment with you can be avoided. The physical examination is usually one of the last steps, as it is ordinarily the most expensive one.

Job Offer

The job offer to applicants for nonmanagerial and nonprofessional positions is usually made by the personnel office. It is often in writing and contains the terms and conditions of employment. At this point, the offer is either accepted or rejected. If it is rejected, the selection procedure starts all over again.

Orientation

The first day on the new job is frustrating to anyone. Therefore, a new employee should be carefully introduced to the job. A job description should be given to him or her and explained in detail. Proper instructions, training, and observation will help start the employee off on the right foot. A tour of the facilities and a look at the firm's product or service should help the new employee understand where he or she fits into the scheme of things.

The new employee needs to know the firm's objectives, policies, rules, and performance expectations. Frequent discussions should be held with him or her during the orientation program to answer questions and to assure proper progress.

A formal interview with the new employee may be appropriate at some point during the first week. Other interviews can be held during the probationary period, which is usually from three to six months. The purposes of these interviews should be to correct any mistaken ideas that the employee may have about the job, and to determine whether he or she feels that you and your people are fulfilling your commitments.

During the probationary period, you should compare the new employee's performance with your expectations. You may also start to point out any shortcomings, as well as strong points. Another formal meeting should be held at the end of the probationary period. This is the time to decide whether or not to keep the person as a permanent employee. If your decision is positive, point out the employee's strong and weak points. Encourage her or him to keep improving. If your decision is negative, make the parting as pleasant and graceful as possible.

Did you notice that this formal meeting was held with John Wolf in Case 10-1? But the outcome was not too pleasant.

TRAINING AND DEVELOPING EMPLOYEES

One of the most basic responsibilities of supervisors is training and developing employees. Not only must new workers be trained in the details of the new job, but also current employees must be retrained and their skills updated to meet rapidly changing environments and job requirements.

> *For example, Reynolds Metals has a program of continuous employee training, including home study to keep employees apprised of current developments. For example, nearly all its headquarters' supervisory staff receive training in the firm's EEO policies.*[6]

Why train employees? Training should result in (1) reduced employee turnover, (2) high job satisfaction, (3) increased productivity, (4) increased earnings for the employee—and the employer, (5) less supervision required as the employee becomes more self-reliant, and (6) decreased costs for materials, supplies, and equipment due to errors.

> *For example, Bill Saul, chairman of Remmele Engineering, Inc., an automation-equipment manufacturer, states that it is profitable to hire and train employees. The Minneapolis, Minnesota employer says: "Every time we bring in a new, well-trained employee, he can . . . bring in $90,000 in new sales. [At that rate,] it doesn't take long to recoup training costs."*[7]

How to Determine Training Needs

A major problem with training is identifying *who* needs *how much* or *what type* of training. There are many ways to identify training needs. Some of the more practical ways are (1) supervisor's recommendations, (2) analysis of job requirements, (3) analysis of job performance, and (4) employee suggestions. A **training needs survey** may be conducted by asking supervisors to state their needs on a prepared form or by using interviews.

How to Train Employees

Once you know the employees' training needs, how do you train them? There are many ways a supervisor can train employees, including (1) on-the-job training (OJT), (2) apprenticeship training, (3) internship training, and (4) outside training.

ON-THE-JOB TRAINING (OJT). **On-the-job training** is the most widely used way to train and develop employees because it involves the employees in actually performing the work under the supervision and guidance of the supervisor or a trained worker or instructor. Thus, while learning to do the job, a person is also a regular employee producing the good or service that the business sells. This form of training always occurs, whether it is consciously planned or not. While the methods used vary with the one doing the training, in general, OJT involves

1. Telling the worker what is to be done.
2. Telling him or her how to do the job.
3. Showing how it is to be done.
4. Letting the worker do the job under the trainer's guidance.
5. Telling—and showing—the learner what he or she did right, what he or she did wrong, and how to correct the wrong activity.
6. Repeating the procedure until the learner has mastered the job.

As with other aspects of supervision, there are many advantages and disadvantages of OJT. What are some of these? The main *advantages* are that production is carried while the employee is training and that OJT results in low out-of-pocket costs. Also, no transition from classroom learning to actual production is required.

On the other hand, OJT has the *disadvantages* of the poor learning environment provided by the production area and the excessive waste caused by lack of skill and/or mistakes. While supervisors handle most OJT, they are not necessarily the best ones to do it. Their primary emphasis is on performing the operating tasks of the job, and they are only secondarily concerned with training. For this reason, if possible, another capable employee—or even an outside trainer—should be assigned this responsibility. Also, there should be a definite follow-up procedure to evaluate the results of the training and to serve as a basis for improving future development.

APPRENTICESHIP TRAINING. **Apprenticeship training** blends the learning of theory with practice in the techniques of the job. If job proficiency can be developed only over a long period of classroom instruction and actual learning experiences on the job, this training method should be used. It usually lasts from two to seven years of both classroom learning and on-the-job training.

For example, Remmele Engineering (see previous example) has its own 6,000-square-foot training center where up to 20 "students" spend up to a year in classroom training and working on relatively simple jobs.

INTERNSHIP TRAINING. Combining on-the-job training at a cooperating business with education at a school or college, **internship training** is generally used for students who are prospective employees for marketing or clerical positions or who are being prepared for management positions. But this method can be used for higher-level positions, too. For example, the Georgia Institute of Technology's co-op program prepares students for engineering positions and also provides income to help them meet the cost of their education. Internship training gives students a chance to see if they would like to go to work for the company, and it gives management a chance to evaluate the student as a prospective full-time employee.

OTHER TYPES OF TRAINING. Some job activities are so technical or specialized that they cannot be taught effectively on an informal basis by the supervisor. Instead, learners are sent to some outside source, such as a school, college, or equipment manufacturer, to learn the job. Drafting, computer programming, and income tax accounting are some jobs of this nature.

Outside Assistance Available for Training

Where can you go for help in training employees? There are many outside programs available to help with training. For example, the National Apprenticeship Act of 1937, administered by the Bureau of Apprenticeship and Training in the Labor Department, sets policies and standards for apprenticeship programs. Also, all states have some form of **vocational-technical education programs** whereby vocational-technical schools, business schools, and junior colleges conduct regular or special training classes. Through such programs, potential employees can become qualified for skilled jobs such as machinist, lathe operator, computer service technician, and legal assistant.

Other training activities for new employees are the **vocational rehabilitation programs** sponsored by the U.S. Department of Health and Human Services (HHS) in cooperation with state governments. These programs provide counseling, medical care, and vocational training for physically and mentally handicapped individuals.

Many outside consultants are now available to help train and develop employees and managers. See the Comprehensive Case for Part VI for an example of how these consultants function.

A new program, the Job Training Partnership Act (JTPA), underwrites the most important public training programs currently being used to help employers with training activities. They are developed and effectively controlled by **private-industry councils (PICs)** and funded by block grants to the states. The PICs are headed by company executives and local business people, who probably know more than anyone else about what is needed to train people in the skills used in their areas. The funds provided must go for training, including on-the-job training, and none of these funds can be used for stipends or wage supplements. In addition to getting cash reimbursement for hiring and training through PICs, firms can also get an investment tax credit to offset the cost of hiring eligible workers.

One of the first employers to use JTPA was Hilti, Inc., a Tulsa, Oklahoma maker of fastening systems used in the construction industry. It received some $80,000 in federal assistance, through the Tulsa-area Private Industry

Training Council, to help offset the $434,000 cost of retraining 50 employees in new skills. After six months of training, the workers became machine-tool operators; were used in heat treating, plating, and inspection; and held various support positions.[8]

This does not complete the staffing function. In the next chapter, we will explain how to evaluate employees' performance and compensate them for that performance.

CHAPTER REVIEW

The chapter has presented some thoughts on selecting, training, and developing new employees. Subjects covered include responsibility for selecting and developing employees, planning personnel needs, finding capable employees to fill jobs from inside and outside the firm, complying with equal employment opportunity laws, selecting employees for specific jobs, orienting new employees, and improving performance through training and development.

In general, the personnel department is responsible for personnel planning, recruiting, and handling the details of staffing. Supervisors have to requisition needed workers, interview applicants, make the preliminary selection, orient new workers, and train new and current employees. In planning personnel needs, job specifications are prepared showing the duties of the job, authority, responsibilities, and working conditions, along with the personal characteristics required of a person to do the job.

Employees are obtained from within by upgrading present employees or by transferring or promoting people from other units, using job posting if feasible. Workers are recruited from outside by using such sources as former employees, friends and relatives of present workers, personal applications, competing firms, labor organizations, public or private employment agencies, and educational institutions.

Minorities, women, older workers, the handicapped, and Vietnam veterans are protected by various laws and regulations. The Equal Employment Opportunity Commission is the primary agency that enforces these laws.

The procedure for selecting employees for specific jobs includes (1) a requisition from the supervisor, (2) preliminary screening out of obvious misfits, (3) the applicant's completion of an application form, (4) employment testing, (5) various interviews by the supervisor and personnel officer, (6) checking of references, (7) a preliminary selection made by the supervisor, (8) the final decision to hire, usually made by some higher official, (9) a physical exam, and (10) a job offer. If the offer is accepted, the new employee proceeds to (11) job orientation by the supervisor.

One of the most basic responsibilities of supervisors is training and developing employees—both new and currently employed—as such training has many benefits for both employees and employer. Training methods include on-the-job training, apprenticeship training, internship training, and training given by outside institutions.

Assistance in training is available from many sources, especially state and federal government agencies. Apprenticeship programs are covered by the National Apprenticeship Act of 1937, while the recent Job Training Partnership Act (JTPA) underwrites local training efforts developed by private-industry councils. The federal government also works with states to provide vocational rehabilitation programs for the handicapped, and most states offer some form of vocational-technical education programs to train workers for skilled occupations.

QUESTIONS FOR REVIEW AND DISCUSSION

1. What are some of the advantages and disadvantages of filling jobs from within the firm?
2. How do you distinguish among upgrading, transferring, and promoting employees?
3. What specific outside sources can be used for finding new employees?
4. How do EEO laws affect recruiting and selecting employees?
5. Name and explain the steps in the suggested procedure for selecting workers for specific jobs.
6. How would you prepare for and conduct an effective interview with an applicant?
7. What are some sources of references that may be used in investigating applicants' backgrounds?
8. Why should a physical examination be required of an applicant?
9. How should new people be introduced to their jobs?
10. Discuss the need for training and development for (a) new employees and (b) current employees.
11. Describe several types of training and tell what sort of jobs they are best suited for.
12. What is the responsibility of supervisors for training their employees?
13. How can training needs be determined?
14. How can the effectiveness of training be evaluated?

LEARNING EXERCISE 10–1
LOUIS KEMP: THE RECALCITRANT EMPLOYEE

Alan Strong, the supervisor of a small state employment office in north Louisiana, had to fill a vacancy for an interviewer. He had engaged in extensive recruiting efforts and spent considerable time trying to find a capable person. Finally, the state personnel officer strongly recommended a young man named Louis Kemp, whom he had interviewed at the home office. After an interview with Kemp, Strong hired him to interview clients coming into the office.

Kemp had a B.A. in social science and was 29 years old. His experience during the four years since he graduated had been on jobs that required little or no responsibility. Recently he had worked for two years as a rodman on a seismograph crew. For two seasons before his employment with the seismograph company, he had been employed as a ticket-clerk helper at a cotton gin.

Strong supervised only five subordinates. After Kemp was employed, Strong explained the job to him for "a few hours"; then Kemp was on his own. Later, he was very reluctant to talk to Strong or the other employees about the operations of the office or any other subject. Upon the completion of his probationary training period, the quality and quantity of Kemp's work failed to meet the standards set by Strong. Strong discussed the problem with Kemp and attempted to offer additional assistance in solving his problem.

Strong knew that Kemp needed further training. Because of Kemp's lack of knowledge of the activities of his new employment, it would take him a little longer to meet the expected job standards. Therefore, a program of on-the-job training and development was designed with these factors in mind. After three or four months, however, Strong decided this was not the answer. Kemp continued to insist that he liked his work and would give no reason for not meeting the expected job goals. Strong requested the aid of his district supervisor and of the staff personnel at the state office. After they interviewed Kemp, they held a joint conference with Strong. It was decided that an entirely new approach would be taken with the recalcitrant employee: Kemp would be given free rein and responsibility on the job, and Strong would follow up on the results after a period of several months. The results showed no improvement!

Answer the following questions:

1. What do you see as the main problem?
2. What probably caused the problem?
3. What would you do with Kemp now?
4. How would you deal with him?

LEARNING EXERCISE 10–2
NEW-JOB BLUES

After over 20 years as a full-time wife and mother, Elaine had taken her first job outside the home. She was well qualified for the job, having taken an accounting course at a business school and passed with flying colors. Still, on her first day of work, confronted by unfamiliar office equipment and 20 strangers whose preoccupation with their own work made them seem unfriendly and unhelpful, she was feeling shaken and discouraged and would have liked to turn around and go home.

Answer the following questions:

1. What would you do if you were Elaine's supervisor?
2. Assume that you had an employment interview with Elaine for 30 minutes and had indicated to the personnel officer that she was your first choice for the position. Personnel has notified you that she has been offered the position and that she has accepted it, and that today will be her first day on the job. Assume that she has just walked into your office to begin her first day. Role-play your initial meeting with Elaine now that she is a member of your department.

ENDNOTES

1. Adapted from Leon C. Megginson, *Personnel Management: A Human Resources Approach*, 5th ed. (Homewood, IL: Richard D. Irwin, 1985), p. 435.
2. Curtis E. Tate, Jr., Leon C. Megginson, Charles R. Scott, Jr., and Lyle R. Trueblood, *Successful Small Business Management*, 3d ed. (Plano, TX: Business Publications, 1982), p. 183.
3. For further details, see "Labor Letter," *The Wall Street Journal*, April 28, 1987, p. 1; and Dianna Solis, "Immigration Cops: New Law Puts Task of Enforcement on Employers," *The Wall Street Journal*, May 7, 1987, p. 33.
4. For these guidelines, see "Adoption by Four Agencies of Uniform Guidelines on Employee Selection Procedures (1978)," *Federal Register* 43 (August 1978): 38290–38315.
5. See Victor Lipman, "New Hiring Tool: Truth Tests," *Parade Magazine*, October 7, 1979, pp. 14ff.
6. "Chief Executives Report on How Training and Development Pay Off in Their Organizations," *Training/HRD* 16 (October 1979): 81ff.
7. "In Search of Survival," *Inc.*, November, 1985, p. 90.
8. Frank Leslie, "Hilti First to Participate in Retraining Program," *Tulsa World*, April 3, 1983, pp. G-1 and G-4.

SUGGESTIONS FOR FURTHER READING

Borinstein, D. I. "Sparking Self-Esteem." *Management World* 12 (April 1983): 36–37.

Brother, Joyce. "How to Get the Job You Want." *Parade Magazine*, November 16, 1986, pp. 4–6.

Fader, Shirley Sloan. "When You Are Doing the Hiring." *Working Woman*, February, 1985, pp. 48–50.

Glicken, M. D. "A Counseling Approach to Employee Burnout." *Personnel Journal* 62 (March 1983): 222–25.

Kahn, Joseph P., and Susan Buchsbaum. "The Training Imperative." *Inc.*, March, 1986, pp. 119–22.

Mitchell, Constance. "Vocational Schools Ready for New Jobs." *USA Today*, August 24, 1984, p. 3B.

Pres, Aric, and Tessa Namuth. "First the Lie Detector and Then the Chemicals." *Newsweek*, January 27, 1986, p. 57.

Tracy, Eleanor J. "Heading for the Big Time in the Part-Time Game." *Fortune*, April 29, 1986, p. 112.

11
APPRAISING AND COMPENSATING EMPLOYEES

OBJECTIVES

After reading and studying the material in this chapter, you should be able to:

- Explain what employee performance appraisal is and how it operates.
- Describe some methods of appraising employee performance.
- Discuss why compensation is important to both employees and employers.
- Explain how employee wages are determined.
- Debate the pros and cons of the comparable-worth concept of wages.
- Discuss how job evaluation is involved in compensating workers.
- Name three possible effects of evaluation on employee morale.
- State two reasons why performance appraisals are usually difficult to carry out during the interview.

IMPORTANT TERMS

performance appraisal *or* merit rating *or* efficiency rating *or* service rating *or* employee evaluation
peer rating *or* mutual rating system
rating scale
employee-comparison method
paired-comparison technique
appraisal interview
wage surveys
single rate
rate range
time wages *or* day work
incentive wages

exempt employees
nonexempt employees
prevailing wage rate
cost-of-living adjustments (COLAs)
consumer price index (CPI)
comparable worth *or* pay equity
job evaluation
employee benefits
experience rating
maternity leave
paternity leave
flexcomp
cafeteria benefit plans *or* smorgasbord benefit plans

CHAPTER OUTLINE
CASE 11–1. WHEN THE TRANSFER BACKFIRES (A)

I. THE ROLE OF PERFORMANCE APPRAISAL IN SUPERVISORY MANAGEMENT
   A. Why is performance appraised?
      1. How performance appraisal operates

2. Purposes of performance appraisal
   B. Who should do the performance appraisal?
      1. The employees themselves
      2. Subordinates
      3. Peers
      4. The immediate supervisor
   C. Traditional methods of performance appraisal
      1. Rating scale
      2. Employee-comparison methods
   D. The appraisal interview
   E. Newer ways of appraising performance
II. COMPENSATING EMPLOYEES
   A. Importance of compensation
      1. To employees
      2. To employers
   B. Roles played by compensation
      1. To attract capable employees
      2. To motivate employees to perform
      3. To retain capable employees
   C. Types of wages
   D. Factors affecting wage rates
      1. Factors affecting what an employer has to pay
         a. Governmental factors
         b. Collective bargaining
         c. Cost-of-living adjustments (COLAs)
         d. Comparable wage rates
         e. Market conditions
      2. What affects an employer's ability to pay
III. THE COMPARABLE-WORTH ISSUE
IV. USING JOB EVALUATION TO SET WAGE RATES
   A. Some problems with using job evaluation
   B. The job-evaluation procedure
V. EMPLOYEE BENEFITS
   A. Legally required benefits
      1. Social Security
      2. Workers' compensation
      3. Unemployment insurance
   B. Voluntary benefits
      1. Pay for time not worked
      2. Health protection and insurance provisions
      3. Retirement income
   C. Flexible benefits
Chapter Review
Questions for Review and Discussion
Learning Exercise 11–1. What Do You Want from Your Job?
Learning Exercise 11–2. When the Transfer Backfires (B)
Suggestions for Further Reading

CASE 11–1
WHEN THE TRANSFER BACKFIRES (A)[1]

Jane Smith abruptly rose and stormed out of the office of Robert Trent, the director of purchasing at a major eastern university. As she made her hasty exit, Trent began to wonder what had gone wrong with a seemingly perfect plan—one that would have rid his department of a "problem" employee. How could his well-constructed plan, using the university's formal transfer system, have failed so miserably, leaving him with an even more unmanageable situation that could possibly lead to litigation?

It had all begun in January, when Trent decided that something must be done about Smith's performance and attitude. The process was made a little more awkward by the university's not having a formal employee performance-appraisal policy and program. This left each department with the right to develop and conduct its own employee appraisals. This meant that each department could choose whether or not to appraise an employee, as well as choose the format and procedure to be used.

In January, Trent decided to conduct an appraisal of Smith. After writing down some weaknesses in her performance and attitude, he called her in to discuss them. He cited the various weaknesses to her, but, admittedly, most were highly subjective in nature. In only a few instances did he give specific and objective references, and he did not give Smith a copy of his findings. During the appraisal interview, he even hinted that possibly she didn't "fit in" and that she "probably would be much happier in some other place." In any event, he was satisfied that he had begun the process for eventually ridding the department of her. He reasoned that, if all else failed, this pressure would ultimately force her to quit. At the time, he hardly noticed that she was strangely quiet through the whole meeting.

As time went by, Smith's attitude and performance did not improve. In March, Trent was elated to learn that an opening existed in another department, and that Smith was most interested in transferring. The university's formal transfer policy required that Trent complete the Employee Transfer Evaluation Form—which he gladly did. As a matter of fact, he gave Smith mostly "outstanding" ratings on all the performance and attitude factors. He was so pleased at having the opportunity to use the transfer system that he called the other department manager and spoke glowingly of Smith's abilities and performance. Although he had been the purchasing director

This case illustrates a problem faced by all supervisors—appraising employee performance. Appraising performance and compensating employees are two of the less pleasant aspects of supervisory management. Yet an employee's performance is always being appraised, either formally or informally, poorly or well. Whenever a worker is praised or reprimanded, is given a wage increase or passed over for one, is promoted or not promoted, or is transferred, laid off, or discharged, his or her job performance has been appraised and a value judgment made about it.

We saw in Chapter 10 how employees are selected and trained. This chapter looks at the overall topic of appraising employee performance and taking action based on that performance. Specifically, it discusses the role of performance appraisal in supervisory management, compensating employees, job evaluation, pricing jobs, and the role of employee benefits.

THE ROLE OF PERFORMANCE APPRAISAL IN SUPERVISORY MANAGEMENT

Because performance appraisal is so important to organizations, more enlightened managers are now trying to upgrade their appraisal programs. In fact, most employers have already developed some form of formal program for improving employee performance, growth, and development.[2]

Why Is Performance Appraised?

Performance appraisal is the process used to determine to what extent an employee is performing the job in the way it was intended to be done. Some other frequently used terms for this process of appraising employee performance are **merit rating, efficiency rating, service rating,** and **employee evaluation**. Regardless of the term used, the process always has the purpose of seeing how actual employee performance compares to the ideal or standard.

HOW PERFORMANCE APPRAISAL OPERATES. If employees' output can be physically measured, there is little need to formally appraise employees, because their rewards can be based on their actual output. However, many jobs today do not lend themselves to physical measurement. Therefore, the supervisor tries to determine what personal characteristics an employee has that lead him or her to behave favorably and have satisfactory performance. As you can see from Figure 11–1, the process works as follows: An employee has (1) personal qualities that lead to (2) job behaviors that result in (3) worker performance, which (4) the

FIGURE 11–1   HOW PERFORMANCE APPRAISALS OPERATE

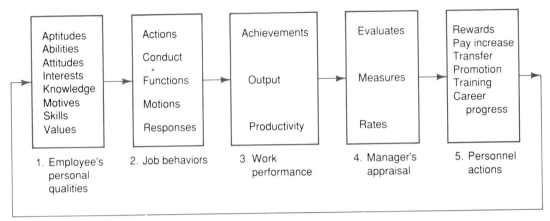

Aptitudes Abilities Attitudes Interests Knowledge Motives Skills Values	Actions Conduct Functions Motions Responses	Achievements Output Productivity	Evaluates Measures Rates	Rewards Pay increase Transfer Promotion Training Career progress
1. Employee's personal qualities	2. Job behaviors	3. Work performance	4. Manager's appraisal	5. Personnel actions

Source: Leon C. Megginson, *Personnel Management: A Human Resources Approach,* 5th ed. (Homewood, IL: Richard D. Irwin, 1985), p. 418.

manager appraises, which results in (5) some kind of personnel action being taken.

An employee's qualities are abilities, attitudes, interests, skills, and values. These qualities lead the employee to take certain actions or make certain motions which result in output or productivity. The manager appraises the employee's performance and then rewards the employee through a pay increase, transfer, promotion, training and development, or career progress.

PURPOSES OF PERFORMANCE APPRAISALS. Some specific reasons for appraising employee performance are (1) to serve as a basis for granting wage increases, (2) to help identify employees for promotions, transfers, layoffs, or discharges, (3) to validate selection techniques in order to meet EEO/AA requirements (as discussed in Chapter 10), (4) to determine the employee's training and development needs, (5) to provide a basis for reducing the work force if necessary, and (6) to improve communication between the supervisor and employees. Appraisal for these purposes is usually done by comparing the performance of one employee to that of others. Therefore, the role of the supervisor is to judge employee performance as the basis for taking some kind of administrative action.

Notice in Case 11–1 how Robert Trent manipulated the appraisal of Jane Smith to get her transferred. While we do not condone the method he used, the case does show how performance appraisal can be used as a basis for administrative action.

Performance appraisals can also be used for development purposes, such as to provide a basis for giving advice, coaching, or counseling so that employees will have a better expectation on the job, or a basis for career planning and development. When used for these purposes, performance appraisal is usually done by comparing the employees' actual performance to some previously determined work standard(s). In such cases, the role of the supervisor is that of a counselor, mentor, or instructor; and the appraisal should serve to motivate employees by giving them a better understanding of their job responsibilities, of what is expected of them, and of their training needs.

Who Should Do the Appraisal?

There are many individuals or groups who can do performance appraisals, but appraisals are most frequently done by the employees themselves, by subordinates, by fellow employees, or by the employees' immediate supervisor. For our purposes, performance appraisals done by the immediate supervisor are the most important. Since we have mentioned the others, however, we will discuss them briefly so that you will be aware of their possible use.

THE EMPLOYEES THEMSELVES. A growing trend among more progressive organizations is to let employees, especially managers, rate themselves. These ratings, which are not usually a part of the employee's regular performance appraisal, help encourage their personal career planning.

At Citibank, a senior manager simply hands subordinates an evaluation form and asks them to fill in their own ratings. Apparently, this method works well because, as one manager said, "It's amazing how honest people are. They even put in things that are detrimental to their own progress and promotion." As a safeguard, however, the senior manager makes the final review of the ratings.[3]

SUBORDINATES. If the only purpose of a performance appraisal is to improve employer-employee relationships, it may be useful to let subordinates rate their own supervisor. This method is also helpful to supervisors who really want to improve their performance, especially their interpersonal relationships.

PEERS. Peer rating allows employees to rate one another. Under this method, each employee secretly appraises the performance of the other members of the work group. The supervisor then tabulates the results for a given employee, as provided by the other employees. This method is often called the **mutual rating system**.

THE IMMEDIATE SUPERVISOR. The most frequently used method of appraising performance is the rating of employees by their immediate supervisors, which is a part of every supervisor's responsibility and one that cannot be avoided.

Immediate supervisors are in the best position to know the job requirements and to know how well an employee is meeting them; thus, a supervisor can make the best judgment about the need for the employee to improve his or her performance. A study by the Conference Board found that 95 percent of the respondents were appraised by their immediate supervisor.[4]

Traditional Methods of Performance Appraisal

We indicated earlier that employee performance is always being appraised, either formally or informally. For the purposes previously discussed, however, *formal* appraisals are preferred by most managers. This method provides a record that can be used for any action resulting from the appraisal. Hence, formal performance appraisals are now conducted by most firms at regular intervals of every six months or a year.

There are many traditional approaches to performance appraisal. Most of them are aimed at attaining greater objectivity in the appraisal and reducing the influence of chance, as shown in Figure 11–2. Two of these traditional methods are explained in detail. They are (1) the rating scale, and (2) the employee-comparison method.

RATING SCALE. The oldest and most prevalent type of performance-rating procedure is the **rating scale**. An example of one type of rating scale is presented in Figure 11–3. Every 6 or 12 months, employees are rated on a number of

FIGURE 11–2   SUSPICIONS CONFIRMED

FIGURE 11–3   A TYPICAL RATING-SCALE APPRAISAL FORM

EMPLOYEE EVALUATION FORM

Employee Name _Fred Willis_   Position _Chief Engineer, Materials Research_

Period covered by evaluation: from _6/1_ to _7/1_

	Unsatis-factory (1)	Meets Minimum (2)	Average (3)	Above Average (4)	Out-standing (5)	Score
1. Quality and thoroughness of work		✓				2
2. Volume of work				✓		4
3. Knowledge of job, methods, and procedures				✓		4
4. Initiative and resourcefulness				✓		4
5. Cooperation, attitude, and team-work			✓			3
6. Adaptability and ability to learn quickly					✓	5
7. Ability to express self clearly in speaking and writing			✓			3
8. Planning, organizing, and making work assignments		✓				2
9. Selection and development of subordinates		✓				2
10. Morale and loyalty of subordinates			✓			3

Total Score _32_

What steps can this employee take to improve his work? _Employee is an eager, innovative, resourceful person whose eagerness sometimes causes him to sacrifice quality of work. While highly talented, must learn to delegate more technical work to subordinates and assume more managerial tasks himself._

Other comments: _Employee has been in position about 7 months. This is his first managerial job, and some problems in making the adjustment were expected._

Total score:
10-15 Unsatisfactory
16-25 Meets Minimum
26-35 Average
36-45 Above Average
46-50 Outstanding

Supervisor's signature _Paul Batson_
Title _Head, Engineering Research_
Employee's signature _Frederick R. Willis_
Approved by _Horace Wilhelm_
Title _Director, Research & Development_

Source: Donald C. Mosley and Paul H. Pietri, Jr., *Management: The Art of Working with and through People* (Encino, CA: Dickenson Publishing Co., 1974), p. 144. Reproduced with permission of Donald C. Mosley and Paul H. Pietri, Jr.

characteristics, such as quality of work, attitude toward work, ability to get along with others, judgment, and other characteristics the organization considers important. Each characteristic may be rated on a point scale ranging from 5 for "exceptional" performance down to 1 for "very poor" performance. The points are totaled and the results are used to compare subordinates' performance and to point out areas where improvement is needed.

The major advantage of the rating-scale system is its simplicity, but several disadvantages are also evident. A score of 35 for one employee does not necessarily mean that he or she is more effective on the job than Fred Willis (the employee named in Figure 11–3), who received a total score of 32. Moreover, different supervisors may have different standards in mind for "above average" or just "average" work. In addition, supervisors may tend to rate their people high because it makes themselves look good, or because they honestly feel that their people are "above average" or need a salary increase.

For example, one of the authors of this textbook was on a hospital's personnel committee a few years ago. After a year and a half with no general salary adjustments, the committee decided to give a maximum raise of 6 percent. The managers and supervisors were told that each employee's increase would be based on appraisals by that employee's supervisor (which were done every six months.)

Of the appraisals received from the nursing department, 97 percent were "outstanding." These appraisals were returned to the director of nursing for an explanation. Her comment was, "Our supervisors thought their nurses deserved a good raise after going without one for 18 months."

EMPLOYEE-COMPARISON METHODS. To overcome the disadvantages of the rating scale, various **employee-comparison methods** are used. These differ from the rating-scale system in that supervisors are required to rank each of the people in comparison to others in terms of *performance* and *value* to the organization. Thus, someone must end up being first, another second, and so on, down to the last employee. Some managers have modified this approach by selecting, say, the top third, the middle third, and the bottom third of the work group, and putting each employee in one of those groups.

One variant of the employee comparison method is the **paired-comparison technique**. Suppose a supervisor has five subordinates: Harrison, Jackson, Santos, Troy, and Willard. If the supervisor wants to appraise Harrison, the supervisor will compare Harrison with Jackson, Harrison with Santos, Harrison with Troy, and Harrison with Willard. The process is repeated until each subordinate has been compared with each of the others. The number of times one subordinate is ranked over another is recorded, and the result is an overall ranking as to who received the most votes, the next most votes, and so on. This technique probably provides a more realistic appraisal than the other methods mentioned, but it is more complex and is difficult to do when the supervisor has a large number of employees.

The Appraisal Interview

Typically, as a supervisor you would be required to communicate the results of performance appraisal to your employees in an **appraisal interview**. This seems compatible with the objective of providing feedback on workers' progress and subsequent improvement on the job. However, it is the appraisal interview that supervisors like least about their job. This fact, plus the poor way it is often handled, has caused this interview to be criticized heavily for damaging relationships between supervisors and subordinates.

The appraisal interview used to be along the lines of "Call the person in and tell him or her what needs to be straightened out and what's expected." Today, however, interviewers are expected to aim at cooperation, constructiveness, and greater understanding. Most experts recommend the use of nondirective interviewing techniques in conducting appraisal interviews. But let us look at what tends to happen during the typical interview, even though it is conducted according to the rules of good performance-appraisal interviewing.

> *Once a year Gloria Rogers calls her employees in one at a time for the appraisal interview.*[5] *Both parties tend to "psych up" for this event. Rogers plans what she's going to say, and the subordinate tends to be apprehensive about what he or she is going to hear. At the beginning, Rogers tries to put the employee at ease by talking about the weather, the latest major-league baseball game, or the employee's family. The employee knows that this is just the prelude to getting down to serious business—and tends to resent the delay.*
>
> *Then Rogers explains her overall appraisal in broad terms. Initially she'll mention some good aspects of the employee's performance and give the employee a chance to express his or her views. Next, Rogers enumerates the employee's weaknesses and past failures. She allows the employee to explain these. Then she explains what steps are needed to improve the employee's performance. At this point, she may ask for the employee's ideas on improvement.*
>
> *One variation of the procedure allows the employee to give his or her own self-evaluation and compare it with Rogers' evaluation after it's given.*

This conventional approach to the appraisal interview is emotionally upsetting for both the supervisor and the employee. There is no doubt in the employee's mind that he or she is on the hot seat, and that there's little point in disagreeing with the supervisor about her judgments. It's best simply to remain submissive and accept the criticism, even if the employee disagrees with it.

Supervisors likewise tend to feel anxiety over performance appraisal. As management theorist Douglas McGregor points out,

> Managers are uncomfortable when they are put in the position of "playing God".... [We become] distressed when we must take responsibility for judging the personal worth of a fellow man. Yet the conventional approach to performance appraisal forces us not only to make such judgments and to see them acted upon, but also to communicate them to those we have judged. Small wonder we resist.[6]

The authors of this textbook have talked with numerous supervisors who suffer the double-barreled discomforts of performance appraisal. These supervisors dislike being appraised by their own bosses, and they dislike appraising their subordinates—or at least telling them the results. All this may lead to appraisal inflation. For example, in one company, when supervisors were required to give their appraisals to their subordinates, their appraisals of their subordinates suddenly jumped remarkably.[7] Yet research shows that one group of employees, who took some form of constructive action as a result of performance appraisals, did so because of the way their superior had conducted the appraisal interview and discussion.[8]

Newer Ways of Appraising Performance

In recent years the traditional approach to appraising subordinates' work has been supplemented by "Management by Objectives," or MBO (as discussed in Chapter 2), also known as *joint target setting, appraisal by results*, and other terms. The supervisor's role in this approach is to help subordinates grow and fit their aims into the supervisor's broader objectives—and ultimately those of the organization. The tone of this approach is positive rather than negative, constructive rather than destructive.

Subordinates themselves are heavily involved in their own self-appraisals and can see on a weekly or even daily basis the extent of their development toward the targets that have been set. They are thus actively involved in self-appraisal as they help establish their own goals, evaluate their strong and weak points, and periodically measure their own progress.

COMPENSATING EMPLOYEES

As stated earlier, one purpose of appraising employee performance is to help determine employee compensation. Compensation is another important part of managing human resources and is therefore an integral part of supervisory management.

Importance of Compensation

Of all supervisory problems, compensating employees is probably the most complex and difficult, because it involves many emotional factors as well as economic and rational ones. Although compensation is important to the nation's economy, we will only look at its importance to employees and employers.

TO EMPLOYEES. Compensation in the form of wages and benefits is the primary—and often the only—source of income for employees and their families. And, as the opening quotation from Carlyle indicated, the concept of fairness demands that employees receive "a fair day's wages for a fair day's work." There are probably as many complaints from employees about the *relative* amount of their income as there are about the *absolute* amount, for everyone wants to be treated fairly when it comes to pay. While employees' absolute level of income determines their standard of living, the relative income indicates status, prestige, and worth.

TO EMPLOYERS. Wages and benefits are also becoming increasingly important to American businesses because of foreign competition; deregulation of transportation, finance, and energy industries; and the tightening of the economy. No longer can wages be increased without a corresponding increase in productivity, and the cost is passed along to the consumer in the form of higher prices. Indeed, employers paying a noncompetitive wage rate will soon find themselves in financial trouble because employee compensation and other types of costs interact with the revenue to determine an employer's profit or loss.

Since the turn of the century, the ratio of employee earnings to business income has remained relatively constant at around 50 percent of the sales dollar, and the labor costs have constituted about 70 percent of the total cost of production.[9] Therefore, the primary way to increase employee earnings is to increase productivity and the company's sales and profits. In summary, to be fair to all, the employer should pay wages high enough to attract, motivate, and retain qualified employees, while at the same time keeping wages low enough to ensure adequate profits to expand productive facilities, attract new capital, and permit consumer satisfaction with the price.

Roles Played by Compensation

The amount and form of compensation play several roles. The more important of these are (1) to attract capable employees, (2) to motivate employees to perform more effectively, and (3) to retain capable employees.

Before you read any further, complete Learning Exercise 11–1, "What Do You Want from Your Job?," at the end of this chapter. Then return to this section and continue your reading.

TO ATTRACT CAPABLE EMPLOYEES. Most employers try to remain competitive, both in their industry and in their community, by paying salaries and benefits that are similar to those paid by other employers. Thus, they try to find out what the average salaries are for different types of positions. This is done by means of **wage surveys** which determine the "going rate" for jobs in the local labor market and in the industry. If it is not feasible to conduct a wage survey, an employer may use published wage-survey information from sources such as trade associations and the United States Department of Labor.

It can be argued that most job applicants probably do not know the exact wages and benefits offered by different employers for similar jobs, and therefore the compensation rate isn't important. But we believe that prospective employees do compare job offers and pay scales before making decisions about where to work. Those applicants who receive more than one job offer will probably compare the amounts of compensation offered and choose the firm that offers them the best deal.

Which argument do you think is correct? Consider your own answers to Learning Exercise 11–1. What did you put as the number one factor in choosing your first job? Was it "good salary"? You might want to check with some of your fellow students to see how they answered the question. In our research with upper-level business students since 1957–58, over 50 percent of them have answered that "good salary" was number one in over 97 percent of the cases.

TO MOTIVATE EMPLOYEES TO IMPROVE PERFORMANCE. According to the equity theory of motivation (see Chapter 8), employees who believe that the employer's pay system, including wages and benefits, is "fair and equitable" to them will contribute more to the employer than those who do not. Moreover, the expectancy theory of motivation, which is based on the law of effect, states that employee behavior that leads to reward tends to be repeated, while behavior that is not rewarded—or leads to punishment—tends not to be repeated. Thus, when an employee's income is what he or she expects, that employee will perform better.[10]

Our conclusion to the question "Does money motivate?" is that until employees satisfy their physical and safety needs, compensation does serve as a strong motivator; but above that level, money (especially day wages) tends to decline in importance.

TO RETAIN CAPABLE EMPLOYEES. After capable employees have been attracted, and after compensation has motivated them to perform, compensation can also act to retain them, especially if it is in the form of favorable employee benefits. While many factors cause employees to leave an organization, inadequate compensation is certainly one of those factors. Therefore, to retain good employees, an employer must be sure that his or her employees' compensation is equitable not only in relation to that offered by other employers, but also in relation to employees in the same organization. To maintain this system of equity and job satisfaction, some form of job evaluation is generally used. (We will discuss this later in the chapter.)

Types of Wages

There are many types of wages used to compensate employees. Among the more popular types are (1) a single rate, (2) a rate range, (3) day work, or time wages, and (4) incentive wages.

When a **single rate** is used, everyone who performs the same job is paid the same wage, regardless of the level of performance. The single rate is used in many industries, especially those that are unionized such as the automobile assembly, trucking, steel, trade, and service industries. It is also used for many occupations such as the crafts, production workers, and maintenance personnel.

Rate ranges consist of a minimum and maximum range of wage rates for a given job, with employees paid at different rates depending on how well they perform. The rate paid to an individual is usually determined by some form of performance appraisal, as discussed earlier. Rate ranges are used for most technical, professional, and office workers, as well as for most government employees.

There are only two bases on which to compensate employees, namely, (1) the amount of time the worker spends on the job and (2) the amount of output the employee produces during a given period of time. The first of these methods, **time wages** or **day work**, pays the employee for the amount of time spent on the job, regardless of the output during that period of time. The second method, **incentive wages**, pays the employee according to the amount of goods and services that the employee produced, or the employee's output.

In general, unions prefer single rates rather than rate ranges for the same type of job because single rates tend to maintain unity among workers. Unions also tend to favor day work, or time wages, rather than incentive wages. While unions will accept incentive wage plans that are based on group output rather than individual output, they insist that such plans be established according to the union's standards.

Factors Affecting Wage Rates

In general, employers will pay their employees (1) what they think they should, (2) what they have to, and (3) what they are able to. What most employers think they *should* pay is "competitive wages."

FACTORS AFFECTING WHAT AN EMPLOYER HAS TO PAY. There are many factors affecting what an employer has to pay an employee. The most important factors are (1) governmental factors, (2) collective bargaining, (3) cost-of-living adjustments (COLAs), (4) comparable wages, and (5) market conditions.

Governmental factors. Governmental laws, rules, and regulations largely determine what an employer has to pay workers. Some of these laws are the Fair Labor Standards Act, commonly called the Wage and Hour Law; the Walsh-Healey Act; the Davis-Bacon Act; the Equal Pay Act; and EEO/AA laws, such as the Civil Rights Act, the Vocational Rehabilitation Act, and the Veterans' Readjustment Act.

The Fair Labor Standards Act covers all employees working in interstate commerce, federal employees, and some state employees. Some employees, referred to as **exempt employees**, including executives, administrative and professional employees, outside sales personnel, and other selected groups, are not covered by the provisions of this law. All other employees, called **nonexempt employees**, are covered and must be paid the basic minimum wage ($3.35 per hour at the time of this writing). If employees work over 40 hours in a given workweek, they must be paid one and one-half times their regular rate of pay for each hour worked over 40 hours. However, there are provisions for employing full-time students at rates lower than the minimum wage. This law also prevents child labor. For example, age 14 is the minimum working age for most nonfarm jobs. On nonhazardous jobs, persons of age 14 and 15 can work no more than 3 hours on a school day, 8 hours on any other day, or 40 hours per week. Those who are 16 and 17 years old can work in nonhazardous jobs for unlimited hours.

The Davis-Bacon Act and the Walsh-Healey Act have different provisions. Construction firms with government contracts or subcontracts in excess of $2,000 are covered by the Davis-Bacon Act, while other employers with government contracts exceeding $10,000 are covered by the Walsh-Healey Act. These acts differ from the Fair Labor Standards Act in that the rate of pay is set by the Secretary of Labor, and overtime is paid at "time and a half" for all hours worked over 8 hours in one day *or* over 40 hours in a given week. This rate of pay is called the **prevailing wage rate** in the area and approximates the union wage scale for the area in the given type of work.

Public policy now prohibits discrimination in pay unless it is based on performance. For example, the Equal Pay Act prohibits different rates of pay for men and women doing the same type of work. Title VII of the Civil Rights Act prevents discrimination based on race, color, religion, sex, or national origin. The Age Discrimination in Employment Act prohibits discrimination against persons 40 years of age and older. Finally, the Vocational Rehabilitation Act prohibits discrimination against handicapped persons.

Collective bargaining. When unions are involved, basic wages, job differentials, individual rates of pay, and employee benefits tend to be determined through the collective-bargaining process. The actual amount of compensation is determined by the relative strength of the union and the employer. However, even nonunionized employers are affected by the wage rates and the amounts of benefits paid by unionized firms.

Cost-of-living adjustments (COLAs). Since 1948, **cost-of-living adjustments (COLAs)** have been included in many union contracts. Under a COLA arrangement, wages rise in direct proportion to increases in the **consumer price index (CPI)**, which measures changes in the price of a group of goods and services that make up the typical consumer's budget. Such arrangements have been popular in the automobile, communications, electrical, mining, steel, transportation, and rubber industries, just to mention a few. Also, many government employees have similar arrangements. COLAs are more popular when inflation increases rapidly, as it did in the late 1970s and early 1980s.

Comparable wage rates. As indicated earlier, an employer must pay wage rates that are comparable to those paid in the area, the industry, and the occupation. If an employer pays less than the prevailing area rate, employees will move to the higher-paying jobs. The same is true for employers in a given industry, such as steel, rubber, and automobile manufacturers, which are known as high-pay industries. Finally, there tends to be a relationship between wages for people in given occupations, such as professional and technical workers, managerial personnel, and sales personnel, regardless of who their employer is.

Market conditions. The basic law of economics applies to wages. That is, as the supply of workers goes up relative to demand, wage rates tend to go down; and when the supply of workers goes down relative to demand, wage rates go up.

WHAT AFFECTS AN EMPLOYER'S ABILITY TO PAY. In spite of the above factors, individual wages are based on what the employer can afford to pay, or the amount of profit the employer makes. This profit, in turn, is based on the productivity of the employees, prices charged, and the volume of goods sold or services provided. Unless there is profit, there cannot be high wages, regardless of what happens outside the organization.

THE COMPARABLE-WORTH ISSUE

In spite of laws prohibiting unequal pay for men and women doing the same job, two recent pay equity studies found that for every dollar earned by white men in 1985, white women working full time earned only 63 cents; black women, only 56 cents; and Hispanic women, only 53 cents.[11] There is much controversy as to the cause of this disparity. The problem, according to advocates of "pay equity," goes far beyond equal pay for the same job. The real issue is: *Are women being systematically underpaid for work that requires the same skills, knowledge, and responsibility as jobs performed by men, for which they receive higher pay?*

Advocates say the issue involves **comparable worth**, or **pay equity**, which evaluates work by a formula of points for the amount of education, effort, skill, and responsibility required for an individual job. These points are then used, along with job evaluation, to set salary rates. Critics say such wage adjustments would destroy the market forces of supply and demand. The arguments of advocates and critics of the "comparable worth issue" are shown in Figure 11–4.

FIGURE 11–4 SHOULD JOBS OF "COMPARABLE WORTH"
RECEIVE COMPARABLE PAY?

Women's groups believe that the principle of "equal pay for work of equal
value" has been violated, in that whole classes of jobs—such as those in the
clerical area—are undervalued because they have traditionally been held by
women. They want this practice changed so that pay for all jobs will be based
on their value to the business or community, rather than on who holds the jobs.

The arguments *for* comparable pay for comparable work are

1. If one employee contributes as much to the firm as another, he or she should
   be paid the same.
2. It is needed to raise women's pay, which is now only about 65 percent of
   men's.
3. It will give women greater internal job mobility.
4. This is one way to further women's career ambitions.
5. It would serve to motivate women to be more productive.

The arguments *against* comparable pay are

1. Federal law only requires *equal* pay for *equal* jobs.
2. It violates a firm's structured job-evaluation system.
3. Employers must pay salaries competitive with those of other employers,
   which are based on what employees produce and on the economic value of
   the work performed.
4. Women receive less than men because two-thirds of new employees are
   women, and they always receive less than more senior employees.
5. It is practically impossible to determine accurately the real value of a job.

Source: Leon C. Megginson, *Personnel Management: A Human Resources Approach,* 5th ed.
(Homewood, IL: Richard D. Irwin, 1985), p. 479.

*Do you think jobs of "comparable worth" should receive comparable pay?
Which arguments in Figure 11–4 do you accept? Why?*

Where does the issue stand now? Although the United States Supreme Court
has acknowledged comparable worth as a valid legal doctrine,[12] and 29 states

have conducted job-evaluation studies addressing pay equity, resulting in implementation of pay equity plans in 16 states, the issue is still hotly debated. Even women's groups are divided on the issue. The National Organization for Women (NOW) did not support a bill introduced in the United States Senate in 1983 that would have required comparable worth in federal jobs.[13] On the other hand, labor unions active in the public sector—especially the American Federation of State, County, and Municipal Employees (AFSCME)—are actively pushing the concept. The Equal Employment Opportunity Commission (EEOC) unanimously decided in 1985 that comparable worth should not be recognized as part of the Civil Rights Act of 1984.[14] The Ninth United States Court of Appeals rejected the doctrine of comparable worth in 1985, in spite of a study which showed that women in state governments were paid 20 percent lower wages than men on jobs requiring the same skills and efforts.[15]

USING JOB EVALUATION TO SET JOB RATES

Job evaluation is a process used to determine the relative value of jobs to an employer in order to determine more objectively the earnings of employees doing given jobs. It is used to develop a fair and equitable scale of wages—especially for new employees—to determine the relative value of each job to the organization as a basis for determining individual wage rates and to satisfy EEO requirements. It also provides information for determining the qualifications needed for a given job in order to make more effective employee selections, promotions, demotions, and job changes.

Some Problems with Using Job Evaluation

While it is possible to obtain a reasonable degree of equity by using job evaluation, there are several problems involved with the process. First, the value of various occupations to an employer cannot be precisely measured by means of the same yardstick. Also, it is difficult to measure the relative value of work done by scientific, technical, professional, and managerial personnel. Finally, it is difficult to evaluate the worth of one job to the organization without considering its relationship to other jobs.

The Job-Evaluation Procedure

The usual procedure for using job evaluation to arrive at job rates or ranges is to do a job analysis, grade the jobs, price each job, and administer the resulting program. As shown in Table 11–1, the process of job analysis results in job descriptions, which are then translated into job specifications that can be used as the basis for hiring new employees. These job specifications are then grouped into job grades, with jobs of the same relative value in the same grade. These job grades are then given a price based on the company's overall wage rate. These wage rates or ranges become the value of the job. By appraising the performance

TABLE 11-1   STEPS IN THE JOB-EVALUATION PROCEDURE

Step	Procedures and Products Used	Resulting Product
Step 1: Analysis	Job analysis→job description→	Job specifications*
Step 2: Grading	Job specifications + job evaluation and appraisal of the worth of job→ job ratings→	Job grades
Step 3: Pricing	Job grades + overall wage rate→	Job wage rates, or ranges
Step 4: Administering	Job wage rates or ranges + appraisal of performance or qualities of each employee→	Individual wage rate

*These specifications can be used as the basic for performing the job-evaluation procedure, or they can be used to prepare a statement of the personal qualifications needed in a person to perform the job. This statement then becomes the basis of the recruitment and selection procedure.

Source: Leon C. Megginson, *Personnel Management: A Human Resources Approach,* 5th ed. (Homewood, IL: Richard D. Irwin, 1985), p. 482.

of each employee, his or her individual wage rate within the wage range is determined.

EMPLOYEE BENEFITS

Employee benefits are the financial rewards and services provided to employees in addition to their regular earnings. In practice, the use of this term is so broad that it might easily extend from steady employment at fair wages up to the payment of tuition for employees attending university courses or to free psychiatric or legal assistance. One way of classifying these benefits is according to whether they are legally required or are voluntary on the part of the employer.

Legally Required Benefits

Employers are required by law to provide Social Security, workers' compensation, and unemployment insurance for all employees. Each of these types of legally required benefits is explained below.

SOCIAL SECURITY. The Social Security system is in reality two separate systems. One provides retirement benefits, and the other provides disability, survivors', and Medicare benefits. To be eligible for the program, a worker must have contributed taxes into the system for 10 years (or 40 quarters).

Benefits are financed by a payroll tax paid by both employer and employee. The tax rate, the earnings base on which it is paid, and the benefits are subject to frequent congressional changes. The tax rate for 1987 was 7.15 percent of the first $43,800 paid to each employee, with both the employer and the employee paying that amount. Thus, the maximum tax paid by any employee was $3,131.70, and the employer paid an equal amount. At the same time, the maximum retirement benefit at age 65 was $789. Each year retirees receive an increase in their retirement income at a rate based on the increase in the consumer price index.

WORKERS' COMPENSATION. All states have passed laws requiring workers' compensation. These laws protect employees and their families against permanent loss of income and high medical payments resulting from accidental injury or illness resulting from the job. The primary purpose of these laws is to keep the cause of the accident out of the decision to pay the benefits; that is, payments are made whether or not the fault was that of the employer or the employee. The amount to be paid for a given condition, such as loss of a hand or arm, is also stipulated in the law.

Workers' compensation funds are primarily provided through employer contributions to a statewide fund. A board exists to review cases and determine eligibility for compensation. Employers may also purchase insurance from private insurance companies to supplement these state funds. In general, employees are able to recover all medical expenses and up to two thirds of the income loss due to disability or missed work.

UNEMPLOYMENT INSURANCE. Included as a provision of the Social Security Act is unemployment insurance. In most states, unemployment insurance requires that states provide unemployed workers with benefits from a fund of payroll taxes imposed on employers. The amount paid into the fund by the employers varies according to the unemployment rate within the state and the employer's record of unemployed workers, called its **experience rating**. In order to receive benefits under the law, the unemployed worker is required to register for employment at a United States employment office and usually must have worked for a certain period of time before becoming unemployed.

Voluntary Benefits

In addition to the legally required benefits, many employers voluntarily provide other benefits. Some of these are in the general areas of payment for time not worked, health protection, and retirement income.

PAY FOR TIME NOT WORKED. Most employers today grant their employees pay for time not worked under certain circumstances. These benefits take several forms such as paid vacations, paid holidays, paid sick leave, pay for jury duty, and paid compassionate leave such as to attend a funeral.

A growing issue is **maternity leave**, which is treated the same as sick leave; that is, the pregnant employee is entitled to time off with pay. This practice was required by law under the Pregnancy Discrimination Act, which was passed in 1978. Another emerging issue is whether to grant **paternity leave**, which permits new fathers to take *unpaid* leave to help take care of the new baby. Some of the more progressive firms, such as AT&T, IBM, and Procter & Gamble, already provide paternity leave.

HEALTH PROTECTION AND INSURANCE PROVISIONS. Another group of benefits provides for medical and hospital care, along with pay, while an employee is sick. These benefits also include payments to an employee's beneficiary in case of the employee's death. Group medical, surgical, and dental plans are very popular with employees but are expensive for management. Most employers are now taking steps to limit these payments. Life insurance is another popular benefit received by many employees today. Group life insurance plans usually provide for death benefits to the employee's beneficiary and are usually based on the employee's income.

RETIREMENT INCOME. A trend toward early retirement in the United States has developed. As this trend continues, employers are adopting various pension plans to help employees supplement their Social Security or other retirement benefits. The employee is usually helped by being provided with preretirement and postretirement counseling (see Chapter 12 for details) and a stipulated payment for the rest of the employee's life.

Flexible Benefits

Many employers are now using **flexcomp**, which is a method of providing employees with flexible benefit packages. Called **cafeteria benefit plans** or **smorgasbord benefit plans**, they provide each worker with an individualized benefit package. Under these plans, all employees receive a statement of the total dollar amount of benefits they are entitled to, along with the amount required for legally required benefits. Each employee then tells the employer how to allocate the balance among the programs available. Some advantages of this program are that (1) workers are more aware of the total value of their benefits (now averaging about 37 percent of each employee's total wages), and (2) workers can choose which programs they want, resulting in worker satisfaction and benefit packages more effectively tailored to individual needs.

Although employees are carefully selected, trained, evaluated, and compensated, they sometimes have problems with which they need help. In Chapter 12, we will present some ideas on counseling such employees.

CHAPTER REVIEW

An employee's performance is always being appraised, either formally or informally. This chapter has dealt with formal performance appraisal—why it is done, who should do it, and methods of appraisal. Also discussed were the subject of compensation, including its importance, the roles it plays, types of wages, factors affecting wage rates, the issue of comparable worth, use of job evaluation to set wage rates, and employee benefits, both legally required and voluntary.

The purpose of performance appraisal is to compare employee performance to a standard or ideal—a sort of personnel quality control. Performance appraisal is more critical for employees whose output cannot be easily measured. Specific reasons for appraising employee performance are (1) to provide a basis for some administrative action, such as a pay increase, promotion, transfer, layoff, discharge, or recommendation for training or development, and (2) to justify these actions for EEO/AA purposes.

Performance appraisal can be done by employees themselves, by subordinates, or by employees' peers, but it is usually done by the immediate supervisors since they are most familiar with their employees' work. Traditional methods of performance appraisal include rating scales, which compare performance to a standard, and employee-comparison methods, which compare employees to one another.

One of the hardest jobs of supervisors is the appraisal interview, which is used to communicate the results of the appraisal to employees. A supervisor's reluctance to criticize employees may lead to appraisal inflation. One solution to this problem is the use of MBO, in which employees are involved with supervisors in setting their own goals and appraising their own performance.

Another difficult management task is determining compensation. Compensation is important to employees because it determines both their standard of living and their status, and to employers because it represents such a large proportion of costs. The amount and form of compensation play several roles: to attract capable employees, to motivate employees to perform more effectively, and to retain capable employees. To help attract capable employees, wage surveys are used to determine competitive wage rates for the area and industry. To encourage performance, employees need to believe that their compensation is equitable in comparison with what others receive. Good employee benefits can be an incentive to employees to remain with the organization.

Types of wages include the single rate for a given job and a rate range, with the actual pay based on seniority, experience, performance, or some other criterion. These rates may be paid on a straight hourly basis—day work or time wages—or by incentive wages, which are based on output.

Wage rates are affected by what employers think they should pay, what they are compelled to pay, and what they are able to pay. Their intentions, for good or ill, are greatly affected by governmental factors, collective bargaining, the standard and cost of living in the area, comparable wages, and supply and demand. However, what they can pay is ultimately limited by productivity and profitability.

Despite laws requiring equal pay for the same job, women continue to be paid less than men, partly because compensation for jobs held primarily by women tends to be lower than that for "men's" jobs. This has led many proponents of "pay equity" to insist that equal pay be offered for jobs of "comparable worth." To establish the "worth" of a job, a complex process of job evaluation is needed; and accuracy and objectivity for this process is very difficult to achieve.

Employee benefits are noncash forms of compensation. Those that employers are legally required to provide are Social Security, workers' compensation, and unemployment insurance. Voluntary benefits usually include pay for time not worked, health protection and insurance, and retirement income. A modern trend is toward a flexible benefit policy that allows employees to choose their own benefits up to a certain value.

QUESTIONS FOR REVIEW AND DISCUSSION

1. Evaluate the statement that "an employee's performance is always being appraised."
2. What is performance appraisal, and what are some of the other names for it?
3. What are some of the purposes of performance appraisal?
4. a. Name at least four persons or groups that do performance appraisals.
   b. Why would each of these be used?
5. What are rating scales, and how are they used?
6. What are employee-comparison methods, and how are they used?
7. Why is compensation so important to
   a. employees?
   b. employers?
8. What are the roles played by compensation? Explain each.
9. Distinguish between
   a. single rates and rate ranges.
   b. time wages and incentive wages.
10. Discuss at least five factors affecting wage rates.
11. Should jobs of "comparable worth" receive comparable pay? Defend your answer.
12. What is job evaluation, and what are some problems with its use?
13. Name and describe the three legally required employee benefits.
14. What are some of the more popular "voluntary" employee benefits?
15. What is flexcomp, and how does it work?
16. What steps can a supervisor take to prepare for a performance appraisal interview?
17. What should a supervisor do when an employee asks a question regarding pay equity?

LEARNING EXERCISE 11–1
WHAT DO YOU WANT FROM YOUR JOB?[16]

In the chart shown on page 289, please rank the employment factors in their order of importance to you at three points in your career. In the first column, assume that you are about to graduate and are looking for your first full-time job. In the second column, assume that you have been gainfully employed for 5 to 10 years and that you are

Employment Factor	As You Seek Your First Full-Time Job	Your Ranking 5–10 Years Later	Your Ranking 15–20 Years Later
Employee benefits	_____	_____	_____
Fair adjustment of grievances	_____	_____	_____
Good job instruction and training	_____	_____	_____
Effective job supervision by your supervisor	_____	_____	_____
Promotion possibilities	_____	_____	_____
Job safety	_____	_____	_____
Job security (no threat of being dismissed or laid off)	_____	_____	_____
Good salary	_____	_____	_____
Good working conditions (nice office surroundings, good hours, and so on)			

presently employed by a reputable firm at the prevailing salary for the type of job and industry you are in. In the third column, try to assume that 25 to 30 years from now you have "found your niche in life" and have been working for a reputable employer for several years. (Rank your first choice as "1," second as "2," and so forth, through "9.")

Answer the following questions:

1. What does your ranking tell you about your motivation now?
2. Is there any change in the second and third periods?
3. What are the changes and why do you think they occurred?

LEARNING EXERCISE 11–2
WHEN THE TRANSFER BACKFIRES (B)[17]

After incorrectly appraising Jane Smith's performance as mostly "outstanding" in order to get her transferred to another department, Robert Trent was shocked when her transfer was turned down. To further complicate matters, Trent realized that he must face Smith in May when it would be time to discuss annual pay raises, which would include both merit pay considerations and cost-of-living adjustments. This would be even more difficult in light of the fact that Jane's performance and attitude had not improved since the January appraisal. If anything, they were worse.

    Trent had just finished the May meeting with Smith by telling her the bad news: on the basis of both performance and attitude, she should not be recommended for the cost-of-living or merit pay increases for the new year beginning July 1. Smith, armed with the transfer evaluation forms (completed and given to her in March), threatened to use all internal and external systems for organizational justice due her.

As Trent pondered this dilemma, he fully recognized Smith's unique status within the university community. She was the wife of a distinguished, tenured professor of business, and this situation provided additional pressure. As if this were not enough, he had to contend with the office social process pivoting around a kaffeeklatsch group that was greatly influenced by Smith. It was not unusual for the former director of purchasing (who had retired after 25 years of service) to attend these gatherings. Of course, Smith had kept this group fully apprised of her continuing troubles with "this new, young purchasing director who is hardly dry behind the ears."

Answer the following questions:

1. What are the facts Trent must consider now?
2. What avenues are now open to Trent?
3. What does this case say to you about the need for supervisors to act morally?
4. Do you believe that some supervisors are untruthful where recommendations are concerned? Explain.
5. What three functions are salaries meant to perform?
6. To what extent should employee appraisals be used in salary adjustments? Explain.

ENDNOTES

1. Prepared by M. T. Bledsoe, Meredith College, and reprinted from Leon C. Megginson, *Personnel Management: A Human Resources Approach*, 5th ed. (Homewood, IL: Richard D. Irwin, 1985), pp. 451–52.
2. "HMR Update," *Personnel Administrator* 28 (June 1983): 16.
3. Megginson, *Personnel Management*, p. 422.
4. *Appraising Managerial Performance: Current Practices and Future Directions*, Conference Board Report No. 723 (New York: Conference Board, 1977), p. 26.
5. Name has been disguised.
6. Douglas McGregor, "An Uneasy Look at Performance Appraisal," *Harvard Business Review* 35 (May–June 1957): 90.
7. L. Stockford and W. H. Bissell, "Factors Involved in Establishing a Merit Rating Scale," *Personnel* 26 (September 1949): 97.
8. H. H. Meyer and W. B. Walker,, "A Study of Factors Relating to the Effectiveness of a Performance Appraisal Program," *Personnel Psychology* 14 (August 1961): 291–98.
9. Sidney Weintraub, "A Law That Cannot Be Repealed," *Challenge* 10 (April 1962): 17–19.
10. William E. Reif, "Intrinsic versus Extrinsic Rewards: Resolving the Controversy," *Human Resources Management* 14 (Summer 1975): 7ff.
11. Desda Moss, "Study: Sex, Race Still Affect Wages," *USA Today*, February 26, 1987, p. 3A.
12. *Washington County, Oregon* v. *Gunther*, June 1981.
13. Robert B. Hershey, "The Wage Gap Between Men and Women Faces a New Assault," *Louisville Courier-Journal*, November 6, 1983, pp. 1 and 4.
14. Pete Yost, "EEOC Rejects Comparable Worth as Means to Judge Discrimination," *Louisville Courier-Journal*, June 19, 1985, p. B–1.
15. "U.S. Courts Say 'No' to Comparable Worth," *Resource* (American Society for Personnel Administration pamphlet), 1985.

16. Adapted from Leon C. Megginson, Donald C. Mosley, and Paul H. Pietri, Jr., *Management: Concepts and Applications*, 3rd ed. (New York: Harper & Row, 1989), Chapter 11.
17. Bledsoe, op. cit.

SUGGESTIONS FOR FURTHER READING

Borinstein, D. I. "Sparking Self-Esteem." *Management World* 12 (April 1983): 36–37.

Galante, Steven P. "Employers Acquiring a Taste for Providing Benefit 'Menus'." *The Wall Street Journal*, July 21, 1986, p. 21.

"Mandatory Retirement Will Be Retired." *Changing Times* 40 (October 1986): 9.

Posner, Bruce G. "Pay for Profits." *Inc.* 40 (September 1986): 57–60.

Sheets, Kenneth R. "GM's Bonus Babies." *U.S. News & World Report*, March 2, 1983, pp. 42–43.

Yancey, Matt. "Study: Most New Jobs Pay Less Than $7,000 a Year." *Mobile Register*, December 10, 1986, p. 11–C.

12
COUNSELING EMPLOYEES

OBJECTIVES

After reading and studying the material in this chapter, you should be able to:

Explain the role of counseling employees in supervisory management.
Describe the counseling process.
Identify and discuss the areas in which counseling is needed.
State what employee-assistance programs (EAPs) are and explain their benefits.
Explain some of the limits to the use of counseling.
Discuss some problems involved in counseling.
Explain the benefits that the employee and the supervisor receive from counseling.
Show how counseling can be made more effective.

IMPORTANT TERMS

counseling
conference
occupational stress
employee-assistance programs
   (EAPs)
job burnout
alcoholism

cross-addiction
drug abuse
accident-prone workers *or*
   injury repeaters
outplacement *or* disengagement
empathy

CHAPTER OUTLINE

There are two ways supervisors can handle problems. They can (1) use the "human-relations approach" of appealing positively to subordinates to do what needs to be done, or (2) use power and lay down the law, telling workers what *has to be done*. The first method is called *counseling*; the second is referred to as *discipline* and will be covered in Chapter 13.

THE ROLE OF COUNSELING IN SUPERVISORY MANAGEMENT

Counseling is found in all areas of life. When people visit a doctor, lawyer, or minister, they usually seek counsel. Often, when employees seek out their supervisor, they need counseling. The purpose of counseling by a supervisor is to help employees do a better job and to give them an accurate evaluation of their standing in the organization. Counseling also provides employees with an understanding of their relationships with their supervisor and co-workers.

Counseling by a supervisor involves communication, motivation, discipline, and the use of psychological methods to give professional advice to subordinates. Almost every supervisor, regardless of his or her area of responsibility, is constantly involved in performing this function. Unfortunately, not all supervisors are adequately skilled or professionally trained to do such counseling effectively.

The primary question facing supervisors is *not* whether to counsel subordinates, but where to draw the line between what is considered to be valid influence and what is not. There is no definite answer to this question, for it is one that must be answered by each individual.

Under what circumstances do you think a supervisor can legitimately counsel an employee without invading the employee's privacy?

In the course of helping and leading employees—and that is the supervisor's primary job—many things happen that can make a human being a better person, a more effective worker, and a more cooperative individual within a group. Counseling has come to be accepted as a very important part of this leadership function. It occurs at all levels and with all subordinates.

WHAT OCCURS DURING THE COUNSELING PROCESS?

By definition, **counseling** is professional guidance of one individual by another, using psychological techniques, especially the interview. Note that supervisory counseling operates in a conversational setting between the supervisor and the employee. You can talk with one person and draw that person out. But if another person joins in, it is no longer counseling—it is a **conference**, which is a meeting of two or more people to discuss matters of common concern.

What occurs between two people when counseling takes place? Notice in Figure 12–1 that thoughts, ideas, and words are going from one person to another,

FIGURE 12–1   WHAT COUNSELING INVOLVES

THOUGHTS, IDEAS, FEELINGS, EMOTIONS, ATTITUDES, AND WORDS

but that each person has feelings that are not being spoken. Feelings, emotions, and attitudes—some of which may be threatening—are being exchanged. There are things being said, and there are some things being left unsaid. The exchanges that take place during counseling are not limited to the conscious processes. Usually a great deal occurs at the subconscious level. However, enough happens at the conscious level to allow the supervisor doing the counseling to proceed with good judgment and a sense of direction.

Finally, counseling involves the whole person. We need to emphasize at this point that all of us are physical, mental, and spiritual beings driven by two systems of motivation: conscious and subconscious. What the counselees feel, believe, or perceive to be true is important because, to them, it is true.

> *Joan Biren's work output had fallen off sharply during the past several weeks, as had her attendance and "spirit."[1] She seemed complacent and did not appear to have her heart in her work. When her supervisor had a counseling session with her to find out what the problem was, the supervisor was shattered to learn that she was the problem—at least from Joan's point of view. It seemed that two brand-new employees had been given newer, more modern equipment than Joan, who had seen this as a slap in the face and was quite bitter about it.*
>
> *The supervisor explained that within a month everyone in the department would have new, upgraded equipment. She said that it had just seemed to make more sense to start the new employees on the new equipment first to avoid having to retrain them later. Joan would probably have new and better equipment within a week or so, she added.*

Note that what was important in this example was what Joan thought, not the actual facts.

AREAS OF EMPLOYEE COUNSELING

Counseling is involved in virtually all aspects of the supervisor-employee relationship. It begins with the hiring phase and does not end until the employee leaves the company. Sometimes counseling may even extend into the employee's retirement. Yet there are certain areas where counseling is practiced more frequently than in others. These areas are (1) job performance, (2) physical illness, (3) mental or emotional illness and stress, (4) alcohol and drug abuse, (5) safety, (6) absenteeism, (7) layoff or termination, (8) retirement, and (9) career planning. Figure 12–2 shows that the most common reasons for counseling are (1) alcohol and drug abuse, (2) retirement, (3) emotional stress, (4) termination, and (5) career planning. Another important area—disciplinary cases—will be discussed in Chapter 13.

Job Performance

Knowing how we are doing on our jobs is one of our greatest desires as employees. Therefore, supervisors should frequently inform their employees of their work

FIGURE 12–2   REASONS FOR EMPLOYEE COUNSELING

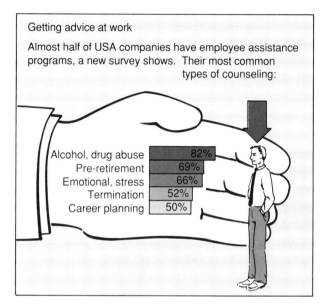

Getting advice at work

Almost half of USA companies have employee assistance programs, a new survey shows. Their most common types of counseling:

Alcohol, drug abuse   82%
Pre-retirement   69%
Emotional, stress   66%
Termination   52%
Career planning   50%

Source: Copyright, 1986 USA TODAY. Reprinted with permission.

progress. One of the ways to do this is the appraisal interview, discussed in the previous chapter. After appraising the performance of an employee, the supervisor should discuss the results with the employee in order to motivate the employee to build on strengths and eliminate weaknesses. For instance, one study in a large manufacturing firm showed that employees who improved their performance as a result of performance appraisals did so because of the way their supervisors had conducted the appraisal interview.[2]

Also important, however, is day-to-day discussion of the problems an employee encounters. An effective supervisor will help that employee solve work problems, plan to improve output, and find ways to improve quality.

Physical Illness

Counseling in the area of physical illness involves seeing to it that employees are well when they come to work and continue to stay so while on the job. Management is concerned about the health of employees because, if they are not well, they cannot perform their assigned tasks.

An employee of the Illinois Central Gulf Railroad complained to one of the authors of this textbook about another employee who wouldn't stay home when he was sick. "He comes to work sneezing, wheezing, and coughing and says to us, 'I'll lick this cold if it kills me.' Instead of killing him, it makes the rest of us sick so that we have to lose time."

If you were the supervisor, what would you say or do to the sick employee?

One particularly difficult aspect of this area of counseling is to know when a physical impairment reaches the point where the ill person is no longer employable or must take sick leave. Many ailments may cause a gradual deterioration; therefore, the supervisor must decide whether the reduced efficiency of the ill employee can no longer be tolerated and whether definite action must be taken. This type of decision requires value judgments that cannot be made easily, as shown in the following examples:

> *John Wilson was a shift supervisor of the catalytic cracking units for a Texas refinery.[3] On his last round of the units, he was told by Bill Barnes, the first-class operator of Unit No. 3, that everything was okay. But Ray Moore, Bill's assistant, had said that the unit was dangerously losing pressure, and Bill wouldn't let him do anything about it. John checked again with Bill, who assured him that everything was fine.*
>
> *Bill Barnes, 62 years old, had worked for the refinery for 30 years. Recently he had become crippled with arthritis and couldn't walk, so he directed the unit's operations from a chair in the center of the control room. While Bill tended to "let the unit run itself," management ignored it because he had been a top-notch operator, and the other operators "carried" him. John and other managers had often discussed retirement with Bill, as nothing could be done to improve his condition. But Bill insisted that he could do the job.*
>
> *Two hours later, Bill called John to say they were reducing the rate of operations because of a "slight problem." By the time John got to the unit, the pressure was so dangerously low that he immediately shut the unit down. At the end of the workday, Bill was told not to come to work until he was called. Management had decided to offer him early retirement. If he chose not to accept it, he would be terminated.*

Mental or Emotional Illness—and Stress

In our culture there are many external pressures, tensions, and stresses that result in mental or emotional problems for employees. Also, the pressure to succeed, the pace of events, and the many problems in modern business add stress on the employee's mind, which is already suffering from the pressures of family, social, religious, and governmental problems. Here is one indication of how severe these external pressures are: According to the American Medical Association, of the four primary illnesses—heart disease, mental illness, alcoholism, and cancer—

the first three are directly related to stress and strain. And even cancer *may* be indirectly caused by these factors![4]

Of course, all of us will be emotionally upset at one time or another. The fact that we are mildly disturbed emotionally does not mean that we need hospitalization or psychiatric treatment. Yet sometimes the work situation may cause us so much stress that we have difficulty coping with it. The sources of our emotional problems may be physical disorders, some handicapping disability, interpersonal conflicts, or other factors in the work environment. These problems are referred to as **occupational stress**. If any of these factors interfere with an employee's job performance, the supervisor must become a counselor. The supervisor may counsel the employee to make possible improvements in job behavior or to seek professional advice, depending on the severity of the employee's behavior deviations.

Counseling programs—called **employee assistance programs (EAPs)**—are rapidly increasing in United States companies. For example, Tandem Corporation, faced with the growing popularity of its EAP, hired an outside counseling firm and provided employees a toll-free number to call for assistance with problems. Participation in Exxon's program increased from 2 percent to 5 percent in four years. And 13 percent of Steelcase, Inc.'s employees took advantage of its comprehensive program in just one year. One reason for this increase is workers' perception that "it's okay to use EAPs."[5]

Related to the problem of occupational stress is **job burnout**, which is physical and/or mental depletion significantly below one's capable level of performance. This increasingly severe problem is a major cause of worksite antagonisms and conflict, as well as absenteeisms. To help combat this problem, management should design periods of rest from responsibility for stressful jobs, or rotate employees into less pressured jobs.[6]

Chemical Dependency

An increasingly costly problem facing employers—in terms of both economic and human factors—is chemical dependency. This dependency results in two different, but related, diseases: alcoholism and drug addiction. As shown in Figure 12–2 on page 297, the most common reason for counseling is alcohol and drug abuse. This finding was verified by Columbia University's Center for Social Policy and Practice in the Workplace, which also found that alcohol and drug abuse are the most common problems handled by EAPs.[7]

ALCOHOLISM. For a long time, alcoholism was viewed as essentially a moral issue calling for social censure and punishment. In 1956, however, the American Medical Association (AMA) recognized **alcoholism** as a *disease* resulting from drinking alcoholic beverages to the point where normal functioning is impaired. In a recent survey, the National Center for Disease Control found that 10 percent of men and 3 percent of women were "heavy drinkers," averaging at least two drinks per day.[8]

In spite of these facts, many supervisors often go to great lengths to protect alcoholic employees, considering them simply to "have a bit of a drinking problem." Some supervisors refuse to make performance appraisals during an alcoholic employee's "bad times." Or they may fail to record the employee's symptoms until these become chronic. However, if a supervisor faces up to this problem and if the company has an enlightened and consistent policy toward such employees, the problem of alcoholism is usually reduced.

An enlightened company policy toward alcoholism usually begins by recognizing that it is a disease. Then the supervisor can take the following steps:

1. Identify the symptoms by which the alcoholic employees can be recognized early, as shown in Figure 12–3.
2. Set up a treatment program to assist such employees.
3. Set limits of tolerance—including immediate discharge—if an employee doesn't take the treatment.

FIGURE 12–3 EARLY SIGNS OF ALCOHOLISM

- Excessive tardiness for work, with invalid or improbable excuses.
- Increasing frequency and length of absences, especially on Mondays.
- Slackening work pace.
- Declining quantity and quality of performance.
- Increasing frequency and intensity of arguments with colleagues.
- Poor, "fuzzy," or irrational decisions.

Where alcoholism is detected early and where alcoholic employees can be forced to take treatment or lose their jobs, companies are usually successful in combating this problem. However, one especially difficult aspect of this problem is **cross-addiction**, in which alcoholics are addicted to other chemical substances.

Alcoholism costs industry over $15.6 million annually in absenteeism and medical costs. Moreover, the losses from inefficiencies and slowdowns, from interpersonal problems, and from the need to discharge highly trained and skilled alcoholic employees cannot even be estimated!

DRUG ABUSE. According to Peter Bensinger, former head of the United States Drug Enforcement Agency and now partner in a drug and alcohol abuse consulting firm, absenteeism is 2.5 times greater, medical claims are 3 times higher, and accidents are 3 to 4 times more likely among alcohol and drug abusers.[9] While **drug abuse** is still less prevalent than alcoholism, it poses a different problem for supervisors. Drugs are more difficult for industry to contain because when the dope addict gets into an organization, the pusher is often close behind. Or the drug users themselves may sell drugs to other workers to provide money for their own habit.

The drug problem is found all the way from the newest, lowest-level employees up to, and including, senior executives who have been with the firm for a long time. Many companies such as airlines, railroads, utilities, and steel mills, and others where safety is paramount, are now running drug screens on applicants, instituting company-wide education programs, helping those who are discovered to be on drugs to improve themselves, and hiring and rehiring employees certified to be ex-addicts. While many of these procedures are not proving very effective, some are.

Within a year after Carpenter Technology Corporation began screening job applicants for drug use at its Bridgeport, Connecticut, steel mill, attendance went up and disciplinary problems went down. During the first year, 28.5 percent of prospective hourly and salaried employees tested positive for alcohol or drugs. Most cases—51 percent—involved marijuana. [10]

Safety

Many safety engineers now believe that accidents are as much a product of human factors as of improper working conditions or the employees' physical condition. Studies indicate that there are **accident-prone workers** (often called **injury repeaters**) with personality types and recognizable syndromes peculiar to them (see Figure 12–4). Such personalities can be identified during the selection procedure. Yet it is not always feasible to be this selective, nor is it always desirable to refuse to hire otherwise capable workers solely because they may have accidents. Therefore, safety is one of the more important areas of employee counseling.

It appears that a short test to determine accident-proneness is now possible if equal employment opportunity laws will permit it. But for those injury repeaters who are currently employed or will be hired, counseling is a desirable and necessary method of reducing injuries. Such counseling could take the form of

FIGURE 12–4   CHARACTERISTICS OF THE ACCIDENT-PRONE PERSONALITY

- Bluntness, abruptness, impatience
- Feeling of superiority to institutions and other people
- Contempt for warnings, rules, and regulations
- Disdain for pain
- Emotional insecurity
- Aggressive personality
- Hostility toward self
- Poor motivation
- Instinctive mavericks
- Age 20 to 24
- Poor motivation

Source: See Leon C. Megginson, *Personnel Management: A Human Resources Approach*, 5th ed. (Homewood, IL: Richard D. Irwin, 1985), pp. 408–9, for further details and clarification.

pointing out that their actions can be prevented and that it is in their best interest, as well as the company's interest, to attempt to do so.

Absenteeism

Absenteeism has always been a problem for supervisors, but today it is becoming more critical. Some of this loss of work is unavoidable for various reasons. Yet the avoidable part is substantial and needs to be controlled. As indicated earlier, much lost time is caused by illness brought on by the worker's reaction to stress in the work situation. If loss of work is the result of the employee's negligence or lack of responsibility, the supervisor may correct it through counseling. If absenteeism is caused by physical illness, the employee may be referred to the medical staff, if available. If absenteeism is caused by mental illness, the employee may require outside professional treatment.

Layoff or Termination

An area of counseling that has grown in importance since the 1982–83 recession is **outplacement** or **disengagement**, which are terms used for counseling people who are laid off or terminated. Since this activity is one of the most difficult— and yet important—aspects of the supervisor's job, the task often falls on the personnel office. But counseling should begin before termination. If it fails, or if the termination is inevitable and based on factors beyond the employee's control, help may be given in seeking another job or preparing the outplaced employee to make the needed psychological adjustments.

Retirement

It was expected that amendments to the Age Discrimination in Employment Act essentially prohibiting mandatory retirement would cause many people to continue working. Instead, a "retirement revolution" seems to be occurring, and these retiring employees need counseling. One Bureau of National Affairs (BNA), Inc., survey found that 36 percent of responding firms had a preretirement counseling program.[11] The topics usually covered included (1) financial planning, (2) earning money after retirement, and (3) health problems.

While many people still believe that retiring is harmful, a study at the Veterans Administration Outpatient Clinic in Boston found no significant difference in health change between a group of retirees and a group that continued working.[12]

Career Planning

More enlightened employers are now having supervisors help employees plan their careers. The usual activities involve identifying and tracking promising employees, designing appropriate educational and training programs for them, and notifying them of opportunities and paths for development and advancement.

LIMITS TO THE USE OF COUNSELING

There are certain limits to the use of counseling that supervisors should consider. Essentially, these limits are (1) to stay clear of strictly personal problems, except to the extent that they influence work, (2) to restrict counseling to the employee's job performance, and (3) to keep counseling as specific as feasible.

Avoiding Discussion of Personal Problems

Very often, when a supervisor counsels an employee about poor work performance, the employee brings personal problems into the discussion and complains about them. It is good that the employee trusts the supervisor, but this practice can be harmful. How? Sometimes when you begin to tell a friend about your personal life and shortcomings, you tend to open up and tell more than you intend to. Later, you may decide that it was a mistake to reveal so much of yourself. Then you may dislike your friend because he or she knows things about you that make you feel ashamed or guilty. When you become aware of these feelings, you resent the friend who made you face reality and are inclined to avoid that person and sacrifice the former friendship.

Of course, we're not saying that a supervisor should never listen to an employee's personal problems. However, the supervisor must be certain that the work relationship will stand up in spite of what the employee has confided. Finally, if the supervisor gives advice on personal problems (such as divorce, problem children, or buying and selling property) and the employee suffers a loss as a result, the supervisor and the company may be open to legal damages. Some companies, recognizing the close relationship between family problems and work problems, have set up in-plant family counseling services with outside professional counselors. Kennecott Copper has such professional counselors. Employees who discussed their problems with these counselors had a decrease of 75 percent in work-related costs and 55 percent in health-care costs. Their attendance also improved by 52 percent.[13]

Dealing with Job Performance Only

In general, counseling of employees should be concerned principally with their work relationships, performance, reliability, dependability, thoroughness, efficiency, ability to get along with co-workers, and related activities. Counseling should be restricted to factors that detract from job performance rather than include all factors of the entire work environment.

STOP AND THINK

To what extent is Kennecott Copper's program really related to personal problems?

Giving Specific Comments

Counseling should emphasize the feelings and perceptions of both the employee and the supervisor, as well as the work situation. Yet the supervisor's comments should be as specific as possible. Instead of telling an employee, "Your job performance is poor," you can say, "You reached only 75 percent of your work goal," or "You have been tardy or absent x times." In this way, the employee has something concrete to work on during the performance-appraisal interview and when improving job performance. Table 12–1 shows how general comments can be turned into specific ones.

TABLE 12–1   GENERAL VS. SPECIFIC COUNSELING COMMENTS

General	Specific
You must improve your attitude toward customers.	You must make customers feel relaxed and comfortable.
You must do better on your production.	Your work must increase 15 percent to reach standard.
You've got to do a better job of communication.	You must notify me in advance when you can't keep an appointment.
You need to improve your cooperation with the production supervisors.	You must give the production supervisors a time estimate as to when you reasonably expect to complete a job.

SOME PROBLEMS INVOLVED IN COUNSELING

As with any other leadership activity, there are some problems involved in the counseling process. These must be carefully handled for the counseling to be most effective.

Reluctance to Point Out an Employee's Weaknesses

One of the problems involved in employee counseling is the supervisor's reluctance to talk about an employee's weaknesses and shortcomings. Basically this reluctance is the result of people's distrust of one another—their dread of sitting down and telling another person how badly he or she is doing. They feel that they will make a mess of things or, worse still, cause the counselee to stop liking them. Ironically, this rarely happens if the proper supervisor-subordinate relationship has been established.

Emotional Involvement

Even very intelligent employees may get scared in a counseling session. While the supervisor may take it for granted that the counselee is understanding everything being discussed, this may not be true if the employee is scared or uneasy. This is particularly true if the employee is insecure and feels threatened in any way. For this reason, emotional involvement on the part of the supervisor must be kept at a minimum during counseling.

Employee's Request to be Criticized

A problem may arise when a subordinate asks the supervisor to criticize the former's performance. The employee may want attention or want to get away from the job and so asks for an "evaluation of how I'm doing." In the first place, counseling is not criticism. Figure 12–5 shows that criticism is not the same as counseling (compare with Figure 12–1 on page 295). In the second place, if the subordinate catches the supervisor off guard and wants to be criticized, in all probability that is the time when counseling should be postponed. Perhaps it would be better for the supervisor to study the subordinate's record (particularly of recent problems), to think the matter over, and to set a more appropriate time for sitting down and talking freely. The supervisor should think of counseling as a constructive effort to help build a stronger and better working relationship with the subordinate.

Conflict of Values

All of us have value systems that are made up of our way of thinking about individuals or ideas. We have our own beliefs, convictions, and perceptions of truth or what is right, and our own ideas about the worth of such things as hard work, overtime, or loyalty to the employer. A value system provides us with a shock absorber to cushion us against many of the unpleasant aspects of life. When

FIGURE 12–5 EXAMPLES OF CRITICISMS

counseling threatens the subordinate's value system, it threatens the foundations of his or her life. A supervisor must take these fixed attitudes into consideration when counseling an employee. Otherwise, the counseling may backfire. That is, the employee may not pay attention and may even become belligerent.

Has this ever happened to you when you were "counseled" by an unsympathetic teacher?

Overreliance on Counseling

Counseling can be potentially dangerous if employees become "hooked" on it. That is, employees may seek their supervisor for counsel because they assume that the supervisor is able and *willing* to give it. If the results of the counseling satisfy them, they may seek out the supervisor every time they need help, instead of doing things for themselves. That is, their independence may deteriorate.

Transference of Employee Problems

Finally, there is the possibility that one problem may lead to another. For example, if a subordinate has a drinking problem and is counseled to overcome it, he or she may begin to have periods of depression. That is, when counseling is provided successfully, it does not necessarily guarantee that the employee is cured. He or she may only escape into another problem area, as shown in Figure 12–6.

BENEFITS OF COUNSELING

Both those being counseled and those doing the counseling receive many benefits from *effective* counseling sessions if there's a certain amount of basic trust and respect between the two parties. Some of these benefits are discussed here.

Reduces Anxiety, Fear, and Distrust

When areas of misunderstanding and apprehension are cleared up, counseling reduces anxiety, fear, and distrust. Counseling tends to develop a better working relationship and strengthen it. Counseling also tends to get disturbed relationships back on a smooth basis.

> *The employees in Jim's department were surly and "soldiering" on the job. Jim started counseling with them on a one-to-one basis. The problem was that the workers saw some machines from the plant being crated up and shipped to*

FIGURE 12–6   TRANSFERENCE OF PROBLEMS

another plant. Thinking their plant was closing, they became unproductive. When Jim explained that new equipment was on order to upgrade their jobs, the problem was cleared up.

Encourages Cooperation

People can work alongside one another and coordinate their efforts but still not have effective cooperation. Yet cooperation is necessary in all organizations. When situations are clarified, when misunderstandings are cleared up, and when uncertainty and confusion are eliminated, cooperation is encouraged.

A student was hired part-time as an orderly in a local hospital's emergency room. When asked to do cleaning and other routine jobs, he griped that it was beneath his dignity as a college junior to do those jobs. When the head nurse explained that she only asked him to do things that she—as an RN— didn't have time to do, and asked him to cooperate with her and the other employees, his work improved.

Gives Sense of Direction

Counseling often reveals for the first time certain capacities that an employee has been unaware of possessing. The supervisor may detect them, bring them out into the open, and counsel the employee to develop those qualities that are desirable. If the better qualities can be cultivated effectively, the supervisor may discover that this employee should be working in a higher capacity because of such assets or qualities.

On the other hand, an employee may discover through counseling that he or she has certain drawbacks, handicaps, unpleasant traits, or antagonistic attitudes that adversely affect his or her interpersonal relationships and personal success. When the supervisor points them out to the employee in a constructive fashion, the employee may for the first time see why he or she has had such a hard time in getting along or moving ahead. Thus counseling gives employees a sense of personal direction.

> *Mary was unhappy as a secretary in a department store, and her work was only mediocre. After her supervisor pointed out the problem and counseled with her, Mary asked for a transfer to the jewelry sales section. Her work is now satisfactory, and she's pleased with her higher income.*

Stimulates Personal Growth

Counseling stimulates growth in the employee because, as areas for progress are indicated, she or he can begin to grow and advance. Likewise, as weaknesses and handicaps are pointed out, the employee can work to overcome them.

> *Ann Green, lab technician, was 30 years old. She had two children and a husband who was an "off-and-on" student, an "off-and-on" worker. Ann had a B.S. degree with some graduate work in biology. Ann worked by herself in one part of the lab doing chemical assay work. Gradually, the quality and quantity of her work declined, and the lab became more disorganized. Her superior counseled her to complete her graduate degree and be promoted to a more responsible position, which Ann did.*

Counseling also stimulates growth in the supervisor. It helps the supervisor learn by enriching his or her capacity for leadership. It helps the supervisor treat everyone differently, for one cannot counsel without perceiving the uniqueness of every individual. The benefit that the supervisor derives from counseling is just a specific instance of the general rule that one cannot help another person without helping himself or herself in some way. Thus, counseling provides a feedback of results.

> *In the example noted above, Ann Green's supervisor had a sense of achievement when Ann completed her graduate degree and was promoted into supervision.*

MAKING COUNSELING MORE EFFECTIVE

If counseling is such an important part of supervision, how can it be made more effective? While each supervisor must develop his or her own methods, there are some general guidelines. Also, each firm should provide the supervisors with some detailed guides.

To begin with, a supervisor must decide how much an employee means to the organization when the counseling becomes an involved and continuous process.

An employee can be counseled once, twice, or many times, but the supervisor must decide whether this employee has reached the maximum degree of efficiency with the firm. Conversely, has this employee reached the minimum acceptable behavioral level? Is this employee a chronic sorehead, a troublemaker? Is this employee out to destroy the organization? If so, the supervisor had better be the first to know it. The employee can be counseled and given a fair and equitable period of time to correct his or her deficiencies. In extreme cases like this, the supervisor may consult with his or her own boss concerning what course of action to take. But the action must be in line with company policy.

Acting Naturally

You can't read a book about counseling or hear someone speak on the subject and then imitate the author or speaker and expect to be effective. In performing this leadership function, supervisors should act as they normally do with their subordinates. They should act naturally, as shown in Figure 12–7. The supervisor cannot be formal or mechanical with the subordinate and achieve the desired objective. The leadership technique that will get the job done must be used, but this technique will vary with the person being counseled, as well as with the situation.

Empathizing with the Counselee

Effective counseling is based on the ability to put oneself in another person's place. This ability is called **empathy**. Essentially, empathy is a feeling toward the other person that makes it easier to know what to say (or what not to say) to him or her. It is knowing that when a troubled person comes to you for counsel, you should sit down, listen, and help him or her find a way out of the problem.

FIGURE 12–7   ACT NATURALLY WHEN COUNSELING AN EMPLOYEE

Empathy is one of the most useful assets that supervisors can have when counseling subordinates. The supervisor should feel some of the employee's feelings and be more understanding, more sincere, and more forthright in trying to help the person. Sometimes counseling demands straight talking; sometimes it demands drawing a person out; and sometimes only a kind word may help build up the person's ego. Remember, putting yourself in the other person's place is empathy, not sympathy.

Listening Attentively

You can't "fake it" with subordinates. So one requirement for effective counseling is to *really* listen. The basic rule for the counseling supervisor is to keep the mouth shut and the ears and eyes open. The supervisor should sense what is really bothering the employee. In other words, listen to what the person says, but listen also for what is *not* being said, because a person often does not talk about what is really on her or his mind. It is here that a supervisor can use the "active listening" techniques that you read about in Chapter 6.

Strengthening the Employee's Ego

Finally, when you find that an employee needs counseling about a certain problem, you should start the corrective interview by pointing out the employee's strengths rather than weaknesses. A little praise is needed to soften the criticisms you may have. Build up the employee's ego by personally relating to him or her. Then get the employee to tell you what is really wrong. Figure 12–8 summarizes some practical suggestions for the corrective interview.

FIGURE 12–8   SUGGESTIONS FOR THE CORRECTIVE INTERVIEW

- State the purpose of the interview.
- Identify the situation or behavior that you want changed.
- Listen to the employee's point of view; help him or her talk.
- Get agreement on the problem.
- Get the employee's involvement in determining a solution.
- Have the employee summarize the corrective action.
- Reinforce the changed behavior.

CHAPTER REVIEW

A certain number of employees in all firms have personality difficulties that result in stress and strain. Sometimes these stresses are connected with the job, but equally often they result from home problems, relations with other employees, the general makeup of the individual, or the pressures caused by the complexities of present-day living. To meet the needs of such people, many large firms employ industrial counselors, whose activities are set apart from the usual grievance and industrial relations machinery. In the vast majority of organizations, however, this important activity must be performed by the employee's supervisor.

The most important thing for a supervisor to keep in mind is: With whom do the employees have a good relationship? If it is with their superior, he or she is the one to counsel them; if it is with someone else, that person should be the counselor. It should be recognized that tensions and frustrations are not inherently "wrong"; we pay a price for everything we do or get, and these frustrations are the price we pay for motivation.

Although counseling is exceedingly important (probably *because* it is important), it is equally difficult. For this reason, either specially trained counselors should be used or supervisors should have special training in counseling. More important, supervisors must know when to do it and when not to because, when a person's inner being becomes "disrobed" before another person, he or she can become very resentful. Thus, the very objective of counseling may be self-defeating.

QUESTIONS FOR REVIEW AND DISCUSSION

1. What is the supervisor's role in counseling, and why is counseling important?
2. "When a third party comes into the picture, it is no longer counseling." Comment on this statement.
3. What are some of the areas where counseling is needed?
4. What are employee assistance programs, and how effective are they?
5. "Counseling should avoid personal problems."
   a. What is the reason behind this statement?
   b. What is the limitation of this statement from the supervisor's point of view?
   c. What is a reasonable limitation on dealing with an employee's personal life during counseling?
6. What are some of the benefits that can be expected from effective counseling?
7. How can counseling be made more effective?

LEARNING EXERCISE 12–1
PERSONAL PROBLEMS

An office manager was hired by a group of physicians in a small town in Kansas to head the employees at their private clinic. The office manager supervised a receptionist, two nurses, a lab technician, and a typist.

The receptionist was married and had three children. She was quite capable in her work and seemed to get along with everyone, including the patients. However, she began to receive many phone calls during work hours. Word got around that it was her husband who was calling her so often; everyone knew that he was an alcoholic. At times he kept her on the phone at great length, and she would ask the other employees to answer the other lines.

It eventually got to the point where the receptionist could not make appointments for patients or handle the incoming calls as she should. One day the doctors asked the office manager for suggestions in dealing with this situation.

Answer the following questions:

1. If you were the office manager, what suggestions would you make?
2. If you were one of the doctors, what action would you take based on your suggestions as the office manager? Explain.

LEARNING EXERCISE 12–2
EMPLOYEE ASSISTANCE*

Dennis P. Kennedy was in over his head. An employee facing a personal crisis had come to him for help, and suddenly Kennedy was in the uncomfortable role of playing psychiatrist. "I got to thinking, as a supervisor, what background do I have to give personal advice? Yet the problem was affecting her job performance," recalls Kennedy, vice-president and treasurer for Paysaver Credit Union of Melrose Park, Illinois.

Paysaver lifted this burden from Kennedy and other supervisors with an innovative solution by contracting with an outside source for employee counseling. For $8,000 a year from Paysaver, 47 employees and their family members are entitled to use the Employee Resource Centers (ERC), a non-profit family counseling service staffed by social service professionals. The fee includes three sessions per employee, normally priced at $50 an hour. Follow-up visits are priced according to income.

The contacts are confidential—ERC tells Paysaver only how many employees use the service and the kinds of problems treated. Amy S. Bayer, controller for Paysaver, stresses that ERC is not offered "in lieu of medical benefits, but as an important addition." Paysaver's agreement with ERC also includes individualized training sessions for supervisors and seminars for employees on such issues as conflict resolution, effective communication, and stress management.

Answer the following questions:

1. What are the advantages and disadvantages to a small company of a program such as ERCs?
2. Will dependence on outside counseling make the relationship between employees and their supervisor less close?

LEARNING EXERCISE 12–3
JANE'S POOR PERFORMANCE

Assume that you are Jane Beck's supervisor. You were going to push her for promotion this year, but she has been performing poorly on the job lately. This is completely

*© 1985 *Venture Magazine* Inc.

unlike her. Her recent work is probably the poorest you've seen so far. This situation has to improve immediately because of the new demand for efficiency in your department. You decide to call Jane in and have a talk with her. You know that her unusually poor work just can't continue!

Role-play this situation with another student. Show how the counseling *should* proceed. After the role play, ask yourself such questions as: When can you terminate this type of interview? How did you feel during the interview?

LEARNING EXERCISE 12–4
THE SLOPPY REPORT

The following exchange took place between Charlene Rowe, a supervisor, and her employee, Leonard Busche, who had been "called on the carpet."[14]

Rowe: Come in, Leonard. Have a seat. (*Leonard sits down.*) I suppose you're wondering why I want to talk to you.

Busche: Yes, I guess I am.

Rowe: Well, Leonard, recently a little thing has come up that I want to know your feelings about. Remember the Adamson report?

Busche: What about it?

Rowe: To be frank with you, Leonard, there was a lot of disagreement on the figures that were used, and the boss wants the whole thing done over. It wasn't up to the level of reports you've been turning out in the past; I have to admit that myself. But I wanted to hear your views about it.

Busche: Well, there isn't much to say. I sort of figured it would get bounced anyway. I wasn't tickled about the damn thing either. (*Getting a little emotional.*)

Rowe: You weren't pleased with it either?

Busche: Heck, no, I wasn't! Look, it takes about 25 to 30 hours, at least, for me to write up a report like that—even when I've already worked up the figures! You know how long I spent on that report? About five hours! And I wasn't as sure on the figures as I should have been either.

Rowe: You didn't get to put in much time on the report, is that it?

Busche: No, I didn't. In fact, I don't blame them for bouncing it at all. Like I said, it was a lousy job. But it won't be the last lousy job they'll get from me unless I get some help down here. There's no way I can run a research department and do the odds and ends that get sent my direction! When we were a smaller outfit, it was possible, but not now. What the heck does everybody expect from me anyway?

Rowe: You're saying that you have too many assignments, then?

Busche: Yes, that's exactly what I'm saying! (*Getting hot under the collar.*) I'm expected to do everybody's odds and ends. Production wants this, marketing wants that, cost accounting wants something else. Then along comes the Control

Committee and their darned report. They give me a week's notice to get it out. I know I'm running a staff department, but there's no way a person can handle all I've been doing lately. And this was a sloppy report, I know. But it won't be the last.

Rowe: Leonard, you know how we've counted on you in the past for these reports. Frankly, they're very important, and you've been doing such a great job on them. Is there any way we might be able to work out this problem?

Busche: How we might work it out? Yeah, give me three new people. (*Only half joking.*)

Rowe: You think extra help would do it?

Busche: Oh, I don't know. I guess we could handle it all if production would get off my back. Whenever they want something, they get the VP to call me and tell me how badly they need it in short order. That's what happened on the Adamson report. I had to finish it in three days. Millican [vice president for production] called with a rush job to be done and said that Henderly would be up to see me with the details. I guess I haven't got the guts to say, "No, I can't do it on such short notice." How do you say that to a VP?

Rowe: It's hard to turn down a VP. Do you feel that I could help in any way?

Busche: Well, you have a lot more say with Millican than I do. But he's sure a bull-headed type.

Rowe: Well, let me worry about that, Leonard. I'll have a talk with him. And if he comes up with another of these "emergencies" that you honestly can't handle, explain to him as best you can that you can't get it out that fast. But offer to talk with me about it. If he still insists, then let me know and I'll talk with him.

Busche: Well, that might get Mr. Millican pretty hot, but it'll sure take a lot of pressure off of me, boss. (*Looking somewhat relieved.*) When Millican calls on short notice, I'll still do my best to work it in. But if I can't handle it, I'll level with him like you said. Somehow I feel a lot better getting this thing out. I was really getting in a rut.

Rowe: Well, Leonard, it's my job to help. You think that this will help your load on the regular Control Committee reports?

Busche: Yeah, I don't think there'll be as much trouble. I hope there'll never be another sorry one like that Adamson report. It was lousy and I knew it. (*Standing, ready to leave.*)

Rowe: Well, Leonard, I'm glad we were able to work this thing out. (*Leonard leaves.*)

Answer the following questions:

1. Do you believe Charlene Rowe handled the interview well or poorly? Why?
2. What should Charlene have done differently? Explain.

ENDNOTES

1. Name disguised at her request.
2. H. H. Meyer and W. B. Walker, "A Study of Factors Relating to the Effectiveness of a Performance Appraisal Program," *Personal Psychology* 14 (August 1961): 291–98.
3. Name disguised.
4. Robert L. Noland, *Industrial Mental Health and Employee Counseling* (New York: Behavioral Publications, 1973), pp. 11–12.
5. "Labor Letter," *The Wall Street Journal*, October 15, 1985, p. 1.
6. David T. Cook, "The 'Ideal' Job: Meeting Problems Is All a Part of It," *Christian Science Monitor*, April 26, 1982, p. 15.
7. "Labor Letter," *The Wall Street Journal*, October 15, 1985, p. 15.
8. "Study: Seven in 100 Are Heavy Drinkers," *USA Today*, February 13, 1987, p. 10A.
9. Pat Guy, "What Tests Can and Can't Do," *USA Today*, November 19, 1985, p. 5B.
10. "Steel Mill's Drug Tests Help It Improve Hiring," *USA Today*, November 19, 1985, p. 5B.
11. "ASPA-BNA Survey No. 39: Retirement Policies and Programs," *ASPA Bulletin to Management*, January 24, 1980, p. 1.
12. Michel Briley, "Retirement: Is It Hazardous to Your Health?" *Modern Maturity* 27 (February-March 1984): 22–24.
13. "Employee Counseling Pays Off," *Behavioral Sciences Newsletter*, November 13, 1978.
14. Names are disguised.

SUGGESTIONS FOR FURTHER READING

Clarke, Adline. "Substance Abuse Said Costly to Businesses." *Mobile Press Register*, February 13, 1987, p. 18–A.

Hale, Ellen. "Your Work May Improve with Age." *USA Today*, March 19, 1986, p. 9A.

McGovney, W. C. *Selecting the Right Supervisor: Guidelines for Non-Discriminatory Hiring Practices*. Chicago: Society for Visual Education.

Muniz, P., and R. Chasnoff. "Counseling the Marginal Performer." *Supervisory Management* 27 (May 1982): 2–14.

Norton, S. D. "Performance Appraisal Advice for the New Supervisor." *Supervisory Management* 27 (June 1982): 30–34.

Toufexis, Anastasia. "Giving Goodies to the Good." *Time*, November 18, 1985, p. 98.

13
HANDLING DISCIPLINARY PROBLEMS

OBJECTIVES

After reading and studying the material in this chapter, you should be able to:

State three reasons why discipline is necessary.

Define discipline.

Name and discuss the differences between positive and negative discipline.

Classify disciplinary problems according to the number and frequency of occurrences, and the severity of their consequences.

Describe and discuss how discipline is imposed under judicial due process.

Explain the supervisor's disciplinary role.

IMPORTANT TERMS

discipline
punishment
positive discipline
negative discipline
malicious obedience
due process
minor infractions

major violations
intolerable offenses
progressive discipline
graduated scale of penalties
hot-stove rule
disciplinary layoff *or* suspension
termination-at-will

CHAPTER OUTLINE
CASE 13–1. THE SUSPECTED MENTAL CASE

CASE 13–1
THE SUSPECTED MENTAL CASE

When the production superintendent's phone rang at 2:00 a.m., the southwestern Texas plant's shift supervisor, Pedro Gonzalez, was on the phone.[1] Pedro said,

Mr. Jelinek, will you please come help me out with a problem here? John Pohl, one of our mechanics, has called me twice since I came to work at 11:00 p.m., insisting that someone's trying to kill him. He claims that someone tried to drop an elevator bucket on him around midnight, and it missed him by only two feet. I investigated and concluded that a bucket had been raised to a high platform by the maintenance department and had fallen due to vibration. Because it didn't seem logical that anyone could be on the platform at the time the bucket fell, I dismissed the incident as an accident.

But John came to me again about an hour ago, charging that someone had thrown a pop bottle at him while he was working on a loader. He claims he saw the assailant and chased him around the mill building but lost him. He didn't recognize the person because it was dark in the area. There was a smashed bottle, but all of the operators said they'd seen no disturbance. Either someone's trying to injure John or he's a mental case. I'm inclined to believe the latter.

Jelinek promised he'd be there in about 45 minutes. He suggested keeping John in the office for his own safety.

On the way to the plant, Jelinek reflected on the fact that John had been an employee for about a year, appeared to be a quiet, unassuming person, and had done excellent work.

Jelinek was unable to get any more significant information from John, Pedro, or the other workers. During the questioning, however, Pedro, who appeared to be slowly losing patience, accused John of making up the story to attract attention. John, of course, denied the charge and stated that he felt the company just didn't appreciate the seriousness of the situation. Someone was trying to take his life.

John was permitted to go outside the office and talk with the union's president and the shop steward, who had arrived by this time. After a few minutes, the union president returned and said to Jelinek, "He's crazy as a loon. And we don't like him casting suspicion on the other employees by claiming someone's trying to kill him."

How would you like to handle this situation? It's not really so different from many other "people problems" with which supervisors must continuously deal. In this case, counseling by a supervisor (see Chapter 12) would probably be of little value, so the exercise of effective discipline comes into play. This chapter deals with this important aspect of supervision.

NEED FOR DISCIPLINE

Effective job performance requires maintaining discipline by both managerial and nonmanagerial employees. In fact, most employees prefer to work with a well-organized, well-trained, and well-disciplined group rather than with one that is not. The reason employees want to work in a disciplined environment is that they benefit from discipline and suffer from disorder. Also, while not necessarily wanting to be personally punished, workers do want to be supervised "not too much—but also not too little."[2] Successful supervisors know how to find the middle road that allows their subordinates to know exactly what they can and cannot do. These generalizations may lead to confusion unless the question, "What is discipline?" is answered. Let's now discuss that question.

WHAT IS DISCIPLINE?

When asked the meaning of the word *discipline*, like most people, you probably think of "punishment." But this is only one of the many meanings of the word, for there is also a positive element in discipline. *Discipline* is related to the word *disciple*, meaning "follower," which, in turn, is derived from the word *discere*, meaning "to learn." The implication of this meaning is that good discipline is based upon good leadership.

Practical Definitions

In this chapter, the term *discipline* will be used to refer to any of these three concepts: (1) self-control, (2) conditions leading to orderly behavior in a work environment, or (3) punishment for improper behavior. Many companies say in their discipline policy that "**discipline** is training that corrects, molds, or perfects knowledge, attitudes, behavior, or conduct." We agree with this overall definition.

DISCIPLINE AS SELF-CONTROL. *Self-control* implies the orderly growth and development of a person to be able to adjust to meet certain needs and demands. For example, athletes become disciplined when they've trained to the point of being ready for the big game. Astronauts train for years until they know exactly what is expected of them; then they are able to react as they should during an actual flight. You are disciplined if you do the intensive study that's necessary for you to pass your courses, as well as do the other things required of you.

Self-discipline usually results from the actions—rather than the words—of the supervisor or higher-level managers, as the following example shows.

The manager of a franchise selling and installing metal buildings had a problem with employees taking extra-long lunch breaks. When he complained about it to his supervisors, one of them had the courage to say, "We could correct the problem more easily if you didn't take two-hour lunches yourself."

DISCIPLINE AS ORDERLY BEHAVIOR. The second meaning of discipline refers to the condition necessary to obtain orderly behavior in an organization. This implies keeping order and individual employee control among a group of workers by using methods that build morale and *esprit de corps.*

Have you had a class where order prevailed, seemingly without any effort on the part of the teacher or anyone else? Then, have you had one where conditions tended to be chaotic? Which did you prefer? Why?

DISCIPLINE AS PUNISHMENT. The third meaning of discipline—**punishment**—refers to a negative result which a person receives after an undesirable act or omission. The function of punishment is not to change past behavior but to prevent a recurrence of the undesirable act or omission in the future. Notice how this is shown in the following example, where a head nurse in a Jackson, Mississippi, hospital recalls a difficult disciplinary problem.

One Saturday evening when staffing was short, a severe explosion and fire occurred at a petrochemical plant near us. As the injured were being admitted, we became very busy, especially the burn unit, which needed another nurse.

James Keiller,[3] the only male nurse on duty, was versatile and able to care for most patients. I asked him to work in the burn unit because of its heavy patient load. He became very angry and stated that, if he wasn't needed in his assigned unit, he would go home. He said that I was unfair and that I always asked him to do extra work because he was the only male nurse in the house.

I informed him that it would mean termination if he left a nursing unit understaffed. But he checked out and left. When I had time later that evening, I wrote out his termination slip.

The punishment, Keiller's discharge, was intended to prevent the nursing unit from being understaffed in the future.

Positive and Negative Discipline

As can be seen from these definitions, discipline can be positive and constructive, or it may be negative and restraining. In either case, discipline is the force that prompts an individual or a group to comply with policies, rules, regulations, and procedures that are needed to attain the organization's objectives.

Positive discipline is an inner force that promotes emotional satisfaction instead of emotional conflict. It provides workers with greater freedom of self-expression and results in coordination and cooperation with a minimum need for formal authority. Positive discipline can best be achieved when group objectives and procedures are well known and are a basis for individual behavior. It usually results from the supervisor's effective use of motivation, leadership, and communication. Figure 13–1 is a classic example of positive discipline that has been in effect at a Canadian plywood mill for several years.

Tampa Electric Company uses positive discipline to "turn around" problem employees. First, they are given a day off, with pay, to think over their behavior and decide whether they really want to work for the company. Upon returning to work, the problem employee meets with his or her supervisor and tells what he or she is going to do. Then it is impressed on the employee that

FIGURE 13–1   HOW A PLAN FOR POSITIVE DISCIPLINE OPERATES

1. When an employee does something meriting punishment, there are casual, private reminders from the departmental supervisor in a friendly but factual manner.
2. If a second transgression occurs within four to six weeks, the reminders are repeated.
3. A third occurrence within a "reasonable time" (usually four to six weeks) leads to another discussion, this time with a shift supervisor involved. At this point, an attempt is made to determine the roots of the employee's problem. For example,
   a. Does the worker like the job?
   b. Is the worker unable to tolerate the work routine?
   c. Are there personal or domestic problems?
   d. Is the worker able and willing to abide by the rules in the future?
4. If a fourth incident occurs within six to eight weeks, the worker's supervisor and the plant superintendent have a "final" discussion with the individual.
   a. The worker is informed that another incident will result in termination.
   b. A record of this discussion is sent to the worker's home.
5. Continued "good performance" over a period of several months leads to a clearing of the record,
   a. One step at a time.
   b. In reverse order.
6. Applying Skinner's "reinforcement" principle, when there is *any* improvement the supervisor lets the worker know it is appreciated.

Source: Reprinted by permission of the *Harvard Business Review*. An exhibit from "Discipline Without Punishment Lives" by John Huberman (July-August 1975). Copyright ©1975 by the President and Fellows of Harvard College; all rights reserved.

whatever happens is his or her own fault. This process is enough to make most employees turn around. Those who don't are given the chance to resign, as they just don't fit into the company's program.

A lazy mechanic was recently given the day off to think about his behavior. At first he thought the "paid holiday" was wonderful. When he realized the company was in earnest, he made up his mind to straighten up and fly right.[4]

Negative discipline involves an outer force or influence. This force will often cause a person to change outwardly, but not mentally and emotionally, in an isolated situation. Or it may cause a person to change *only* for events that continue to occur over a period of time. In fact, it sometimes results in **malicious obedience**, whereby an aggrieved employee does exactly what he or she is told to do, even knowing that the order given is faulty and will result in getting things fouled up.

Negative discipline need not be extreme, and it is best used *only* when the positive type fails. Unfortunately, some organizations rely on negative discipline almost exclusively (see Figure 13–2). The choice as to which type of discipline to use depends upon each supervisor, and the effective supervisor will vary the type of discipline used to suit the subordinate or the situation involved.

Which form of discipline do you think the production superintendent in Case 13–1 should use with the disturbed mechanic? Why?

FIGURE 13–2 NEGATIVE DISCIPLINE

Discipline as Due Process

The United States Constitution guarantees every United States citizen due process under law. Essentially, **due process** assures that you receive justice under the following conditions:

1. Rules or laws exist.
2. There are specific, fixed penalties for violating those rules, with progressive degrees in the severity of penalties.
3. Penalties are imposed only after a hearing is conducted for the accused, at which time the extent of guilt is determined after considering the circumstances of the situation.

Unions have insisted that this same process be used within organizations in disciplining employees; even nonunion employers now use it. Therefore, today most arbitrators will uphold a disciplinary action if it can be shown that (1) the rules are reasonable, (2) the penalty is related to the severity of the offense, and (3) the worker was given a fair hearing. Due process also assumes that the employer has the right to have a well-disciplined work environment and the right to administer discipline when rules are violated. Of course, where there's a union, its representative wants to be present when a member is disciplined. Disciplinary due process is explained in more detail later in this chapter.

Did you notice in Case 13–1 that the union president and the shop steward were present when John was being disciplined?

CLASSIFICATIONS OF DISCIPLINARY PROBLEMS

Disciplinary problems can be classified in only two basic ways: (1) according to the number and frequency of their occurrences, and (2) according to the severity of their consequences.

Number and Frequency of Occurrences

The Personnel Policies Forum of The Bureau of National Affairs, Inc., studied the most serious disciplinary problems in manufacturing, nonmanufacturing, and nonbusiness organizations. It found that in 79 percent of the organizations surveyed, from the standpoint of frequency and number of occurrences, the worst disciplinary problems in all organizations were absenteeism and tardiness. A lack of productivity and poor work habits and/or attitudes were reported by 11 percent of the organizations, and 16 percent reported other problems.[5]

Severity of Consequences

In terms of the severity of their consequences, there are three categories of disciplinary problems: (1) minor infractions, (2) major violations, and (3) intolerable offenses.

MINOR INFRACTIONS. When they happen in isolation, **minor infractions** do little harm or result in few serious consequences. But they may be serious when they happen frequently or in connection with other infractions.

Absenteeism and tardiness are the most frequently committed minor infractions. These problems involve workers who are not present when they are needed and who have an apparent disregard for others. Other minor infractions are taking too long for breaks, leaving early, littering, slowing down production, distracting others with shouts (or "horseplay"), and poor or careless performance. Operators, laborers, and service personnel have the highest rate of minor infractions, while technical and professional employees and managerial personnel have the lowest rate.

MAJOR VIOLATIONS. Disciplinary problems that substantially interfere with orderly operations are called **major violations**. Some of the most frequent major violations involve lying, cheating, stealing, sleeping during working hours, willfully punching someone else's time card, violating safety rules, doing personal work on company time, and failing to carry out an order.

In a previous example, James Keiller was given a direct order by the head nurse. Notice that he was warned and given a chance to change his mind about checking out when he was needed in the burn unit. What type of disciplinary problem did he commit?

INTOLERABLE OFFENSES. When the disciplinary problems are of such a drastic, dangerous, or illegal nature that they severely strain or endanger employment relationships, they are called **intolerable offenses**. These problems are so grave and their consequences so serious that they usually result in *immediate* discharge. The situation and the nature of the organization's operations tend to determine what is considered to be an intolerable offense. In other words, what is acceptable at one time or in one industry may not be acceptable at another time or in another industry.

Some examples of intolerable offenses are fighting that results in serious harm to others; serious theft, including using company property to make something for personal use on company time; willful destruction of property; smoking in an area of inflammables if a "No Smoking" sign is posted; possession of, and threatening to use, deadly weapons; and the use of hard drugs and narcotics on the job. Look at the following example in which a head nurse in a large nursing home in Illinois recalls a dreadful problem with Babs, a loyal but addicted registered nurse.

Babs's recent pattern of behavior was characterized by a state of being "high" and happy for a day or two, then extreme depression followed by slightly slurred speech and muttering to herself.[6] One afternoon, she went to the medicine room and picked up a bottle of capsules. She clutched them eagerly, saying, "Ah, what would I do without you." Then she dropped a bottle of syrupy liquid on the floor. Finally, she shakily asked if she could go home. I told her to get a good night's sleep and see me in the morning at 10:00.

She was calm and back to normal the next morning. She said, "I realize you have no choice but to let me go, but please, please help me." Apparently her problems began when she had difficulty getting to sleep and was given a prescription for sleeping pills by her doctor. Because she was still sleepy when she awoke, she took a pep pill. This made her nervous, so another doctor prescribed a tranquilizer. Now she needs them all and takes so many that she rarely feels or acts normally.

Both my department head and the personnel officer suggested that I fire her immediately!

HOW DISCIPLINARY DUE PROCESS OPERATES

As indicated earlier, disciplinary due process involves three steps. First, rules are established that will result in punishment if they're violated. Second, fixed penalties are set for each rule that's violated (the penalties usually vary according to their degree of severity and how many times the rule is broken, as shown in Table 13–1). Third, the penalty is imposed only after the employee is given a fair hearing.

TABLE 13–1 EXAMPLE OF DISCIPLINARY PROCEDURE USING GRADUATED PENALTIES

Offenses	*Enforcement*			
Minor	**First Action Step**	**Second Action Step**	**Third Action Step**	**Fourth Action Step**
Minor infractions that do not do great damage or have serious consequence when viewed individually but may be considered serious when accumulated.	Education and informal warning(s) by first-line supervisor.	Warning in presence of union representative by first-line supervisor.	Warning or written reprimand by higher supervision in presence of union representative; and/or suspension up to 2 days.	Becomes a major offense and is handled accordingly. (Does not necessarily involve immediate suspension.)

Major	**First Offense**	**Second Offense**	**Third Offense**	
Violations that substantially interfere with production or damage morale; or when seriousness of offense is apparent to a reasonable mind; or an accumulation of minor offenses.	Step 1: Immediately remove employee from job and have report to higher supervision. Step 2: Suspension up to 5 days, plus a written reprimand or written final warning, if necessary.	Step 1: Immediately remove employee from job and have report to higher supervision. Step 2: Written final warning. Suspension up to 10 days, or discharge if final warning was given for first offense.	Step 1: Immediately remove employee from job and have report to higher supervision. Step 2: Discharge	

Intolerable	**First Offense**	**Pointers**		
Offenses of a criminal or drastic nature which strain employment relationship or would be outrageous to most people.	Step 1: Immediately remove employee from job and have report to industrial-relations department. Step 2. Discharge	1. Economic penalties (such as suspensions, transfers, discharges) should be imposed only by higher supervision after consultation with industrial-relations department. 2. Written final warnings should always be accompanied by an economic penalty. 3. To be considered a second offense, violations should occur within a year of the first offense.		

Source: Reprinted, by permission of the publisher, from "Does the Penalty Match the Offense?" by Walter Collins and Herman Harrow, *Supervisory Management* 3 (September 1958): 20. © 1958 by American Management Association, Inc., New York. All rights reserved.

Establishing Rules of Conduct

If employees are to maintain self-discipline, they must know what they can and can't do, and they must know it in advance. Therefore, most progressive organizations publish rules, usually in their *Employee's Handbook*. The Bureau of National Affairs study mentioned earlier found that 85 percent of the organizations published rules. Table 13–2 shows one such list of actual rules (and penalties).

TABLE 13–2   SHOP RULES AND PENALTIES OF A LARGE NATIONAL MANUFACTURING COMPANY

Rules	1st Offense	2nd Offense	3rd Offense
Stealing private or company property	Discharge		
Material falsification of any company record	Discharge		
Gambling on company property	Discharge		
Fighting on company property	Discharge		
Refusal to obey orders of supervisor	Discharge		
Deliberate destruction or abuse of company property	Discharge		
Reporting to work or working while under the influence of intoxicating beverages or narcotics or other drugs or having possession of same on company property	Discharge		
Possession of weapons on company premises	Discharge		
Immoral conduct on company property	Discharge		
Sleeping during working hours	Discharge		
Absent three consecutive days without notice	Voluntary termination		
Willfully punching somebody else's timecard	Discharge		
Leaving premises during work hours without permission	Discharge		
Personal work on company time	Written warning	2 days layoff	Discharge
Personal conduct at work dangerous to others	Written warning	2 days layoff	Discharge
Solicitation for any cause during working time without permission	Written warning	2 days layoff	Discharge
Distribution of literature during work hours or in areas of work without permission	Written warning	2 days layoff	Discharge

TABLE 13–2   (continued)

Rules	1st Offense	2nd Offense	3rd Offense
Repeated failure to punch timecard	Written warning	2 days layoff	Discharge
Visiting other departments during work hours without permission	Written warning	2 days layoff	Discharge
Stopping work before break time, lunch time, or quitting time or not performing assigned work	Written warning	2 days layoff	Discharge
Posting, removal or tampering with bulletin board notices without authority	Written warning	2 days layoff	Discharge
Threatening, intimidating, coercing, or interfering with employees or supervision at any time	Written warning	2 days layoff	Discharge
Poor or careless workmanship	Written warning	2 days layoff	Discharge
Leaving early and/or failure to be at assigned work area at the start of shifts, breaks, and/or meal periods	Written warning	2 days layoff	Discharge
Using abusive language or making false or malicious statements concerning any employee, the company, or its products	Written warning	2 days layoff	Discharge
Distracting the attention of others or causing confusion by unnecessary shouting, catcalls, or demonstrations in the plant	Written warning	2 days layoff	Discharge
Littering or contributing to poor housekeeping or unsanitary or unsafe conditions on plant premises	Written warning	2 days layoff	Discharge
Negligence of safety rules or common safety practices	Written warning	2 days layoff	Discharge
Restricting output or intentional slowdown	Written warning	5 days layoff	Discharge
Unexcused absence	Written warning		
Unexcused tardiness	Written warning		

Receipt of any combination of five (5) of the above offenses within a one (1) year period will result in the employee's automatic discharge. Written notices or warning or other disciplinary action shall not be used as a basis for further discipline after the employee has maintained a clear record of conduct for one year.

Source: *Employee Conduct and Discipline*, Personnel Policies Forum Survey No. 102 (Washington, D.C.: The Bureau of National Affairs, Inc., August 1973), p. 30.

Determining Penalties

The types of penalties to be used, as well as the way they're used, are usually determined in consultation with the union. What results is usually termed **progressive discipline,** which means using a graduated scale of penalties. If there's no union, the penalties result from management's philosophy of how to treat employees, as well as from the fear of the entry of a union or government action. The normal steps of a progressive-discipline policy are:

1. *Oral warning* that does not go into the employee's record.
2. *Oral warning* that goes into the employee's record.
3. *Written reprimand,* which usually comes from some level above the supervisor.
4. *Suspension,* which usually consists of a layoff lasting from a day to a number of months.
5. *Discharge,* which is the ultimate penalty, constitutes a break in service, and wipes out the employee's seniority. Most supervisors are reluctant to use it because it is the economic equivalent of the death penalty. As discharge also affects the worker's family, justification must be strictly established because discharge is almost always subject to the grievance procedure and arbitration.

Some other infrequently used penalties are demotions, transfers, and the withholding of benefits such as promotions, raises, or bonuses.

Unions, personnel managers, and most supervisors favor using a **graduated scale of penalties**, which means that punishment for a given violation becomes progressively more severe as it is repeated. Under such a plan, the first time an intolerable offense is committed, the employee is discharged.

Were James Keiller and Babs in the previous examples given a graduated scale of penalties?

For less serious acts, punishment becomes more severe after the first, second, and third time. The penalty may be, first, an oral warning; second, a written warning; third, suspension; and fourth, discharge.

Imposing the Penalty Only after a Fair Hearing

Once the grounds for disciplinary action have been established, it becomes necessary for supervisors to follow the correct procedure in taking any action against an employee. In other words, discipline must be properly administered in accordance with previously established and announced rules and procedures. Penalties should be based upon specific charges, with notices given to the employee and the union, if there is one, usually in advance of management's attempt to take corrective action. The charges, and their underlying reasons, should be definite and provable. There should be provisions for a prompt hearing, witnesses, protests, and appeals. Finally, adequate remedies should be available to employees whose punishment has failed to meet the requirement of "fair play."

In summary, the main provisions in the proper disciplinary procedure are (1) to make definite charges, (2) to notify the employee (and union), in writing, of the offense, and (3) to have some provision for the employee to answer charges either by protest or appeal.

To what extent was the proper disciplinary procedure used in Case 13–1 and in the other examples given in this chapter (James Keiller, the male nurse, and Babs, the RN)?

THE SUPERVISOR AND DISCIPLINE

Whether or not they are in unionized firms, supervisors must exercise varying degrees of discretion when recommending or imposing penalties on employees. Supervisors must deal with mistakes according to what the mistakes are and under what circumstances they were made. Mistakes resulting from continued carelessness call for disciplinary action. Honest mistakes should be corrected by counseling and positive discipline, not by punishment. These should be corrected in a way that will help the employee learn from the mistakes and become a more proficient and valuable worker. In the following example, a supervisor in a New Jersey chemical company has the right attitude about discipline.

I don't like calling my first discussion on minor offenses an "oral warning." I'll use the term "oral discussion" or "oral review," where I point out what's expected of a person and where I think he or she is falling down. I try to emphasize that I'd like to hear what the employee's perspective of the situation is, which will sometimes make a difference in how I see what the employee has done. But I don't like using that "warning" terminology in my first discussion—it's just too negative. What I'm trying to do is to get employees to change their behavior and focus on the positive side of things. But if their performance doesn't change, I'll move to an oral or a written warning on the progressive discipline scale.

The Supervisor's Disciplinary Role

A supervisor is responsible for instilling a desire for self-discipline in subordinates. If subordinates are not required to face up to the realities of their jobs, their goals, their resources, and their potential, they are in a poor position to function properly and make their best contribution to the organization. It's surprising how quickly "organizational" problems melt away when interpersonal forthrightness is applied.

When applying discipline, the supervisor must consider these points:

1. Every job should carry with it a certain margin for error.
2. Overconcern with avoiding errors stifles initiative and encourages subordinates to postpone decisions or avoid making them altogether.
3. A different way of doing something should not be mistaken for the wrong way of doing it.

Finally, a supervisor is more likely to avoid administering severe disciplinary action than a higher-level manager because of the likelihood of generating undesirable effects. Other managers, including some personnel managers, take a stronger—perhaps more punitive--position on matters of discipline.[7] A possible explanation is that supervisory managers are inclined to give stronger consideration to individual circumstances and behavior than are top managers. Also, supervisors are somewhat reluctant to follow rules strictly for fear they'll lose the cooperation of their employees if they're too severe.

Principles of Effective Discipline

Four important principles of effective discipline are discussed in this section. These principles are often referred to as the **hot-stove rule**, which draws a comparison between touching a hot stove and experiencing discipline. The four principles are (see Figure 13–3):

1. You know what will happen if you touch a hot stove (carries warning).
2. If you touch a hot stove, it burns you right away (is immediate).
3. A hot stove always burns you if you touch it (is consistent).
4. A hot stove doesn't care whom it burns (is impersonal).

CARRIES WARNING. Employees should know what is and what is not expected of them. This means that there must be clear warning that a given offense will lead to discipline, and there must be clear warning of the amount of discipline that will be imposed for an offense.

Supervisor C.D. Yates has long ignored a safety rule that the employees wear short-sleeved shirts while operating their machines.[8] In fact, for over a year, several employees have routinely worn long-sleeved shirts in the department. After learning of an injury in another department caused by an employee's

FIGURE 13–3 THE HOT-STOVE RULE

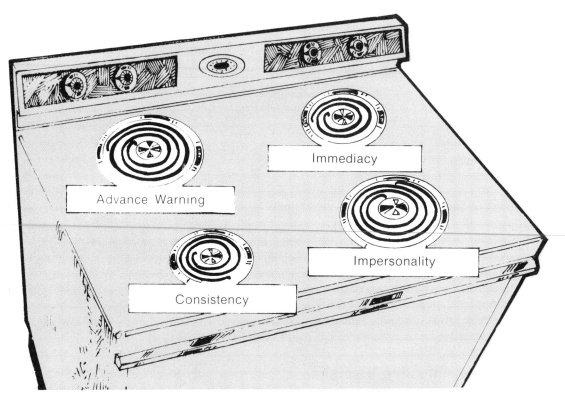

Source: Based on concepts in Theo Haimann and Raymond L. Hilgert, *Instructor's Manual— Supervision: Concepts and Practices of Management*, 3d ed. (Cincinnati: South-Western Publishing Co., 1982), pp. 334–37. Reproduced with permission.

long-sleeved shirt being caught in a conveyor belt, Yates immediately writes up warnings to five employees in his department who are wearing long-sleeved shirts.

If you were one of the five employees, would you consider Yates's action fair? Probably not. Since the safety rule was so openly ignored, it was the equivalent of no rule at all. For adequate warning to take place, Yates needs to communicate to his employees that, while the rule has been ignored in the past, it will begin to be enforced in the department. If you were an outside arbitrator, how would you rule? Why?

IS IMMEDIATE. The supervisor should begin the disciplinary process as soon as possible after he or she notices a violation. This is important for the following reasons:

1. An employee may feel that he or she is "putting one over" on the supervisor and may try to violate other rules.
2. An employee may feel that the supervisor is too weak to attempt to enforce the rules.
3. An employee may feel that the supervisor doesn't consider a rule important enough to justify enforcing it. Thus, all the other employees may be encouraged to break or stretch the rule as well. It is not surprising to find an employee responding, "Well, I've been doing this for several days (or weeks) and nobody's said anything about this to me before."

IS CONSISTENT. This principle means that for similar circumstances, similar discipline should be administered. If two people commit the same offense under the same circumstances, they should receive the same punishment.

Helen had a very poor absenteeism record.[9] Recently she missed work for two days without a legitimate excuse. Considering her past record, this offense would justify an immediate one-week suspension. However, her skills were badly needed by the supervisor, since the department was "snowed under" by a tremendous backlog of work. Helen was given only an oral warning.

What will Helen's supervisor do when another worker misses work for two days without a legitimate excuse? If the supervisor is inconsistent, he or she will risk being labeled as "playing favorites" and lose credibility with employees. Does this mean a supervisor always has to dish out identical penalties for similar offenses? Note that we said the supervisor must be consistent, *as long as circumstances are similar.* An employee's past record is a major factor to consider.

Two employees were caught drinking an alcoholic beverage on the job. The rules clearly prohibit this. For one employee, it was the first such offense; for the second worker, it was his third in the past year. Is the supervisor justified in giving the second employee a more serious penalty than the first? You bet the supervisor is!

What are the pros and cons of giving an employee a "break" regarding discipline?

IS IMPERSONAL. As a supervisor, you shouldn't get into personalities when administering discipline. You need to be as objective as possible. Moreover, after administering discipline to an employee, try to retain a normal relationship with that person. Two common mistakes supervisors make in imposing discipline are apologizing to or "bawling out" employees. Remember, you're supposed to be disciplining the act, not the person. Your focus is upon *getting the employee's work behavior consistent with the rules.*

Applying Discipline

Two of the more difficult aspects of the supervisor's job are (1) laying off a worker for disciplinary reasons and (2) discharging an unsatisfactory employee. Yet these aspects are part of supervisory management, unpleasant though they may be.

DISCIPLINARY LAYOFF. If an employee has repeatedly committed major offenses and previous warnings have been ineffective, a **disciplinary layoff**, or **suspension**, is probably inevitable. Such a layoff involves a loss of time—and pay—for several days to workers. This form of discipline usually comes as a rude shock to workers. It gets their attention! And usually it impresses upon them the need to comply with the organization's rules and regulations.

Because this form of discipline is quite serious and involves an enormous penalty—loss of pay—most organizations limit power to use it at least to the second level of management; often the human-resources manager is involved as well.[10] Yet supervisors have the right to recommend such action.

Not all managers believe the layoff is effective, and some seldom apply it as a disciplinary measure. First, they may need the worker to continue production. Second, they may feel that the worker will return with an even more negative attitude. Still, when properly used, it is an effective disciplinary tool.

DISCHARGE. In 1884, a Tennessee court established the **termination-at-will** rule whereby an employer could dismiss an employee for any reason—or even for no reason at all—unless there was more explicit contractual provision preventing it.[11] The reasoning behind this decision was: If an employee can quit work for any reason, then the employer should be able to discharge for any reason.

But recent legislative enactments and court decisions, as well as union rules and public policy, have swung the pendulum of protection away from the employer and toward the employee by limiting the termination-at-will rule.[12] Most union agreements have a clause detailing "just cause" for disciplinary discharge and define the order in which employees can be laid off. EEO/AA regulations do essentially the same.

In general, court decisions suggest that the safest (legal) grounds for discharge include incompetent performance that does not respond to training or accommodation, gross or repeated insubordination, excessive unexcused absences, repeated and unexcused tardiness, verbal abuse of others, physical violence, falsification of records, drunkenness or drug abuse on the job, and theft.[13]

Since discharge is the economic equivalent of the death penalty, supervisors may only recommend it. The discharge must be carried out by top management—usually with the advice and consent of the human-resources manager.

Do you remember that Bill Morrow in Case 1–1 had the authority to recommend layoffs and discharges to higher management but couldn't order them himself?

Unions are quite involved in discipline when they represent the employees. Also, the union's disciplinary procedure is now followed in many nonunionized organizations. These topics will be covered in the next chapter.

CHAPTER REVIEW

If counseling problem employees does not correct the problem, then discipline must be applied. Discipline is necessary for supervisory success and plays an important role in holding an organization together. This chapter has shown that discipline is closely related to supervisory leadership, communication, and motivation.

Employee discipline is a process of control which is either internally or externally imposed. As such, it is a method of maintaining management's authority, and this authority is necessary to keep the enterprise operating effectively. Discipline may be positive or negative. Positive discipline provides workers with greater freedom of self-expression and results in cooperation and coordination with a minimum need for formal authority.

Management's view of this control function has switched from the traditional one, of discipline as punishment, to the modern approach, which considers discipline as self-controlled, orderly behavior, and tries to apply training that corrects and strengthens the worker. Unions have played a major role in bringing about this change in philosophy, especially by insisting on due process with stated rules, specific penalties, and an orderly procedure for assessing guilt and punishment. The rules usually fall into groups of (1) minor infractions, (2) major violations, and (3) intolerable offenses. Penalties vary from an oral warning, an oral warning with a written record, a written reprimand, a suspension, and a discharge. The last is rarely used because it is the economic equivalent of capital punishment. Usually a graduated scale of penalties is imposed that increases with the severity of the penalty and the frequency of violation.

The impact of unions shows up not only in company policy, but also in the supervisor's role, regardless of whether or not the firm is unionized. But no matter how much influence the unions have had on the disciplinary process, the right to discipline is still management's responsibility. The main change is that today supervisors must be sure they follow the due-process procedure. The supervisor is the major element and influence in disciplinary action.

In spite of all progress, discipline is still largely negative, operating through penalties for wrong behavior rather than rewards for right action. Therefore, to be effective, discipline must be enforced. The manner of enforcement, in turn, acts upon the morale of the organization. One of the most difficult tasks of management is to strike an acceptable balance between severity and leniency in administering discipline.

Four principles of effective discipline, which are referred to as the "hot-stove rule," are that (1) discipline should carry advance warning, (2) discipline should be immediate, (3) discipline should be consistent, and (4) discipline should be impersonal.

When lesser forms of discipline are ineffective, it may ultimately be necessary to resort to layoff or discharge of an employee. Usually such action is restricted to higher levels of management or the personnel department, and it is important to be sure that due process has been observed and that there is just cause for such action.

QUESTIONS FOR REVIEW AND DISCUSSION

1. Why is discipline important in organizations?
2. What is discipline? Define it in at least three ways.
3. To what extent is the concept of self-control important as a means of discipline?
4. What is the necessary condition for obtaining orderly behavior in organizations?
5. How do you distinguish between positive and negative discipline?
6. What is the judicial due process of discipline, and why is it so important?
7. What is the union's role in the disciplinary process?
8. Why are penalties set down in a graduated scale?
9. What procedure should be followed in administering discipline?
10. Why should disciplinary layoff and discharge decisions be restricted to higher levels of management?
11. If you are now working, or have worked before, explain the disciplinary procedure used by your employer.

LEARNING EXERCISE 13–1
POOR INTERPERSONAL RELATIONSHIPS

The division superintendent of a large plant was faced with a disciplinary problem in a certain department of his division. Here is his account:

In one department there are two workers who are badly needed by my division of the plant. Because of the nature of our work, it is important that the members of that department work as a team. At the present time, that department is not producing as efficiently as it could because of the relentless bickering between these two workers. They are constantly sore at each other, and hurt feelings usually result. Each feels offended, resented, and irritated by the other. In short, these two have a personality clash and apparently are unable to function together.

The first employee has greater seniority (by two years) and more education (two years at a junior college) and is older (by five years). The second worker has only a high-school education but is more capable of performing the job and is better able to relate to other employees.

Alone, and at different times, each was asked about his feelings toward the other. Then each was asked to be more understanding of the other and to try to work in greater harmony. They were told that the job had to be done, that they had to try to work together for the good of all, and that their present conduct toward each other could not be tolerated.

My department supervisors and I concluded that if, after I had talked to both workers, they could not work out their differences and work in harmony, I would be left with two or three choices. One solution would be to have them work on different shifts. Another possibility is to transfer one of them to another department. A last resort would be to discharge one or both of them.

The real problem is to decide what to do and then to do it. It will be a difficult problem determining which one will be transferred or fired, since help for this department is not readily available. The factors to be considered in the solution are fault, seniority, capability, and individual personality. These factors would have to be considered carefully, and a decision would have to be made that would be suitable and based upon the facts.

Answer the following questions:

1. If you were the division superintendent, what would you recommend doing with the two bickering employees? Why?
2. How would you implement your decision? In what order would you implement it?
3. What does this exercise illustrate about the need for a disciplined work environment?

LEARNING EXERCISE 13–2
ROY ROBARD: THE CHIEF TECHNICIAN

Roy Robard was the chief technician in the research laboratory of a medium-sized genetic engineering company in Texas. He recounted the following details when asked about his main problem as a supervisor.

I was employed here for three years as a technician before being promoted to chief. During those years, I'd become quite close to one of the other technicians

(I'll call him Al) and considered him a good friend. We'd been hired at about the same time and enjoyed many of the same things, both on and off the job. We ate together daily and spent much of our spare time together.

I think that part of our problem began when the previous chief resigned. Al and I both applied for the job. According to our department head, I was given the job because of my education, experience, and performance.

One day during lunch break, Al and I had an argument about his refusal to clean up the work area after some experiments were completed. Although the clean-up wasn't messy or repugnant, it was usually done by lower-level workers, but none were available that day. He flatly refused to do it, stating that he was not supposed to do that type of work because it wasn't in his job description. This was not true, and I pointed that out to him. He became even more vocal and antagonistic. I asked him again to do the duty and he refused. He did, however, do the duty after he cooled off and realized he was wrong.

After thinking over the whole situation and conferring with my department head, I called Al back in to discuss the problem. We began calmly and slowly but built to a "head of steam." We both conceded some ground and came to the mutual agreement that he should follow instructions or look for employment elsewhere.

Two days later he resigned, and I felt bad, thinking that I had probably been too harsh with him. Later, I found out that he had divulged to other personnel all the secrets I had trusted him with, and he had been doing so ever since I had been promoted.

Answer the following questions:

1. Evaluate the way Roy handled Al.
2. Would you have handled Al differently? Why?
3. What does this exercise show about the need for self-discipline, especially by supervisors?
4. Assume that you are Roy and that Al has not resigned but has agreed to follow instructions from you, as directed. However, you have *just learned* that he has not performed the duty in question. He was not at his work station when you entered it. A co-worker said to you, 'He told me he'd quit before he does that job again. As far as I know, he hasn't even started it." Role-play the meeting that you will hold with Al.

ENDNOTES

1. Name disguised at the request of the company, a medium-sized petrochemical plant.
2. For further details, see Irwin H. McMaster, "Unusual Aspects of Discipline," *Supervision* 36 (April 1974): 19.
3. Name disguised.
4. Laurie Baum, "Punishing Workers with a Day Off," *Business Week*, June 16, 1986, p. 80.
5. *Employee Conduct and Discipline*, Personnel Policies Forum Survey No. 102 (Washington, DC: The Bureau of National Affairs, Inc., August, 1973), pp. 1–2.
6. Name disguised.

7. See Philip C. Shaak and Milton M. Schwartz, "Uniformity of Policy Interpretation Among Managers in the Utility Industry," *Academy of Management Journal* 16 (March 1973): 77–83.
8. The name of this supervisor in a Michigan auto-parts plant has been disguised.
9. Name disguised.
10. For further details, see Leon C. Megginson, *Personnel Management: A Human Resources Approach,* 5th ed. (Homewood, IL: Richard D. Irwin, 1985), pp. 376–77.
11. *Payne* v. *Western & A.R.P. Co.,* 81 Tenn. 507 (1884).
12. S. A. Youngblood and G. L. Tidwell, "Termination-at-Will: Some Changes in the Wind," *Personnel* 58 (May-June 1981): 24.
13. For a state-by-state guide on how easily an employer can fire a worker, send $21.50 to Jill Henderson, CUE, 1331 Pennsylvania Ave., N.W., Suite 1500, North Lobby, Washington, DC 20004, for a copy of the National Association's publication, *Employment Law in the 50 States.*

SUGGESTIONS FOR FURTHER READING

Baum, Laurie. "Punishing Workers with a Day Off." *Business Week*, June 16, 1986, p. 80.

Belohlav, J. "Realities of Successful Employee Discipline." *Personnel Administration* 28 (March 1983): 74–77.

Brophy, Beth. "What Boss Calls Bad Conduct Must Fit Law." *USA Today,* March 6, 1985, p. 5B.

Caruth, D. "This Matter of Discipline." *Supervisory Management* 28 (April 1983): 24–31.

Fenn, Donna. "The Lord of Discipline." *Inc.* 7 (November 1985): 82ff.

Pulich, M. A. "Train the First-Line Supervisors to Handle Discipline." *Personnel Journal* 62 (December 1983): 980–86.

Suters, Everett T. "The Toughest Job Around." *Inc.* Volume 8 (October 1986): 138–40.

14
THE SUPERVISOR
AND LABOR RELATIONS

OBJECTIVES

After reading and studying the material in this chapter, you should be able to:

Explain what is meant by labor relations.

Name several areas of organizational life affected by unions.

Trace the development of unions in the United States.

Name and explain the basic laws governing labor relations.

Describe union objectives and discuss the methods used to achieve those objectives.

Name three things that a supervisor must know in order to live with the union agreement.

IMPORTANT TERMS

labor union

labor relations *or* union-management
  relations *or* industrial relations

craft union

industrial unions

employee associations

unfair labor practices

union shop

closed shop

agency shop

maintenance-of-membership clause

right-to-work laws

employees' bill of rights

union authorization card

bargaining agent

collective bargaining

mediator

arbitrator

strike

picketing

lockout

union steward

seniority

grievance procedure

CHAPTER OUTLINE
CASE 14-1. IN UNION THERE IS STRENGTH

All your strength is in your union,
All your danger is in discord;
Therefore be at peace henceforward,
And as brothers live together.
Henry Wadsworth Longfellow

CASE 14–1
IN UNION THERE IS STRENGTH[1]

A wise man had seven sons who were smart, personable, and otherwise attractive, but they had one common fault—they were constantly fighting and squabbling with one another, even when being attacked by others outside the family. One day, the father decided to teach them a lesson. He called them together, gave each one of them a long wooden stick, and said to each one, in turn, "Break this stick over your knee." Each one of the sons broke his stick with very little effort.

Again, the wise man handed each son a stick, but this time said to them, "Bind the seven sticks together in a bundle." They did as he asked. "Now try to break the sticks," he said to each son as he handed him the bundle. None of them could break the bundle of sticks. "Remember," he said, "In union there is strength."

The opening quotation and case illustrate one of the most basic reasons why unions are needed. Just as the individual sticks can be broken, so individual employees cannot compete with the employer's resources by themselves. But when united, as the sticks were united into a bundle, the individual employees can successfully compete with management. Unions exist for many reasons, including (1) employees' need for recognition, (2) political pressures, and (3) lack of good, fair supervisory practices and management policies.

A **labor union** is an organization of workers banded together to achieve economic goals, especially increased wages and benefits, shorter working hours, and improved working conditions. The individual employee has very little bargaining strength when negotiating alone with the employer. But when employees band together to form a labor union, they are better able to protect their interests and to achieve their economic goals. That is why unions exist in the United States and other countries.

It is impossible to cover everything about dealing with unions in one chapter, but we will include the most important ideas to help you understand the supervisor's role in labor relations. Even if you are—or expect to be—a supervisor in a nonunion firm, you need to understand how labor relations affect supervisory activities and relationships, for they affect nonunion employers as well.

Did you notice in Chapter 13 that, even in nonunion firms, supervisors use judicial due process in applying discipline?

WHAT ARE LABOR RELATIONS?

Terms such as **labor relations, union-management relations,** and **industrial relations** are often used to apply to the relationships between employers and their unionized employees. In this text, these terms will be used interchangeably.

The growth of unionism has forced managers—especially supervisors—to change many of their ways of dealing with employees, especially in matters concerning wages, hours, working conditions, and other terms and conditions of employment. Managers of unionized companies are constantly challenged by union leaders in these areas. Those challenges force supervisors to consider the rights of workers in developing and applying policies. Thus, management's freedom of choice has been greatly limited. For example, managers can no longer reward an employee on the basis of favoritism or punish one without just cause.

Labor relations are more than a mere power struggle between management and labor over purely economic matters that concern only themselves. Instead, hurt feelings, bruised egos, disappointments, and the hopes and ambitions of workers, managers, and labor leaders are involved. Also, these relationships affect and are affected by the total physical, economic, social, technological, legal, political, and cultural environment in which they occur.

Recall the last serious strike you can remember, such as the air controllers' strike in the summer of 1981, or the National Football Players Association's strike, or a teachers' strike. Did it affect you in any way, either directly or indirectly? Even if it didn't affect you, what were the economic, social, political, and cultural effects on your community? Did any workers in nonaffected organizations lose jobs or wages? Did any companies lose output or go out of business? Were the sales at retail stores hurt? Were tax receipts reduced? Was there any violence? Did it affect any social or cultural events? Were there any political effects?

HOW UNIONS DEVELOPED IN THE UNITED STATES

In general, employees were treated well in the early colonies because of the severe shortage of skilled labor. By the late 1800s, however, this had changed. The high birthrate, rapid and uncontrolled immigration, the concentration of wealth and industry in the hands of a few businessmen, political abuses by some employers, and the large numbers of workers in crowded industrial areas led to many abuses. These included long hours, hard labor, unsafe and oppressive working conditions, crowded and unsanitary living conditions, low pay with no job security, and abuses of working women and children.

Early Union Activities

As Case 14–1 illustrates, individual employees are weak and powerless when acting by themselves. Although there were labor unions in the United States as early as 1789, they tended to be small, isolated, and ineffective craft unions. A **craft union** is a union of workers in a specific skill, craft, or trade.

More concerted action and stronger efforts were needed to improve the workers' plight. So several of the craft unions joined together in 1869 to form the Knights of Labor—the first nationwide union. Because its leadership was considered quite radical, it was only moderately successful. A more conservative national union was formed in 1881, and it was named the American Federation of Labor (AFL) in 1886. Under the leadership of Samuel Gompers, the AFL grew and had great impact through World War I. The basic concepts of unionism were developed under his leadership. When asked what unions wanted for their members, Gompers invariably replied "More."

Period of Rapid Union Growth

During the 1920s and early 1930s, business became so powerful that workers were again exploited. They were hired, rewarded, punished, and fired at the whim of first-line supervisors, many of whom often acted brutally. Therefore, several laws were passed in the 1930s which forced management to recognize unions and protected workers from exploitation (see pages 346–350 for details). Until that time, the AFL and its affiliates were organized on the craft basis. Union growth was thus limited, as there were few craft workers left to organize. But some workers had started organizing **industrial unions**, in which all the workers in an industry, such as coal, belonged to the same union whether they were craftsmen, unskilled workers, or clerical employees. These unions broke away from the AFL in 1936 to form the Congress of Industrial Organizations (CIO).

Because of laws favorable to workers, the demand for workers resulting from World War II, and the prosperity which followed that war, union membership grew rapidly until the mid-1940s. Then, as Figure 14–1 shows, it grew more slowly through the mid-1950s.

Recent Limited Union Growth

Although total union membership was increasing through the mid-1950s, the percentage of all workers belonging to unions started leveling out shortly after World War II. For this and other reasons, the AFL and the CIO combined in 1955, with George Meany as president of the newly formed AFL-CIO.

FIGURE 14–1   MEMBERSHIP OF NATIONAL UNIONS AND MEMBERSHIP AS A PERCENTAGE OF THE TOTAL WORK FORCE*

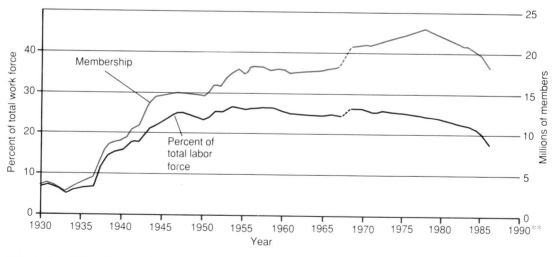

* Exclusive of Canadian membership. The broken lines beginning in 1967–68 indicate the fact that employee associations which bargain collectively were first reported then.
** Estimated from various news stories and Congressional hearings.
Source: U.S. Department of Labor, Bureau of Labor Statistics.

Membership again began to grow in the 1960s, when new types of unions developed. Government, white-collar, agricultural, and service employees, as well as professionals, formed **employee associations** which functioned as labor unions. Consequently, there are now around 20 millon members of unions and employee associations, which is around 18 percent of the total labor force.

Nearly four out of five workers don't belong to a union. Why do you think this is so?

LAWS GOVERNING LABOR RELATIONS

The legal basis of union-management relations is provided by the National Labor Relations Act of 1935 (called the Wagner Act), as amended by the Labor-Management Relations Act of 1947 (the Taft-Hartley Act), the Labor-Management Reporting and Disclosure Act of 1959 (the Landrum-Griffin Act), and others. This complex of laws sets public policy and controls labor relations. Table 14–1 shows the coverage, basic requirements, and agencies administering these laws. We'll provide only a few more details about them in the text.

Basic Labor Laws

In this section we will examine why the basic labor laws were passed. We will also point out the important features of these laws and explain how they were administered.

WAGNER ACT. The National Labor Relations Act (Wagner Act) was passed to help protect employees and unions by limiting management's rights. It gave workers the right to form and join unions of their own choosing and made collective bargaining mandatory. It also set up the National Labor Relations Board (NLRB) to enforce the law. While the act defined specific **unfair labor practices** that management could not commit against the workers and the union, it had no provision for unfair practices that unions might commit against workers and management. As a result, many union abuses arose. One major abuse was that unions could impose requirements as to how employees could get, or keep, a job. Many managers, as well as employees, assumed that the right to join a union carried with it the right not to do so. This assumption was changed during World War II when agreements such as the union shop, the closed shop, and the agency shop became legal.

Under a **union shop** agreement, all employees must join the union within a specified period—usually 30 days—or be fired. Under a **closed shop** agreement,

TABLE 14–1 BASIC LAWS GOVERNING LABOR RELATIONS

Laws	Coverage	Basic Requirements	Agencies Involved
National Labor Relations Act, as amended (Wagner Act)	Nonmanagerial employees in non-agricultural private firms not covered by the Railway Labor Act, and postal employees	Employees have right to form or join labor organizations (or to refuse to), to bargain collectively through their representatives, and to engage in other concerted activities such as strikes, picketing, and boycotts; there are unfair labor practices which the employer and the union cannot engage in.	National Labor Relations Board (NLRB)
Labor-Management Relations Act, as amended (Taft-Hartley Act)	Same as Above	Amended NLRA; permitted states to pass laws prohibiting compulsory union membership; set up methods to deal with strikes affecting national health and safety	Federal Mediation and Conciliation Service
Labor-Management Reporting and Disclosure Act (Landrum-Griffin Act)	Same as Above	Amended NLRA and LMRA; guarantees individual rights of union members in dealing with their union; requires financial disclosures by unions	U.S. Department of Labor

Source: Extracted from F. Ray Marshall, Allan G. King, and Vernon N. Briggs, Jr. *Labor Economics*, 4th ed. (Homewood, IL: Richard D. Irwin, 1980), especially Chap. 16; and Leon C. Megginson, *Personnel Management: A Human Resources Approach*, 5th ed. (Homewood, IL: Richard D. Irwin, 1985), pp. 118–19. ©1980 and 1985, respectively, Richard D. Irwin, Inc.

all prospective employees must be members of the recognized union before they can be employed, and all current employees must join within a specified time in order to retain their jobs. In an **agency shop**, all employees must pay the union dues even if they choose not to join the union. The **maintenance-of-membership clause** says that once an employee joins the union, he or she must maintain that membership as a condition of employment.

Do you have trouble seeing the difference between a union shop and a closed shop? As you can see from the definitions, in a union shop, management employs the people it chooses and then these people become members of the union. In a closed shop, management must accept the workers sent by the union.

TAFT-HARTLEY ACT. Following World War II, with evidence of the abuse of power by some union leaders, Congress passed the Labor-Management Relations Act (Taft-Hartley Act) in 1947. This Act greatly changed the Wagner Act by making it more evenhanded, so that unions as well as management could be charged with unfair labor practices.

The Taft-Hartley Act prohibited the closed-shop agreement, except in the construction and shipping industries. Also, Section 14(b) of this Act gave states the right to pass laws prohibiting the union shop. By 1987, 21 states had used Section 14(b) to pass **right-to-work laws** giving the right to join or refuse to join a union without being fired. The states with right-to-work laws are highlighted in Figure 14–2.

LANDRUM-GRIFFIN ACT. In 1959, Congress passed the Labor-Management Reporting and Disclosure Act (Landrum-Griffin Act), which tries to prevent corruption and abuse of employees by some union leaders and managers. It provided an **employees' bill of rights** that protects employees from possible abuse by some unscrupulous managers and union leaders.

Rights Under the Basic Laws

Employees, unions, and employers have certain specified and implied rights and privileges under the basic labor laws. Figure 14–3 contains the rights of employees. Figure 14–4 shows what *unions cannot do* and Figure 14–5 shows what *employers cannot do* (see page 350).

FIGURE 14–2   STATES WITH RIGHT-TO-WORK LAWS

☐ states with "right-to-work" laws

FIGURE 14–3   RIGHTS OF EMPLOYEES

- To organize.
- To bargain collectively.
- To expect no discrimination against employees by management because they are union members.
- To expect no discrimination against employees by management if they bring charges of unfair labor practices against the employer.
- To get a job without first being a member of a union.
- Not to join a union unless the union and the employer have signed a valid union shop agreement in one of the states that do not have right-to-work laws.
- Not to be charged exorbitant initiation fees and dues by a union with a valid union-shop agreement.
- To receive financial reports from the union.

How the Basic Labor Laws Are Administered

The five-person National Labor Relations Board (NLRB) has the power to enforce the basic labor laws. The functions of the NLRB are (1) to certify unions as the exclusive bargaining agent for employees and (2) to see that unfair labor practices are not committed, or are punished. Its specific duties are:

FIGURE 14-4   UNFAIR LABOR PRACTICES OF UNIONS

■ To coerce employees into, or restrain them from, engaging freely in union activities.
■ To force management to discriminate against employees in violation of the law.
■ To refuse to bargain in good faith.
■ To require managers to pay money for work not done.
■ To engage in a strike or boycott to force management to commit illegal acts.
■ To charge excessive initiation fees and dues where there is a union shop.

FIGURE 14-5   UNFAIR LABOR PRACTICES OF EMPLOYERS

■ To interfere with, restrain, or coerce employees who exercise their rights under the law.
■ To dominate or interfere with the forming or administering of unions, or to contribute support to them.
■ To discriminate in hiring or in any other terms of employment in such a way as to encourage or discourage membership in a union.
■ To discharge or otherwise discriminate against employees for filing charges against the employer or testifying under the law.
■ To refuse to bargain with the union representative.

1. To hold an election to establish the bargaining agent for employees of a given firm.
2. To investigate charges of unfair labor practices against the employer or the union.
3. To issue complaints against either management or labor.
4. To prosecute unfair labor practices and determine guilt.
5. To assess fines and prison sentences.
6. To ask federal courts to control activities of both management and labor by citing them for contempt.

UNION PRINCIPLES, OBJECTIVES, AND METHODS OF ATTAINING OBJECTIVES

The main reason why unions exist is to protect individual workers from the economic power of an employer or employer groups. Unions try to achieve certain objectives for their members and follow certain principles to achieve them.

Samuel Gompers, the AFL's first president, identified the following basic principles upon which unionism is based: (1) strength through unity, (2) equal pay for the same job, and (3) employment practices based on seniority. If any one of these principles is threatened, the union and its members will fight back, as these are cardinal, nonnegotiable beliefs.

These basic principles of unionism are the bases for the practical objectives unions have for their members. These goals are (1) higher pay, (2) shorter hours of work on a daily, weekly, or annual basis, (3) improved working conditions, both physical and psychological, and (4) improved security, both of the person and of the job.

How do unions achieve their objectives? The usual methods they employ are (1) to organize a firm's employees, (2) to become recognized as the employees' exclusive bargaining agent, (3) to engage in collective bargaining, (4) to go on strike or threaten to strike, and (5) to process grievances and arbitration. Let us explain each of these methods.

Organizing Employees

First, the union leader must persuade the employees of a firm to organize and join the union. The union organizer tries to get the employees to do this by signing a **union authorization card**.

UNDERSTANDING THE SITUATION. Supervisors should first of all recognize that most union organizers are competent professionals who are committed to their work. By attending seminars and other programs, union organizers become expert in the provisions of the labor laws and in organizing techniques. Their international headquarters conducts continual research and supplies the organizers with current and effective information and carefully conceived and tested techniques. Carefully planned, methodically executed, and well-financed campaigns have replaced the heavy-muscled past attempts by amateurs to organize workers by intimidation or force.

The employer, and the conscientious supervisor in particular, may be shocked when first hit by the realization that a union is moving in to organize employees. The supervisor may be greeted by workers, including some of the oldest and most trusted employees, carrying placards at the gates to the plant. The manager is often personally hurt, angered, and confused by this sudden defection. A natural reaction would be to strike back hard and fast against this threat. But precipitous action can result in losing the contest before the issues are drawn. Instead, managers must know what to do—and, perhaps even more important, what *not* to do.

Bobby Sutton managed Quality Service, a small hauling and delivery firm in California.[2] *His father had just bought it from an aging proprietor who had let the business slide. The elder Sutton had retained the employees—a secretary, a clerk, two warehouse workers, and three drivers. A month had passed when Marvin Wiley, an organizer for the Teamsters Union, came in and demanded that Bobby recognize the union as the bargaining agent for the firm's warehouse workers and drivers. Marvin said that most of them had joined the union and wanted it to represent them. Also, the firm owed each of them $400 in back wages in order to bring them up to the union scale. Bobby indicated that he had no evidence that the workers either belonged to* *or wanted to belong to a union. When Marvin threatened to take the workers out on strike, Bobby said he'd consider them absent without permission and fire them if they walked off the job. Marvin said "You'd better not do that," and left.*

Bobby was quite upset and shaken by the incident. While he was trying to figure out what to do, Joe, a driver, came in to talk about the situation. Joe said he and the two warehouse workers did not want to join but that they were being pressured by Marvin and Bill, another driver. Bill was quite dissatisfied and was actively pushing the others to sign up. The third driver, Tony, was neutral and would do what the majority wanted to do.

Going back to his office, Bobby felt betrayed by Bill and Tony.

WHAT ORGANIZERS DISLIKE TO FIND IN AN ORGANIZATION.   Union organizers have found that certain factors effectively reduce their chances of organizing employees and gaining union recognition. Therefore, they dislike finding the following in a targeted firm:

1. Employees who strongly believe that managers and supervisors are fair and are not taking advantage of them.
2. Employees who take pride in their work.
3. Good performance records kept by the management, for employees feel more secure when they know that their efforts are recognized and appreciated.
4. No claims of high-handed treatment, for employees respect firm but fair discipline.
5. No claims of favoritism that is not earned by higher performance.
6. Supervisors who have established good relationships with subordinates. Union leaders know that good supervisor-subordinate relations stifle organizing attempts.

As you can see, *supervisors are the key persons as far as employees are concerned; so they are an employer's first line of defense against the entry of a union.* The wise selection of supervisors is obviously very important, with leadership abilities being given more consideration than production abilities in their selection. Once selected, supervisors should be given a substantial pay differential from their subordinates. They should also get support from their superiors for the orders they give and the decisions they make, because unhappy supervisors can do tremendous harm to an employer's labor relations.

THINGS TO DO BEFORE THE UNION CALLS.   There are many things supervisors and other managers can do to minimize the chances of employees joining a union—if that's their wish. The most important ones are

1. The company and its higher-level managers must pay close attention to supervisors, for they're the key to successful labor relations. Treat them right, keep them well informed, support their relationships with their subordinates, and make them an integral part of the management team.
2. Make sure that no item in the wage-benefit package lags far behind the norm for the area and industry.

3. Improve employee benefits as quickly, and as extensively, as is feasible.
4. Review jobs frequently to see if they need to be upgraded because responsibilities or working conditions have changed.
5. Make sure employee facilities are adequate, safe, well-lighted, well-ventilated, and reasonably clean.
6. Keep records of good—and bad—performance by employees, and have programs for boosting employee performance, loyalty, and morale.
7. Be firm but fair when imposing discipline.
8. Provide a practical release valve, such as a grievance committee, for employee frustrations and complaints.
9. Be alert for any complaints of abuse or favoritism by employees or supervisors.
10. Establish clear-cut lines for two-way communications with all employees.
11. Have clear, definite, and well-communicated work rules, making sure that their wording doesn't violate NLRB or EEO/AA rules.
12. Use discretion in hiring new employees.

Notice throughout the above list the importance of good supervisory practices. It cannot be said too strongly that first-line supervisors play an integral role in making unions unnecessary!

A research study found some marked differences in attitude between "pro-union" and "pro-employer" workers. In general, "pro-employer" workers showed a greater need for achievement, perfection, and success; a higher level of independence; a drive for endurance; and an identification with management. "Pro-union" workers showed a greater need for, and dependence upon, attention, sympathy, and support from someone other than themselves. Their achievement level was low, as was their endurance.[3]

About a week after the incident at Quality Service took place (see pages 351–352), Marvin Wiley walked in, slapped a contract on Bobby Sutton's desk, and said "Sign it!" After reading it, Bobby refused, saying he couldn't live with it or he'd go broke. He said he was already paying near the union scale; he would pay the workers more when he could afford it and if they deserved it. Marvin said, "We'll see about that!" and angrily stalked out with the unsigned contract in his hand.

Bobby decided that if he was to keep the union out, he'd have to get rid of Bill. As business was slow during the winter months, Bobby laid Bill off, telling him he'd rehire him when things picked up. Bobby would drive the third truck, if this became necessary.

Things went well for Bobby during the next four years. Business grew and he had to add personnel. Each time he interviewed an applicant, he'd inquire as to the applicant's attitude toward various organizations, including unions. If the applicant showed a favorable attitude toward unions, Bobby would find a reason for not hiring him or her.

WHAT TO DO WHEN THE UNION ENTERS.   A frequently used tactic to gain recognition is for the union organizer to meet with the supervisor and hand over some signed authorization cards. Then, as illustrated in the case of the Quality Service firm, the union representative says he or she represents the workers and asks to be recognized as the workers' exclusive bargaining agent to sign or negotiate a contract.

Most labor-relations specialists suggest that supervisors *not touch or examine the cards*, for if they do, this action can be construed as their having accepted the union as the workers' agent. Nor are the supervisors to make any comments to the union representative. If the representative says, "Are you refusing to recognize the union?" the supervisor should reply, "Any comment concerning the company's position must await full consideration of the matter by higher levels of management." Then, if they are asked for, the supervisor should give the name, address, and phone number of the company's labor-relations manager. Of course, as soon as the representative leaves, the supervisor should inform his or her boss about this. Figure 14–6 contains some suggestions as to what you may legally do when a union tries to organize your employees. Some things you *should not* do are listed in Figure 14–7.

FIGURE 14–6   THINGS YOU MAY DO WHEN A UNION TRIES TO ORGANIZE YOUR COMPANY

1. Keep outside organizers off premises.
2. Inform employees from time to time of the benefits they presently enjoy. (Avoid veiled promises or threats.)
3. Inform employees that signing a union authorization card does not mean they must vote for the union if there is an election.
4. Inform employees of the disadvantages of belonging to the union, such as the possibility of strikes, serving on a picket line, dues, fines, assessments, and rule by cliques or one individual.
5. Inform employees that you prefer to deal with them rather than have the union or any other outsider settle grievances.
6. Tell employees what you think about unions and about union policies.
7. Inform employees about any prior experience you have had with unions and whatever you know about the union officials trying to organize them.
8. Inform employees that the law permits you to hire a new employee to replace any employee who goes on strike for economic reasons.
9. Inform employees that no union can obtain more than you as an employer are able to give.
10. Inform employees how their wages and benefits compare with those in unionized or nonunionized concerns where wages are lower and benefits are less desirable.
11. Inform employees that the local union probably will be dominated by the international union, and that they, the members, will have little to say in its operations.
12. Inform employees of any untrue or misleading statements made by the organizer. You may give employees corrections of these statements.

FIGURE 14–6   (continued)

13. Inform employees of any known racketeering, Communist, or other unde-sirable elements that may be active in the union.
14. Give opinions on the unions and union leaders, even in derogatory terms.
15. Distribute information about unions such as disclosures of congressional committees.
16. Reply to union attacks on company policies or practices.
17. Give the legal position on labor-management matters.
18. Advise employees of their legal rights, provided you do not engage in or finance an employee suit or proceeding.
19. Declare a fixed policy in opposition to compulsory union membership contracts.
20. Campaign against a union seeking to represent the employees.
21. Insist that no solicitation of membership or discussion of union affairs be conducted during working time.
22. Administer discipline, layoff, and grievance procedures without regard to union membership or nonmembership of the employees involved.
23. Treat both union and nonunion employees alike in making assignments of preferred work or desired overtime.
24. Enforce plant rules impartially, regardless of the employee's membership activity in a union.
25. Tell employees, if they ask, that they are free to join or not to join any organization, so far as their status with the company is concerned.
26. Tell employees that their personal and job security will be determined by the economic prosperity of the company.

Source: Leon C. Megginson, et al., *Successful Small Business Management*, 5th ed. (Plano, TX: Business Publications, 1988), Chapter 13, Appendix B. Reproduced with permission of Business Publications, Inc.

FIGURE 14–7   THINGS YOU MAY NOT DO WHEN A UNION TRIES TO ORGANIZE YOUR COMPANY

1. Engage in surveillance of employees to determine who is and who is not participating in the union program; attend union meetings or engage in any undercover activities for this purpose.
2. Threaten, intimidate, or punish employees who engage in union activity.
3. Request information from employees about union matters, meetings, etc. Employees may, of their own volition, give such information without prompting. You may listen but not ask questions.
4. Prevent employee union representatives from soliciting memberships during nonworking time.
5. Grant wage increases, special concessions, or promises of any kind to keep the union out.

FIGURE 14–7 (continued)

6. Question a prospective employee about his or her affiliation with a labor organization.
7. Threaten to close up or move the plant, curtail operations, or reduce employee benefits.
8. Engage in any discriminatory practices, such as work assignments, overtime, layoffs, promotions, wage increases, or any other actions that could be regarded as preferential treatment for certain employees.
9. Discriminate against union people when disciplining employees for a specific action, while permitting nonunion employees to go unpunished for the same action.
10. Transfer workers on the basis of teaming up nonunion employees to separate them from union employees.
11. Deviate in any way from company policies for the primary purpose of eliminating a union employee.
12. Intimidate, advise, or indicate in any way that unionization will force the company to lay off employees, take away company benefits or privileges enjoyed, or make any other changes that could be regarded as a curtailment of privileges.
13. Make statements to the effect that you will not deal with a union.
14. Give any financial support or other assistance to employees who support or oppose the union.
15. Visit the homes of employees to urge them to oppose or reject the union in its campaign.
16. Be a party to any petition or circular against the union or encourage employees to circulate such a petition.
17. Make any promises of promotions, benefits, wage increases, or any other items that would induce employees to oppose the union.
18. Engage in discussions or arguments that may lead to physical encounters with employees over the union question.
19. Use a third party to threaten or coerce a union member, or attempt to influence any employee's vote through this medium.
20. Question employees on whether or not they have been affiliated or signed with the union.
21. Use the word *never* in any predictions or attitudes about unions or their promises or demands.
22. Talk about tomorrow. When you give examples or reasons, you can talk about yesterday or today instead of tomorrow, to avoid making a prediction or conviction which may be interpreted as a threat or promise by the union or the NLRB.

Source: Leon C. Megginson, et al., *Successful Small Business Management*, 5th ed. (Plano, TX: Business Publications, 1988), Chapter 13, Appendix C. Reproduced with permission of Business Publications, Inc.

Becoming Recognized as the Employees' Bargaining Agent

The union then tries to become recognized as the employees' exclusive bargaining agent. A **bargaining agent** is the employees' representative who deals exclusively with management over questions of wages, hours, and other terms and conditions of employment. This means that the union has the *sole* right and legal responsibility to represent *all* of the employees—nonunion members as well as union members—in their dealings with management.

Management may voluntarily recognize the union or may be forced to accept it because of the union's superior bargaining strength. But ordinarily a secret-ballot election is conducted by the NLRB when requested by the union or the company. If 30 percent or more of the eligible employees sign authorization cards or a petition requesting a representation election, the NLRB will conduct one. If a majority of the voting employees vote for the union, it is named the exclusive representative of the employees in their dealings with management.

TECHNIQUES USED BY UNION ORGANIZERS.   The most common technique employed by union organizers in obtaining union recognition is to compare the target company's practices to the items in the contracts that the union has with other companies, perhaps in an entirely different industry. If the terms of employment in the target company lag far behind, the union has a ready-made argument. Of course, the organizer will bore in on those parts of the wage/benefit package that will make the employer look bad.

WHAT UNIONS USUALLY OFFER EMPLOYEES.   Union organizers appeal to five main desires of employees:

1. *Job protection.* Unions stress that they constantly try to assure employees a job— or at least an income—for a lifetime. With the current generous employee benefits enjoyed by most employees, many of them seem more interested in job security than in higher pay rates. But there are exceptions to this generalization.

   For example, unionized employees at an Alcoa plant in Mobile, Alabama, voted to permit the plant to close rather than take cuts in income and benefits. They received quite high unemployment compensation, as well as supplemental payments from the company, for three years.

2. *Interference running.* Unions assure employees that they will act as their agents in grievances and disputes. They will "go to bat" for employees and have the "know-how" to protect their interests.

3. *Participation in management.* Unions insist that they can and will give employees a greater voice in deciding the policies, procedures, and rules that affect them and the work they do.

4. *Economic gains.* Higher wages, reduced hours, and better benefits, however, are still at the top of an organizer's checklist.

5. *Recognition and participation.* Knowing that "pro-union" workers need and are dependent upon attention, sympathy, and support, union organizers promise

employees that they'll have greater recognition and participation through union activities.

It was once believed that the problems and frustrations of female clerical workers were their own concern—to be borne in silence. This attitude changed in 1973, when Karen Nussbaum, a clerk-typist at the Harvard Graduate School of Education, organized 10 clerical workers into a group known as "9 to 5." Now, "9 to 5" is a nonunion, membership advocacy group, and many of its members belong to District 925 of the Service Employees International Union. Karen Nussbaum is one of the top women of the AFL-CIO.[4]

ADDITIONAL PRECAUTIONS FOR SUPERVISORS. Besides the "can do" and "cannot do" factors listed in Figures 14–6 and 14–7 on pages 354–356, there should be nothing in personnel policies and work rules that the NLRB can construe as "anti-union." For example, suppose a company has the following sign displayed: "No solicitation at this company." This sign can actually be ruled an unfair labor practice unless it's clearly worded and is enforced against all types of solicitation, not just the union organizer.

Also, solicitations from and distribution of union literature to employees can only take place at the work area during nonworking hours and not in nonwork areas such as locker rooms and parking lots. Of course, managers can prohibit non-employees from being on company property at all times.

Next, supervisors and anyone in a position to reward or punish voting employees should stay away from the voting area during a representation election.

Finally, neither threat of reprisal nor any promise of reward should be given before the election, although it's permissible to tell employees what has happened at other plants where workers unionized—if it's factual.

During its fifth year of operation, things were booming for Quality Service (see pages 351–352 and 353). Bobby Sutton had 22 employees, including 3 office employees, 7 warehouse workers, and 12 truck drivers. His father had bought another firm in a nearby city, and Bobby was running both businesses with a supervisor at each location. Bobby had contracted to buy five new trucks and was trying to hire new drivers for them, but the number of capable drivers available for employment was quite limited.

After hearing nothing from the union for four years, Bobby was surprised when Marvin Wiley walked in and laid down authorization cards from five warehouse workers and two drivers. Marvin said, "Bobby, the last time I was here, you said you couldn't afford to unionize. But now you're the largest delivery firm in town. I think your people had better be working under a contract."

Again, Bobby refused to accept the union as the representative of his employees. The seven employees subsequently petitioned for an NLRB election, but lost it by a vote of 6 for the union and 13 against it. From then on, Bobby and his supervisors became more concerned about employee relations.

Collective Bargaining

Once the union is recognized as the employees' bargaining agent, it starts negotiating with management to try to reach an agreement (which in effect is a contract between the company and the union). In general, **collective bargaining** is the mutual obligation of the representatives of the employer and the employees to meet at reasonable times and places and to confer in good faith over wages, hours, and other terms and conditions of employment. The representatives of the two parties are only required to meet in a reasonable place, usually a hotel or motel, and at reasonable times—usually the firm's normal daily working hours. They must negotiate in good faith by making valid offers and counteroffers about any question involving wages, hours, and other "terms and conditions of employment." And once an agreement is reached, it must be signed if both parties want to—which they usually do.

It's a "must" that supervisors be consulted at each step of this bargaining procedure. They should carefully examine every union proposal — and management's counterproposal—to see how these would affect their relationships with the employees. Also, supervisors should be consulted about concessions to be asked of the union negotiators.

If no agreement is reached, an *impasse* develops, with neither side able to win. At this point there are three alternatives: (1) to call in an outside **mediator**, provided by the Federal Mediation and Conciliation Service, who tries to bring the parties together; (2) to agree to bring the issue to an outside **arbitrator**, who will make a binding decision, or (3) for the union to go on strike or for management to stage a lockout.

Conducting a Strike or Lockout

The ultimate strategy used by the unions to achieve their objectives is the strike. A **strike** occurs when employees withhold their services from an employer in order to get something. The striking employees tell the public why by means of **picketing** (walking back and forth outside the place of employment, usually carrying signs).

Most union leaders *do not like to use the strike*. It is costly, it carries a certain stigma for those walking the picket line, and it is potentially dangerous to the union because of the possible loss of membership and power if the strike fails. In fact, only a very small percentage of some 12,000 contracts being renewed annually result in strikes. Although the strike itself is the ultimate device in collective bargaining and is the technique resorted to when all other methods of resolving differences fail, the *threat of a strike* is a continuing factor in almost all negotiations. Both the union and the employer frequently act as if one could occur.

Just as the union can call a strike if it isn't satisfied with the progress of negotiations, so can management stage a lockout. A **lockout** is the closing of company premises to the employees and refusal to let them work.

Reaching an Agreement

When an agreement is reached, a document is prepared which becomes the "contract" among the company, the union, and the workers. It usually contains clauses covering at least the following areas:

1. Union recognition.
2. Wages.
3. Vacation and holidays.
4. Working conditions.
5. Layoffs and rehiring.
6. Management prerogatives.
7. Hours of work.
8. Seniority.
9. Arbitration.
10. Renewal clause.

Specifics are set forth in each of these areas, and rules are established which should be obeyed by management and the union. The "management prerogatives clause" defines the areas in which supervisors have the right to act, free from questioning or joint action by the union.

LIVING WITH THE AGREEMENT

Once the agreement is signed, managers and supervisors have to *live with the contract* until it is time to negotiate a new one. Therefore, all management personnel—especially first-level supervisors—should be thoroughly briefed on its contents. Meanings and interpretations of each clause should be reviewed, and the wording of the contract should be clearly understood. Supervisors' questions should be answered to better prepare them to deal with labor relations matters.

Supervisors' Rights Under the Agreement

Supervisors should view the agreement as the "rules of the game," for it spells out what they can and cannot do. Thus, they should take a positive view of what they *can do* rather than the negative one of what they *cannot do*. While all agreements differ in detail, they tend to give supervisors the following rights:

1. To decide what work is to be done.
2. To decide how, when, and where it will be done.
3. To determine how many workers are needed to do the work safely.
4. To decide who will do each job, as long as the skill classifications and seniority provisions are observed.
5. To instruct, supervise, correct, and commend employees in the performance of their work.
6. To require that work performance and on-the-job personal behavior meet minimum standards.

7. To recommend promotions and pay increases, as long as they do not violate the union agreement.
8. To administer discipline according to the agreed-upon procedure.

If uncertain as to their authority, supervisors should check with the firm's personnel or labor-relations experts. But supervisors need to have a working knowledge of the agreement's details because the employees and their advocate, the union steward, will be aware of these details.

Would you rather be a supervisor in a unionized or a nonunionized company? Why?

The Supervisor and the Union Steward

The **union steward**, a union member who's been elected by other members to represent their interests in relations with management, is the supervisor's counterpart. He or she is the link between the workers and their union, and between the union and the company, especially in case of controversy. The steward is at the same level in the union hierarchy as the supervisor is in the company hierarchy. Thus, as equals, they must maintain production operations within the framework of the agreement.

Frequently the goals of the steward and the supervisor conflict, for the supervisor's job is to obtain maximum productivity while the steward's aim is to protect the workers' interests — including not working too hard, or not working themselves out of a job. Also, the supervisor represents the company and its interests to workers who play the dual roles of employees of the company and members of the union. The steward represents the union's position to the workers and to the company.

The Role of Seniority

As stated earlier, one of the most basic union principles is **seniority**, which means that workers who have been on the job the longest get preferred treatment and better benefits. This is one of the supervisor's greatest challenges: how to maintain high productivity while assigning work, especially preferred jobs and overtime, to the most senior employee, who is not necessarily the most capable worker. Also, whom does the supervisor recommend for promotion — the most capable worker or the most senior employee? These issues, plus discipline, lead to most grievances against the supervisor.

Handling Employee Complaints

In unionized companies, employees' complaints take the form of grievances. The **grievance procedure** is a formal way of handling these complaints. In nonunionized companies, employees may present their complaints to their supervisors for proper disposition.

GRIEVANCE PROCEDURES.   Figure 14–8 shows a typical grievance procedure, such as is usually found in unionized organizations. The form and substance of the grievance procedure depend upon several factors:

1. The industry (the old-line, "smoke-stack industries," such as steel, auto, and transportation, have the most formal and rigid procedures).
2. The size and structure of the organization (the larger, more highly structured organizations have the most formal and inflexible procedures).
3. The union (the older, craft-oriented unions tend to want a highly structured procedure).

There are usually five steps in a formal grievance procedure in a unionized organization. However, the *actual* number of steps taken will depend on the number of managerial levels existing in the organization and whether or not the grievance is submitted to arbitration.

1. *Step 1* in a formal procedure begins with the employee complaining to the supervisor over a presumed wrong. From the employee's viewpoint, the supervisor may

FIGURE 14–8   TYPICAL GRIEVANCE PROCEDURE IN A
UNIONIZED ORGANIZATION

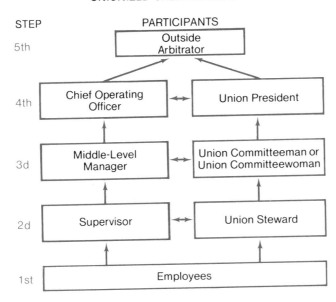

be violating the labor agreement or doing something that dissatisfies the employee. If the supervisor straightens out the matter satisfactorily, that's the end of the grievance.

2. Usually the employee goes to the union steward to present a grievance, not to the supervisor. The steward then tries to obtain satisfaction from the supervisor. This is *Step 2*. The vast majority of grievances are settled at this stage.

3. In *Step 3*, the union committeeman, committeewoman, or business agent tries to resolve the complaint with middle management such as a department head.

4. In *Step 4*, the union president and the chief operating officer try to resolve the difference. If they succeed, that ends the grievance.

5. If the chief operating officer and the union president cannot resolve the grievance, it is submitted to outside arbitration. A mutually agreed-upon arbitrator makes the decision. This is *Step 5*.

COMPLAINT PROCEDURES IN NONUNIONIZED ORGANIZATIONS.   Most nonunion organizations do not have specific provisions for handling employee complaints. However, many of them have formal complaint procedures that are in many ways comparable to the formal union grievance procedures. They permit complaints to go beyond the supervisor to committees composed of higher-level executives, which usually include the personnel officer, or even to top executives. However, they do not provide for arbitration since the primary purpose of their procedures is to assure fairness in employee relations and to improve employee attitudes rather than to interpret personnel policies and practices. These procedures are frequently found in public organizations.

Supervisors can help improve employee-employer relationships if they understand the types of employees who are more prone to file complaints or grievances. For example, the more sensitive people are, the more apt they are to file. Younger employees who are better educated but lower-paid tend to file more often, as do employees with less service who are also veterans.[5]

CHAPTER REVIEW

Labor relations are particularly important to supervisors, for supervisors are the managers who must deal with operative employees on a day-to-day basis. A company usually has good labor relations if the supervisors have good relationships with employees.

Union membership and activities grew slowly in the United States until the formation of the AFL. Then they grew steadily until they leveled off after World War I. They mushroomed during the period from 1935 to 1950, when favorable laws were passed and industrial unions became popular. Since then, they have grown more slowly.

The basic law governing labor relations is the Wagner Act, which gives workers the right to freely join unions of their choosing and to engage in concerted actions to achieve their goals. The Taft-Hartley Act prohibits the closed shop and provides for states to pass right-to-work laws prohibiting the union shop. The Landrum-Griffin Act provides employees with a bill of rights that protects them from exploitation by management and unscrupulous union leaders. These laws are administered by the National Labor Relations Board (NLRB), the Federal Mediation and Conciliation Service, and the U. S. Department of Labor. The NLRB tries to prevent the unions and management from using unfair labor practices.

Union objectives are higher pay, shorter hours of work, improved working conditions, and improved security. In achieving those objectives, unions organize (or recruit) a firm's employees into a union, then try to become their exclusive bargaining agent in dealing with management, usually through an NLRB secret-ballot election. Unions have greater difficulty organizing employees in firms that have effective supervisors and good employee relations. Management can try to keep the union out as long as its policies and actions stay within the law.

When the union becomes the bargaining agent, it bargains collectively with representatives of management over wages, hours, and other terms and conditions of employment. Supervisors are critical to success at this point; so they should help formulate demands to be made of the union, evaluate proposals made by the union, and be kept informed of progress being made in the negotiations. If the two parties can't agree and reach an impasse, they can (1) call in an outside mediator, (2) agree to send the issue to an arbitrator, who'll make a binding decision, or (3) conduct a strike or a lockout. Most negotiations end with an agreement, which becomes the contract between management and the employees.

It's then primarily up to the supervisor to live with the contract. If there's disagreement in interpreting the agreement, it goes to the grievance procedure. If agreement isn't reached within the company, the issue goes to an arbitrator to resolve it.

QUESTIONS FOR REVIEW AND DISCUSSION

1. Define labor relations.
2. When did unions grow the fastest? Why?
3. Why has union growth tended to stabilize?
4. How do you interpret the union membership trends shown in Figure 14–1 on page 345?
5. Do you believe that union power will increase or decrease in the future? Why or why not?
6. Name the laws that form the legal basis for labor relations, and explain their general provisions.
7. What are some unfair labor practices that management sometimes commits?
8. What are some unfair labor practices that unions sometimes commit?
9. What are the primary objectives of unions?

10. What are the methods used by unions to achieve their objectives?
11. What are the differences among the union shop, the closed shop, and the agency shop? Are these differences really significant? Explain.
12. What provisions are usually included in a labor agreement?
13. Describe the typical grievance procedure.

LEARNING EXERCISE 14–1
LABOR TRIES TO REBOUND WITH NEW STRATEGY[6]

Desperate to reverse its steep decline, American labor has embarked on a new strategy to concentrate power in its high command. The plan could make organizing efforts in factories and offices more effective by ending competition among AFL-CIO affiliates to unionize the same group of workers.

Until now, labor unions have often wasted enormous amounts of money and effort fighting among themselves for new members. In Ohio in 1985, 11 unions spent more than $15 million battling one another to represent 41,000 public employees. Each year, unions feud among themselves to organize workers at about 150 privately owned companies. "Unions have talked it over, and if they couldn't agree on who could organize what, they have slugged it out," says Charles McDonald, the AFL-CIO director of organizing. As a result, says Ray Abernathy, a consultant to the Service Employees International Union (SEIU), "it's expensive and it sours the potential members," who may then veto all the unions seeking to represent them.

To halt the slide in union membership, the AFL-CIO Executive Council is taking more responsibility for its 93 affiliates. Now, if two or more unions clash over organizing the same workers, they can submit their dispute to a mediator picked by the federation. Should mediation fail, the matter goes to an AFL-CIO umpire. The unions must abide by the umpire's ruling or face sanctions.

The new policy is a startling departure from union autonomy established a century ago by the AFL's first president, Samuel Gompers. But labor's declining fortunes— unions represent one in five U. S. workers, compared with one in three 30 years ago—are forcing today's labor chiefs to take a new look. "I think people are willing to give up some of their own prerogatives to see some gains important for us all," says Karen Nussbaum, an SEIU district president.

Will the strategy produce significant union gains? Labor watchers aren't sure. Says John T. Dunlop, a Harvard University professor, "It can make a contribution to either increase the extent of organizing or reduce the cost of organizing so that resources are available for other purposes."

Answer the following questions:

1. Why do you think union membership has declined?
2. What are some results of this decline?
3. Do you think labor's new strategy will work?
4. What can unions do to reverse the decline in membership?

LEARNING EXERCISE 14–2
DIVISION OF LABOR

Historically, craft unions demanded "craft integrity," whereby a craftsworker would do the work only in his or her own craft and would not touch any other work. This division of labor sometimes puts supervisors in a dilemma. The following is quoted from the production vice-president of an industrial firm:

The division-of-labor concept has drifted into real labor union difficulties today. Although at one time it was true that more production could be maintained with workers doing only one phase of a complicated manufacturing process, automation has now taken over most of those hand-operated jobs. The jobs that are left don't lend themselves to individual crafts or specialists. In the modern plant, practically the only hand jobs left are in maintenance; and, in most cases, the worker whose responsibility it is to fix things needs to be a jack-of-all-trades. Automation will turn history back to the handyman, or else maintenance will be contracted out to service people.

For example, a recent cost study was taken in our plant on cleaning the burner on a 50-gallon hot water heater. The heater originally cost $475. After employees belonging to seven different crafts (operator, insulator, pipe fitter, instrument man, sheet metal worker, electrician, and carpenter) had worked for over eight hours, the job was still not completed. At that time, the total labor was $550. The shop steward informed the maintenance supervisor that the craftsmen would have to work overtime to ensure hot water in the change house because this was the contract.

A local plumber quoted a firm price of $45 to clean and adjust the burner. The union leaders told the supervisor that if we allowed the plumber to do the job, the workers would go on strike.

Answer the following questions:

1. What is your evaluation of the sentence, "Automation will turn history back to the handyman, or else maintenance will be contracted out to service people"?
2. What steps should management take when automation is increasing at such a rapid rate? Under these conditions, what is the responsibility to the affected workers on the part of
   a. management?
   b. unions?
   c. the workers themselves?
3. Evaluate this problem from the point of view of
   a. a union leader
   b. a supervisor
   c. a top manager
4. How would you attempt to resolve the dilemma faced by management in this exercise?

ENDNOTES

1. *Aesop's Fables*, "The Bundle of Sticks."
2. Name disguised at the company's request.
3. Joseph P. Cangemi, et al., "Differences Between Pro-Union and Pro-Company Employees," *Personnel Journal* 55 (September 1976): 451–53.
4. For further details, see Leon C. Megginson, *Personnel Management: A Human Resources Approach*, 5th ed. (Homewood, IL: Richard D. Irwin, 1985), pp. 554–55.
5. Phillip Ash, "The Parties to the Grievance," *Personnel Psychology* 23 (Spring 1970): 13–37.
6. Joe Rosenbloom III, "Labor Tries to Rebound with New Strategy," *Inc.*, September 1986: 17.

SUGGESTIONS FOR FURTHER READING

Blake, Robert R., and Jane S. Mouton. "Developing a Positive Union-Management Relationship." *Personnel Administrator* 28 (June 1983): 23–31 and 140.

English, Carey W. "Unions-Employers Try New Paths to Labor Peace." *U.S. News & World Report*, March 12, 1984, p. 74.

Esten, M. *The Unions*. New York: Harcourt, Brace & World, 1967.

Feddacker, B.S. *Labor Guide to Labor Law*. Reston, VA: Reston Publishing Co., 1980. See especially Chapter 6.

Lynch, Larrie. "Unions Step Up Recruiting." *USA Today*, February 11, 1985, p. 3A.

Rosenbloom, D. H., and Jay M. Shafritz. *Essentials of Labor Relations*. Reston, VA: Reston Publishing Co., 1985.

Tidwell, Gary L. "The Supervisor's Role in a Union Election." *Personnel Journal* 62 (August 1983): 640.

Zuckerman, M.J. "Women-Run Union Due to Get Charter." *USA Today*, February 23, 1984, p. 3A.

COMPREHENSIVE CASE FOR PART IV
FOREMAN STEVE*

At approximately 8:45 a.m. on Friday, Amos and Louis, two employees of an automobile assembly plant, were seen sitting in the corner of an operations office that was designated as a "No Smoking" area. As foreman Steve was passing the window of the office, he noted with alarm that Louis was smoking. "No Smoking" signs were posted at the entrance to the office and on one wall of the office. All employees had been warned orally that smoking was not permitted.

Foreman Steve turned and entered the office. He noted that Amos was sitting in a corner of the office with his back to Louis and that Louis was sitting on a desk with a lighted cigarette in one hand. Steve walked up to Louis and asked him what excuse he had for smoking in a "No Smoking" area. Louis immediately jumped up, shook his fist at Steve, and loudly exclaimed, "If you don't mind your own business, you'll find a fist planted in your face." Amos sat with his back to Louis and Steve

---

*Names have been disguised.

throughout the entire incident and pretended not to see what was going on around him.

Late in the morning, around 11 a.m., in recounting the incident to his supervisor and the superintendent, Steve stated that he was so shocked he hardly knew what to say because he and Louis had worked together for 15 years. Instead of answering Louis back, Steve said, he bit his tongue, said nothing, and immediately left the area. He felt certain that Louis would come back later in the day and apologize for his actions, since Louis had been a very unstable employee for several years. Louis had had many outbursts of temper and periods of surliness.

By Friday afternoon, it had become common gossip in Louis's group that he had really "told Steve off," and that Steve had had to stand there and take it. One employee remarked to another foreman as he left the plant, "Steve really took a licking from Louis."

As soon as he arrived on the job Monday morning at 6:45 a.m., Steve asked for another meeting with his supervisor and the superintendent. Again the entire incident was related. Steve apologized for bringing the matter up a second time, but Louis had not come in Friday to make amends. The weekend had passed without further developments, and now Steve felt some disciplinary measures should be taken. It was obvious to Steve's supervisor and the superintendent that something drastic had happened, because several of the foremen had heard an account of the incident on Friday.

The superintendent knew that Steve, 62 years old, with 18 years' company service, had always been fair, impartial, strict, and a most truthful foreman. Also, Steve was highly thought of by almost all of the hourly workers, the other foremen, and those members of management above him.

Conversely, Louis had been known as a very unpredictable employee who would often do the unexpected. He would favor the company one week and turn against it the next; he was known to have distorted the truth in the past; and he was respected by few of his fellow employees.

At 10:30 a.m. on Monday, Louis was called into the superintendent's office, along with the union steward. Louis was asked to explain his actions on Friday morning. Louis claimed he did not know what incident he was being asked about and could not recall having talked to Steve at all on Friday. Under further questioning, Louis became rather indignant. The union steward insisted that unless proof of insubordination could be furnished, Louis should be allowed to return to work with no questions asked.

After requesting a recess, the supervisor and the superintendent went to another office and called Amos in for questioning. Asked to relate the incident of Friday morning between Steve and Louis, Amos grinned and stated that he "did not see anything or hear anything." He maintained this attitude throughout the questioning, and it was decided that he would not testify in Louis's behalf. It then became a matter of the word of the employee, Louis, against that of the foreman, Steve.

The management representatives reentered the office where the union steward was talking to Louis. Louis was notified that he was being suspended from work without pay for two weeks for insubordination and for threatening a member of management.

The union immediately filed a grievance. After the grievance was processed through the established procedure, up to the plant manager, it was decided that "the suspension was justified." The grounds for this justification was Steve's long-standing reputation for integrity and the fact that Louis had incriminated himself by bragging openly about his actions. Upon receiving management's response, the union considered taking the case to arbitration.

Answer the following questions:

1. How would you evaluate Steve's handling of the situation? That of the supervisor and the superintendent?
2. If the case went to arbitration, outline the strengths and weaknesses for (a) the company, and (b) the union.
3. Assume that you were the arbitrator of the case. What would you rule, and why?

PART V

CONTROLLING

15
EXERCISING CONTROL

OBJECTIVES

After reading and studying the material in this chapter, you should be able to:

- Explain how supervisory control works.
- Identify the different types of standards.
- Explain the importance of strategic control points.
- Discuss how preventive control works.
- Explain the concept of management by exception.

IMPORTANT TERMS

standard
tangible standards
numerical standards
monetary standards
physical standards

time standards
intangible standards
strategic control point
preventive controls
management by exception

CHAPTER OUTLINE
CASE 15–1. LOST CONTROL

CASE 15–1
LOST CONTROL

Supervisor Hans Higgins was visibly upset. A week ago he'd told production superintendent Phil Amos that his maintenance department would be able to complete a 5- to 6-hour overhaul of a critical machine. Several production departments would be affected, but there was ample material in process to keep them busy until the overhauled machine could be brought back on line prior to the incoming 5 p.m. shift.

On the day the machine was to be overhauled, Hans had assigned 3 of his 12 mechanics to the job and gone about his workday feeling that things were in good shape. Naturally he expected the job to be finished in plenty of time for the next shift. At 3:00 p.m., Hans decided to routinely check out his crew's progress. Hoping to find the job pretty much completed, he was shocked to find it way behind schedule! Only two people had been on the job most of the day. His senior mechanic had received an emergency call from home at about 11:00 a.m. and had not returned. To make matters worse, the two remaining mechanics discovered that an important replacement pump was not in stock, and the piece had to be ordered from a local supplier. The supplier had promised delivery by noon, but the pump still had not been received.

About this time, the production superintendent drifted by and asked Hans how the job was coming along. Hans told him the bad news about the snags and indicated there was some question as to whether they'd be able to complete the job as scheduled. The superintendent responded, "I don't want to hear your excuses, Hans. You told us it could be done and it better get done. This won't sell with Lowry [plant manager]. If this machine isn't on line by 5:00 p.m., it will tie up 50 people who come on for the next shift. Those people can't sit around here twiddling their thumbs waiting for your people to finish the job as promised."

Hans knew, as the superintendent walked off, that even if the pump were on hand, it would be almost impossible to complete the job by 5:00 p.m. As he looked at his two mechanics, each of them shrugged his shoulders as if to say, "Don't blame us. It's not our fault."

Hans Higgins was caught flat-footed by his crew's lack of progress on the machine overhaul job, wasn't he? Like Hans, many supervisors get caught by surprise when things seemingly blow up their plans. It was crucial to complete the overhaul by 5:00 p.m. If Hans had used the principles involved in controlling, which we will discuss in this chapter, the job would likely have been completed as scheduled. And he wouldn't be in his present crisis.

In this chapter we will give you a broad overview of what is involved in the control function. In Chapter 16 we will examine some specific areas of control that are crucial for supervisors.

WHAT IS CONTROL?

Have you ever driven a car on an unfamiliar highway and come to an unmarked fork in the road? Your map doesn't show it, there are no numbers, and you have nobody to ask for information. You then choose one route and drive for miles before you find a marker that confirms you've taken the correct route. What a relief!

Managers and supervisors are often in a similar quandary. They go along not knowing whether they are on the right road or not. Unfortunately many of them find they are headed in the wrong direction, but it's too late to do much about it. They don't have the advantage of periodic road markers to tell them whether they're on track or not because they haven't established any. You might think of control as consisting of road markers that tell you whether your department's performance is moving in the correct direction.

In Chapter 1 we defined *controlling* as the management function that involves comparing actual performance with planned performance and taking corrective action, if needed, to ensure that objectives are achieved. In Chapter 2 we also indicated that planning and controlling might be thought of as "Siamese twins" because they are so closely related. Planning sets the ship's course, and controlling keeps it on course. When a ship begins to veer off course, the navigator notices this and recommends a new setting designed to return the ship to its proper course. That's how supervisory control works. You set goals or targets and receive information on whether they are being accomplished as planned. If not, you make adjustments designed to enable you to still accomplish your goals.

Examples of Controls

We live in a world of controls. Circuit breakers in our homes and offices are examples of controls. When an electrical overload occurs, the system adjusts by shutting itself down. Security alarm systems send out signals when a protected area is violated. The dashboard on your car contains numerous controls to warn you when something is not the way it's supposed to be—low oil pressure, overheated engine, alternator malfunction, keys left in car, seat belt not on, and so on. Figure 15–1 illustrates a number of other common examples of control with which you are familiar.

FIGURE 15–1   SOME COMMON EXAMPLES OF SUPERVISORY CONTROL

- At the end of the workday, a production supervisor spends 30 minutes examining a printout showing each employee's output, quality, and scrap. The supervisor notes those employees whose performance is below par and will discuss it with them tomorrow.
- A nursing supervisor studies a survey completed by all patients who were housed in her ward in the past six months. The survey lists items such as nurses' friendliness, professionalism, appearance, and a number of other factors related to their job performance.
- A maintenance supervisor tours the building, examining the progress of each worker or work team.
- After a college football game, the head defensive coach monitors the game films several times, assigning performance grades to each defensive player. Players graded below 60 reflect areas to which the coach must devote special attention during the week's practices.

Importance of Controls

You've perhaps heard the old adage, "Things never go as planned." That's one primary reason why supervisors need to perform the controlling function effectively. You might think of control as being important because of the many variables that can occur to put things off track. Supervisors need to be aware of progress being made on important jobs and to make necessary adjustments along the way.

Murphy's Laws (shown in Figure 15–2) seem to be found everywhere. Because anything involving humans or things put together by humans is imperfect, good control is necessary to monitor progress and to make intelligent adjustments as required.

FIGURE 15–2   MURPHY'S LAWS

- Left to themselves, things always go from bad to worse.
- There's never time to do it right, but always time to do it over.
- If anything can go wrong, it will.
- Of the things that can go wrong, the one that will is that which is capable of the most possible damage.
- If you think nothing can go wrong, you have obviously overlooked something.
- Of those things that cannot go wrong, the most unlikely one is that which will.
- Inside every large problem are many small problems struggling to get out.
- Any object will fall so that it lands in the one spot where it is capable of doing the most damage.

Did you note the two unplanned events—the emergency absence of a senior mechanic and the pump which was not on hand—that occurred to set back the machine overhaul job in Case 15–1?

STEPS IN THE CONTROLLING PROCESS

The controlling process involves the several steps illustrated in Figure 15–3. Note that Step 4 may involve going back to any of the previous three steps. This means that the corrective action taken may entail modifying the original standard, changing the frequency and manner of measuring performance, or achieving more insight into the possible cause of the problem. Let us examine the details involved in each of these steps.

Step 1. Establish Performance Standards

This first step of the controlling process is really a "planning" step. You set your sights on something you want to accomplish, which then becomes the target you shoot for.

As a supervisor, you exercise control against some standard or goal. A **standard** is a unit of measurement that can serve as a reference point for evaluating

FIGURE 15–3   THE PROCESS OF CONTROL

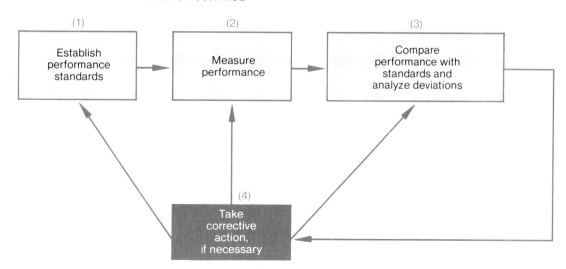

results. Properly communicated and accepted by employees, standards become the bases for the supervisor's control activities.

TYPES OF STANDARDS. Standards can be either *tangible* or *intangible*. **Tangible standards** are standards that are quite clear, concrete, specific, and generally measurable. For instance, when you say, "I want the machine on line by 3:00 p.m.," this is very specific and concrete. The machine is either on line at 3:00 p.m. or it's not.

Tangible standards can be further categorized as numerical, monetary, physical, and time-related. **Numerical standards** are expressed in numbers, such as number of items produced, number of absences, percentage of successful sales calls, or number of personnel successfully completing training. **Monetary standards** are expressed in terms of dollars and cents. Examples of monetary standards are predetermined profit margins, payroll costs, scrap costs, maintenance costs, and so on. **Physical standards** relate to quality, durability, size, weight, or other factors concerning physical composition. **Time standards** include the speed with which the job should be done. Examples of time standards include printing deadlines, scheduled project completion dates, and rates of production.

Referring to Case 15–1, what standards were involved in the machine overhaul job?

Note that there may be some overlap among the types of tangible standards. For instance, when you say, "I want the machine on line by 3:00 p.m.," you have obviously communicated a time standard, but you might also think of it as a numerical standard because time is expressed numerically. Monetary standards are also expressed numerically, as are physical standards.

In contrast to tangible standards, **intangible standards** are not expressed in terms of numbers, money, physical qualities, or time because they relate to human characteristics and are difficult to measure. Examples of intangible standards are a desirable attitude, high morale, ethics, and cooperation (see Figure 15–4). Intangible standards are nonetheless important and pose special challenges to the supervisor, as the following example illustrates.

Supervisor Maude Leyden of the State Employment Office overheard one of her newer employment counselors, David Hoffman, berating a job applicant. The tone of his voice was domineering, as though he were scolding a child, although the applicant was perhaps 30 years his senior. She heard David conclude the interview with, "Now don't you come back here and bother us

FIGURE 15–4 CONTROLLING INTANGIBLE STANDARDS

until you've had someone fill this form out properly for you. That's not what I'm paid to do!"

After the applicant left, Maude listened to David's explanation of what had just happened. He said he'd had a lot of pressure that day and had grown very impatient, acknowledging his curtness with the applicant. Maude told him that he had not handled himself in a professional manner and discussed what he should have done differently. Later in the day, David was to call the applicant, apologize, and offer to be of further help.

It's much more difficult to clearly explain an intangible standard, such as "interviewers must observe professional conduct with clients" than to tell someone that the standard is "to produce 500 bolts a day," isn't it? For example, just what *is* professional conduct? Is it patience, friendliness, courtesy, keeping level-headed? Certainly, it is less specific than "producing 500 bolts daily." But difficult as it may be, every supervisor has to establish, communicate, and control some types of intangible job standards.

Employee cooperation, employee attitude, employee personal hygiene, and mature employee behavior are some typical intangible standards that organizations and individual supervisors must control. Can you think of additional ones?

HOW STANDARDS ARE SET. Standards can be set in many ways. The supervisor frequently sets standards on the basis of familiarity with the jobs being performed by his or her employees. The supervisor normally has a pretty good knowledge of the time required to perform tasks, the quality necessary, and the expected employee behavior. This is especially true for supervisors who have been promoted through the ranks. For those who aren't technically knowledgeable about the work performed in their department, there are a number of ways to become familiar with standards. You can gain insights from past records of performance, if available, and from fellow supervisors, employees, and your own boss. Figure 15–5 presents the types of standards that can be used for a variety of positions.

FIGURE 15–5   TYPES OF STANDARDS FOR VARIOUS POSITIONS

Position	Type of Standard
Bank teller	Monetary (balance), time (speed of teller line), physical (orderliness of work area)
Postal letter carrier	Time (hours taken to complete run)
Waiter in large restaurant	Physical (appearance), time (speed), intangible (courtesy and friendliness)
Real estate salesperson	Monetary (volume), numerical (number of listings and closings)
Offensive-line football coach	Numerical (yards per game rushing), intangible (leadership with players)
Upholsterer in manufacturing plant	Numerical (number of units completed), physical (quality of units)
Third grade teacher	Intangible (appearance, classroom behavior), physical (quality of lesson plans)

For many jobs performed by employees, certain staff departments will exercise strong influence over standards. The industrial engineering department, for example, may utilize systematic studies of movements and speed of workers to set quantity and time standards. The quality control department may establish standards for finish, luster, or precision. Cost accounting may establish standards for material costs or scrap. Thus, many of these standards are already established for the people that you will supervise.

Staff departments will also have a hand in setting standards for supervisors to follow. For example, the budget department may help set standards regarding your material costs and payroll costs. Personnel may set standards regarding the quantity and quality of grievances and turnover in your department. How well you will be able to meet your departmental standards reflects the amount of control that your own boss will employ over your activities.

Step 2. Measure Performance

While setting standards is an essential first step in control, by itself it doesn't go far enough. A supervisor must actually monitor performance to ensure that it complies with the standards established. Two important issues the supervisor must determine are (1) How often should performance be measured? and (2) How should the performance be measured?

HOW OFTEN TO MEASURE. An important control decision a supervisor must make is how often to measure performance. Sometimes this decision is already made by the system, as shown in the two examples.

> *Kay Davis, sales manager of City Motors, needs only to look at the sales chart prominently displayed on the sales floor outside her office to see how her sales personnel are doing. The chart lists each salesperson's number of new and used cars sold for the week and the month, as well as sales volume.*
>
> *The production control room at DAVO company provides a constant reading of activity on each of the production floor's operating machines. At any point in time, a production supervisor need only visit the area to receive a printout of the work performed by any of the operators up to that time.*

Notice that in each example given above, performance is constantly monitored. But don't get the idea that a supervisor should spend the entire day constantly monitoring performance. Instead, the supervisor should establish strategic control points. As shown in Figure 15–6, a **strategic control point** is a point in an activity when performance is measured sufficiently early so that the necessary corrective action can be taken to accomplish the objective. You ask

FIGURE 15–6   SETTING STRATEGIC CONTROL POINTS IN THE CONTROL PROCESS

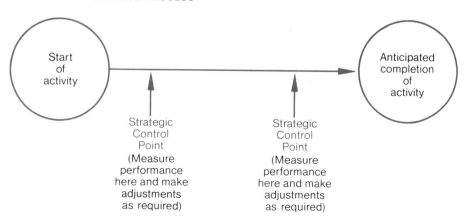

yourself: Considering the importance of the job being done, at what point do I need to know the progress being made so that I can make the required adjustments and still complete the job as planned?

Certain types of jobs, such as maintenance, personnel, and sales, don't lend themselves to frequent measurement of progress. Measurement takes time unless an automated system is in place. Moreover, some jobs are more crucial than others, with more at stake. For example, it is more crucial to monitor effectively the work of a person who assembles parachutes than the work of a sales representative or a clerical worker.

Note in Case 15–1 that Hans Higgins had not given much thought to establishing any strategic control points on the machine overhaul job. What key control points would you recommend? If these had been established, would the job have gone awry?

HOW TO MEASURE. There are several basic ways for a supervisor to measure performance. These are:

1. Personal observation.
2. Written or oral reports of subordinates.
3. Automatic methods.
4. Inspections, tests, or samples.

Note that in Case 15–1, supervisor Hans Higgins used personal observation as the control technique. Might he have used any other methods? Which? Why?

Some supervisors work in an area where their entire work group is situated close together. A supervisor can easily rove among the workers, observing their performance. In other departments, however, the supervisor may have workers spread out in various locations, which makes direct observation impractical. Consider a sanitation supervisor whose eight work crews collect garbage on various routes throughout the city. In such cases, these supervisors must depend upon written or oral reports, or occasional inspections, as the primary means of measurement. Here is what one sanitation supervisor said:

> *How do I know if my crews are doing the job properly? Mainly by the complaints I get from people whose garbage isn't picked up as scheduled or whose cans are thrown around with litter scattered. That's the main way I know what's going on directly in the field. Sometimes I will drive around and make an occasional inspection. We also have an annual survey done of our residents to see if our people are considered friendly, efficient, and courteous.*

Sales supervisors may seldom see their salespersons if the sales work takes them outside the office. As a result, salespersons are required to fill in reports about the number of calls made, sales results, travel expenses, customer comments, and numerous other matters. These reports are received by supervisors or the home office staff. Many salespersons, in fact, complain that they are required to do too much paperwork!

When you are not in frequent contact with your employees, the idea is to come up with some meaningful, valid way to measure results. But you will need to make sure the measurements are reliable. Because of pressures to conform to standards, employees may attempt to falsify reports to make themselves appear better. Here is one example:

> *Several years ago, a nationally respected youth organization set very high membership goals for their local offices. The results were spectacular until it was discovered that a number of local chapters considerably upped the actual number of new members enrolled so as to avoid looking bad.*

In other words, you have to be careful about attempts to beat the control system. People may extort money, falsify documents, and even distort oral reports. For example, you might ask an employee to give you an oral report on a job's progress, and he or she will tell you "Everything's just fine, boss," when, in fact, it may not be.

Step 3: Compare Performance with Standards and Analyze Deviations

Unfortunately many supervisors receive information that demonstrates a serious departure from standards, but make little effort to understanding what caused the deviation. Failure to meet standards may result from a variety of causes. A supervisor needs to understand the reasons for below-par performance. Many supervisors hurriedly jump to conclusions about the causes of problems; as a result, the corrective action they take is ineffective.

> *For example, suppose that the quality control standard to produce a certain part is 99/100. This means that there should be no more than one defective product per hundred units produced by a worker. You just received notice from the quality department that, of the last 200 units produced by your employee, Kevin Rae, almost 13 percent were defective.*

What could have caused this problem? Could it have been poor materi-als? Might Rae's equipment be the cause? Is this like Rae? What will you do about it? These are some questions you have to ask yourself. Simply to give Rae an oral or written warning may be highly inappropriate and may not correct the problem!

It is important to find out the opinions of those familiar with or close to a particular problem in order to determine why standards are not being met. For example, an employee's explanations or those of other employees or fellow supervisors might be obtained. Frequently, people in other departments can add insight. Here is what one supervisor said:

I was all set to really chew out Emily. She had an important job to complete for me this morning and didn't show up as scheduled. Fortunately, before I made a fool of myself, I learned from one of her friends that she'd gotten here early and the plant manager had asked her to do an important job. I checked this out with the plant manager, and sure enough that was the case. She was supposed to notify me but had just forgotten.

Step 4. Take Corrective Action if Necessary

The final step in the control process is to take corrective action if necessary. You have undoubtedly seen many athletic contests turn completely around after halftime. This is due to the corrective action taken by the coach—the modifi-cation, adjustments, and fine-tuning done in response to problems encountered earlier.

The supervisor's job is much like that of a coach. Adjustments, fine-tuning, and perhaps even drastic actions are necessary to pull off important tasks or to maintain standards. Examples of corrective actions a supervisor may take include such things as the following:

1. Making a decision to retrain a new operator whose performance has not progressed as expected.
2. Shifting several employees from their normal jobs to help meet a deadline on another.
3. Counseling an employee whose performance has recently been below standard.
4. Reprimanding an employee for failure to adhere to safety rules.
5. Shutting down a piece of equipment for maintenance after a check of defective output is traced to it.

TWO IMPORTANT PRINCIPLES OF SUPERVISORY CONTROL

In this section we shall look at two important principles of control. These are the principles of preventive controls and of management by exception.

Preventive Controls

Preventive controls are actions taken before or during the course of a job to prevent things from going wrong. Essentially they are up-front actions that supervisors take to ensure that standards will be met.

Think back to Case 15–1 and supervisor Hans Higgins' predicament with the machine overhaul. Listed below are two problems that occurred to throw the machine overhaul badly off schedule and a preventive control for each.

1. *Problem 1:* Key operator leaves the job due to an emergency, leaving the crew shorthanded.
   Preventive control: Establish a system whereby the supervisor must immediately be notified when a worker leaves the job.
2. *Problem 2:* An important replacement pump needed in the overhaul of the machine was not on hand and needed to be ordered from a local supplier.
   Preventive controls: Keep on hand an inventory of critical machine parts, have a checklist of parts needed, and have these parts on hand prior to beginning the overhaul.

Assume that, as supervisor Hans Higgins, you have just called the supplier and ordered the pump. What preventive control could you use to ensure its delivery by 12 noon?

Figure 15–7 lists some tips for establishing preventive controls in your department. Note that the first step is to zero in on your goals or "plans." Again, you see how importantly linked the planning and controlling processes are.

FIGURE 15–7   TIPS FOR ESTABLISHING PREVENTIVE CONTROLS

1. Identify your department's major goals.
2. Identify those factors most crucial to accomplishing your department's major goals. These may be factors such as properly running machinery and equipment, availability of raw materials, availability of key personnel, or a balanced demand for your department's services.
3. Determine the *most likely problems or circumstances* that could prevent the items identified in No. 2 from occurring. These could be factors such as machine breakdowns, absence of key personnel, or stripping of capacity for your department's output.
4. Develop a plan for preventing those items listed in No. 3 from occurring. You might consider inputs from your employees, staff personnel, immediate supervisor, peers, and others in arriving at your preventive control plans.

Management by Exception

A story found in many books on effective management is taken from the Old Testament account of the exodus from Egypt. As the story goes, Moses was having difficulties spending his entire day resolving disputes among his people. Little progress was being made in the search for the Promised Land. Moses' father-in-law, Jethro, told Moses that what he was doing was not good, that he would wear himself out. What Moses must do was to choose able persons from all the people, some of whom would rule thousands, some hundreds, some fifties, and some tens. These leaders would handle small and routine decisions; the great matters would be brought to Moses. Moses took his father-in-law's advice and established the system, and the Israelites emerged from the wilderness and reached the Promised Land. This is the first recorded use of the principle of management by exception.

Under **management by exception**, a supervisor focuses attention upon the most critical control needs and allows employees to handle most routine deviations from the standard. Figure 15–8 shows that the key issue is whether a deviation is "exceptional."

In reading about time management in Chapter 20, you will learn how to set priorities for activities, depending on their importance, and to focus your efforts on top-priority items. Management by exception works essentially the same

FIGURE 15–8   MANAGEMENT BY EXCEPTION

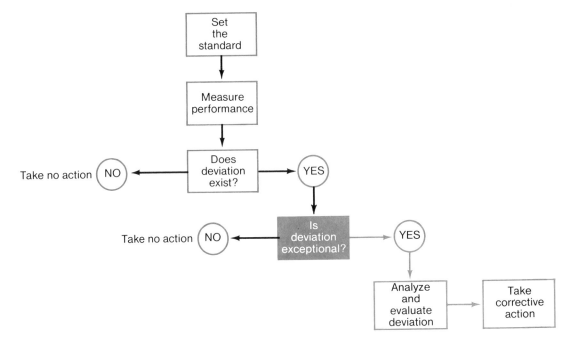

way. Your attention should focus on exceptional, rather than routine, problems. Before reading further, examine the situation shown below.

Suppose you are a sales supervisor and your departmental sales goal is 800 units weekly (or 3,200 units monthly). Each of your eight sales reps, then, has a goal of 100 units weekly (or 400 units monthly). At the end of the first week, your sales results are as follows:

Salesperson	Weekly Goal	Units Sold
A	100	105
B	100	95
C	100	90
D	100	102
E	100	102
F	100	88
G	100	98
H	100	115
Total = 800		795

What corrective action will you take?

Managers who practice management by exception might do absolutely nothing about the situation given above. "But wait!" you say. Look at Salesperson C, who performed 10 percent below standard and Salesperson F, who was 12 percent below standard. Certainly you as the supervisor should do something about these two reps, shouldn't you?

Of course, a supervisor should be aware of these deviations. However, recall that only the first week has gone by. It is probably fairly normal to find such deviations in a single week. The supervisor would probably be more interested in the monthly benchmark of 3,200 units. With three weeks to go, the supervisor who gets too involved after Week 1 may be overreacting. Naturally, the supervisor will keep an eye on sales data in the upcoming weeks to watch whether or not Salespersons C and F improve their performance. In this situation, the assumption of management by exception is that Salespersons B, C, F, and G realize that they're below standard and will be working to improve.

Suppose that at the end of the second week, sales results are as shown:

Salesperson	Weekly Goal	Week 1	Week 2
A	100	105	107
B	100	95	101
C	100	90	97
D	100	102	101
E	100	102	117
F	100	88	84
G	100	98	99
H	100	115	126
Total =	800	795	832

Things seem to have perked up, and, with the exception of Salesperson F, everyone is in reasonable shape. As supervisor, you'd be justified in entering the control process with Salesperson F, as the red flag has reddened. You may want to discuss this person's results, trying to identify actions that produce below-standard results and develop a plan of corrective action.

Note that Salesperson H has been setting the standards on fire, averaging more than 20 percent above standard the first two weeks. This performance is also an exceptional departure from standard. What's behind these results? Is Salesperson H using some techniques that will work for others? Is this person's territory so choice that it becomes easy to make the standard? Should you modify the standard for Salesperson H because of this? Management by exception, then, can work in both favorable and unfavorable deviations from standard.

In one sense, you might think of management by exception as a form of delegation, which indeed it is. Some common additional examples of management by exception are given below.

A sales clerk has authority to make merchandise returns to customers for up to $30. Any amount over this figure must be brought to the supervisor's attention for approval.

As long as a pressure gauge reads within certain limits, the employee monitoring the gauge makes corrective decisions. But, when the reading becomes abnormally high, the supervisor is to be notified.

CHAPTER REVIEW

Controlling is the supervisory process of making things happen that were planned to happen. Because of the many variables involved in executing and carrying out plans, supervisory control is an essential part of the management process.

Four steps are involved in the controlling process. These are to (1) establish performance standards, (2) measure performance, (3) compare performance with standards and analyze deviations, and (4) take corrective action if needed. Standards can be tangible (numerical, monetary, physical, and time) or intangible (attitudes, ethics, morals). They can be established by supervisors and staff departments. Supervisors measure performance through direct observation; written or oral reports by subordinates; automatic methods; and inspections, samples, or tests. It is important that the supervisor establish strategic control points, which permit sufficient adjustments or corrective actions to allow the plan still to be accomplished.

Two important control principles were discussed: preventive controls and management by exception. Preventive controls are actions that prevent or minimize the effect of things that can go wrong. Management by exception focuses supervisory attention upon exceptional departures from standard rather than routine variances.

QUESTIONS FOR REVIEW AND DISCUSSION

1. In what ways are planning and controlling related?
2. A supervisor says, "I don't have to worry much about controlling. My view is that, if you plan a job properly, things will go right; so you don't have to worry about control." Discuss.
3. Identify the four steps involved in controlling.
4. Give an example of each type of standard listed below.
   a. numerical standard
   b. monetary standard
   c. physical standard
   d. time standard
   e. intangible standard
5. Reflect on Case 15–1. Hans Higgins is supervisor of a maintenance crew of 12 persons who work in different parts of the plant. How can he possibly know what's going on in order to exercise proper control?
6. In what ways do certain staff departments influence the supervisor's exercise of "control"? Give an example.
7. Discuss the concept of preventive control.
8. In *management by exception* the supervisor focuses on exceptional deviations from standard rather than every deviation. Doesn't this mean that employees will grow lax when they realize that they can perform below standard as long as it's not *too far* below? Discuss.

LEARNING EXERCISE 15–1
THE OVERCONTROLLING SUPERVISOR

As a new operations supervisor, Clarise Rogers was very conscientious about wanting to do a good job and pleasing her own boss. She spent a large part of the day watching her employees perform their jobs, roving from one to another's work station. She inquired about how things were going and tried to engage in friendly small talk.

One day a senior operator asked to see Clarise in her office. The operator said, "We know you mean well, but there's no need for you to be constantly checking up on everybody. We had one of the best departments in this company under Morgan [the previous supervisor], and she stayed off our backs. We're professionals and we don't need somebody constantly looking over our shoulders. We're gonna do a good job for you. Just give us some breathing space."

Answer the following questions:

1. What should Clarise do?
2. Suppose Clarise had just taken over one of the poorest-performing departments in the company. Would this make a difference in the control techniques she should use? How?

LEARNING EXERCISE 15–2
CONTROLLING ABSENTEEISM

Anna McIntyre had been named head nurse of the University Hospital pediatrics department yesterday. She would officially begin wearing the head nurse's cap in one week, when Carla Smith, the present head nurse, would be reassigned to a new department being created. Anna reflected on the conversation she'd had with Gail Sutherland, Director of Nursing, when Gail offered her the position. "Anna," Gail had said, "you'll be taking over a department that has 8 percent absenteeism as compared to only 2 percent for other nursing units in the hospital. This has always been a problem, and Carla never could handle it—that's a major reason she was transferred. I want you to make it your number-one priority."

Anna reflected on Carla's performance as head nurse. Carla had always been a skilled, competent nurse, but since being promoted to head nurse in pediatrics, she had just been too soft. Many nurses had taken advantage of her good nature—Carla found it impossible to discipline, and the situation in pediatrics had begun to deteriorate. Finally, when Gail Sutherland was hired as nursing director, a number of personnel changes had been made, Carla's among them. Anna knew from her own experience that absenteeism had been high in the department. It was especially true of weekend work, and Carla never took action, even when it was obvious that personnel were making petty excuses.

Answer the following questions:

1. What additional information should Anna attempt to find out regarding the absenteeism problem?
2. Advise Anna on the steps she should take to control absenteeism.

3. What types of standards should she use?
4. What strategic control points should she establish?

SUGGESTIONS FOR FURTHER READING

Bittel, L. R. *Management by Exception*. New York: McGraw-Hill Book Company, 1964. This is a classic on the subject.

Daft, Richard L., and Norman B. Macintosh. "The Nature and Use of Formal Control Systems for Management Control and Strategy Implementation." *Journal of Management* 10 (Fall 1984): 43–66.

LaForge, Lawrence R., and Lester R. Bittel. "A Survey of Production Management Supervisors." *Production and Inventory Management* 24 (Fourth Quarter 1983): 99–112.

Machalaba, Daniel. "Up to Speed: United Parcel Service Gets Deliveries Done by Driving Its Workers." *The Wall Street Journal*, April 22, 1986, pp. 1 and 23.

Waldon, Barry. "The Human Side of Control." *Supervisory Management* 30 (June 1985): 34–39.

Walton, Richard E. "From Control to Commitment in the Workplace." *Harvard Business Review* 63 (March-April 1985): 77–84.

16
CONTROLLING PRODUCTIVITY, QUALITY, AND SAFETY

OBJECTIVES

After reading and studying the material in this chapter, you should be able to:

▪ Explain the concept of productivity.
▪ Identify causes of the declining productivity rate in the United States.
▪ Outline the steps that supervisors can take to increase productivity.
▪ Explain the difference between quality assurance and quality control.
▪ Explain how quality circles work.
▪ Identify ways that supervisors can achieve better quality.
▪ Describe the supervisor's role in promoting safety.

IMPORTANT TERMS

productivity
quality assurance
robot
computer-assisted design (CAD)

computer-assisted manufacturing
  (CAM)
quality control
quality circles

CHAPTER OUTLINE
CASE 16–1. PRODUCTIVITY INCREASE OR ELSE

I. IMPROVING PRODUCTIVITY AND COST CONTROL
  A. Defining productivity
    1. Example A: Increasing output
    2. Example B: Decreasing input
    3. Example C: Increasing output and decreasing input
  B. Why productivity is important
  C. Declining rate of American productivity
  D. Who is to blame for the declining rate of American productivity?
    1. Management
    2. Government
    3. Individual workers
    4. Unions
  E. The supervisor's role in improving productivity
  F. The supervisor's role in cost control
  G. Three recent productivity improvement methods
    1. Robotics
    2. Computer-assisted design (CAD)
    3. Computer-assisted manufacturing (CAM)
II. ACHIEVING AND CONTROLLING QUALITY
  A. Quality assurance and quality control
  B. Quality—a concern of all organizations
  C. The supervisor's role in achieving quality
    1. Let employees know you expect quality performance
    2. Involve workers in achieving quality
      a. How QCs operate
      b. Characteristics of effective QCs
III. PROMOTING EMPLOYEE SAFETY
  A. What OSHA does
  B. Factors influencing safety
    1. Organization size
    2. Type of industry
    3. People
  C. Causes of accidents
  D. The supervisor's role in promoting safety
Chapter Review
Questions for Review and Discussion
Learning Exercise 16–1. The Case of Bill Wesley
Learning Exercise 16–2. Ranking Departmental Goals
Learning Exercise 16–3. Over Budget
Suggestions for Further Reading

> You can never inspect quality into products.
> You can only build it into them.
> *Akio Morita, Chairman, Sony Corporation*

CASE 16–1
PRODUCTIVITY INCREASE OR ELSE

As the financial community saw it, GFF had acquired Triaz, Inc., mainly to gets its hands on the latter's breadwinner division that served the aerospace industry. For years, Triaz had been a leading manufacturer of control devices, pumps, and gauges serving the automotive and marine divisions. In the last seven years, though, Triaz had shifted gears, emphasizing the aerospace and government industries. In the previous year, the latter industries had accounted for 45 percent of total revenues, but over 70 percent of the profits.

About two months after the acquisition, Al Jackson, general manager of the division, was expected to dispose of, or eliminate, marginally performing divisions, one of which was the Boaz facility. Boaz produced a variety of pumps for the automotive and marine industries. In the previous year, Boaz had lost $8 million on volume of $50 million in sales. The plant was one of the oldest in the Triaz group, having been built in the 1920s. Two months after the GFF acquisition, Bert Mayfield, the newly named vice-president and general manager of Boaz, and a former financial manager with Triaz, addressed the 200-plus managers of the division:

What I've just heard from New York is not very good news, people. It boils down to this: We have 12 months to turn things around at Boaz or we're all gonna go. We'll be sold, or if nobody wants us, we'll be shut down for good. These GFF folks know their stuff. Among the main things they're aware of are some that I already knew, namely:

1. Our average costs are the highest in the industry—this includes our cost of goods sold as well as administrative costs. It costs us 12 percent more to make a pump than our competitors. These costs have severely affected our bottom line.
2. Our cost of reworked parts—products that had to be reworked or scrapped because of poor quality—has increased steadily over the past five years and is significantly higher than our competitors'.
3. The quality of our finished products has deteriorated. Once we had among the most reliable products on the market. But a recent survey GFF conducted showed that customers now rank us fourth in quality out of six firms we compete with. Last year, we lost two long-time

major contracts because of quality problems with the products we shipped to them.

4. Our safety performance at Boaz is at the bottom of the industry.

After a brief pause, Mayfield continued:

Each department is going to have to make a significant contribution to productivity if we are to meet this challenge. In other words, we all have to become efficient at our jobs. I'll be meeting with all department heads, asking them to develop plans for increasing their department's productivity by 15 percent or more—that's the idea. We've got to get our costs back in line, our quality up, and those lost-time accidents down. Our line supervisors will play a big part in this, but everybody has to improve—production, purchasing, maintenance, engineering—you name it. We're all in this together, and if everyone shares the responsibility, we'll make it. If we don't, . . .

It sounds as if this plant has a challenge, doesn't it? The fact that the unit cost in this plant is 12 percent over that of its competitors certainly didn't happen overnight. But only now has the plant decided to exercise control, and it may be too late.

Notice the important role that department heads and line supervisors are expected to play in raising departmental productivity through their controlling function. This chapter focuses on several key areas of control that concern supervisors: productivity and costs, quality, and safety.

IMPROVING PRODUCTIVITY AND COST CONTROL

Productivity has been an "in" word in American business for the past ten years. Another name for it is efficiency. We hear about productivity at work, read about it in magazines and newspapers, and hear it discussed on television. It has become the subject of business- and government-sponsored seminars. Also, "productivity centers" have sprung up around the country to research the subject.

Defining Productivity

Basically **productivity** is a measure of inputs as compared to outputs. It tells you how efficiently a system is performing. For example, your car's gas mileage is a productivity measure of energy performance. For a certain input, say one gallon of gas, your car achieves a certain output, say 22 miles of travel. The 22 MPG is thus the productivity measure of your car's energy performance. How is this useful? Well, you now have a basis to (1) compare your car's performance to that of other cars and (2) compare your car's present performance to its own previous performance. For example, if your MPG were to fall to 15, you would know that your car's performance had fallen, and you would need to determine the reasons. This assumes, of course, that such an energy loss is important to you!

Productivity is expressed as a ratio, that is, output is divided by input. In our example of the auto's gas mileage, the ratio looks like this:

$$\frac{\text{Total miles (220)}}{\text{Number of gallons (10)}} = 22 \text{ MPG}$$

STOP AND THINK

What would be some meaningful input/output relationships for the following departments in a manufacturing company: (a) maintenance department, (b) safety department, (c) typing pool, and (d) security force?

In business organizations, such input-output performance measures are also available. Some of these are shown in Table 16–1. Generally when you hear about people in business discussing "improved productivity," they are probably talking about Item 6 in Table 16–1. That is what the plant manager had in mind in Case 16–1 when he said that the plant needs to increase productivity by 15 percent. What the plant manager is hoping for is that, at the end of the next 12-month period, its productivity ratio would look like this:

$$\frac{\text{Total value of goods/services (output)}}{\text{Total costs (input)}} = \begin{array}{c} \text{15\% more than} \\ \text{previously} \\ \text{accomplished} \end{array}$$

TABLE 16–1   EXAMPLES OF PRODUCTIVITY MEASUREMENTS

Input	Output
1. Energy used in BTUs	1. Number of pounds fabricated
2. Number of hours of plantwide safety meetings	2. Number of accidents
3. Labor hours spent in preventive maintenance	3. Lost hours due to unscheduled machine breakdown
4. Cost of raw materials	4. Number of finished goods produced
5. Total labor hours of work force	5. Total quantity of goods produced
6. Total costs	6. Total number (or value) of goods or services produced

Basically there are three ways to accomplish the 15 percent productivity increase desired at Boaz. These are:

1. *Increase* the value of total output without changing the value of the total input.
2. *Decrease* the value of the total input without changing the value of the total output.
3. *Increase* the value of the output *and decrease* the value of the input.

To illustrate these three ways, assume that a department of Boaz produces 48,000 units (output) at a cost for raw materials, energy, and labor of $24,000. Thus, the productivity ratio is:

$$\frac{48,000 \text{ units (output)}}{\$24,000 \text{ (input)}} \;=\; 2.0 \text{ productivity ratio}$$

To achieve a 15 percent increase in productivity, you would need to raise the final ratio by 0.3 (= 2.0 × 15%). In other words, you would need a final productivity rate of 2.0 + 0.3 = 2.3 to achieve a 15 percent productivity increase.

EXAMPLE A: INCREASING OUTPUT. One approach to attaining the productivity increase is to hold the line on costs while increasing output. How much additional output is needed to reach your new productivity rate of 2.3? This can be calculated by the following steps:

(a) $\dfrac{\text{Total units}}{\$24,000} \;=\; 2.3$

(b) Total units $=$ 2.3 × $24,000

(c) Total units $=$ 55,200

Since you are presently producing 48,000 units, you would have to produce 7,200 additional units without increasing costs to attain the 15 percent productivity increase.

EXAMPLE B: DECREASING INPUT. Another approach is to maintain present output while reducing costs. How much do you need to reduce costs to attain the 15 percent increase? This can be calculated by the following steps:

(a) $\dfrac{48,000 \text{ units}}{\text{Costs}} \;=\; 2.3$

(b) Costs $=$ 48,000/2.3

(c) Costs $=$ 20,870

Thus, if you can produce the 48,000 units at a cost of $20,870, this would provide the 15 percent productivity ratio improvement. You would have to maintain your production of 48,000 units while reducing costs by $3,130 (or $24,000 − $20,870).

EXAMPLE C: INCREASING OUTPUT AND DECREASING INPUT. Suppose that you feel fairly locked into your costs but could reduce them by $1,000. How much will you then have to increase output to achieve the 15 percent productivity increase?

$$(a) \quad \frac{\text{Total units}}{\$24,000 - \$1,000} = 2.3$$

$$(b) \quad \frac{\text{Total units}}{\$23,000} = 2.3$$

$$(c) \quad \text{Total units} = 2.3 \times \$23,000$$

$$(d) \quad \text{Total units} = 52,900$$

Thus, reducing costs by $1,000 and increasing output by 4,900 units (52,900 − 48,000) would also provide the 15 percent productivity increase.

Why Productivity Is Important

Productivity is important for several reasons. From an individual company's standpoint, increased productivity translates into lower prices, larger market share, and greater profits. The firm's stronger financial position puts it in better shape to invest in research and development, to utilize newer advanced technology, to pay better wages and benefits, to have better working conditions, and so on.

Assume that a company's workers produce an average of 100 kudgits each per hour. Each worker's pay and benefits amount to $10 per hour. This means that the labor cost of each kudgit is $10/100, or $0.10 per kudgit.

Now suppose that the company discovers an improved work method that enables each worker to produce 20 additional kudgits per hour. Note what this productivity increase does to average labor costs. It reduces them to $10/120 or $0.0833 per kudgit. Since labor costs typically account for 30 to 60 percent of a company's expenses, increasing the efficiency of labor is very important to a company's success.

On a larger scale, productivity is very important to our nation. In the international market, companies from the United States compete with firms from other nations. Increased productivity in the United States keeps prices down, reduces inflation, and increases our standard of living. Productivity is thus very important to the economic growth and health of the United States.

The official productivity measure of the United States is based on labor output and input per hour. This is the productivity that is announced each month by the government and discussed in the media. Basically, it is the ratio of the total output of the nation's goods and services to the total hours of labor that went into producing those goods and services.

Declining Rate of American Productivity

The productivity of American workers is higher than that of any other country's workers, despite what you may have heard. However, as shown in Figure 16–1, productivity in some industries has actually declined in recent years. What has happened in machine tools is especially discouraging because they are so important to other production.

Although the productivity of Japanese workers is much touted, actually the Japanese worker produces only about two-thirds of the output of the American worker. Canadian workers rank next to American workers, as they produce about 95 percent of American workers' output.

What troubles many people, though, is that we have been losing our edge

FIGURE 16–1 GROWTH IN OUTPUT PER EMPLOYEE HOUR IN SELECTED
INDUSTRIES FOR A FIVE-YEAR PERIOD

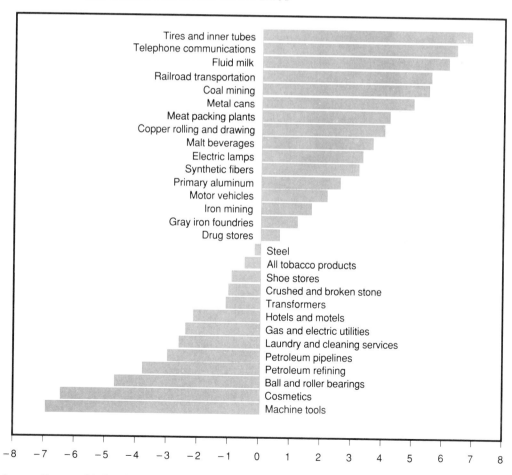

Source: Bureau of Labor Statistics.

in productivity. For example, Figure 16–2 shows that in recent years a number of countries have been closing in on the United States in productivity. Now you have an idea why we hear so much about the productivity of the Japanese — their productivity gains have been much sharper than those made by the United States. European countries also have been closing in on that record.

FIGURE 16–2   PRODUCTIVITY INCREASE OF UNITED STATES LAGS BEHIND OTHER COUNTRIES

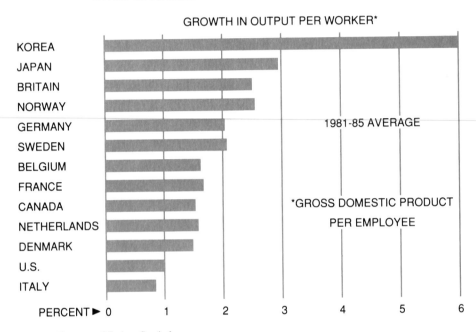

Source: Bureau of Labor Statistics.

Who Is to Blame for the Declining Rate of American Productivity?

The reason for the declining rate of productivity in the United States is difficult to pinpoint. A number of possible causes are associated with management, government, individual workers, and unions.

Who do you think is chiefly to blame for the declining rate of productivity in the United States? Management? Government? Workers? Unions?

MANAGEMENT. Some experts place much of the blame for the decline in American productivity on poor management. They say that modern managers have lost their aggressiveness and are not the risk takers they once were. Updated, state-of-the-art equipment is a major productivity factor for a business, and management has in numerous cases been unwilling to invest funds in such equipment or in the research and development needed to invent more efficient equipment. The steel industry in this country is a good example of an industry whose top management has been unwilling to spend the dollars necessary to keep up with the more modern plants, equipment, and processes of other countries such as Japan and West Germany. As a result, our steel industry is not as cost-effective as that of other countries and has lost its once dominant position in world markets.

GOVERNMENT. Others blame the federal and state governments. They say our productivity decline began—and has continued— because of the many rules and regulations that businesses have had to comply with. They argue that the huge amounts of spending on items such as safety and health, environmental control (pollution equipment, for example), and increased MPG for American-made cars have diverted expenditures that normally would have gone into more efficient labor-saving technology, equipment, and plants. Moreover, many new positions, such as EEO specialists, record keepers, and clerks, which were created to meet government requirements, do not directly contribute to output.

INDIVIDUAL WORKERS. Others say that the characteristics and attitudes of workers at all levels and of all types have changed in the United States. They point out that workers have lost the work ethic leading to "a fair day's work for a fair day's pay." This tendency is reflected by the poor quality of work performed, high absenteeism rates, and low-level commitment to their jobs. Moreover, the average age of individual workers in today's work force is younger than that in the past years. This lack of experience results in lower efficiency and productivity.

UNIONS. Perhaps you, as well as many others, blame unions as the primary culprit for our productivity decline. We read and hear about many cases in which unions resist improved technology and new work methods, protect jobs that are considered nonproductive, and generally resist labor-saving techniques and efficiencies. Few experts, however, place primary blame on unions for productivity decline. If anything, unions have been losing rather than gaining influence in recent years. For example, many industries with little, if any, union strength—such as agriculture, wholesale trade, or retail trade—have also suffered productivity declines similar to those of the more traditionally unionized industries. While shouldering some of the blame, unions certainly don't seem to be the major problem.

So then, who's to blame? In all probability, each of these factors has played a part in our productivity decline.

The Supervisor's Role in Improving Productivity

Regardless of who is to blame, supervisory management has a large role to play in improving productivity. But how do you do it? Suppose that your department has 20 employees who produced a total of 10,000 units last year. Under your plant manager's new mandate, you must increase production to 11,500 units. How will you go about this? You could do some of the things shown in Figure 16–3, many of which have already been discussed elsewhere in this text.

FIGURE 16–3 IMPROVING EMPLOYEE PRODUCTIVITY

- Train employees. Can their abilities be upgraded?
- Clearly communicate the need for high standards so that workers understand what is expected of them.
- Use motivation techniques to inspire workers to increase output. Pride, ego, and security are several important motivators available.
- Eliminate idleness, extended breaks, and early quitting time.
- Build in quality the first time work is done. Lost productivity results when items are scrapped or need to be reworked to salvage them.
- Work on improving attendance and turnover in your work group.
- Reduce accidents. Accidents normally require lost-work time due to investigations, meetings, and reports—even if the employee does not suffer a lost-work-time injury.
- Seek to improve production measures. Will process or work-flow improvements help? Try to get your employees to contribute ideas.
- Try to eliminate or reduce equipment or machinery breakdowns. Preventive maintenance is important here.
- Exercise good control techniques. Follow up performance and take corrective action promptly.

The Supervisor's Role in Cost Control

As we pointed out earlier, the productivity of a department is based on its total outputs and total inputs. Since costs represent major inputs, this explains why upper management is so often cost-conscious. Supervisors direct the operating work of an organization; thus, they occupy a key position in controlling a firm's cost in labor hours and efficiency, maintenance of machinery and equipment, supplies, energy, and other matters.

Budgets are one example of aids that help supervisors to control costs (see Table 16–2). Different budgets are normally prepared for sales, production, scrap, equipment, grievances, lost-work-time accidents, and the like. Moreover, they may be set for different time periods such as a week, a month, a quarter, or a year. Since a budget reflects expected performance, it becomes a basis for evaluating a department's performance.

TABLE 16–2   PERFORMANCE REPORT

Name of department	Fabrication	Performance period	November 198–
Budgeted output	15,700 lbs.	Budgeted scrap	152 lbs.
Actual output	15,227 lbs.	Actual scrap	120 lbs.
Variance	− 473 lbs.		+ 32 lbs.

Item	($) Actual	($) Budgeted	($) Variance
Direct labor	$32,000	$32,000	$ 0
Overtime	1,500	1,000	− 500
Supplies	500	385	− 115
Maintenance & repairs	4,250	3,000	− 1,250
Utilities	1,300	1,200	− 100
Scrapped material	1,200	1,520	+ 320
Total	$40,750	$39,105	− $1,645

Assume that you are supervisor of the fabrication department in Table 16–2. If you were really trying to "tighten up" costs, which activities in your department would you focus on? Why?

Note that, in Table 16–2, the supervisor's department has performed well in some "cost" areas and not so well in others. Output is off by 473 pounds, overtime is 50 percent higher than budgeted, and maintenance and repairs are also over budget. On the plus side, the department has been efficient in using raw materials.

Budgets are not set in stone but must take into account unusual occurrences that affect performance. An investigation of the unfavorable variances in Table 16–2 may reveal that the supervisor or the workers could have done little to avoid them. For example, perhaps a crucial piece of equipment had faulty parts, causing the high repair costs; or perhaps the high overtime resulted from an unexpected weekend job thrust upon the supervisor with little notice. A budget does, however, serve as an important supervisory tool to signal areas that may need attention.

A most important recent development has proved especially helpful to supervisors in achieving effective cost control. This development is the use of management information systems (MIS). It is now possible for supervisors in some circumstances to have available up-to-the-minute cost data on payroll, raw materials, utilities, and other costs as nearby as a computer monitor or printer. MIS will be discussed in detail in Chapter 17.

Three Recent Productivity Improvement Methods

Despite our lagging productivity growth, three productivity improvement measures have recently come into use in manufacturing firms. These improvements, which have been due to advances in computer and machinery technology, are (1) robotics, (2) computer-assisted design (CAD), and (3) computer-assisted manufacturing (CAM).

ROBOTICS. A **robot** is a machine, controlled by a computer, that can be programmed to perform a number of repetitive manipulations of tools or materials. The best-publicized use of robots has been in the automotive industry, where robots perform welding, painting, and other operations. Estimates are that by 1990 industries will employ almost 100,000 robots. Today, it's estimated that robots—often called "iron-collar workers"—operate for around $5.00 an hour, which is considerably less than the $15 to $20 (including benefits) paid to many employees.[1]

In addition to the $15 hourly payroll cost savings of robots, can you think of any other advantages they offer over human employees? Disadvantages?

COMPUTER-ASSISTED DESIGN. **Computer-assisted design (CAD)** refers to computerized systems that enable designers to utilize computer screens in designing three-dimensional parts and systems. In some systems, for instance, designers use a special electronic pen to sketch directly on a computer screen. Here modifications can be readily made after subjecting the design to various tests. When the optimum design is obtained, it can then be converted to a physical model or prototype. CAD technology thus enables greater design flexibility and speedier, less costly design decisions.

COMPUTER-ASSISTED MANUFACTURING. In **computer-assisted manufacturing (CAM)**, special computers assist automated machines or equipment in performing the necessary processes or sequences of actions for production. CAM can be reprogrammed to enable machinery to easily produce different specifications on a product or part. Whereas proper planning and coordination would normally take hours, CAM equipment can be programmed to make proper adjustments within seconds. CAM is especially useful when small orders of customized products must be made. Once the computer is programmed, the electronic signals control the machine processor, resulting in the correct sequence of steps to properly complete the task.

ACHIEVING AND CONTROLLING QUALITY

Recently "quality" has become a major focus of organizations throughout the United States. There are a number of reasons for this increased quality-consciousness, some of which are the following:

1. Attention has been drawn to the enormous cost associated with poor quality. Some estimates are that American manufacturers spend two cents of every sales dollar just to rework poor-quality parts. This figure doesn't even include the costs of items that have to be scrapped as unusable (see Figure 16–4).
2. The high quality of many foreign products (such as high-quality Japanese automobiles and electronic devices) has cut greatly into the market share of United States firms.
3. Groups such as the Consumer Product Safety Commission and other organized consumers have been formed to "police" quality with their great power through public opinion, boycotts, adverse publicity, and legal action.

FIGURE 16–4

Quality Assurance and Quality Control

Sometimes the terms *quality assurance* and *quality control* are used interchangeably. However, they are not the same thing. **Quality assurance** is the entire system of policies, procedures, and guidelines that an organization institutes so as to attain and maintain quality. It involves such factors as product design, employee training, purchase of materials, maintenance of equipment, and employee attitudes toward quality. For example, policies to be used in making the product standards for purchases of raw material are a part of quality assurance, as are policies that encourage the supervisor to use quality circles.

Quality control, on the other hand, consists of the measurements that are designed to see if the desired quality is being met. When a supervisor inspects a worker's progress or products made, quality control is being exercised. Typically, quality control uncovers problems *after* they have occurred.

Quality—A Concern of All Organizations

We frequently think of "quality" as something that is of concern only to manufacturers of products such as autos, appliances, or electronic devices. This is not the case. As shown in Figure 16–5, evidences of poor quality exist in all kinds of organizations such as department stores, hospitals, and hair salons. Moreover, all departments of an organization, such as purchasing, maintenance, or accounting, should be concerned about quality.

FIGURE 16–5   EXAMPLES OF POOR QUALITY SERVICE

- Telephone installer incorrectly installs telephone in your house.
- Accounts receivable clerk cannot locate a customer's account. Customer is calling long distance to clarify item on a bill.
- Hospital patient receives medication 20 minutes late, delaying scheduled surgery.
- Hair salon runs 30 to 45 minutes late for each appointment.
- Purchasing agent orders wrong piece of equipment or is lax at processing and/or following up on orders.
- Restaurant server is slow, unfriendly, and unfamiliar with items on menu.
- Salesperson does not have authority to take a personal check for payment and cannot find anyone to approve it.
- Hotel room is smelly, a light bulb is burnt out, and the television set doesn't work.
- Cost accounting department's data are too old, don't include relevant information, and are impossible to interpret.

The Supervisor's Role in Achieving Quality

Motivating workers to perform high-quality work consistently is one of the most difficult jobs a supervisor faces. Two ways to do this are to (1) let employees know you expect quality performance and (2) involve workers in achieving quality.

LET EMPLOYEES KNOW YOU EXPECT QUALITY PERFORMANCE. Many firms, to use an expression, try to *inspect* quality into their products or services rather than "make it right" the first time. Fortunately, some companies and supervisors emphasize the right way from the start by stating their high-quality expectations of a job and beginning with the training of new personnel.

A large bank trains its new tellers not only in the technical aspects of the job, but also on how to interact with customers. In a number of trial runs, a customer walks up to the teller to complete a hypothetical transaction. The teller's actions are observed by a number of trainees and the trainer, and a critique is given of the way the customer was handled. Frequently an experienced teller will demonstrate how the situation should have been handled. Included are such actions as smiling, looking directly at the customer, calling the customer by name, and efficiently handling the transaction. As a result, the bank's quality expectations are instilled in new tellers.

The best place to make an impact regarding your "quality" expectations is with the new employee. Yet many current employees may have spotty quality records. What can you do about this? We can surely tell you one thing *not* to do! To ignore poor-quality performance results in the following:

1. The employee concerned gets the message that you don't expect any better or that mediocre quality is acceptable to you.
2. Other employees will also assume that mediocre performance is acceptable.

Assuming that workers know what the quality standards are, you *must* exercise supervisory control over quality (see Figure 16–6). Sometimes a quality control specialist will help a line supervisor determine the quality of workers' perfomance. However, in many departments, the supervisor must play the key role.

FIGURE 16–6

INVOLVE WORKERS IN ACHIEVING QUALITY. Today, Japan's products set exceptionally high standards of quality. And, as indicated in Figure 16–2 on page 400, Japan's productivity rate has more than doubled that of the United States in recent years. A major factor has been Japan's ability to harness the creative potential of its employees through employee involvement.

One of the important tools in the Japanese management system has been the quality circle, or QC, concept, which has gained favor in the United States since it was introduced by Honeywell, Inc., and Lockheed in 1974. Today well over 1,000 companies in the United States have adopted the QC concept as a means of addressing problems related to the quality of products or services, productivity, costs, and quality of work life. **Quality circles** are small organized work groups meeting periodically to improve organizational productivity and effectiveness.

HOW QCs OPERATE. A group of four to ten volunteers meets (usually once a week) to find ways to improve some aspect of the organization's performance. As shown in Figure 16–7, quality circles follow these steps:

1. The first thing they do is identify problem areas.
2. They select the problem that is to be solved first.
3. They individually and collectively gather as much information as they can about the problem and study how it can be used to solve the problem.
4. They plan how to solve the problem.
5. They present their proposed plan to the responsible manager(s).
6. The plan is implemented.
7. The results of the improvement are studied.
8. They determine whether the results are successful.
9. If they are successful, the changes are made a permanent part of the operating procedure.

> *Ford Motor Company and the UAW have set up over 1,000 Employee Involvement Groups (EIGs) in 68 plants across the country to carry out the theme "Quality is Job 1." The members of one group at the Kansas City, Missouri, assembly plant, for example, used their skills to refine the fit-and-finish procedure needed to build the new Ford Tempo.*

CHARACTERISTICS OF EFFECTIVE QCs. Figure 16–8 presents the overall characteristics of effective quality circles. For best results, membership in a QC should be voluntary. Problems and opportunities can be brought up by QC members, higher management, or staff personnel. QC sessions are neither gripe nor bull sessions, and the groups receive training in decision-making techniques. Among these techniques are:

1. Cause-and-effect diagrams for helping to break apart a problem systematically.
2. Pareto diagrams, which are vertical bar graphs that visually pinpoint major problems.

FIGURE 16–7   HOW QUALITY CIRCLES OPERATE

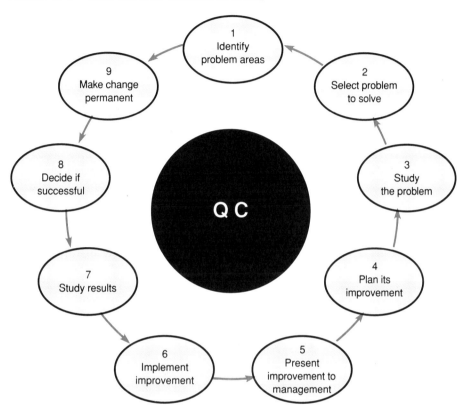

Source: Leon C. Megginson, *Personnel Management: A Human Resources Approach,* 5th ed. (Homewood, IL: Richard D. Irwin, 1985), 318.

FIGURE 16–8   CHARACTERISTICS OF EFFECTIVE QUALITY CIRCLES

- Managers at *all* levels, especially at the top, should be committed to the concept and give it their unqualified support.
- Only volunteers should be allowed to participate in the program.
- Projects undertaken should relate directly—or at least indirectly—to participants' work.
- Project should be team efforts, not individual activities.
- Participants should be trained in quality-control and problem-solving techniques.
- Circle leaders should be also trained in group dynamics and leadership work as a group.
- QC groups should be given feedback—in the form of results—regarding their recommendations and solutions.

3. Statistical quality control techniques.
4. Checksheets for researching problems in an orderly manner.

Many companies provide these circles with the right to call in staff experts for information or expertise as needed.

The kinds of QCs we have been discussing are those that are implemented formally and require top management's approval and commitment. Individual supervisors may, however, capture the spirit of a QC on their own. As one manager of a hotel convention center commented:

The best quality ideas come from the people who are directly involved in the work. Frequently, poor quality is not caused by something they directly control. We noted that many clients would come in for a meeting and change the room arrangement at the last minute. The clients would get flustered, as did our people.

The problem was that our meeting coordinator would talk with the client, usually by phone, and take instructions as to how the meeting room needed to be set up. There was much room for interpretation as to just what the client wanted, and these last-minute changes would drive everyone nuts. It was one of our workers who suggested that we come up with a form showing the basic ways to arrange a meeting room. Now the client indicates a preferred arrangement and returns it, signed, to our coordinator. We now have something definite to go by and have had only one or two cases all year where we've had these last-minute changes.

The lesson here is to seek out workers' advice on how to improve the quality of their work. Since they are so directly involved in the work, they frequently have excellent suggestions.

Today we are seeing a tremendous emphasis being placed on quality. Management is beginning to find that the Japanese system of *building* quality into products through employee involvement is far better than inspecting quality into products.

We have seen cases where the Japanese can buy an American plant and immediately turn around poor quality performance. Sanyo recently took over a Warwick color television plant in Arkansas and cut its product defect rate from 30 percent to 2 percent in about two months. Was this done with substantial changes in the plant's process or equipment? Major changes in personnel? The answer is no. Management turned it around by generating enthusiasm for quality and actively involving operating employees in the quality process.[2]

PROMOTING EMPLOYEE SAFETY

The final aspect of supervisory control that we will discuss in this chapter is employee safety. This is a subject that has been in the business limelight in recent years, primarily as a result of the government's passage of the Occupational Safety and Health Act (OSHA) in 1970. But management has had an interest in employee safety for over a century since safety, efficiency, and productivity are closely related.

Should the following kinds of organizations really be concerned about occupational safety and health: (a) banks, (b) supermarkets, and (c) department stores?

What OSHA Does

OSHA stands for the Occupational Safety and Health Administration. This federal body was created by passage of the Occupational Safety and Health Act and went into effect in April 1971. In the past, different states had different emphases on occupational health and safety. So the federal government stepped into the picture to provide uniformity and to ensure enforcement. Basically, OSHA ensures that state governments, labor, and management provide consistently safer and healthier working conditions for employees.

OSHA requires organizations to keep safety logs and records of illnesses and injuries incurred on the job (see Figure 16–9). OSHA also has the right to develop standards, to conduct inspections to see that standards are met, and to enforce compliance by issuing citations and penalties against organizations that fail to comply. OSHA also provides help by performing pre-investigations upon invitation from the organization.

Factors Influencing Safety

Several factors affect job safety. Among these are (1) organization size, (2) type of industry, and (3) people.

ORGANIZATION SIZE. The safest places to work are the smallest and largest organizations. Companies with under 20 employees or over 1,000 employees have had better safety statistics than medium-sized organizations.

What do you think accounts for the better safety performance in large companies of, say, 10,000 employees as contrasted to those with 100 employees?

FIGURE 16–9 RECORD KEEPING REQUIRED BY OSHA

OSHA No. 101
Case or File No. ----------

Form approved
OMB No. 44R 1453

Supplementary Record of Occupational Injuries and Illnesses

EMPLOYER

1. Name _____Bradley Pulp & Paper Company_____
2. Mail address _____P.O. Box 1420_____Sherman_____Texas 75090____
   (No. and street)   (City or town)   (State)
3. Location, if different from mail address _____

INJURED OR ILL EMPLOYEE

4. Name __Herman_____L._____Jackson___ Social Security No. _414-26-1000____
   (First name)   (Middle name)   (Last name) Sherman   Texas 75090
5. Home address __707 Eighth Street_____
   (No. and street)   (City or town)   (State)
6. Age ____38_____ 7. Sex: Male__✓_____ Female_____ (Check one)
8. Occupation ___Painter_____
   (Enter regular job title, *not* the specific activity he was performing at time of injury.)
9. Department ____Bleach Plant_____
   (Enter name of department or division in which the injured person is regularly employed, even though he may have been temporarily working in another department at the time of injury.)

THE ACCIDENT OR EXPOSURE TO OCCUPATIONAL ILLNESS

10. Place of accident or exposure _____Sherman_____Texas_____
    (No. and street)   (City or town)   (State)
    If accident or exposure occurred on employer's premises, give address of plant or establishment in which it occurred. Do not indicate department or division within the plant or establishment. If accident occurred outside employer's premises at an identifiable address, give that address. If it occurred on a public highway or at any other place which cannot be identified by number and street, please provide place references locating the place of injury as accurately as possible.
11. Was place of accident or exposure on employer's premises? ____Yes_____ (Yes or No)
12. What was the employee doing when injured? ___Employee had been cleaning pipes in preparation for___
    (Be specific. If he was using tools or equipment or handling material,
    painting. As he put his stepladder down, sodium hypochlorate dripped inside his face shield and went into his
    name them and tell what he was doing with them.)
    right eye.
13. How did the accident occur? ___above_____
    (Describe fully the events which resulted in the injury or occupational illness. Tell what
    happened and how it happened. Name any objects or substances involved and tell how they were involved. Give
    full details on all factors which led or contributed to the accident. Use separate sheet for additional space.)

OCCUPATIONAL INJURY OR OCCUPATIONAL ILLNESS

14. Describe the injury or illness in detail and indicate the part of body affected. _____
    (e.g.: amputation of right index finger
    chemical burn in right eye
    at second joint; fracture of ribs; lead poisoning; dermatitis of left hand, etc.)
15. Name the object or substance which directly injured the employee. (For example, the machine or thing he struck against or which struck him; the vapor or poison he inhaled or swallowed; the chemical or radiation which irritated his skin; or in cases of strains, hernias, etc., the thing he was lifting, pulling, etc.)
    sodium hypochlorate
16. Date of injury or initial diagnosis of occupational illness _____July 16, 1980_____.
    (Date)
17. Did employee die? _____No_____ (Yes or No)

OTHER

18. Name and address of physician ___Dr. Harry W. Myers_____Sherman, Texas 75090____
19. If hospitalized, name and address of hospital _____

Date of report ____July 16, 1980___ Prepared by ___Joseph Dixon_____
Official position ____Supervisor_____

Source: U.S. Department of Labor.

In a small firm the owner or manager is more personally involved with employees and tends to take on the role of safety officer. Very large firms have strong resources available, such as safety departments, whose sole mission is employee safety. Medium-sized firms have neither the direct personal involvement of the top manager nor the resources available to create full-fledged safety departments. The person assigned to oversee the safety function more than likely has additional job responsibilities. Thus, the safety focus may be diluted by other important assignments.

TYPE OF INDUSTRY. The type of industry in which you work also has a large influence on safety. Table 16–3 shows some difference in rates of occupational injury and illness among various industries. Note the high rates for lumber and wood products, metal fabricating, and general building contractors. However, the more serious cases involving numerous lost workdays occurred in the water transportation and anthracite mining industries.

TABLE 16–3   OCCUPATIONAL INJURY AND ILLNESS RATES:
SELECTED INDUSTRIES, 1983

Industry	Total Cases[*]	Lost Workdays[*]
Anthracite mining	6.7	470.4
General building contractors	14.8	118.2
Lumber and wood products	18.3	163.5
Chemicals and related products	5.5	42.3
Printing and publishing	6.6	44.6
Railroad transportation	8.2	76.9
Water transportation	10.8	229.9
Communications	2.9	27.1
Retail trade	7.3	46.7
Banking	1.6	8.2
Auto repair, services, garage	7.1	52.3
Textile mill products	7.4	51.4
Fabricated metal products	15.1	96.5

*Per 100 full-time workers.
Source: Bureau of the Census, *Statistical Abstract of the United States* (Washington, D.C.: U.S. Government Printing Office, 1986), 426.

PEOPLE. The attitudes of managers and supervisors strongly influence safe work performance. Moreover, employees themselves are important factors, as certain types tend to have more accidents. Studies of accident-prone employees show that:

1. They are relatively young (age 20 to 24).
2. They are more likely to be single.
3. They are emotionally insecure.
4. Their motivation is low.
5. They have aggressive egos.
6. They tend to show hostility toward themselves.

Causes of Accidents

What causes on-the-job accidents? Basically job-related accidents are caused by three types of factors: human, technical, and environmental. *Human factors* include such things as horseplay, fighting, carelessness, use of drugs, poor understanding of equipment or processes, the thrill of taking risks, poor attitudes, and fatigue. *Technical factors* include unsafe mechanical, chemical, or physical conditions such as defective tools and equipment, poor mechanical construction or design, or improper personal protective equipment (safety shoes, glasses, or mechanical guards or shields). *Environmental factors* are those that surround the job such as poor housekeeping, inadequate lighting and ventilation, or management pressure and stress to increase output.

The Supervisor's Role in Promoting Safety

Good safety practices among employees help the supervisor in many ways. For one thing, on-the-job injuries can take up much of a supervisor's time. There are accident reports to fill out, meetings to investigate the injury, and recommendations to be made (see Figure 16–10). Furthermore, the work group's productiv-

FIGURE 16–10 PERSONAL INJURY INVESTIGATION

Injured:	Fred Hanna
Position:	Lab Assistant
Presiding:	L.C. Smithson, Technical Supt.
Date of meeting:	4/15/8–
Time of meeting:	2:34 p.m.
Place of meeting:	Plant Conference Room
Present:	L.C. Smithson (Technical Supt.), Fred Hanna (injured), Jim Berry (Housekeeping), Tom Ahens (Safety Director), Kim Jernigan (Supervisor)
Nature of injury:	Fractured distal end of radius, right arm
Lost time:	42 days (estimated)
Accident time and date:	4/13/8– at 7:15 a.m.
Cause of injury:	Floor was wet—appeared to be water. Investigation revealed that bags of Seperan (a synthetic polymer) had been rearranged during the 7:00 p.m.–11:00 p.m. shift. One bag was torn, and its contents had trickled onto the floor causing it to be exceptionally slippery when washed at end of shift. Janitor noticed but did not flag it or attempt to remove hazard as he noted at end of his shift.

Corrective steps/recommendations:
1. Apply grit to slippery areas; mark with appropriate warning signs.
2. Remind incoming shift personnel of hazardous conditions.
3. Communicate to incoming shift personnel any job priorities.
4. Store Seperan in a more remote area of the plant.

ity suffers when an injured employee is being treated or is recovering from an accident. Temporary or full-time replacements must be recruited, selected, and trained. Even then, an inexperienced worker is unlikely to be as productive as the more experienced employee being replaced. Thus, safety is definitely linked to productivity.

The supervisor, as top management's link with operating employees, plays a crucial role in employee safety. He or she is accountable for safety, just as for output or quality. Good safety control by the supervisor begins with a positive attitude, as shown in the following example:

"Safety is very important around here and especially in my work unit," said Vera Edwards, a machine tender for Supreme Manufacturing. "When you drive into the parking lot, a large sign shows our company's safety record for the week and the year. Our supervisor is always talking safety, we have safety meetings monthly, and there are posters and signs throughout the work area. Our supervisor also makes us toe the line in following safety rules. He can really be tough on you when he catches you bending a rule such as not using your goggles or failing to put on your machine guard."

Figure 16–11 shows a number of steps that supervisors can take to improve safety performance in their departments. Even though supervisors play a critical role in controlling safety, they cannot do it alone. Top management must be

FIGURE 16–11   WHAT SUPERVISORS CAN DO TO INCREASE SAFETY PERFORMANCE

- Recognize the need for safer equipment and work methods.
- Establish and communicate safety goals for the department.
- Clearly communicate safety requirements to all employees.
- Make sure new employees thoroughly understand equipment and safety rules.
- Prohibit use of unsafe or damaged equipment.
- Encourage safety suggestions from your workers.
- Post safety bulletins, slogans, and posters to reinforce need for safety.
- Refuse to let rush jobs cause relaxed safety standards.
- Set proper example. Don't bend safety rules yourself.
- Conduct periodic safety meetings, with demonstrations by employee safety specialists or insurance representatives.
- Refuse to tolerate horseplay.
- Compete with other departments in safety contests.
- Report to employees accidents that occur elsewhere in the company.
- Encourage reporting of unsafe conditions.
- Make regular safety inspections of all major equipment.
- Enforce the rules when they are broken—take appropriate disciplinary action to demonstrate your safety commitment.
- Thoroughly investigate all accidents and attempt to remedy the causes.
- Develop a system for rewarding or acknowledging excellent safety conduct.

committed to factors such as proper plant layout and design, safe machinery and equipment, and good physical working conditions.

CHAPTER REVIEW

Controlling productivity, quality, and safety are key parts of a supervisor's job. The extent to which the supervisor accomplishes these tasks will strongly influence his or her overall effectiveness.

Productivity is a measure of outputs over inputs. When it is used in a companywide sense, it refers to the value of a company's total units or services produced as compared to its total costs of producing them. Productivity as measured by the federal government is based on the average labor hour output among the nation's industrial and business firms.

The United States has the highest productivity per labor hour in the world. However, the rate of our yearly productivity increases has been declining. Among the causes of this decline in the United States are the unwillingness of industry to invest in upgraded equipment; federal and state government rules and regulations requiring much capital spending by industry on nonproductivity-improving technology such as environmental control and health and safety; and work-force characteristics such as changed work-ethic values. A number of productivity-improving actions that supervisors can take include upgrading workers' skills through training, improved worker motivation, better use of machinery and equipment, improved quality, and the prevention of accidents.

Cost control is also an important measure of a supervisor's productivity. One helpful device is a budget, which shows expected outcome for a given period and is expressed in numbers. Cost reduction can be attained by combining certain jobs, reducing scrap, achieving better quality production, and focusing upon large-cost items rather than numerous smaller ones. Robotics, computer-assisted design, and computer-assisted manufacturing are three recent productivity enhancement measures that have been used in manufacturing firms.

A second major area discussed in the chapter was quality. *Quality assurance* is the entire system of policies, procedures, and guidelines an organization institutes so as to attain and maintain quality. On the other hand, *quality control* consists of after-the-fact measurements to see if quality standards are actually being met. Good quality is important not only in manufacturing, but also in service organizations. Many firms try to inspect quality into their activities rather than emphasize the importance of performing the job properly the first time. The supervisor must communicate the high quality expectations and standards. Frequently workers themselves have excellent insight into how quality can be improved; therefore, supervisors should tap this expertise.

Quality circles are groups of 5 to 12 employees and a supervisor who meet to address and resolve work-related problems. Originated in Japan, they have become increasingly popular in the United States in dealing with problems related to product and service quality, cost effectiveness, and quality of work life.

Employee safety has become especially important to organizations in recent years, especially since the passage of the Occupational Safety and Health Act in 1970. The Occupational Safety and Health Administration, charged with enforcing compliance with the law, sets standards and regulations, requires organizations to maintain safety logs and records, conducts inspections, and has the authority to issue citations and penalties for violations found. Generally, the smallest and the largest organizations are the safest in which to work, and the nature of some industries makes them much more likely to have higher injury-incidence rates than others. Statistics show that accident-prone employees are single, young, and not highly motivated; are emotionally insecure; have aggressive egos; and tend to show hostility toward themselves.

Accidents on the job can be caused by human factors such as carelessness or fatigue; by technical factors such as defective tools or equipment; and by environmental factors such as poor housekeeping or lighting. Good safety performance is essential to increase productivity for several reasons. First, accidents require the supervisor to spend much time filling out reports, attending meetings, and attempting to eliminate or control causes. Second, injured employees are nonproductive while being treated or recovering from lost-work time. Replacement workers, when hired, are not likely to be as efficient as the more senior, experienced employees being replaced.

The supervisor can be active in controlling safety in a number of ways. Among these are clearly communicating safety standards, emphasizing the importance of safety through meetings, being alert to identifying and remedying equipment or conditions, and taking corrective action when safety rules are violated.

QUESTIONS FOR REVIEW AND DISCUSSION

1. What is meant by productivity?
2. Name three causes of the recent declining rate of productivity in the United States.
3. Recently there have been strong productivity gains among white-collar workers in clerical jobs. What developments do you think have caused these jobs to become more productive?
4. Are "quality assurance" and "quality control" the same thing?
5. Paul Juran, one of the leading "gurus" of quality in the United States, says that the typical company spends 10 to 15 percent of its total sales volume on poor quality. Assuming this is true, why haven't companies done anything about it?
6. What does OSHA do?
7. Name four characteristics of effective quality circles.
8. A supervisor made this comment: "My people know the safety rules, and they're supposed to be mature adults who can take care of themselves. I don't have the time to go out and give pep talks about safety. If they violate the rules, they're the ones who suffer, not me. I spend my energy on more important things, like seeing to it that quality is met, meeting our production goals, and training new operators." Evaluate this supervisor's viewpoint.

LEARNING EXERCISE 16–1
THE CASE OF BILL WESLEY

The operations in a manufacturing plant involved a five-stage batch process of material that contained a high percentage of caustic soda. One duty of the operators was to move this material in open buggies to the proper chute located in the floor. Then the material was dumped through the chute to equipment on the floor below, where the next stage of the process took place. At two stages in this process, the material was light and fluffy, and there were occasional backdrafts through the chutes, causing it to fly.

Up until a year ago, the safety rules only required that goggles be worn when unloading the material, since it was during this stage that the greatest possibility of eye injury existed. The wearing of goggles at other times was up to the operator's discretion. However, there had been three cases of minor eye irritations among the workers. Consequently, a new safety rule was established a year ago. It required the operators to wear goggles whenever they were near exposed material.

Katherine Michaels, who had been supervisor for the past two years, was bothered because everyone went along with the new safety rule except Bill Wesley, the most senior operator at the plant. Wesley was an outstanding operator and had had only one minor injury in his 20 years of service. Because of his experience and performance, Wesley was looked up to by the rest of the workers. His resistance to the new rule caused some difficulty in selling it to the other operators because they respected Wesley's opinions. Wesley's contention was that one need not wear goggles except when unloading the caustic material. However, after much discussion, Wesley agreed to go along with the new rule.

During the past six months, Michaels had seen Wesley on four occasions without his goggles on. On a half-dozen other occasions, Michaels felt that Wesley had put the goggles over his eyes only when Michaels came on the floor. Michaels's doubts were confirmed three days ago when she came upon Wesley unexpectedly and saw him bob his head to shift the goggles from his forehead to his eyes.

Answer the following questions:

1. Why do you think Bill Wesley is violating the new rule?
2. What action would you recommend to Katherine Michaels? Support your reasoning.

LEARNING EXERCISE 16–2
RANKING DEPARTMENTAL GOALS

Visit with one or more supervisors, either individually or as a group, at a plant in your community. Ask the supervisors to rank the following objectives used in supervising their departments in order of priority at this time.

	Rank
Production output	_____
Production quality	_____
Employee safety	_____
Cost reduction (supplies, payroll)	_____

	Rank
Employee relations	_____
Reduction in scrap and waste materials	_____
Good housekeeping	_____
Preventive maintenance of equipment	_____
Other	_____

After completing this project, compare your list with those of other students.

Answer the following questions:

1. What might account for the differences in rankings?
2. Which of the items on the list relate most directly to productivity? Discuss.

LEARNING EXERCISE 16–3
OVER BUDGET

Barbara Bayne had just received a printout of her department's budget and expenditure for the past month. It wasn't good news, as three major items of the budget showed major overages, as shown below:

	Percentages Over Budgeted Amount
Personnel labor costs (overtime)	20
Supplies (paper, tablets, pads)	15
Telephone (long distance)	20

Barbara knew her boss wouldn't be pleased at these results, especially since just last month he had announced to all department heads that they needed to keep an eye on their budgets because the corporate office was really trying to "tighten things up."

It was the first time that such control had been exercised in the three years that Barbara had been department manager; in fact, it was common knowledge that some departments consistently "overspent" by as much as 25 to 30 percent. She pondered her meeting with her boss.

Answer the following questions:

1. Why would management allow departments to consistently overspend and take no corrective action?
2. What might be some explanations for the expenditure overruns in Barbara's department?
3. What does the case tell you about Barbara's control of costs?

ENDNOTES

1. James H. Donnelly, James Gibson, and John Ivancevich, *Fundamentals of Management* (Plano, TX: Business Publications, 1987), 472.
2. Yoshi Tsurumi, "Productivity: The Japanese Approach," *Pacific Basin Quarterly* (Summer 1981): 7.

SUGGESTIONS FOR FURTHER READING

Blake, Robert R., and Jane S. Mouton. *Productivity: The Human Side*. New York: AMACOM, 1981.

Gochenour, D. L., Jr., W. D. Wyant, P. E. Wyant, and B. N. Windor. "Energy Audit Turns up Many Opportunities for Energy Savings in Manufacturing Plant." *Industrial Engineering* 13 (December 1981): 46–52,110 + .

Himes, Gary K. "For Greater Profits, Cut Expenses." *Supervision* 43 (May 1981): 14–17.

LeBoeuf, Michael. *The Productivity Challenge*. New York: McGraw-Hill Book Company, 1982.

Puckett, Allen E. "People Are the Key to Productivity." *Industrial Management* 37 (September-October 1985): 12–15.

Sinha, Madhav, and Walter O. Willborn. *The Management of Quality Assurance*. New York: John Wiley & Sons, 1985.

Stoner, James A., and Charles Wankel. *Management*. Chapter 8, "Operations Management and Productivity." Englewood Cliffs, NJ: Prentice-Hall, 1986.

17
MANAGEMENT INFORMATION SYSTEMS AND THE COMPUTER

OBJECTIVES

After reading and studying the material in this chapter, you should be able to:

- Explain what a management information system is.
- Differentiate between data processing and management information systems.
- Describe how a management information system assists in planning, organizing, and controlling.
- Discuss the impact of the microcomputer on management information systems.

IMPORTANT TERMS

management information systems (MIS)
data processing system
economic order quantity (EOQ)
mainframe computer
minicomputer
microcomputer

hardware
software
computer network
word processing
spreadsheet
database management

CHAPTER OUTLINE
CASE 17-1. OUT OF CONTROL

CASE 17-1
OUT OF CONTROL

Production supervisor Fred Henderson had been with Auto Electronics for some nine years and had always seemed to be on top of his job. Fred's department produced various electrical components such as alternators and starter motors used in the assembly of automobiles. Production runs were typically short, lasting from two to five days. Each production run consisted of a specific type of component, and several thousand were produced in each run. Fred had recently run into a string of problems, including being called to the office of Rob Augustine, manufacturing vice-president, where Fred had been tactfully told to get things "straightened out." This had never happened to him before because Fred had always gotten favorable results, even given the high pressure of daily "fire fighting" that took place on the production floor. It seemed that problems had really gotten out of hand two months earlier when Auto Electronics had expanded its product line, increased its production by about 15 percent, and hired 17 new production operators.

Fred's problems resulted from many things, but the three most pressing problems were these:

1. Production runs had always been scheduled in response to incoming orders. But current inventory counts, given the expanded lines, were so inaccurate that they were seldom checked to determine whether a current order could be filled from present stock.
2. No overall purchasing strategy existed to ensure that appropriate raw materials were on hand. As a result, material shortages frequently arose; unfinished inventory would be piled up around the production area waiting until the material was received to complete the job.
3. As they occurred, production and sales were manually recorded on 3" × 5" index cards. The production people had difficulty knowing exactly how many components to make in a single run; so overproduction was common.

As Fred left Augustine's office, the message to him had been pretty clear: Fred had to "get on top of things" immediately. What was needed, Fred thought, was something he couldn't handle alone. There had to be better coordination among sales, purchasing, production, and inventory control departments. Auto Electronics simply had not kept pace with the times. To be more accurate, information was needed at a faster pace and everyone had to contribute to it and share in it. But everyone seemed so busy that there seemed no time to pause and restructure. Fred thought: "We're trying to run this operation like it was a small shop in someone's garage. Yet we've become a $100 million company that's as sophisticated as a bunch of school kids at a car wash. We have got to find a better way to manage the problem."

Fred's problems are common in modern organizations. Supervisors and managers face increasing pressures to remain efficient and effective when, in fact, the operations they control have become much more complex. And, like Fred, they become so involved in handling the crises of the hour that they seem to have lost the ability to control the overall job. Frequently, immediate access to information from a single integrated source can enable managers to handle with ease increasingly difficult demands.

This chapter presents an overview of management information systems and their impact on management decision making.[1] Special emphasis is placed on the role of such a system as it affects the supervisor's job.

WHAT IS A MANAGEMENT INFORMATION SYSTEM?

A **management information system (MIS)** is an *integrated system*, usually *computer based*, that *provides information* to management to *assist in decision making*. The four important aspects of this definition are discussed below.

MIS Is an Integrated System

When we say that MIS is an integrated system, we mean that, to be effective, it requires input from various units in an organization. You might think of a central library as being the heart of MIS in which various departments, or users, pool their information to be stored in the system. Then, as information is needed by the various departments, they simply call on the information that has been stored in the system.

MIS Is Usually Computer Based

This is the computer age! Pick up almost any newspaper or magazine—*Business Week, Time,* or *People,* for example—and you will find numerous advertisements for various computers. It wasn't until 1946 that the first all-electronic computer was unveiled at the University of Pennsylvania, and only in 1954 did the first mainframe—Univac—become operational in a business organization, General Electric. In fact, the computer information explosion didn't really occur until the 1970s. Does this mean that management information systems didn't exist before? Not at all. Pre-computer MISs were manual systems that relied on typed or handwritten entries. Many personnel were required simply to keep up with and post data. Today, however, the reduced prices of computers (under $5,000) and their increased capabilities have resulted in a MIS explosion which, for

practical purposes, means that most MISs are computer based. We shall examine
the computer's role more deeply later in this chapter.

*To what extent has the "computer information explosion" affected your life?
What would your life be like without the computer in your residence, auto,
school, or elsewhere?*

MIS Provides Information

The heart of MIS is the information it provides, which is intended to facilitate
managerial decision making. Basically, information results from the processing
of raw data that have been placed in some meaningful format (see Figure 17–1).

FIGURE 17–1   FROM DATA TO COMPUTER TO INFORMATION FOR
DECISION MAKING

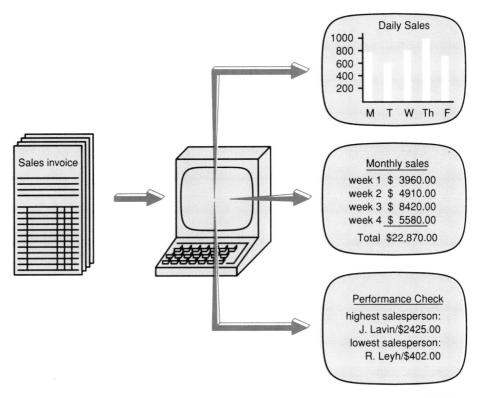

Source: John R. Schermerhorn, Jr., *Management for Productivity*, 2d ed. (New York: John
Wiley & Sons, 1986), 438. Used with permission.

You can get a better idea of the importance of information by noting the important criteria for desirable information listed below and shown in Figure 17–2.

1. *Accessible.* Information should be relatively easy to obtain, without undue effort.
2. *Relevant.* The information should be meaningful and pertinent in and of itself.
3. *Clear.* The information should be in a format easily understood, specific, and unambiguous.
4. *Accurate.* The information should be precise and dependable for accuracy; free from error.
5. *Objective.* The information should be unbiased; free from intended persuasion of other parties.
6. *Timely.* The information should be available when needed and sufficiently current to aid recipients.

FIGURE 17–2 DESIRABLE CHARACTERISTICS OF MANAGEMENT INFORMATION

ACCESSIBLE

RELEVANT

CLEAR

ACCURATE

OBJECTIVE

TIMELY

MANAGEMENT INFORMATION

MIS Aids Decision Making

MIS doesn't simply produce information for its own sake. The nature of a MIS is to help managers make decisions. This should be obvious when you note the six characteristics of "information" discussed above.

For instance, one type of MIS report might list the names of sales representatives, their present sales volume, and an indicator showing the extent to which each rep has reached his or her sales quota for past and current performance periods. A sales supervisor would be able to immediately identify those persons in need of closer follow-up.

Based on what you read in Case 17–1, what are some types of decisions in which a MIS could be of help in assisting Fred Henderson perform his job as supervisor?

Now that we have identified the four important components of a MIS system, let us examine a real-life application of MIS for one firm.

Air Products and Chemicals, Inc., of Allentown, Pennsylvania, has developed a MIS that monitors customers' inventories of liquefied gases. This is done through a telemetry sensor installed in their tanks. When the gas level drops to a predetermined level, a signal is sent to an IBM PC at Air Products' data center. The customer is identified, as is the gas needed. The MIS then springs into action.

1. It receives the data and automatically schedules delivery to the customer.
2. It sends the data to the inventory department, where current inventory is adjusted.
3. It notifies the production department when inventory levels reach points where production must begin.

Bill Seibel, one of Air Products' managers, states that the system allows the company to maintain a continuing relationship with customers, preventing competitors from getting to first base with a customer. Another manager feels that the system reduces distribution costs because deliveries are made only to customers who actually need products. Since the system keeps Air Products' inventories current and correct, customers do not have to worry about late shipments due to inventory shortages.[2]

DISTINCTION BETWEEN MIS AND DATA PROCESSING SYSTEMS

Many people think that any computerized system that processes data is a management information system. This is not true, however. While there is a frequent overlap between MIS and data processing systems, some clear distinctions can be drawn. For example, **data processing systems** typically focus on producing or processing information such as sales orders, inventory reorder reports, and employee time cards. That is the second phase of the basic flow chart of MIS shown in Figure 17–3.

A true MIS goes one step further by converting the data into meaningful "information" in order to facilitate decision making. Note that Air Products' MIS triggered for management the names of customers and quantities needed, automatically adjusted inventories, and scheduled customer deliveries. Or, consider

FIGURE 17–3 MIS FLOWCHART SHOWING RELATIONSHIP BETWEEN DATA PROCESSING AND MIS

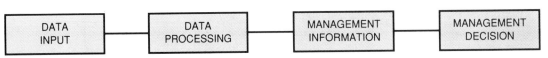

what a MIS can do for a production manager. By properly calling on the MIS, a production manager at any time may be able immediately to see a weekly production schedule for the department, measure progress toward these goals, compare each operator's performance to standards regarding quality, output, and material, and see whether the department's costs conform to a predetermined budget. Thus, while a data processing system is important, it is not the equivalent of a MIS.

WHAT MIS CAN DO FOR MANAGERS AND SUPERVISORS

Managers and supervisors live in fast-paced, action-oriented environments. The core activity they must perform is decision making, and you learned earlier, in Chapter 3, how important "information" is in the decision-making process.

MIS and the Management Functions

MIS assists in decision making by helping managers perform their jobs in a number of ways. We shall examine specifically how MIS assists in performing the planning, organizing, and controlling functions.

PLANNING. As stated in Chapter 2, planning ideally precedes all other management functions. Many supervisors, however, are too busy reacting to daily problems and hence neglect planning. Therefore, if MIS can be used to handle daily problems, especially the more routine ones, the supervisor has more time to use in planning. Let us examine several areas in which planning can be facilitated.

First, MIS can be most helpful in setting goals and objectives in numerous areas (see Table 17–1). For example, MIS can be used to assemble past data and

TABLE 17–1   PERFORMANCE AREAS IN WHICH MIS CAN AID IN GOAL SETTING AND MONITORING OF PERFORMANCE

Functional Area	Specific Performance Goal
Marketing	Sales volume by product
	Sales volume by customer
	Sales volume by salesperson
	Sales volume by order size
Production	Manufacturing costs by department
	Manufacturing costs by product
	Capacity utilization
	Equipment downtime
	Percentage of defects
Personnel	Employee absenteeism
	Employee turnover
	Employee grievances
	Employee wage and salary information

TABLE 17–1 (continued)

Functional Area	Specific Performance Goal
Finance	Return on capital
	Financial ratio analysis
	Cash flow
Purchasing	Orders placed
	Status of deliveries
Inventory control	Current inventory in hand
	Inventory in process
	Storage capacity
Accounting	Budgetary compliance
	Costs incurred by department
	Material, personnel, utility costs

facilitate goal setting in areas such as capacity planning, expansion, budgeting, sales forecasting, and production.

Another useful planning application of MIS is in the area of scheduling. Various MIS programs can allow a supervisor to prepare alternative schedules and select the one that meets work requirements at the lowest cost. This may be the case with production scheduling, inventory scheduling, personnel scheduling, and so on. MIS can help supervisors make use of computerized scheduling tools such as PERT network analysis and Gantt charts. Networks and charts can actually be drawn by the computer (see Figure 17–4).

One particularly important MIS application is assisting in inventory planning. By gathering material utilization data over several months, a MIS can determine at what level each item in inventory becomes "critically low." Collected data can be used to determine when and how much material to order to minimize overall costs. The **economic order quantity (EOQ)** formula considers material utilization rates, consequences of running out of materials, the length of time typically needed to receive orders, costs of carrying materials in inventory, and costs of ordering more materials. The system can determine the most economic quantities of materials to order and when to order them. As a result, (1) material shortages or overstocking rarely occurs, and (2) costs of carrying inventory and placing numerous smaller orders are decreased.

In what other areas of planning should MIS be helpful?

FIGURE 17–4   EXAMPLE OF GANTT CHART GENERATED BY COMPUTER

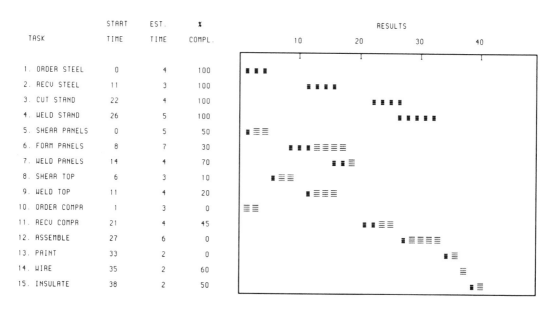

PRODUCTION SCHEDULING GANTT CHART

Press the SPACE BAR to continue

ORGANIZING. A MIS can have a direct impact on the organizing function of management. Because of its ability to provide information so readily, the MIS allows supervisors to alter their own roles and tasks. In fact, the impact of MIS has been to allow supervisors more breathing room to manage their own operations since higher-level mangement can better monitor the performance results of low-level management.

This practice has resulted in greater decentralization. MIS makes it less essential for a manager and his or her work group to be located physically close together. MIS has thus increased the tendency for supervisors to supervise personnel in widespread locations at a single site or even in different physical locations in different cities. Supervisory travel is minimized, and the control function can be exercised by simply keying certain requests into the MIS and reading progress results on a monitor.

In fact, when computerized MIS systems were first introduced, the overall impact was expected to modify the traditional approach to organization. In one of the classic articles on management, written over 30 years ago, Harold Leavitt and Thomas Whisler forecast the impact of computer technology on business organizations.[3] They predicted that the middle management of organizations would be drastically modified by MIS—more so than top and supervisory management. Since middle management's major role was to oversee supervisory management performance, Leavitt and Whisler thought that MIS technology would allow top management, aided by staff personnel, to assume more of this role themselves, thus permitting wider spans of management and reducing the number of middle managers needed. The result was to be an hourglass-shaped organization as contrasted to the traditional pyramidal organizational shape (see Figure 17–5). The results of their forecasts, while true to some extent, have not yet come about to the extent predicted. The middle management level has perhaps been proportionally altered more than other levels; however, the traditional pyramid remains the basic shape of organizations today.

FIGURE 17–5   FORECAST MIS EFFECT ON ORGANIZATION STRUCTURE

Top management

Middle management

Supervisory management

Operating level employees

Staff Personnel: Increased Role

Top management and staff personnel

Middle Management: Diminished Role

Middle management

Supervisory management

Operating level employees

Traditional Pyramid
Organization Prior to MIS

Hourglass Organization
Resulting from MIS

Do you see evidence that Leavitt and Whisler's prediction may be coming true with the mergers and acquisitions now occurring? Often, some middle managers are eliminated when companies combine.

CONTROLLING. Perhaps the controlling function of management has been the single function most affected by MIS. As you may recall from Chapter 15, controlling involves several basic steps:

1. Establishing performance standards.
2. Measuring performance.
3. Comparing performance to standards and analyzing deviations.
4. Taking corrective action if needed.

MIS has had a significant impact on all the steps, but especially steps 2, 3, and 4. Some examples of specific types of control applications are:

1. *Production control.* Production quotas can be entered into the system, and actual production can be compared to the standards set.
2. *Inventory control.* Inventory levels can be constantly monitored; at determined levels (which MIS can help determine), the system can alert management of the need to reorder certain materials to be used in production or to begin production of additional units.
3. *Quality control.* Quality of employees' performance can be evaluated through a variety of charts or comparison, showing projected and actual quality.
4. *Environmental control.* Where certain pollution control or safety measures have been taken, a MIS constantly monitors a variety of areas and signals management when deviations from standards occur.
5. *Budgetary control.* At given intervals, a MIS can provide charts showing performance against standard for items such as cost, production, inventory, absenteeism, turnover, and other financial information.
6. *Financial control.* A variety of financial controls can be employed by MIS, including cash-flow monitoring, ratio analysis, return on sales, profitability ratios, and so on. At the supervisory level, control of costs, productivity, and quality—areas we discussed in Chapter 16—are especially relevant.

Thus, MIS strongly and directly impacts the planning, organizing, and controlling functions that supervisors perform.

Role of the Supervisor in MIS Design

Earlier we stated that, to be of maximum value to managers, the information in a MIS should be timely, relevant, and clear. But who should make decisions as to the ultimate information, its layout, format, and frequency? Should it be the supervisor? Or should it be the MIS or computer specialist?

Many people, from first-line supervisors to top-level mangers, mistakenly think that designing a MIS is the total responsibility of the "computer center," systems analyst, or some specialist skilled in MIS design and computer operations. Nothing could be more incorrect! Computer personnel frequently have little experience in the practice of line management; many, in fact, may not fully understand the specific information required to do a manager's job.

Ideally, then, supervisors should have an opportunity to specify the information needed to help them make decisions. This opportunity carries with it a responsibility, however. If you are asked to participate in the design of a MIS, you will need to do some homework. Some of the questions you might answer to assist in a MIS design should include the following:

1. What types of decisions do I make regularly?
2. What types of information do I need to make these decisions?
3. What kind of information do I regularly receive?
4. What types of information would I like that I don't presently get?
5. How often do I want the information? Daily? Weekly? Monthly? Yearly?[4]

THE COMPUTER AND MIS

As stated earlier, the first business organization to use a giant computer was the General Electric Company at its Appliance Park, near Louisville, Kentucky, in 1954. Since that time, computer use has increased dramatically. In this section, we will examine some key aspects of the computer and its implications for MIS.

Computers: The Basic Terms

It is important that you understand the basics of computer technology. Therefore, in this section we will present some basic terms and their definitions to aid supervisors.

1. The **mainframe computer** is the largest type of computer system. As such, it has the capability to store enormous amounts of information and to process data at the fastest speeds.
2. A smaller version of the mainframe, the **minicomputer** takes up less space (about the size of a small file cabinet). While it originally had less speed or capacity than the mainframe, many minisystems today are more powerful than the mainframes of the 1960s.
3. The **microcomputer** is the smallest type of computer, typically sitting on a desk top. It resembles a typewriter keyboard and has a television-like screen (called a CRT) to display the data (see Figure 17–6). It is the microcomputer that has made MIS so readily available to organizations.
4. **Hardware** is the equipment needed to operate a computer system, including devices such as central processing units, storage devices, printers, and terminals.
5. Programs that issue directions to perform manipulations of data are called **software** (see Figure 17–7). These programs can be written in programming languages, such as BASIC, COBOL, and FORTRAN, and converted to machine language by other software.

New Trends and Developments

The microcomputer and computer-to-computer communications represent the two newest trends in MIS.

THE MICROCOMPUTER. The microcomputer is taking its place in business alongside its larger brothers, the mainframe computer and the minicomputer. Until the early 1980s, only large companies could afford computers. However, the microcomputer changed that. Typical microcomputers today cost less than

FIGURE 17–6   EXAMPLE OF MICROCOMPUTER WITH CRT DISPLAY

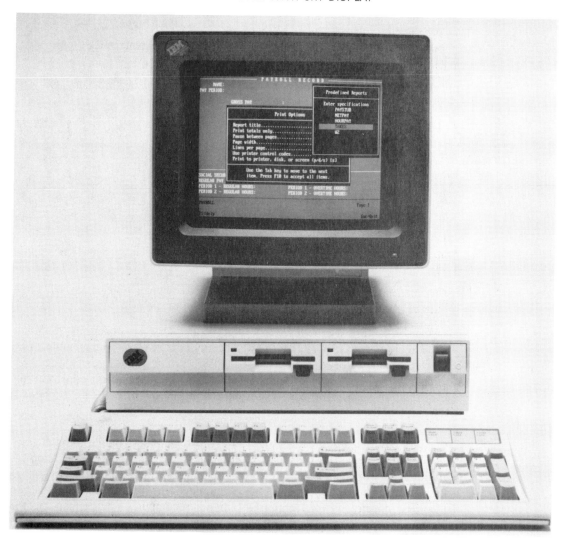

Source: Courtesy of IBM Corporation. Used with permission.

$5,000, making it possible for almost any size organization and many households to afford one. Typical microcomputers have the capability to run large and powerful scheduling, inventory, and production control programs, as well as others.

Printers are available to link up with the microcomputer to provide the user an immediate "hands on" reference of data produced in the system. One of the newest types of printers is the laser printer, which works much like a photocopy machine. An entire page of information is printed from the microcomputer into

FIGURE 17–7 THREE POPULAR SOFTWARE PROGRAMS

The three most popular types of programs or software available for microcomputers are word processors, spreadsheets, and database management systems.

 Word processing software turns the microcomputer into a ready-to-use typewriter at which the supervisor can prepare memos or documents, easily make modifications or corrections, and print the final document on the printer.

 Spreadsheets turn the computer into a large piece of paper with columns that can be manipulated in any number of ways, such as to show inventory levels needed to accommodate various production outputs.

 Finally, **database management** systems provide supervisors with a powerful tool for record keeping. The microcomputer can be programmed to accept various data such as daily absenteeism, quality per employee or component, and hourly output per employee. The data will then be sorted and reported in any manner useful to the supervisor.

the memory of the laser printer, where up to 20 pages per minute can be printed immediately.

One of the fastest-growing uses of microcomputers is in generating graphics. Software programs are available to produce any type of picture imaginable, from Gantt charts to factory layouts. Once a PERT program has been defined, for example, it can be drawn and printed immediately. A supervisor needn't wait for the drafting department to compose it or to build in any changes the supervisor may make in the future.

COMPUTER-TO-COMPUTER COMMUNICATION. Another popular trend in computer use is in organizations that use computers at more than one location. A **computer network** is a system for linking computers so that information can be shared among them. Supervisors' microcomputers at distant work stations can be hooked up directly to a mainframe or macrocomputer, thus enhancing the microcomputer's storage, versatility, and power.

A sales manager can use a minicomputer to tie into Plant X's mainframe to obtain data on current inventory available for immediate delivery to a large customer. This can be done by communicating directly with the mainframe instead of having to go through the inventory control department, thus avoiding time-consuming delays and speeding up decision making.

Even with organizations at different physical locations throughout the country, computers can be linked by ordinary telephone lines so that information can be shared quickly and easily. For example, our sales manager above could just as easily communicate directly with computers at other plant sites to determine their inventory levels and possibly complete a customer's order from locations other than his own. To examine some of the broad applications of computer networking, let us consider how Domino's Pizza uses the system.

Domino's Pizza currently has over 350 computers throughout its franchise system. Domino's uses the computers to free management and employees to concentrate on what they do best—making better pizzas faster. The microcomputers have allowed communications among Domino's four regional offices to be greatly improved—ideas can be readily swapped, and policy manuals and surveys quickly disseminated. The micro network has also been of great help in improving the quality control throughout the system.[5]

CHAPTER REVIEW

A management information system (MIS) is an integrated system, usually computer based, that provides information for management decision making. It is an *integrated* system in that it requires input from various units in the organization. It is typically *computer based*, especially given the recent breakthroughs in the cost of microcomputers. It *provides information* that is accessible, relevant, clear, accurate, objective, and timely. Finally, the nature of MIS is to *aid decision making* by management.

Data processing and management information systems differ in that data processing focuses on "processing of data," while MIS uses a data processing system to put data into an informational format that is decision-oriented.

MIS has primary relevance for the planning, organizing, and controlling functions. Regarding supervisory *planning*, it (1) frees up time to plan, and (2) can aid in future goals and objective setting by easily assembling past performance data. It is especially useful in the area of production scheduling and inventory planning. Regarding the *organizing* function, it (1) allows for wider spans of control, and (2) results in greater decentralization of authority. It has numerous *controlling* applications, including (1) monitoring performance levels, (2) calling attention to problem areas or discrepancies, and (3) assisting in the corrective actions to be taken.

Ideally, the supervisor should play a key role in the design of a MIS since it is the individual supervisor rather than a computer specialist who will use the information.

The computer has had a huge impact on MIS. Two recent computer-related trends have been especially important. One is the development of the microcomputer, which has enabled most business organizations to be overall beneficiaries of cost-effective MIS. Another is computer networking—the ability of computers at different sites to "pool" and "share" information.

QUESTIONS FOR REVIEW AND DISCUSSION

1. What is MIS?
2. What is meant by MIS being an "integrated" system?

3. Distinguish between data processing and MIS.
4. The three functions of management affected by MIS and discussed in the text were planning, organizing, and controlling. MIS is more apt to assist each of the following supervisors in the performance of which single function?
   a. A supervisor of quality assurance.
   b. A bank teller supervisor.
   c. A production scheduling supervisor.
5. What role, if any, should the supervisor play in MIS design?
6. Distinguish between computer hardware and software.
7. What are some possible computer applications for the following departments of a hospital?
   a. Accounts receivable.
   b. Nursing.
   c. Medical records.

LEARNING EXERCISE 17–1
MIS OVERLOAD

The computer information department recently installed a new management information system in the plant where Mary Stone works as a production supervisor. Mary now receives daily reports of production levels and worker hours on every project in the plant. The reports often exceed several hundred pages in length and don't really give Mary any information that she can directly use to supervise her project.

Mary's boss, Ray Johnson, just sent a memo to all production supervisors explaining how much money was spent on the new MIS and how it was designed to provide all the information needed by supervisors to assist them in their jobs. Johnson's memo leaves no doubt that he is very proud of the new MIS and wants all supervisors to use it.

Johnson has just walked into Mary's office and asked how she likes the new MIS.

Answer the following questions:

1. What do you think Mary should tell Ray Johnson?
2. What would you recommend to Ray Johnson if you were in Mary's situation?

LEARNING EXERCISE 17–2
IN THE WAY

Susan Asano, a production supervisor for the past seven years, has been notified by her boss that she has been selected to be on a team to design a new management information system for the plant. The team is to consist of three production supervisors and three people from the computer department. A systems analyst from the computer department is to act as the team leader.

At the first team meeting, the systems analyst states that he doesn't understand why the company president had Susan and her fellow supervisors placed on the team. "You people know nothing about computers or programming. How can you help us do our job? You will just be in the way. If you really want to help, you can just keep your mouths shut."

Answer the following questions:

1. Why do you think the systems analyst made his statements?
2. What action would you recommend to Susan? Support your reasoning.

ENDNOTES

1. Special thanks to Dr. Warren A. Beatty, Assistant Professor of Management, University of South Alabama, for his contribution in writing this chapter.
2. Michelle Louzoun, "Air Products Turns to Computers and the Chemistry's Just Right," *Information Week* (December 22–29, 1986): 28–30.
3. Harold T. Leavitt and Thomas L. Whisler, "Management in the 1980's," *Harvard Business Review* 36 (November-December 1958): 41–48.
4. Adapted from James H. Donnelly, Jr., James L. Gibson, and John M. Ivancevich, *Fundamentals of Management*, 6th ed. (Plano, TX: Business Publications, Inc., 1987), 567.
5. Craig Zarley, "Domino's Pizza: Personal Computers Help Deliver on Productivity Promises," *PC Week* 4 (February 17, 1987): 39.

SUGGESTIONS FOR FURTHER READING

Adams, David R., and Gerald E. Wagner. *Computer Information Systems: An Introduction.* Cincinnati: South-Western Publishing Co., 1986.

Leavitt, Harold J., and Thomas L. Whisler. "Management in the 1980's." *Harvard Business Review* 36 (November-December 1958): 41–48.

Lucas, Henry C. *Information Systems Concepts for Management.* New York: McGraw-Hill Book Co., 1986.

Newman, Michael. "User Involvement—Does It Exist, Is It Enough?" *Journal of Systems Management* 35 (1984): 34–38.

O'Reilly, Charles A. III. "Individuals and Information Overload in Organizations: Is More Necessarily Better?" *Academy of Management Journal* 23 (December 1980): 684–96.

Stern, Robert A., and Nancy Stern. *An Introduction to Computers: Information Processing.* New York: John Wiley & Sons, 1985.

COMPREHENSIVE CASE FOR PART V
THE PARTS PICKER

Shelby Arnold was a parts picker at a distribution warehouse for one of the three largest United States automobile firms. Basically, a picker's job was to move throughout the warehouse, selecting items to complete an order placed by one of the dealerships in the company's tri-state distribution area.

Large dealers' orders ran as long as four or five pages, each page identifying some 10 to 15 different parts ordered in various quantities. The parts ranged in weight from engine blocks weighing several hundred pounds to small screws or gaskets weighing only ounces. Productivity was measured in terms of "lines," or the number of different items picked in a single day. Thus, ten #10532Y gaskets were considered a line, as were ten #65942 fenders.

During a typical day, difficult orders would balance out with lighter ones. Each picker was expected to pick 300 to 350 lines on a given day. "Picked" items were placed in a four-wheel push truck, along with the order, and pushed into the shipping department where a shipper would check the order for accuracy and pack it in boxes or crates for shipment.

Picker errors resulted from either (1) a wrong quantity or (2) a wrong part being picked. For example, an order might call for eight #41796 tail light bulbs, which came two to a package. A picker might fail to notice the "two per package" and pick eight boxes (16 bulbs) in filling the order. Another source of error was transposing item numbers; instead of selecting an X9427Y bolt, a picker might select an X9472Y bolt.

In other cases, the wrong part might be placed in a storage bin or cell. In such cases, the picker would select from the right bin but inadvertently get the wrong item. During and at the end of each day, error slips were forwarded to the picking department from the shipping department, and the errors were corrected. More than two or three errors a day (10 to 15 per week) were considered above standard for a picker.

With this background in mind, let's examine a recent discussion between Harry Frost, picker supervisor, and Shelby Arnold, picker.

Frost: Shelby, come in and have a seat. [*Shelby enters and meekly sits down.*] Shelby, I won't beat around the bush. Recently, your work has been just awful. Just what is your problem?

Arnold: I didn't know I had a problem.

Frost: Well, I'll tell you your problem. Your lines are down and in the past week you've had 17 errors—more than the three or four errors that people should have. We can't tolerate work like that. . . . Now, *there's* your problem. What's going on?

Arnold: Well, nobody told me I was making errors this week. All pickers make a few mistakes, and my lines are down because I've had some tough orders. I have lots of good weeks, but you never say anything about them.

Frost: You're *supposed* to have good weeks. But this week has been a disaster— 17 "E" slips—that's no good and you know it. Now what's your problem?

Arnold: Well, this has been a bad week, I guess . . .

Frost: [*Interrupting*] I'd say it sure *has* been a bad week. Now I'll tell you what. A parts picker isn't a hard position to fill. There are 30 people we could hire tomorrow for your job. It would take three hours to train them. Maybe they'd have a hard time picking your volume for a few days, but they sure wouldn't make 17 errors. Now I'd like to keep you, but there's no way I can do it with this kind of performance. You need to do better—understand? Consider this your final notice. Any questions?

Arnold: . . . No.

The following morning, Harry Frost received a formal grievance filed by Shelby Arnold. It claimed that Frost had not allowed the union steward to be present and had bypassed the first three steps of formal discipline—the oral warning, one written warning, and suspension.

Answer the following questions:

1. How would you evaluate Frost's session with Arnold? What should he have done?
2. Assume that you are Frost's boss, the superintendent. You have just received a copy of the grievance and wish to discuss it with Frost. Role-play the meeting that you would conduct with Frost regarding the grievance.

PART VI

CURRENT CHALLENGES AND OPPORTUNITIES

18
TEAM BUILDING AND MANAGING CHANGE

OBJECTIVES

After reading and studying the material in this chapter, you should be able to:

- Understand what a team is.
- Discuss and be able to compare and contrast two models of participative management.
- Identify the conditions for effective team building.
- Discuss the characteristics of effective team building.
- Discuss how quality-of-work-life programs and quality circles relate to team building.
- Identify the reasons that employees resist change and understand ways to overcome resistance to change.
- Discuss ways in which a supervisor can effectively manage the boss.

IMPORTANT TERMS

team
human-relations model
human-resources model
principle of supportive relationships

quality-of-work-life (QWL)
  program
change
organization change

CHAPTER OUTLINE
CASE 18–1. THE CAREERS OF TWO MANAGERS

I. WHAT IS A TEAM?

II. APPROACHES TO PARTICIPATIVE MANAGEMENT
- A. Human-relations model of participative management
- B. Human-resources model of participative management

III. CONDITIONS FOR EFFECTIVE TEAM BUILDING
- A. Support from top management
- B. Supervisor's ability and attitude

IV. CHARACTERISTICS OF EFFECTIVE TEAM BUILDING
- A. Supervisor's high standards and expectations
- B. Supervisor's use of the principle of supportive relationships
- C. Supervisor's use of the human-resources approach
  1. Quality-of-work-life programs
  2. Quality circles

V. MANAGING CHANGE
- A. Why employees resist change
- B. Overcoming resistance to change

VI. BUILDING A POSITIVE RELATIONSHIP WITH YOUR BOSS
- A. Why managing the boss is important
- B. How to influence the boss

Chapter Review

Questions for Review and Discussion

Learning Exercise 18–1. "Win As Much As You Can" Tally Sheet

Learning Exercise 18–2. Identifying Successful and Unsuccessful Factors in Team Building

Learning Exercise 18–3. Decision by the Group

Suggestions for Further Reading

CASE 18–1
THE CAREERS OF TWO MANAGERS

James Jackson's Career. James Jackson had scored higher on XYZ Life & Casualty's achievement test than any other managerial trainee. The son of a sales manager for a pharmaceutical company, James had been oriented toward a career in sales since high school. His father, convinced that competition is what makes capitalism a successful economic system and that it brings out the best in people, encouraged James to compete in athletic and academic pursuits. Since James was initially unsuccessful in team sports, he concentrated on sports based on individual skill, such as golf and tennis. He was highly successful in these areas. In his schoolwork, James always ranked in the top 10 percent of his class. During college he chose marketing as his major.

Upon graduation, James went to work for XYZ. After completing the managerial training program, he became a highly successful insurance salesman. Eighteen months later, he was promoted to district sales manager in a territory where past sales had been far below potential. James called in his 12 salespersons and gave them a pep talk on the virtues of competition. He then initiated a competitive program whereby the top three salespersons would receive prizes each month; the bottom three would receive a tailender plaque. The rankings of all salespersons were posted each month on the office bulletin board.

Higher management was quite pleased to note that in the first three months of James Jackson's tenure sales increased appreciably. This initial success motivated James to greater efforts to increase performance by having meetings twice a month during which he would give pep talks. He would draw from inspirational "how to get rich quick" books and strongly urge his salespersons to enroll in courses on "how to motivate and influence people."

After six months, sales began leveling off and even declining. At this point, James sent tags to his salespersons' homes, requesting that the tags be placed on furniture as a reminder of the new furniture that could be won in a new promotion campaign. But, much to his dismay, sales continued to decline. The more James tried to stop the reversal, the more turnover among the salespersons increased. Finally, sales dropped below the average experienced under the previous sales manager. At this point, higher management offered James a choice: either accept a demotion to salesperson or leave the company.

John Tyler's Career. John Tyler scored the second-highest of any management trainee on the achievement test at XYZ Life & Casualty. His father had died when John was seven; so his mother was the greatest single influence in his life. Fortunately she was not overprotective and she encouraged John to be independent and to pursue various interests. She actively encouraged him to read and to examine conflicting points of view. As a result, John became an open-minded person, unusually free from prejudice about people and ideas. He was also an excellent student. In college he majored in speech and became a member of the debating team. Although he was keenly interested in sports, he was not an active participant on a varsity team. But he served as manager of the basketball team during his junior and senior years.

Two college experiences later influenced John Tyler's career with XYZ. First, he took a course on small-group dynamics, which was concerned with small-group problem solving and the inner workings of group behavior. This course convinced John that under certain conditions a group could produce a better solution to a problem than an individual could. Second, the school's losing basketball team hired a new coach who used an entirely different approach from that of his predecessor. The new coach constantly stressed the importance of teamwork instead of everyone trying to be a scoring leader. The squad met frequently and discussed how they could improve teamwork and individual performances, coaching with their coach. The result was a more successful season.

When John Tyler joined the insurance company after graduation, his early career was much like James Jackson's. After two years in the field as a salesperson, John was appointed sales manager of a district rated below-average in sales. In his first month, he made it a point to get to know his salespersons individually. He concluded that one of the past problems was that, like his basketball team, the salespersons were competing with one another instead of focusing on an overall goal and competing with other companies. As a result, there had been considerable secrecy among the salespersons regarding prospects, successful sales techniques, and so on.

John tried to create an environment of cooperation so that the group competed against overall sales targets and other insurance companies. He had regular monthly educational meetings in which members learned from one another as well as from him. During these meetings, he introduced team and individual target setting, in which everyone shared in setting the overall sales quota and listened to discussions of targets developed by individuals. They also had role-playing sessions in which they conducted simulated sales calls and coached one another on how to improve. Finally, John also established a group bonus system for members of the team to share (in addition to their individual commissions).

Over a period of time, the team members began sharing all kinds of information and ideas and developed high morale. They began setting high sales objectives, and after a year they became the number-one sales division in the corporation.

This case indicates that sometimes teamwork is stronger than internal competition in working effectively with and through people. As we proceed through the chapter, we will refer to this case from time to time.

Referring to Case 18–1, identify the reasons why John Tyler was successful and James Jackson was not.

Figure 18–1 will give you some insight into why John Tyler was so successful. He used a participative style, involving his entire team in decision making. Unfortunately, many supervisors, for one reason or another, are particularly weak in participative management and team building.

In this chapter we have also included a section on the management of change. To the old saying that nothing is certain but death and taxes, we would add a third word: change. In the past few decades, the world has undergone changes at a faster pace than ever before in the history of humanity. Such changes

FIGURE 18–1 POWER STYLE

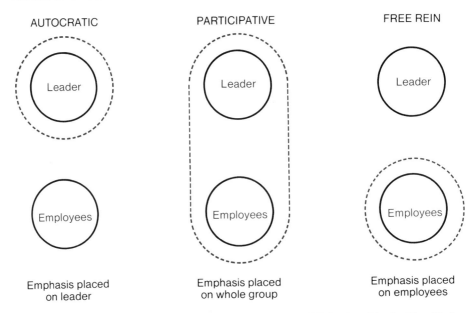

Source: Keith Davis, *Human Behavior at Work: Organizational Behavior,* 6th ed. (New York: McGraw-Hill Book Co., 1981), 136. Reproduced with permission.

are especially significant for the supervisor. Today supervisors are faced with managing employees who are better educated and more skilled than in the past. Also, the values and attitudes of employees have changed; they are more skeptical of authority figures. As we shall see, team building and participative management are keys to overcoming employee skepticism and providing meaningful work for employees.

WHAT IS A TEAM?

Teams are everywhere and run the gamut from Little League sports teams to the management teams of the world's largest corporations. A definition we like is that a **team** is a collection of people who must rely on group cooperation if the group is to experience the most success possible and to achieve its goals.[1]

Reflect on the basketball team mentioned in Case 18–1. John Tyler's coach stressed the importance of teamwork rather than a situation like that shown in Figure 18–2 where everyone is trying to be a scoring leader. A successful team constantly reviews past performances and identifies ways to build on members' strengths and to overcome problem areas. Thus, an important part of team building is the supervisor's ability to diagnose problems and to come up with ways to solve those problems so that the entire team maintains top performance.

FIGURE 18–2   ABSENCE OF TEAMWORK

APPROACHES TO PARTICIPATIVE MANAGEMENT

Almost all managers and supervisors give lip service to the merits of participative management. Actually it is a difficult style to use effectively. However, more companies are emphasizing and providing training in participative management, and it is less of a problem today than it was in the past. Raymond Miles, in his research regarding the use of participative management, provides insight into one difficulty in using this style.[2] He notes that some managers and supervisors, when using participative management, have a human-relations model in mind while others follow a human-resources model. For effective team building, Miles recommends the human-resources model. However, we need to understand the important differences in these approaches.

Human-Relations Model of Participative Management

Figure 18–3 demonstrates the thinking of a supervisor who uses the **human-relations model** of participative management. The basic idea of this model is to use participation as a technique to make people feel happy and important and lower their resistance to formal authority. Essentially, the supervisor uses participative management as a way of gaining cooperation and getting his or her decisions accepted. You might think of it as somewhat manipulative in that the supervisor is really interested in the group's involvement only so long as it is consistent with his or her own ideas!

Let us look at an example of a supervisor who was asked to role-play a situation in front of the class during a management development program. The role-play called for the supervisor to use a participative management style to come up with cost-saving ideas. This supervisor initially approached participative

FIGURE 18–3   HUMAN-RELATIONS MODEL OF PARTICIPATIVE MANAGEMENT

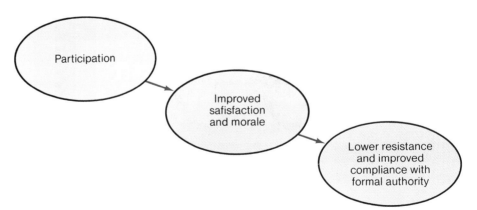

Source: Reprinted by permission of the *Harvard Business Review*. An exhibit from "Human Relations or Human Resources?" by Raymond E. Miles (July/August, 1965). Copyright © 1965 by the President and Fellows of Harvard College; all rights reserved.

management with the human-relations model in mind and then reverted to his basic style.

> *"Good morning," he began. "I've called you together because the plant manager wants our department to develop suggestions for lowering costs in the overall plant and in our own department. I have the following five ideas, and I would like to get your input and reactions to them."*
>
> *The supervisor went on to present his five ideas and asked for reactions. One of the employees was strongly opposed to one suggestion on the grounds that it would actually decrease quality. The supervisor responded, "Lou, if you can't be a member of this team and cooperate, you can get your paycheck and leave any time."*

As a result of the supervisor's reaction, how do you think the other group members would respond to the supervisor's request for input and react to his ideas?

Most supervisors who follow the human relations model would probably not react as strongly as the one mentioned in the example given above. But the basic idea of this model is not really to get incoming ideas from others but to win agreement with one's own ideas (see Figure 18–4).

FIGURE 18–4   USING THE HUMAN-RELATIONS APPROACH

Human-Resources Model of Participative Management

Figure 18–5 illustrates the thinking of a supervisor who uses the **human-resources model** of participative management. The basic idea of this model is that participative management used for *both* routine and important matters leads to improved decision making and departmental effectiveness. The supervisor views subordinates as reservoirs of untapped potential. This model highlights the fact that subordinates' satisfaction comes about as a result of having more meaningful roles in decision making and control.

FIGURE 18–5   HUMAN RESOURCES MODEL OF PARTICIPATIVE MANAGEMENT

Participation → Improved decision making and control → Improved subordinate satisfaction and morale

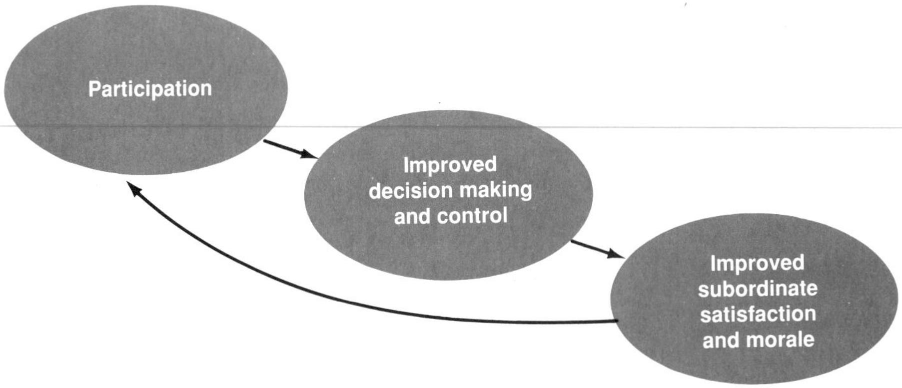

Source: Reprinted by permission of the *Harvard Business Review*. An exhibit from "Human Relations or Human Resources?" by Raymond E. Miles (July/August, 1965). Copyright © 1965 by the President and Fellows of Harvard College; all rights reserved.

Would the human resources model work with all employees—skilled, unskilled, trained, and untrained?

Obviously, it takes time and effort to develop an effective team using the human-resources model. However, it is worth the time and effort, as we saw in the opening case. Recall that John Tyler, over a period of time, developed his team to where he could use a human resources approach. He solicited their views on setting objectives and on ways of improving performance. They responded by becoming the number-one unit in the corporation.

CONDITIONS FOR EFFECTIVE TEAM BUILDING

In Chapter 9, on leadership, we noted that several variables affect leadership style. Those factors are the supervisor's management philosophy, the maturity level of the followers, and the situation. Those factors, together with other factors such as support from top management and the supervisor's ability and attitude, should be considered before the supervisor embarks on a team-building strategy.

Support from Top Management

The most important additional condition for effective team building is support from top management. Because the top management of successful American and Japanese companies has used problem-solving task forces and quality circles, more companies are shifting toward participative management. As we noted earlier, the heart of team building is participative management and collaborative problem solving.

Supervisor's Ability and Attitude

Some people have difficulty mastering the skills required of participative management. Unfortunately, many supervisors confuse participative and permissive approaches. In management development programs, we have used role playing to illustrate leadership styles. We often see a supervisor who is supposed to be playing the role of a participative leader revert to an autocratic style when the role play does not develop the way the supervisor wanted it to go!

The point is that a participative approach may not be "natural" for a supervisor. So, many supervisors cannot use it effectively without proper training. A supervisor must truly believe in participative management, for "faking it" will probably result in more harm than good.

CHARACTERISTICS OF EFFECTIVE TEAM BUILDING

The characteristics of effective team building presented here emphasize the role of first-line supervisors. Several of the points developed in Chapter 7 regarding effective meetings apply equally well here.

Supervisor's High Standards and Expectations

It is well known that a person who expects to succeed in an endeavor probably will succeed. By the same token, a person who expects to fail will do so. What is not so well known is that, in an organization, subordinates are often influenced more by the supervisor's expectations of their performance than by their own.

The supervisor's standards and expectations, communicated in various ways, can create a high-performance climate or a low-performance climate. In either case, the supervisor's expectations will usually be supported and thus become a self-fulfilling prophecy. The *self-fulfilling prophecy* works like this: If you expect low performance from people, you will get it; if you expect high performance, you will get that.

In one of the classic pieces of research on this self-fulfilling prophecy, a welding teacher was told that his group of trainees had a special aptitude for welding. Actually, there was no difference between his group and other groups of trainees. At the end of the training period, which group do you think performed best?

There is an old saying with considerable wisdom in its message: "If you want the best from people, expect it of them."

The late football coach, Paul "Bear" Bryant, is generally considered one of the greatest college coaches of all time. Even though national experts rarely ranked Bryant's incoming recruits among the top 25 recruiting classes in the country, his teams invariably finished in the top ten and, several times, as number one in the country. This success can be attributed to his high standards and expectations and his ability to inspire players to go beyond their potential. Former professional coach "Bum" Phillips stated during Bryant's career, "Coach Bryant doesn't coach football, he coaches people—he can get more out of people than anybody. Like Jack Gaither used to say, 'Bryant could take his'n and beat your'n, and take your'n and beat his'n!' He could win with either group."[3]

Supervisor's Use of the Principle of Supportive Relationships

A crucial factor in developing an outstanding team is the supervisor's practice of the **principle of supportive relationships.** This principle holds that the supervisor's leadership and interactions must be such that each employee views the experience as supportive and one that maintains his or her sense of personal worth and importance.[4] The challenge is for the supervisor to develop a climate of trust, support, openness, and credibility with his or her workers. Figure 18–6 illustrates the opposite climate.

The relationship between a supervisor and employees in a supportive climate is one of ego building rather than ego deflating. The questions in Table 18–1 provide insight as to whether a supervisor is effectively carrying out this principle. If the answers are mostly "yes," then the principle is being applied.

FIGURE 18–6   HOW NOT TO CREATE SUPPORTIVE RELATIONSHIPS

"THANK YOU FOR YOUR KIND SUGGESTIONS. NOW THAT WE HAVE THAT GARBAGE OUT OF THE WAY, LET'S GET DOWN TO BUSINESS."

Source: Cartoon by Fred Maes. Reproduced with permission.

TABLE 18–1   DO YOU PRACTICE THE SUPERVISORY PRINCIPLE
OF SUPPORTIVE RELATIONSHIPS?

Yes	No	
____	____	1. Do employees have considerable confidence and trust in you?
____	____	2. Do you understand employee problems and try to do something about them?
____	____	3. Do you keep your employees informed about matters relating to their jobs?
____	____	4. Do you help your employees get the training they need to do their jobs and/or get promotions?
____	____	5. Do you ask employees' opinions when a problem comes up that involves their work?
____	____	6. Are you friendly and easily approached?
____	____	7. Are you generous in the credit and recognition given to others for their accomplishments and contributions instead of seeking to claim all the credit yourself?

Source: Adapted from Rensis Likert, *The Human Organization* (New York: McGraw-Hill Book Co., 1967), 48–49.

Supervisor's Use of the Human-Resources Approach

In taking the human resources approach to participative management, a supervisor uses his or her group to assist in problem solving and decision making. Problems are recognized and dealt with rather than swept under the rug. The supervisor is convinced that, in certain situations, a group approach to problem solving results in a better decision than the supervisor can make alone. (Do you recall how John Tyler in Case 18–1 used his group to assist in setting overall sales objectives?) Of course, the supervisor is still held accountable for the quality of decisions and their implementation. His or her responsibility is to build an effective team that makes good decisions and carries them out well.

Some people argue that most operative employees simply do not have the ability to contribute to problem solving and decision making. Do you agree or disagree with that viewpoint? Why?

QUALITY-OF-WORK-LIFE PROGRAMS. In response to Japanese competition in the automobile industry, Ford Motor Company and General Motors have worked with the United Automobile Workers union and implemented **quality-of-work-life (QWL) programs**. Essentially a QWL program systematically studies factors such as working conditions, jobs performed, supervision, company policy, and others that affect the conditions of the workplace and its environment. Under the programs at Ford and GM, teams of 3 to 12 workers from different departments focus on diagnosing various QWL problems and recommending solutions to them.

Although commitment to a QWL program comes from top management, action plans are developed by employees and supervisors from below. In one reported study from two plants, the programs resulted in substantial dollar savings and greatly increased supervisor and employee participation in job-related problem solving.[5]

QUALITY CIRCLES. As we indicated in Chapter 16, the quality circle (QC) concept is demonstrating dramatic improvements in quality, productivity, and cost savings for a growing number of organizations. More importantly, QC groups are excellent examples of the team-building concept.

Properly established and led, QC groups enable members to contribute important ideas to their departments and the organization and to derive personal satisfaction from their experiences and contributions. The characteristics that ensure the success of quality circles are similar to those for effective team building. They include teamwork in identifying problems, gathering data, and problem solving. Moreover, there is a feeling of group ownership and belonging, with emphasis placed upon free, open participation by all circle members.

At Honeywell and other organizations, QC groups carry their *esprit de corps* so far as to wear special QC T-shirts, hats, and patches and place stickers on their lockers and autos. The team-building concepts developed in this chapter provide insights for a supervisor on how to be effective as a quality-circle leader.

MANAGING CHANGE

The management of change is directly related to the ideas presented earlier in this chapter. This is because one of the most effective ways to manage change is through team building and participative management. In order to see this relationship, we will first define *change* and *organization change*. Then we will point out the reasons that employees resist change and give suggestions on how to overcome this resistance to change.

Change can be defined in many ways. We define **change** as the process of altering, modifying, or transforming one state, condition, or phase to another. **Organization change** refers to the way an organization adapts to its external and internal environment. Externally, the organization must meet the challenges imposed by such factors as competition, the economy, legislation, and other broader issues. Internally, the organization must deal with changes in technology, in work methods, in employee attitudes, and so forth.

Specifically, what are the ways in which a supervisor can effectively cope with the increasing educational levels of employees and changing attitudes toward authority?

Why Employees Resist Change

In order to compete in a world of rapid change, organizations must change internally. The way internal changes are handled determines whether organizations meet their goals of higher productivity, employee acceptance of new technology, employee motivation, and profits.

Employees resist change for many reasons. Some reasons, such as being transferred, demoted, or let go, are real. Other reasons, such as loss of status or security, are psychological. Figure 18–7 lists some of the common reasons that employees resist change.

Overcoming Resistance to Change

The primary task of management is to create an environment in which employees maintain a positive attitude toward most changes and feel secure enough to

FIGURE 18-7   WHY EMPLOYEES RESIST CHANGE

- Insecurity and fear of the unknown.
- Economic considerations and fear that income level will be adversely affected.
- New work habits or sacrifices that are required.
- Threats to attitudes and beliefs (e.g., when women are hired for jobs previously held by men).
- Loss of status or rank.
- Failure to be notified in advance.
- Failure to see the big picture.
- Rational opposition in that the benefits do not offset the costs.

tolerate other necessary changes. Figure 18–8 highlights the role that participative management plays in creating a positive climate. As the degree of participation with respect to change increases, the resistance to change decreases.

FIGURE 18-8   OVERCOMING RESISTANCE TO CHANGE

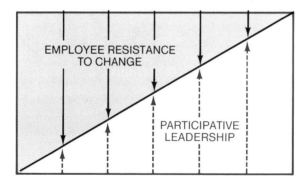

The following suggestions are helpful in developing a positive climate for organizational changes:

1. Condition the employees to expect change.
2. Inform employees well in advance of changes that will affect them. Give them all the facts and an opportunity to think about the changes well ahead of implementation.
3. Let employees participate and become involved early. They can help plan and assist in the details of implementation.
4. If the changes result in economic benefits for the company, share these benefits with employees.
5. Time the changes carefully. For example, just before Christmas would not be a good time to embark on a major change.

6. If employees have strong objections to a change, consider the merits of their viewpoint. There may be problems you haven't anticipated.

7. After changes are implemented, provide follow-up to see that the change is having the desired consequences.

A U.S. airline ran into financial difficulties in 1983. Top management's assessment was that one major problem on the cost side was a collective bargaining agreement reached with the union in 1981. Market conditions had been favorable in 1981, and the union had been granted substantial wage increases.

By 1983, however, market conditions had changed, and the airline was losing money. The president of the airline met with top union officials and explained the financial condition of the company. After verifying the financial plight of the company, the union agreed to work with management in identifying ways to lower costs.

Among other cost-reduction measures, the union agreed to a 15 percent pay cut for all union members until financial conditions improved. Three months after this decision was implemented, all management personnel received an average 10 percent increase in salaries. The union found out about the increase and immediately initiated a work stoppage. This dispute resulted in the president's being fired. A new president was hired who immediately called for a withdrawal of the 10 percent increase and a pay reduction of 15 percent of all management personnel. He stated that, from this point on, all nonunion personnel would share in gains or losses with employees who were union members.

As you can see from this incident, a management decision regarding change must be equitable and reflect a view that promotes the interest of the entire organization.

BUILDING A POSITIVE RELATIONSHIP WITH YOUR BOSS

Although a supervisor can build an effective team even without higher management support, it is much easier to do this when that support is given. The best way to gain that support is to have a positive relationship with your boss—in effect, manage your boss.

Why Managing Your Boss Is Important

Your influence with your boss determines to a large extent the amount of support you receive from higher management. To some extent, it also determines the amount of resources your work team receives to get a job done. For example, if you have a positive relationship with your boss, suggestions from you and those whom you supervise will receive a fair hearing. Your recommendations on promotions will most likely be accepted and implemented. Moreover, your subordinates and peers will perceive you as a person with influence and feel that you are a supervisor who can make things happen.

If you do not have the support and confidence of your boss, you will tend to have people from above "breathing down your neck" and questioning your decisions. There are numerous instances in which a superior bypasses a supervisor and passes out orders directly to the employees reporting to that supervisor. Obviously, in these cases, the superior is violating the chain of command and undermining the supervisor's authority. Many times the reason this happens is that the supervisor has not properly managed his or her boss.

Another key reason why managing your boss is important is that your boss is the primary person who determines your salary increases and decides whether or not you should be recommended for promotion. Because of this, many supervisors attempt to influence their boss through flattery and "apple polishing." Sometimes this tactic can be successful, especially in the short run, but rarely over the long run.

How to Influence the Boss

The best way to influence the boss, however, is not through "apple polishing" but in more meaningful ways that benefit the organization, yourself, and your boss. John Gabarro and John Kotter, in an article in *Harvard Business Review*, address this matter. They emphasize that it is crucial that you as a supervisor understand yourself and your boss. You need to have "a good understanding of the other person and yourself, especially regarding strengths, weaknesses, work styles, and needs."[6]

For example, some bosses prefer to get information in the form of a report so that they can study it before meeting with you. Other bosses prefer to discuss an issue with you so that they can ask questions and then have you follow it up with a memo. Which style does your boss prefer?

Other questions you will need to answer are: What are your boss's goals and objectives? What are the pressures on your boss? How can you help your boss in ways that are beyond your normal job description? What type of leadership style is your boss using?

One of the authors of this textbook recently served as a consultant for a company that was having a number of difficulties involving people in high management and low-level supervision. In a training program conducted for the supervisors, one of the questions addressed was: How can we do a better job of influencing our bosses? Figure 18–9 lists some of the strategies identified as ways for supervisors to influence their bosses more effectively.

If you were asked to name additional strategies that supervisors could use to manage their bosses, what would they be?

FIGURE 18-9   WAYS TO INFLUENCE YOUR BOSS

- Be firm in getting your boss's attention.
- Time your approach—don't just "drop in" to discuss major items. Arrange a set time.
- Have the necessary facts to back up your requests or indicate your performance.
- Stress positive results.
- Call your boss's attention to problems before they become major, but indicate the actions you're taking.
- Keep your boss informed on current progress and anticipated problems.
- Realize that your boss is responsible for the final results.
- Be loyal—even if you disagree with your boss's final decision. Accept it and strive to make it effective.
- Maintain open lines of communication.
- Give your boss positive feedback. Thank your boss for his or her support. If possible, compliment your boss in front of his or her own superior.
- Have your boss attend occasional meetings of your work team so that he or she will better understand this team.

CHAPTER REVIEW

Although leadership is and should be situational, there is a trend in American industry to shift toward more team building and thus increased team effectiveness. Teams are collections of people who collaborate in problem solving and decision making to improve organizational success and effectiveness. A key component in this trend is the successful use of participative management on the part of the supervisor.

There are two distinct models that managers and supervisors have in mind when utilizing participative management: (1) human relations and (2) human resources. Those supervisors following the human-relations model use participation as a somewhat manipulative technique to make people feel useful and important and to lower their resistance to formal authority. On the other hand, those using the human resources approach believe that employees are reservoirs of untapped potential. These supervisors have in mind that participation leads to improved decision making and departmental effectiveness.

Certain conditions are necessary for successful team development. In addition to a reasonable maturity level of the people involved and a situation that calls for group participation and problem solving, support from top management is critical. Moreover, the ability and desire of supervisors and other managers to practice participative management is important. The attitude of the people involved is also significant. Managers and supervisors must be convinced that team building will pay off in dividends for the organization. Management development programs focusing on leadership and group methods of problem solving can help in this regard.

One of the characteristics of effective team building is the supervisor's having high standards and expectations of employees. These standards and expectations need to be made known to the employees to create a high-performance climate. Another characteristic is the supervisor's use of the principle of supportive relationships in dealing with employees. Finally, the supervisor's use of the human resources approach makes for effective team building. QWL programs and quality circles are tools that can be used not only for team building but also for improving quality, lowering costs, and increasing worker productivity.

The use of the above three concepts can assist in the management of change and help overcome employee resistance to change. Insecurity, economic worries, prejudiced viewpoints, ingrained ways of doing things, and not being consulted in advance are some of the reasons employees resist change. There are a number of things that the organization and its supervisors can do to help employees develop a positive attitude toward change. Among these are timing changes carefully, giving employees plenty of advance notice and a chance to participate in the plans for change, considering their objections seriously, following up to make sure that changes are working out as planned, and letting employees share any economic benefits that result from the change.

Finally, the importance of the supervisor's effectiveness in influencing his or her boss was stressed. How well this is accomplished will determine how successful the supervisor is in obtaining the support necessary to maintain a productive work team. It is essential that the supervisor have an excellent relationship with the boss. One of the best ways of establishing an excellent relationship is through loyalty to the boss and good performance.

QUESTIONS FOR REVIEW AND DISCUSSION

1. Define what is meant by a team.
2. Discuss the two models of participative leadership. What are the probable views held by a supervisor who uses the human resources approach regarding the nature of people?
3. One survey indicated that a number of middle-level managers and supervisors prefer that their bosses use the *human-resources* approach with them, but they prefer to use the *human-relations* approach with their subordinates. Why do you think the above attitude is so prevalent? Would it be desirable to change these attitudes of middle-level managers and supervisors? If so, how could it be accomplished?
4. Discuss the conditions for effective team building.
5. One of the characteristics of effective team building is the use of the principle of supportive relationships by the supervisor. What are some specific things a supervisor can do to carry out this principle in working with and through people?
6. What are the major changes that have occurred in the last ten years that have had considerable impact on organizations? Would these changes provide support for

or make a case against the use of team building in organizations? Defend your position.

7. Why is it important for a supervisor to have influence with the boss? What are some ways the supervisor can influence the boss?

LEARNING EXERCISE 18–1
"WIN AS MUCH AS YOU CAN" TALLY SHEET*

The detailed instructions for completing this exercise will be provided by your instructor. If there is no objection to a modest wager, each partnership may want to place a bet, ranging from ten cents to a dollar, on the outcome of the game. The "winner" collects the money at the end of the exercise.

NOTE: For ten successive rounds you and your partner will choose either an X or a Y in the scorecard (see Figure 18–10). The payoff for each round depends on the pattern of choices made in your group. The payoff schedule is given on page 464.

FIGURE 18–10   SCORECARD

	Round	Your Choice (circle)		Cluster's Pattern of Choices		Payoff	Balance
	1	X	Y	__ X	__ Y		
	2	X	Y	__ X	__ Y		
	3	X	Y	__ X	__ Y		
	4	X	Y	__ X	__ Y		
Bonus Round payoff x 3	5	X	Y	__ X	__ Y		
	6	X	Y	__ X	__ Y		
	7	X	Y	__ X	__ Y		
Bonus Round payoff x 5	8	X	Y	__ X	__ Y		
	9	X	Y	__ X	__ Y		
Bonus Round payoff x 10	10	X	Y	__ X	__ Y		

*From an exercise by William Gellermann in J. Pfeiffer and J. Jones, *Structured Experiences for Human Relations Training*, Vol. II, University Associates Press, 1970.

Payoff Schedule

4 Xs:	Lose $1.00 each
3 Xs:	Win $1.00 each
1 Y :	Lose $3.00 each
2 Xs:	Win $2.00 each
2 Ys:	Lose $2.00 each
1 X :	Win $3.00
3 Ys:	Lose $1.00 each
4 Ys:	Win $1.00 each

You are to confer with your partner in each round and make a joint decision. In rounds 5, 8, and 10, you and your partner may first confer with the other partnerships in your group before making your joint decision, as before.

LEARNING EXERCISE 18–2
IDENTIFYING SUCCESSFUL
AND UNSUCCESSFUL FACTORS IN TEAM BUILDING

Divide the class into teams of five or six. Have half the teams develop a list of factors that contribute to successful team building. Have the other teams develop a list of factors that hinder team building. After the reports, be prepared to contribute to the discussion your own experiences with effective and ineffective teams of which you've been a member.

LEARNING EXERCISE 18–3
DECISION BY THE GROUP*

John Stevens, plant manager of the Fairlee plant of Lockstead Corporation, attended the advanced management seminar conducted at a large midwestern university. The four-week seminar was largely devoted to the topic of executive decision making.

Professor Mennon, of the university staff, particularly impressed Stevens with his lectures on group discussion and group decision making. On the basis of research and experience, Professor Mennon was convinced that employees, if given the opportunity, could meet together, intelligently consider, and then formulate quality decisions that would be enthusiastically accepted.

Returning to his plant at the conclusion of the seminar, Stevens decided

*This exercise is taken from John M. Champion and John H. James, *Critical Incidents in Management*, 4th ed. (Homewood, IL: Richard D. Irwin, 1980). Reproduced with permission.

to practice some of the principles he had learned. He called together the 25 employees of Department B and told them that the production standards established several years previously were now too low in view of the recent installation of automated equipment. He gave the employees the opportunity to discuss the altered circumstances and to decide among themselves, as a group, what their standards should be. On leaving the room, Stevens believed that the employees would doubtless establish much higher standards than he himself would have dared propose.

After an hour of discussion, the group summoned Stevens and notified him that, contrary to his opinion, their group decision was that the standards were already too high; and since they had been given the authority to establish their own standards, they were making a reduction of 10 percent. These standards, Stevens knew, were far too low to provide a fair profit on the owner's investment. Yet it was clear that his refusal to accept the group decision would be disastrous. Before taking any action, Stevens called Professor Mennon at the university for his opinion.

Answer the following questions:

1. Critique John Stevens's approach in handling this situation. Include in your answer how you think he should have handled it.
2. If you were Professor Mennon, what advice would you give Stevens?

ENDNOTES

1. William G. Dyer, *Team Building: Issues and Alternatives* (Reading, MA: Addison-Wesley Publishing Co., 1977), 4.
2. Raymond E. Miles, "Human Relations or Human Resources?" *Harvard Business Review* 43 (July-August 1965): 148–63.
3. Paul W. Bryant and John Underwood, *Bear* (Boston: Little, Brown & Co., 1974), vii.
4. Rensis Likert, *The Human Organization: Its Management and Value* (New York: McGraw-Hill Book Co., 1967), 47.
5. Sahab Doyal, "Quality-of-Work-Life Movement in the United States: The Case of the Automobile Industry," in *Proceedings of the Southern Management Association*, ed. Dennis F. Ray (Mississippi State, 1983), 318.

SUGGESTIONS FOR FURTHER READING

Blake, R. R., and J. S. Mouton. "Overcoming Group Warfare." *Harvard Business Review* 62 (November-December 1984): 98–108.

Harris, P. R. "Building a High-Performance Team." *Training and Development Journal* 40 (April 1986): 28–29.

Kennedy, M. M. "Barter with Your Boss [to Win Coveted Assignments]." *Executive Female* 9 (May-June 1986): 44–47.

Mitchell, R. "How Ford Hit the Bull's-Eye with Taurus." *Business Week*, June 30, 1986, pp. 69–70.

Selman, James, and V. F. DiBianca. "Contextual Management: Applying the Art of Dealing Creatively with Change." *Management Review* 72 (September 1983): 13–19.

19
CHANGING TO A PARTICIPATIVE MANAGEMENT CULTURE AND DEVELOPING CREATIVITY

OBJECTIVES

After reading and studying the material in this chapter, you will be able to:

- Define key concepts such as *synergy*.
- Explain the reasons for the success and characteristics of Japanese management.
- Describe what effective participative management is and is not.
- Explain Likert's contribution to participative management.
- Develop skill in carrying out the slip technique and nominal grouping.

IMPORTANT TERMS

participative management	ad hoc task forces
synergy	deferred judgment
ownership	Crawford slip technique
corporate culture	fluency
organization development (OD)	flexibility
System 1, 2, 3, 4	nominal grouping technique (NGT)

CHAPTER OUTLINE
CASE 19–1. THE TURNAROUND CHEMICAL PLANT

> In order that people be happy in their work, these things are needed: they must be for it; they must not do too much of it; and they must have a sense of success in it.
> *John Ruskin*

CASE 19–1
THE TURNAROUND
CHEMICAL PLANT[1]

The Pending Shutdown

In the 1960s, a chemical plant of a major U.S. corporation was built in a rural area of the mid-South. The plant was trying to perfect a product that only DuPont had perfected and successfully marketed until that time. As a consequence of the challenging nature of the assignment, the management group was a carefully selected and highly educated one. For example, three of the top four managers had master's degrees in chemical engineering from Cal Tech, Purdue, and Columbia, respectively.

Three years after the plant was built, operations had still not reached the break-even point. Neither the manufacturing process nor the quality of the product met the standards of the competition. The corporation president indicated to the plant manager that, if a break-even point was not reached within a year, the facility would be closed.

The Consultant's Entry and Approach

Out of a sense of desperation, the plant manager turned to a college professor at a nearby university for consultation. This professor (one of the authors of this textbook) was chosen because the plant's chief chemist had been favorably impressed with a presentation made by this professor at a university-sponsored management development program. At the time, the professor was a young, recent Ph.D. whose doctoral courses had concentrated primarily on industrial relations and economics and whose only experience with managers was coordinating and teaching one university-sponsored management development program. Fortunately, he was familiar with the work of Douglas McGregor and Rensis Likert, and the concepts of these men had formed the foundation of the seminar.

The initial meeting was held with the plant manager, the manager of industrial relations, and an executive from headquarters. The three executives agreed that the plant had the expertise to perfect the process, but that many human problems were getting in the way. They requested a behavioral science seminar focusing on improving leadership styles and teamwork among the management group.

In addition to the seminar, the consultant suggested that key managers be interviewed and asked to identify plant strengths and problems. The seminar would then be tailored to build on strengths and to overcome problems. The plant manager thought that was a great idea and further suggested that a strength/problem profile be developed for the *four* top (key) managers. This would be done by asking subordinates, peers, and the key managers' bosses to give a confidential assessment regarding the key managers' leadership styles. Interviewees were told that all comments would be presented to each manager, but no individual would be identified with a specific comment. Without question, these confidential feedback sessions made the top managers much more receptive to the concepts presented in the seminar.

The interview results revealed the following six problem areas:

1. There were conflicts and friction among the production, technical, and engineering department heads.
2. Several managers, when they made decisions affecting various people, did not communicate the decisions to all the people affected.
3. There were poor interpersonal relations among people on the same level, as well as up and down the line.
4. Several managers demonstrated ineffective leadership, using highly autocratic styles and failing to utilize their subordinates' skills.
5. The organizing function was poorly implemented, with fuzzy definitions of authority and responsibility relationships, bypassing of the chain of command, and too much managerial time devoted to technical rather than management problems.
6. Performance appraisals were performed ineffectively, and there was little effort to involve subordinates in the goal- setting process.

The Miracle

In a dramatic turnaround, the plant reached the break-even point within a year after the initiation of the OD program and met the deadline set by the president of the company. Fourteen months after the initiation of the OD program, a second round of data gathering revealed a consensus that the program was the primary reason for the turnaround.

The second round of data gathering also led to the following actions:

1. A tailored training program implemented for all lower-level supervisors.
2. Assessment of leadership styles for middle-level managers, who were also provided confidential feedback and counseling.
3. Joint target setting implemented for most managers and engineers.
4. Attendance at sensitivity training sessions by the manager of the technical services department to provide better insight into working with people.

The icing on the cake was that a licensing agreement was reached with a Japanese firm to manufacture the product in Japan. The income from this agreement was more than the cost of the facility, land, and equipment at the Deep South plant.

This chapter builds on the previous one and goes further in developing the concepts of participative management. We have added this chapter to the second edition for several reasons. First, participative management is given extensive lip service but is sometimes misunderstood and misapplied in actual practice. Second, there is a widespread movement attempting to shift organizations from autocratic and bureaucratic management systems to participative management systems. This does not mean that the authors of this textbook disagree with contingency or situational leadership theory, which maintains that the appropriate leadership style depends on the situation and the maturity (competence) level of employees. It does mean that, because of forces at work in the external environment (increasing international competition in both price and quality) and in the internal environment (increasing education levels of employees), there are more and more situations that call for a participative management approach and culture.

What are other factors in the external environment and internal environment of organizations that call for the use of participative management?

KEY CONCEPTS AND DEFINITIONS

Since we will be exploring participative management in more depth, it will be helpful to start with a common understanding of terms.

Participative management is taking part or sharing in problem solving or decision making. It can run the gamut from soliciting ideas and suggestions from one or several individuals to delegating to a small group the opportunity to develop recommendations or reach a consensus decision.

Synergy is the concept that the whole is greater than the sum of the parts. In small-group work, the outcome or recommendations would be superior to any set of recommendations made by a group member working alone. In mathematical terms, synergy means that $2 + 2 + 2 + 2 > 8$.

Ownership is the notion that soliciting participation from people affected by a problem or decision results in involvement, commitment, and a strong desire to ensure that the decision is implemented effectively. An analogy is: "If you're on the plane when it takes off, you'll be on it when it lands."

Corporate culture "refers to the set of values, beliefs, and behavior patterns that form the core identity of an organization."[2] Thus, in a participative management culture, there would be widespread acceptance and knowledge at all levels of the values and benefits of participative management, as well as the skills needed to carry it out.

Organization development (OD) is a planned effort, managed from the top, that is designed to increase an organization's effectiveness and health. Many times, OD uses both action research and behavioral science knowledge in designing interventions to enable the organization to build on its strengths and to overcome problems. The opening case is an example of OD in action, utilizing an outside consultant. The OD program in this case was designed to shift the plant in the direction of a more participative management system.

THE JAPANESE CHALLENGE

After World War II and through the early 1960s, American industry and U.S. management were considered the best in the world. In fact, a Frenchman in the 1950s wrote a book called *The American Challenge*. His message was that, unless European managers took lessons from American managers, they would be left behind in the international economic arena. Today, the industry and management that are most admired and envied are not American but Japanese. In the past 20 years, the Japanese have increased their market area in key industries and have a reputation for outstanding quality. For example, the respected publication *Consumer Reports* recently issued its recommendations for 1987 cars. "Of 136 cars and vans judged in the April magazine, *Consumer Reports* recommends only 54, and 36 of them are imports. Twenty-six are Japanese-made."[3] That is, almost 50 percent of the highest-rated cars are Japanese-made.

Characteristics of Japanese Management

In 1981, William Ouchi published a book titled *Theory Z* contrasting American management with Japanese management. He concluded that Japan's relative success is the result of better management. The essence of the Japanese style that Ouchi calls "Theory Z" is long-time employment and widespread participation of employees in problem solving and decision making. He maintains that many American organizations are too "autocratic" in that orders flow from the top down, and people are told to follow rules and procedures and are not encouraged to use their ideas, information, talent, and discretion. Among other characteristics, Theory Z emphasizes long-range planning, consensus decision making, and strong mutual employer-employee loyalty.[4]

The United States is not the only country studying management practices in Japan. An Englishman, Chris Clegg, conducted a study in Japan of a factory that manufactures photocopiers. He was particularly interested in what his findings might mean for companies in the United Kingdom. Figure 19–1 summarizes some of his findings, focusing on human resources synergy. The positive type of synergy represents what Clegg saw happening in the factory in Japan. Unfortunately, the negative type of synergy represents what is taking place in many United Kingdom companies. The challenge is to identify actions that need to be taken in the United Kingdom to turn the negatives into positives.[5]

FIGURE 19–1 TYPES OF HUMAN RESOURCES SYNERGY

	Positive	Negative
Examples of cultural and national characteristics	Very large national investment in education, with large proportions of people entering higher education. Existence of lifetime employment in major companies. People in major companies follow generalist career paths, gaining experience in many functions.	Smaller national investments in higher education. Some lifetime employment exists, but in many cases employment is contractually based and relatively short term. People follow specialist paths, perhaps changing companies to broaden experience.
Management philosophy	Employees share responsibility for the goals rather than means. Employees are an asset. Operators are the local experts.	Employees are responsible for the means. Specialists are experts. Systems are designed to be operator-proof.
Management systems and style	Straightforward, powerful systems exist. Systems help operators and supervisors manage the present. Managers are free to manage the future in a planned way.	Systems are often complex and poorly understood. Managers manage the present. General operational emphasis on managing the present.
Operator roles	Operators are experts who handle problems as they occur. Operators are highly trained.	Operators refer problems to specialists. Training of operators is implicitly regarded as a waste of time.
Opportunities for synergy	Positive relationships exist, characterized by self-sustaining virtuous circles.	Negative relationships exist, characterized by self-sustaining vicious circles.

Source: Chris Clegg, "Trip to Japan: A Synergistic Approach to Managing Human Resources," *Personnel Management* 8 (August, 1986), p. 39. Reproduced with permission.

The Impetus for Japanese Management

American know-how and management techniques have been preached and taught all over the world. Rarely, if ever, have they fallen on such fertile soil as in Japan. The following excerpt from an article by Yukuo Takenaka explains how this happened. It explains how a nation defeated in World War II, a country smaller than Montana, with few natural resources, became the world's quality leader.

> It is little wonder that Japanese industry leaders almost always refer to the United States as "our great teacher." Virtually all the "new" Japanese techniques originated in the United States. The concepts of job enrichment and participative management, for example, were developed by IBM founder Thomas J. Watson in the twenties. In addition, Watson pioneered, in the thirties, what the Japanese call "quality circles." Employee suggestion programs, which in Japan account for many times more cost savings and cost improvement than quality control activities, are also nothing new: Eastman Kodak's suggestion program was launched in 1898. Statistical quality control and the fundamentals of quality science were developed in the thirties by Walter Shewhart and his associates at AT&T.
>
> The concept of continuous improvement in every single thing a company does—a notion now institutionalized in Japan—is the product of the thinking of two former Western Electric engineers, Dr. W. Edwards Deming and Dr. Joseph M. Juran, who were invited to teach statistical quality methods in Japan in 1952. For this, they are today venerated in Japanese manufacturing circles. The highest prize a company can win for excellence in Japan is, in fact, the Deming Award.[6]

DEVELOPING EFFECTIVE PARTICIPATIVE MANAGEMENT

The following sections present in depth the concepts of effective participative management. Examples are provided of companies we have worked with that are using participative management in an effective way.

What Participative Management Is Not

At the beginning of this chapter, we stated that participative management may be the most misunderstood and misapplied approach in industry. Let us examine several of the practices that go under the name but are really not participative management.

First, participative management is not permissive management, whereby the supervisor pretty well allows employees complete freedom to do as they wish. Second, it is not democracy, where employees make all the decisions. Third, as we saw in the previous chapter, it is not allowing employees to participate just so they will be more compliant with formal authority. (We called this the human-relations model of participative management.) Finally, contrary to many beliefs, it is not even the wholesale use of task forces and quality circles so that almost every employee is involved in some type of participation.

As Rosabeth Kanter has noted: "Participation is assumed to be present in an organization only when everybody practices it all the time. So participative vehicles get used where they clearly make no sense—as in one organization of about 1500 exempt employees that had at least 92 identifiable task forces with the exempt ranks."[7]

What do you see as the major deficiencies in having 92 task forces at work with 1,500 exempt employees?

What Participative Management Is

Basically, the philosophy of effective participative management states that, under proper conditions, employees should have the opportunity to make a significant contribution to solving problems, controlling costs, contributing to objectives, and assisting in managing and controlling the business. The philosophy is related to the human-resources model of participative management and McGregor's Theory Y assumptions about people. The philosophy is keenly aware that not all industrial situations call for participation; that people have to be developed and trained before they can effectively participate; and that, to be successful, key line managers and supervisors have to be committed to and involved in the process.

The basic characteristics of effective participative management, which have been developed throughout this book, can be summarized as follows:

1. Top management has to be committed, and all levels are involved through the chain.
2. The managers and supervisors at each level have high standards and expectations. Difficult but attainable objectives are established.
3. Managers and supervisors make use of the principle of supportive relationship.
4. Problems are confronted rather than "swept under the rug." In attacking key problems and issues, appropriate ad hoc forces are used.
5. Communications are effective in all directions—up, down, laterally, and diagonally.
6. As a result of the environment, a participative culture is created, resulting in human development, synergistic decisions, and considerable "ownership" in implementing plans and achieving objectives.

Next, let us turn to the late Rensis Likert's systems framework in which he demonstrated more than anyone else that an effective participative management system can tremendously improve bottom-line results.

LIKERT'S CONTRIBUTION

In the textbook authors' judgment, the late Rensis Likert has been one of the most effective proponents of participative management in the world. For 25 years, Likert served as director of the Institute for Social Research at the University of Michigan. In that capacity, he and his associates did extensive research regarding the working of the human organization.

Four Management Systems

One of Likert's greatest contributions was to identify four management systems operating in organizations. He and his team of researchers were strongly convinced that leadership was a causal variable that, over time, affected end results of factors such as productivity, profits, turnover, and absenteeism. The four management systems, arranged along a continuum, are shown in Figure 19–2.

FIGURE 19–2 LIKERT'S FOUR MANAGEMENT SYSTEMS

System 1	System 2	System 3	System 4
Exploitative-Authoritative	Benevolent-Authoritative	Consultative	Participative

Likert developed a "Profile of Organizational Characteristics" questionnaire that provided descriptive ratings in seven areas: leadership processes, motivational forces, communication, interaction-influence process, decision making, goal setting, and control. A version of this questionnaire is found in the comprehensive case at the end of this part. Although only one of the seven areas specifically focuses on leadership, it is a causal variable that affects the others. Likert and his team found that, the closer an organization is to System 4 (participative groups), the more effective it will be in achieving its end results.

Several studies have since been published documenting successful shifts from Systems 1 and 2 to Systems 3 and 4, with accompanying improvements in performance and satisfaction. The comprehensive case at the end of this part is an example of a successful shift. Following is a brief description of these four leadership styles:[8]

1. *System 1 (Exploitative-Authoritative)*. In **System 1**, top management primarily uses an autocratic style, makes all the decisions, and relies on coercion as the primary motivating force.

2. *System 2 (Benevolent-Authoritative)*. In **System 2**, higher management makes most of the decisions, although some minor implementing decisions may be made at lower levels. A condescending attitude is usually displayed in communicating with subordinates, which results in a subservient attitude toward superiors.

3. *System 3 (Consultative)*. In **System 3**, higher management still reserves the tasks of direction and control, but ideas are at least solicited from lower levels. As a result, up-and-down communications are superior to those in Systems 1 and 2. There is a moderate amount of cooperative teamwork, and certain specific delegated operating decisions are made at lower levels.

4. *System 4 (Participative)*. Under **System 4**, higher management views its role as that of making sure the best decisions are made through a decentralized partic− ipative group structure. These groups overlap and are coordinated by multiple memberships. There is a high degree of trust that allows both superiors and sub− ordinates to exercise greater control over the work situation.

Thus, a key concept of System 4 is the creation of a participative management culture and the use by managers of group decision making and supervision in the management of the work group. It should be noted that System 4 is similar to the type of management found in many Japanese firms. Perhaps the biggest distinction is that, in System 4, each individual manager is still held accountable for his or her decisions and implementations even though decision making is a group process.

Specifically, what was initiated in the opening case that helped the chemical plant shift toward Systems 3 and 4?

The Special Case of Ad Hoc Task Forces

In a System 4 organization, participative management is carried out when appro− priate by the line organization with overlapping group membership. Thus, orga− nization members have experience and have been trained in problem solving and group dynamics. Under these conditions, properly implemented quality circles and ad hoc task forces supplement the formal organization and have the oppor− tunity to make significant contributions.

> *The authors of this textbook have had very good success in helping companies use ad hoc task forces effectively. In one plant where we were helping a shift toward a System 4 organization, we first spent considerable time training and developing all line managers. One of the problems addressed was lack of cooperation between production and maintenance. A task force of both*

maintenance and production supervisors was established to solve the problem and had excellent results. A year later, the maintenance manager established an ad hoc task force composed of one member of each maintenance crew to develop action planning recommendations on issues they identified to improve maintenance efficiency and effectiveness. These recommendations were handled each week by the maintenance manager at his regular meeting with his supervisors. Within two weeks, the task force got feedback on which of the recommendations would be implemented or modified.

This is an example of the System 4 concept at work. Appropriate ad hoc task forces provide the opportunity for the concepts of ownership and synergy to be operative.

DEVELOPING CREATIVITY

Scientists tell us that the right side of the brain provides us with our creative impulses. If we think of ourselves as problem solvers/decision makers, the right side of the brain is the generator of ideas and is where imagination originates. It may be considered the decision maker's prime mover.

On the other hand, the left side of the brain handles logical, analytical, and linear functions and is considered the decision maker's monitor. This is where judgment enters into the process. Unfortunately, you cannot use both at the same time, and many times the left side (monitor) encroaches on the right side (mover) prematurely!

How many times have you been in a meeting to solve a problem and spent an hour debating the pros and cons of the first idea presented to solve it?

In order to gain the maximum benefit from ad hoc task forces, quality circles, or any problem-solving effort, the left side must be restrained initially. The key to doing this is to make use of the concept of **deferred judgment**. This is the idea behind brainstorming, and the secret is to delay judgment while generating ideas. After the ideas have been generated, then it is appropriate to use the monitor side to evaluate and judge which ones are good, cost effective, etc. Two techniques that are very useful in this process are the Crawford slip technique and the nominal grouping technique.

Crawford Slip Technique

The **Crawford slip technique** was developed by Professor C. C. Crawford at the University of Southern California.[9] It makes use of two elements that are important in achieving creativity—fluency and flexibility. **Fluency** is the ability to let ideas flow out of your head like water over a waterfall, and **flexibility** is the ability to use free association to generate or classify ideas in categories. Materials needed are a number of 3" × 5" scratch pads and a number of empty boxes distributed among the participants. The process starts by telling participants that they are about to engage in a new type of problem solving that will generate 50 to 100 new ideas.

For example, this technique was used with the top management of Baldor Electric Company, a very successful company listed on the New York Stock Exchange. Unfortunately, one of the large motors it produced was losing money. The following series of steps was initiated to deal with the problem.[10]

1. Participants were asked not to pause to evaluate ideas and not to generate such thoughts as "We've tried this before."
2. Every participant was given a pad of 3" × 5" slips of paper.
3. In this technique, the leader presents a problem in "how to" form. In the case of Baldor Electric, the problem presented was, "How can we reduce costs on our 300 series motors without affecting quality?"
4. Each person would write down as many answers to the problem as time would permit. After an idea was written on a slip, it was placed in the idea bank (box) anonymously.
5. After ten minutes, the idea boxes were collected and task forces established. In the case of Baldor, there were three task forces, to whom the idea slips were distributed like cards dealt from a deck.
6. Each task force was charged with arranging the ideas in categories, using judgment (left side of the brain) to throw out weak ideas and then developing the good ideas and presenting recommendations to the larger group.

The chief executive officer of the company then judged what ideas were most relevant to solving the problem and decided to implement them. Please note that, although there was considerable participation in the process, one person made the final decision. In many instances, this is a desirable approach in using participative management.

Why in the above case might it be desirable to have the CEO make the final decision on which ideas to implement?

Nominal Grouping Technique

The **nominal grouping technique (NGT)** also makes use of brainstorming, and we have found the technique very effective in developing creativity and generating useful information. It can be used in many different ways. One way we have found useful is to develop a strength-problem profile of the organization, plant, or department. Then, through action planning, steps can be taken to convert problems into strengths.

If the organization is involved in an OD program, nominal grouping can be helpful in generating a strength-problem profile from groups of employees. This profile is very useful in making a diagnosis in the first phase of an OD program.

Under the leadership of Bob Bell, mill manager, and Jack Sims, manager of management development, the Texarkana Mill of International Paper is using management develoment programs to shift to a more participative management culture. In assisting top management of the mill, we used nominal grouping on the last afternoon of a four-day management development program. The way the process works is that we asked participants to take six minutes to respond to the following two questions:

1. What are the strengths of your mill?
2. What are the problems preventing your mill from reaching its potential effectiveness?

We advised participants to identify only problems they could do something about at the mill level. The steps in this process are listed in Figure 19–3.

One nominal group of managers from the IP Texarkana program identified 25 strengths and 22 problems—a very healthy profile. An unhealthy profile would be one in which the group's problems greatly outnumber its strengths. We recall one group in another company that identified only 12 strengths and 55 problems. In the IP group, the top-ranked problems identified are listed on page 480.

FIGURE 19–3   STEPS IN NOMINAL GROUPING

1. Divide into groups of six or nine people.
2. *Without* interaction, list strengths you feel are associated with Question 1, then list the problems for Question 2. (Time: 6 minutes)
3. Select a recorder.
    a. The recorder asks each member, one at a time, to read from his or her card one strength associated with Question 1.
    b. The recorder writes each strength exactly as it is read.
    c. Those having the same strength should raise hands. The recorder checkmarks each strength once for each person raising a hand.
    d. When all Question 1 strengths are recorded, the procedure is repeated for Question 2 problems.
4. Discuss the two lists. Clarify, defend, elaborate, or add other items as needed. (Time: 5 minutes)
5. *Without interaction,* each member lists on an index card the *five* items he or she considers most important with reference to Question 1; do the same for Question 2.
6. The recorder collects and records the votes.

1. Poor communication within and between departments.
2. Slow repair of noncritical equipment.
3. Poor motivation of employees (need for positive, timely feedback).
4. Need to listen more effectively to employees' suggestions.
5. Need to improve training program.

This group then developed action-planning recommendations that went to the mill manager and his management team for consideration and possible implementation. The action plan the nominal group developed is presented as Figure 19–4.

FIGURE 19–4 PROPOSAL DEVELOPED BY A NOMINAL GROUPING TASK TEAM[11] (Members were Keith Dunlap, Ennis Williams, Carl Trichel, and Carl Wilson.)

I. Statement of the problem: Need more effective communication within and between departments.

II. Impact on the mill—what it is costing: The cost is tremendous. For example, several days ago on graveyard shifts, the power house shut down all the diesel-powered compressors to refuel them. The sudden drop in air pressure resulted in approximately 30 minutes lost time on both machines. Proper notification of this situation prior to shutting the compressors down would have significantly reduced these losses. Similar situations exist concerning dirt problems from the pulp mill, sheet quality from the machines to the extruder, liquor quality from the caustic plant to the pulp mill, etc.

III. Alternatives to solving the problem:
1. Develop team concept millwide.
2. Notes from production/maintenance meetings need to be passed on to employees.
3. Oral communication of information.
4. Better reporting in operator logs for oncoming shifts.
5. Specified time during shifts for cross-communication between departments.
6. Suggestion box.

IV. Action plan: Needs to involve everybody, working through department heads, and needs to happen immediately. Requires development of *team* attitude in everyone, because each individual job ultimately impacts all jobs. Department heads must support and force communication downward, leave an "open door" to upward communication.

V. Impact of solving the problem:
1. Reduced downtime.
2. Reduced rejects.
3. Lower costs.
4. More efficiency/fewer losses.
5. Improved morale.
6. Greater equipment reliability.

CHAPTER REVIEW

This chapter has gone further into the development of some of the concepts of participative management. It is not that we disagree with situational leadership theory, but it is because of *increased education of employees* and *increasing international competition* that participative management is found to be the proper approach in more and more situations.

We defined some concepts that are essential in understanding the philosophy of participative management—synergy, ownership, corporate culture, and organization development. We also discussed the Japanese challenge and characteristics of Japanese management. A basic characteristic is widespread participation of employees in problem solving and decision making.

We then discussed the development of effective participative management by first discussing what it was not, concluding that it was not permissive management, democracy, human relations, or total employee involvement in participation. We summarized the basic characteristics of effective participative management.

Rensis Likert, as a proponent of participative management, identified four management systems used in American industry, ranging from exploitative-authoritative (System 1) to participative (System 4). He and his team of researchers concluded that the closer an organization moved to System 4, the better were the end results in financial performance and employee health and satisfaction.

Finally, we examined the special case of ad hoc task forces and emphasized that appropriate use of task forces and quality circles can work with the line organization in developing a participative management culture. We also emphasized the importance of creativity and the appropriate use of the Crawford slip technique and the nominal group technique in carrying out the participative management process effectively.

QUESTIONS FOR REVIEW AND DISCUSSION

1. Define what is meant by *synergy* and *ownership*.
2. Assume that you are taking over a department (22 employees) that is low in both morale and productivity. As manager, what might you do to turn things around?
3. Discuss the reasons that the Japanese have surpassed the Americans in worldwide reputation for effective management? Do you think the United States can regain the reputation it once had? Why or why not?
4. Explain the different functions of the right and left sides of the brain.
5. Contrast and compare (a) participative and permissive management; (b) participative and democratic management.

LEARNING EXERCISE 19-1
DEVELOPING CREATIVITY

Divide the class into teams of three or four. The assignment is for each member of the class to think of as many uses of a paper clip as possible. In the text, we indicated that this process is called "fluency" in generating ideas. Do not evaluate the ideas; just write them down as fast as they come to you. Time allowed is two minutes.

Next, work with members of your team to classify the various ideas into categories. In the text, we called this element "flexibility," and it is useful in developing free associations. Place the ideas your team members have generated into the various categories. Please use free association to add additional ideas. Time allowed is 15 minutes.

Have each team present its categories and the total number of ideas. Give a good round of applause for the most creative and productive team.

LEARNING EXERCISE 19–2
PRACTICING THE SLIP TECHNIQUE

A. If the members of the class are primarily full-time students, follow the steps in the slip technique to answer the following question: How can we best find and obtain a good job upon finishing our education?

B. If the class is part of a supervisory and management development program, follow the steps in the slip technique to answer this question: How can we create a participative culture in our organization?

LEARNING EXERCISE 19–3
STRENGTH/PROBLEM PROFILE OF YOUR COMMUNITY

Divide the class into teams of six. Using the steps in the nominal grouping process, develop a strength/problem profile of your community. Prioritize the top five strengths and problems and present them to the overall class. Be sure that the problems identified are ones the community can do something about.

Next, choose one of the top-ranked problems and develop an action plan to solve it. A good action plan deals with who, what, when, where, and how. Present your action plan to the class.

NOTE: If this assignment is done in class, it will take more than one hour.

ENDNOTES

1. This case is an excerpt from Donald C. Mosley, "System Four Revisited: Some New Insights," *Organization Development Journal* (Spring, 1987): 19–20. Reproduced with permission.
2. Daniel R. Dennison, "Bringing Corporate Culture to the Bottom Line," *Organization Dynamics* 13 (Autumn 1984): 5.
3. Doug Carroll, "Imports, Ford Rate Highest for Reliability," *USA Today* (March 24, 1987): 1B.
4. William Ouchi, *Theory Z* (Reading, MA: Addison-Wesley, 1981).
5. Chris Clegg, "Trip to Japan: A Synergistic Approach to Managing Human Resources," *Personnel Management* 8 (August 1986): 35–39.
6. Yukuo Takenaka, "How the Japanese Did It," *World, The Magazine for Decision Makers* (Peat Marwick, NY) 20 (Nov. 5, 1986): 27.
7. Rosabeth Moss Kanter, "Dilemmas of Managing Participation," *Organizational Dynamics* (Summer 1982): 4–27.

8. Rensis Likert, *The Human Organization* (New York: McGraw-Hill Book Co., 1967), 4–10.
9. The ideas for this section came from Charles H. Clark, *Idea Management: How to Motivate Creativity and Innovation* (New York: AMACOM, 1980).
10. One of the authors of this textbook was introduced to this technique by Mr. Rollie Boreman, Jr., chairman and CEO, and Dr. Robert L. Qualls, executive vice-president, during a consulting assignment with their company, Baldor Electric Company. Since that time, it has been successfully used a number of times.
11. This proposal was developed by IP task force team #2 (Keith Dunlap, Robert Holmes, Ennis Williams, Carl Trichel, and Carl Wilson).

SUGGESTIONS FOR FURTHER READING

Gordon, J. "The Creativity Craze." *Training* 23 (May 1986): 82.

Mutch, W. "Productivity Improvements Begin with Communication." *Plastics World* 44 (June 19, 1986): 55–57.

Rowan, R. *The Intuitive Manager*. Boston: Brown & Co., 1986.

Sullivan, J. J. "A Critique of Theory Z." *Academy of Management Review* 8, No. 1 (January 1983): 133.

20
STRESS AND TIME MANAGEMENT

OBJECTIVES

After reading and studying the material in this chapter, you should be able to:

- Explain why life today makes us particularly vulnerable to stress.
- Describe both the costs and the positive benefits of stress.
- Explain the major causes of stress.
- Compare and contrast Type A behavior and Type B behavior.
- Elaborate on personal ways to cope with stress.
- Discuss ways a supervisor can effectively manage stress within the unit.
- Identify your biggest personal time wasters.
- Explain the steps you can take to manage your time better.

IMPORTANT TERMS

stress
job stress
major life event
Type A behavior

Type B behavior
relaxation response
concept of balance
time management

CHAPTER OUTLINE
CASE 20–1. THE MISSED PROMOTION

CASE 20-1
THE MISSED PROMOTION

Susan Williamson was worried. For the past six months, her husband, Paul, had been a different person from the man she married. Up until that time, Paul had been a cheerful and caring husband and father. He took an interest in their children, was active in church, and had a zest for day-to-day living. In recent months he had been moody, abrupt, and withdrawn. He spent his time at home watching television and drinking beer. He never talked about his job as maintenance supervisor at the ABC Company as he once had. Recently Susan asked if something at work was bothering him and, if so, whether he would discuss it with her. His reply was: "No, there's nothing bothering me! You take care of the house and the children, and I'll take care of the job and making a living!"

Actually the job had been bothering Paul for about a year. Before that, he was considered to be one of the outstanding maintenance supervisors. In those days his two immediate superiors, the maintenance superintendent and the maintenance manager, called on him frequently for advice and used him as a troubleshooter within the plant. Although Paul did not have a college degree in engineering, the maintenance manager had strongly hinted that when the maintenance superintendent retired, Paul would be promoted to his position. The maintenance manager had told Paul that, despite having three engineering graduates in the supervision group, he considered Paul the best in the department.

A year ago, the situation changed. The maintenance manager was transferred to another plant. A new maintenance manager came aboard and, from the start, favored college graduates. Gradually Paul was used less and less for troubleshooting assignments, and his advice was rarely sought. Six months earlier, the maintenance superintendent had retired and a young engineering graduate Paul had trained was promoted to the superintendent's job. It was then that Paul's personality had changed. Paul began sleeping longer each night, often falling asleep in front of the television set. He also developed a tightness in his stomach that was creating a burning sensation.

Paul Williamson's job stress has certainly affected other aspects of his life, hasn't it? A supervisor is particularly vulnerable to on-the-job stress. He or she is on the firing line and has pressures from employees, perhaps a union steward, and higher-level management. A supervisor not only is susceptible to personal stress, but also is in a position to create considerable stress on the employees being supervised. How well stress is managed plays a role in how successful the supervisor will be in achieving organizational objectives.

A number of the concepts we have presented in the book provide insight into how to manage stress. This chapter explores stress in more depth and provides additional insight into managing and coping with the problem.

WHAT IS STRESS?

In the past decade, more attention has been directed toward the unhealthy aspects of both on- and off-the-job stress and its impact on individuals, organizations, and society. For example, the June 16 and 19, 1987, issues of *USA TODAY* devoted special reports to stress and the world of work. In this section, we will define stress, point out its costs, and examine the positive role that stress can play.

Definition of Stress

The medical community for many years neglected to take stress seriously. One of the reasons for this was the lack of an adequate definition of stress and a lack of research into its effects. **Stress** may be defined as any external stimulus that causes wear and tear on one's psychological or physical well-being.[1]

Stress researchers point out that modern men and women sometimes react to the strains of work and everyday life the same way our primitive ancestors did. In the days of the caveman, when there was danger, the body geared itself for either fight or flight. A chemical reaction in the body allowed our ancestors to cope adequately with danger until it was over. The problem for modern men and women is that, because of reactions to external stimuli, some of us maintain a constant fight-or-flight readiness. It would be similar to the anxiety of soldiers in combat, and this causes wear and tear on our bodies.

Jane Coleman was driving to work during the morning rush hour. An irresponsible driver nearly caused an accident by cutting into her lane. By the time she arrived at work, she was already tense; the problem was compounded when she discovered one of her key employees was out with the flu. Two emergencies during the day caused her to end the day anxious and exhausted.

Jane's situation can be duplicated for many of us. Thus, stress can be caused not only by an external stimulus (driving on the freeway) but also by conditions on the job. An excellent definition of **job stress** is "a condition arising from the interaction of people and their jobs and . . . characterized by changes within people that force them to deviate from their normal functioning."[2] Under normal conditions, our body and mind are in a state of equilibrium (see Figure 20–1).

FIGURE 20–1 EQUILIBRIUM AND DISEQUILBRIUM

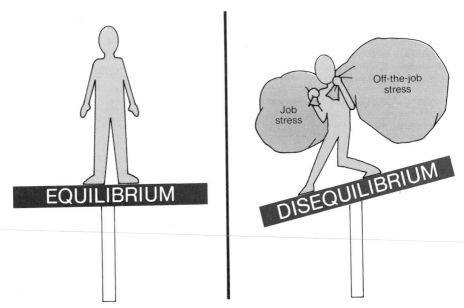

However, as a result of occurrences or events on or off the job, our equilibrium may be disrupted. In attempting to recover from this imbalance, we function differently and sometimes generate a fight-or-flight chemical reaction. Obviously Jane, as a supervisor, cannot leave her job or pick a fight with someone, but the chemical reaction in her body occurs anyway.

The Costs of Stress

It has been estimated that two-thirds of all visits to doctors can be traced to stress-related symptoms. Stress, for example, is a major contributor to heart disease, cancer, lung problems, accidents, cirrhosis of the liver, and suicide. Even the common cold and skin rashes are sometimes related to a person's experiencing prolonged and severe stress. Industry leaders are aware that such symptoms play a major role in absenteeism, accidents, and lost productivity. *Time* magazine notes that "these costs have been estimated at $50 billion to $75 billion a year, more than $750 for every U.S. worker."[3]

Certainly a person under severe and/or prolonged stress cannot function as effectively as a person leading a more balanced life. However, we are not implying that stress is all negative, because a certain amount of stress adds zest to life.

The Positive Aspects of Stress

Some amount of stress is necessary to accomplish anything meaningful. The teams that play in the Super Bowl are certainly in a stressful situation. All of us who have played sports or participated in activities that required speaking to large groups have been in stressful situations. Without question, moderate amounts of stress improve performance. For example, setting difficult but attainable objectives motivates us better than setting easy objectives.

People differ in the amounts and types of stress they can handle. Jet pilots and astronauts thrive in careers that others would find extremely stressful. It is well documented that the supervisor's job is one that is considered to be highly stressful. The secret is to manage stress properly and to develop ways to cope with it.

MAJOR CAUSES OF STRESS

A number of factors contribute to individual stress. Among these are (1) life events, (2) personal psychological makeup, and (3) organizational and work-related factors.

Life Events

Stress occurs whenever we face situations that require changes in behavior and a higher level of activity. It would be impossible to list all the situations that place stress on human beings since the mere fact of living does that. However, researchers have identified major life events that require changes in a person's behavior. These events can be either positive or negative. But, if a large number of these events occur within a year's time, a person becomes particularly susceptible to unpleasant physical or psychological consequences of excessive stress.

Table 20–1 lists a number of stress-provoking life events. A **major life event** is anything that causes a person to deviate from normal functioning. The events are ranked in order of impact on a person's life. The death of a spouse would have the most impact; and minor violations of the law, such as a traffic ticket, would cause the least stress.

TABLE 20–1   LIFE EVENTS FROM THE SOCIAL READJUSTMENT RATING SCALE

Events	Scale of Impact		Scale of Impact
Death of spouse	100	Change in health of family	
Divorce	73	member	44
Marital separation	65	Pregnancy	40
Jail term	63	Sex difficulties	39
Death of close family member	63	Gain of new family member	39
Personal injury or illness	53	Business readjustment	39
Marriage	50	Change in financial state	38
Fired at work	47	Death of close friend	37
Marital reconciliation	45	Change to different line	
Retirement	45	of work	36

TABLE 20–1   (continued)

Events	Scale of Impact	Events	Scale of Impact
Change in number of arguments with spouse	35	Change in work hours or conditions	20
Mortgage over $10,000	31	Change in residence	20
Foreclosure of mortgage or loan	30	Change in schools	20
		Change in recreation	19
Change in responsibilities at work	29	Change in church activities	19
Son or daughter leaving home	29	Change in social activities	18
Trouble with in-laws	29	Mortgage or loan less than $10,000	17
Outstanding personal achievement	28	Change in sleeping habits	16
Wife begins or stops work	26	Change in number of family get-togethers	15
Begin or end school	26	Change in eating habits	15
Change in living conditions	25	Vacation	13
Revision of personal habits	24	Christmas	12
Trouble with boss	23	Minor violations of the law	11

Source: "The Stress of Adjusting to Change" from *The Relaxation Response* by Herbert Benson, M.D., with Miriam Z. Klipper. Copyright 1975 by William Morrow Company, Inc. By permission of the publisher.

Patrick Hogan was a 34-year-old supervisor who seemed to have it all. He had a good job, was happily married, had two children, and was on top of the world. At work, he was highly productive and outgoing and was considered a leading candidate for advancement.

In the course of a year, several events occurred in Patrick's life that completely disrupted his patterns of living. A long-time friend enticed him to invest in a steak house that his friend would operate. The restaurant lost money, and his friend left town, leaving Patrick responsible for the bank note. In order to save his investment, he started moonlighting at the restaurant, not getting home many nights until 1:00 a.m.

While Patrick was struggling with the restaurant, his mother died after a lingering illness. Two weeks after the funeral, his wife had an accident and was confined to bed with a slipped disc. For the first time in his life, Patrick had to prepare meals, wash clothes, and care for the children while at the same time carrying on with his regular job and struggling with the restaurant.

At work, Patrick's behavior changed drastically. He was impatient with his employees and lost his temper quickly. He became depressed and found it difficult to reach decisions about matters that he had previously handled decisively.

If Patrick Hogan talked to you about his situation, what advice would you give him?

In Case 20–1, Paul Williamson also had a drastic change in behavior. Would you give Paul the same advice you give Patrick, or would it be different?

Later in the chapter, we will offer some insight into how both Patrick and Paul could more effectively cope with their situations.

Personal Psychological Makeup

Americans have long been noted for their emphasis on work. The United States has a justifiable reputation as a country where individuals, through hard work, can achieve considerable economic success. This emphasis has led to considerable accomplishments in all facets of life. Some of us have become so caught up in the work ethic that work becomes the end itself rather than the means to an end. New Zealanders say that "Americans live to work and New Zealanders work to live." Our point is that some of us have become "workaholics," and this has behavioral consequences that take a toll over a period of time.

Researchers have identified two basic types of behaviors characterizing people in our society: Type A and Type B.

TYPE A BEHAVIOR. Cardiologists Meyer Friedman and Roy Rosenman first identified the term **Type A behavior**. Type A individuals have two important characteristics. First, they tend to try to accomplish too many things in a short time. Second, they lack patience and struggle against time and other people to accomplish their ends. As a consequence, they become irritated by trivial things. Type A people also have a tendency to be workaholics. Their psychological makeup tends to cause them to be particularly subject to stress over prolonged periods. For this reason, Type A people have a much higher risk factor for heart disease than Type B people.[4]

TYPE B BEHAVIOR. People exhibiting Type B behavior tend to be calmer, to take more time to exercise, and to be more realistic than Type As in estimating the amount of time it takes to complete an assignment. Type Bs also worry less and, in general, desire more satisfaction from their work.[5]

Sample studies of "A" and "B" behaviors indicate that 60 percent of managers and supervisors fall into the category of Type A behavior. Thus, many supervisors are constantly responding to events as if they were in an emergency or life-threatening situation. Managers and supervisors who exhibit extreme Type A behavior patterns tend to practice close supervision and find it difficult to delegate. They are concerned that errors might reflect on past achievements, and so they become excessively task-oriented.[6]

Do you think of yourself as a Type A or a Type B personality? Table 20–2 provides a quiz that will give you a rough idea of your behavioral pattern.

TABLE 20–2   BEHAVIOR TYPE QUIZ

To find out which behavior type you are, circle the number on the scale below that best characterizes your behavior for each trait.

1. Casual about appointments	1	2	3	4	5	6	7	8	Never late
2. Not competitive	1	2	3	4	5	6	7	8	Very competitive
3. Never feel rushed even under pressure	1	2	3	4	5	6	7	8	Always rushed
4. Take things one at a time	1	2	3	4	5	6	7	8	Try to do many things at once, think about what I am going to do next
5. Slow doing things	1	2	3	4	5	6	7	8	Fast (eating, walking, etc.)
6. Express feelings	1	2	3	4	5	6	7	8	"Sit on" feelings
7. Many interests	1	2	3	4	5	6	7	8	Few interests outside work

Total your score: _____   Multiply it by 3: _____

The interpretation is as follows:

Number of Points	Type of Personality
Less than 90	B
90 to 99	B +
100 to 105	A −
106 to 119	A
120 or more	A +

Source: A. P. Brief, R. S. Schuler, and M. V. Sell, *Managing Job Stress* (Boston: Little, Brown & Co., 1981), 87.

Organizational and Work-Related Factors

Throughout this book we have discussed many organizational and work-related factors that cause excessive stress. As shown in Figure 20–2, these may range from an organization's having poorly defined position descriptions to autocratic leadership, and even permissive leadership. If these factors exist in an organization over a period of time, they will cause extensive damage in the form of dissatisfaction, higher turnover, lower productivity, and incomplete goal accomplishment.

FIGURE 20–2   ORGANIZATIONAL AND WORK–RELATED FACTORS THAT CAUSE
EXCESSIVE STRESS

- A highly centralized organization with decision making concentrated at the top.
- Many levels and narrow spans of control.
- Excessive and continuous pressure from higher levels.
- Conflicting demands on lower levels.
- Lack of clarity with respect to organizational and work objectives.
- Widespread autocratic leadership and close supervision.
- Little or no participation in decision making by supervisors and workers.
- Inconsistent application of company policies.
- Favoritism in decisions regarding layoffs, salary increases, promotions, and the like.
- Poor working conditions.
- Poor communication.
- Lack of structure and job descriptions.
- Widespread permissive leadership.

From the list in Figure 20–2, what factor(s) do you think were responsible for the change in Paul Williamson's behavior in Case 20–1?

As the following situation shows, stress can even open an opportunity for union activity.

A union organizer approached several employees from the home office of XYZ Life & Casualty Insurance Company. He was quickly told that they were not interested in joining a union since they had excellent pay, good working conditions, and a high regard for their supervisors.

Six months later, a supervisor retired in the claims department. The new supervisor, after being on the job a month, called two long-time employees into the office and gave them a dismissal notice without a reason for doing so. That night, five employees drove 90 miles for a meeting in another city with the union organizer. Upon their return, they obtained enough employee signatures to force an election to see if the union would represent employees in the XYZ home office.

PERSONAL WAYS TO COPE WITH STRESS

A supervisor can cope with stress in numerous ways. Several methods that have worked very well in the past are (1) physical exercise, (2) the relaxation response, and (3) gaining a sense of control.

Physical Exercise

People who exercise a minimum of two or three times a week are much less prone to the adverse symptoms of stress than those who do not. The exercise should be vigorous to the point of developing perspiration. A person's muscles and circulatory system are not designed for a life of inactivity. If you revitalize your body, you will have much less chance of worrying and becoming upset over events and problems. You can choose from among many forms of exercise— tennis, handball, jogging, walking, swimming, gardening, or simply joining a health and exercise spa.

> *Earlier in the chapter, we highlighted the problems Patrick Hogan was facing and saw how the stress of dealing with these problems had drastically changed his behavior. Patrick's manager noticed the change and counseled him regarding the situation. After Patrick had discussed his circumstances, the manager asked him if he engaged in regular exercise. Patrick answered that he simply did not have the time as a result of having to moonlight at the restaurant.*
>
> *Patrick's manager persuaded him to work out three times a week in the company exercise room (see Figure 20–3). Within two weeks' time, Patrick's on-the-job behavior was back to normal, and he began developing a plan to cope with some of the problems outside of work.*

The Relaxation Response

Several years ago, Herbert Benson, M.D., wrote a book called *The Relaxation Response*. Among other things, the book described a simple meditative technique that helps relieve tensions, enables one to deal more effectively with stress, lowers blood pressure, and, in general, improves physical and emotional health. This technique is particularly useful to supervisors because it is neither time-consuming nor costly. All it involves is finding a quiet place and practicing the technique for 10 to 20 minutes once or twice a day.

Research by Dr. Benson and others validates that the **relaxation response** not only relieves hypertension but also acts as a mechanism for counteracting the stressful events of life that provoke the fight-or-flight response (see Figure 20–4).

FIGURE 20–3   COPING WITH STRESS

In the words of Dr. Benson, the method of bringing forth the relaxation response is as follows:

1. Sit quietly in a comfortable position.
2. Close your eyes.
3. Deeply relax all your muscles, beginning at your feet and progressing up to your face. Keep them relaxed.

FIGURE 20–4   RELAXING AS A MEANS OF COPING WITH STRESS

4. Breathe through your nose. Become aware of your breathing. As you breathe out, say the word "one" silently to yourself. For example, breathe in . . . out, "one," in . . . out, "one," etc. Breathe easily and naturally.

5. Continue for 10 to 20 minutes. You may open your eyes to check the time, but do not use an alarm clock. When you finish, sit quietly for several minutes, first with your eyes closed and later with your eyes opened. Wait a few minutes before standing up.

6. Do not worry about whether you are successful in achieving a deep level of relaxation. Maintain a passive attitude and permit relaxation to occur at its own pace. When distracting thoughts occur, try to ignore them by not dwelling upon them, and return to repeating "one."[7]

Gaining a Sense of Control

Supervisors and others who have a sense of control over their own lives handle stress much better than people who feel they are manipulated by life's events or by other people. These supervisors look at work as only one aspect of life and have other interests. Many of them also have a deep faith in a religion that allows them to cope with adversity. Specifically, some of the things that can be done to gain control are as follows:

1. Planning, which involves looking ahead and identifying both life and short-term goals. It also includes identifying things that are causing stress and identifying ways to alleviate the causes.

2. Getting to know and like yourself. Identify your strengths and interests and pursue activities that capitalize on your strengths.

3. Perceiving situations as challenges rather than problems.

4. Taking a long vacation rather than a series of short vacations.

5. Doing things for others, either through the church or by becoming involved in some kind of volunteer work or youth activities such as Boy or Girl Scouts, Big Brother or Big Sister, or Junior Achievement.

6. Finally, providing yourself with positive reinforcement when you do something well. Treat yourself to a reward when you accomplish something worthwhile.

THE SUPERVISOR AND THE CONCEPT OF BALANCE

The organization as a whole can manage stress by developing organizational strategies that focus on improving such things as communication, organizational structure, and managerial behavior. However, we'd like to focus our emphasis on what a supervisor can do to manage and cope with stress in his or her unit. Our task is made easier because, in previous chapters, we have already dealt with many ways this can be accomplished—effective delegation, effective team building, and effective communication. So our emphasis will be on a concept that, in our judgment, is neglected both in practice and in the management literature—the concept of balance.

Generally the **concept of balance** states that, in many work-related decision areas, the best condition is a state of equilibrium between extremes. The concept does not rule out flexibility. On the contrary, it is a supervisor's ability to be flexible in diagnosing and deciding on a strategy that balances conflicting needs or directions.

Earlier in this textbook, we made a strong case for leadership strategies that are determined by the demands of the situation and the maturity level of followers. We also indicated that in today's business world, with employees having higher educational levels, more and more situations call for a strategy of participative management (team building). It is well documented that prolonged autocratic or permissive leadership will have unfavorable consequences for both organizations and individuals. Figure 20–5 illustrates this point.

FIGURE 20–5   THE CONCEPT OF BALANCE APPLIED TO LEADERSHIP

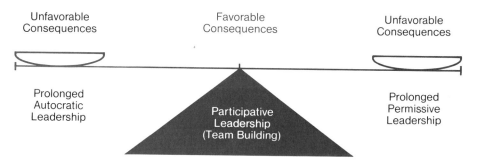

Let's demonstrate the concept of balance by focusing on a leadership example.

The manager of Plant X was of the old school and practiced autocratic leadership. After several months, his leadership style had been adopted by almost all the managers and supervisors under his jurisdiction. Continued and excessive pressure was directed downward through the various organization levels to the operative level. Production met standards for two years, until another new plant moved into the area. Then the new plant received applications from and hired many of the best employees of Plant X.

When production at Plant X fell below standard, the manager increased the pressure. Finally, the home office replaced the autocratic manager with a new person. The new manager examined production in various departments and discovered that Department C had not suffered the production decline and turnover of the other departments. Upon investigation, the new manager found that, while the other supervisors had pushed the pressure downward, the supervisor of Department C had resisted and continued to use a participative-supportive leadership style.

This illustration is based on a true case in which the concept of balance was used effectively by a supervisor. The concept can also be applied in areas of delegation, performance appraisal, communication, and discipline. Obviously it requires the use of good judgment and common sense in its application. The successful use of balance will create an environment where people can grow, develop, and achieve; at the same time, it will alleviate the undesirable effects of excessive stress.

Another example of using the concept of balance relates to how a supervisor copes with anger. Anger is a natural emotion that is especially triggered by stressful conditions. Unfortunately many of us deal with anger in a manner that causes imbalance, and we suffer adverse consequences as a result. If a person becomes angry and erupts with language that is defensive, abusive, or degrading to the other person, then an imbalance has occurred. The following illustration demonstrates how a supervisor used the concept of balance in dealing with anger.

Sales supervisor Linda Williams was taking a coffee break when her boss, Jean Hardy, came in and accused her of a major cost error in dealing with a client. Although Linda became very angry since the accusation was not true, she counted to 10, smiled, and said she would look into it.

At the end of the day, Linda worked off some of her hostility toward her boss by slamming a tennis ball in a game with her son. The next day she looked into the problem and discovered that the error had been made in the accounting department. The error was corrected, and Linda then waited until Friday afternoon to discuss the matter with her boss. She chose this time because she was aware that there was less pressure on Jean at the end of the week. After hearing that the error had been corrected and that it had occurred in the accounting department, Jean apologized to Linda for her angry, incorrect accusation.

Linda demonstrated balance by neither falling into a trap of erupting in anger nor holding her anger within and perhaps taking it out on her family. Surely she was angry, but she transferred the anger to a tennis ball and then used a problem-solving approach in dealing with the matter.

Another way to gain balance and a sense of control is effective time management. Let us turn to this important area.

MANAGING YOUR TIME

In Chapter 1 we said that an organization's three resources are human, physical, and financial. Some management experts would include *time* as a fourth. Make no mistake about it, time is one of the greatest resources a supervisor has. **Time management** is the ability to use one's time to get things done *when* they should be done. Without this ability, all your other management skills are for naught. You may have excellent human relations skills, but poor time management may mean you're so easily distracted that you can't effectively listen to an employee's problems. Or your pressures keep you from thinking clearly enough to use your conceptual skills fully. You may not even be able to take the time to display your technical skills by showing a new employee the ropes. To be effective as a supervisor, then, you must make effective use of your time.

The Time Log: Where Your Time Goes

Time management experts say the best first step in making effective use of your time is to determine where your time actually goes. As shown in Figure 20–6,

FIGURE 20–6 DAILY TIME LOG

DAILY TIME LOG

Name _Harold Stevens_

Date _March 1, 198–_

On this log record each activity that you performed during the workday. Make sure that you include every activity performed such as telephone calls, conversations, rest breaks, reading, and so on. Do this for a period of time long enough to reflect normal "workdays." A week should normally be sufficient.

From – To	Minutes	Type of Activity	People Involved	Priority A	B	C
8:00 – 8:05	5	Talked in hall	Dan, Patsy			
8:05 – 8:15	10	Read status report on work progress				
8:15 – 8:20	5	Checked progress on slow job	Ronald			
8:20 – 8:30	10	Prepared for supt. meeting				
8:30 – 9:30	60	Attended supt. meeting	Dept. heads & Supt.			
9:30 – 9:45	15	Coffee	Al, Peter, Karen			
9:45 – 9:50	5	Tried to return two phone calls -- no luck				
9:50 – 10:02	12	Completed questionnaire from Personnel Dept.				
10:02 – 10:06	4	Went for mail				
10:06 – 10:20	14	Opened & read mail				
10:20 – 10:23	3	Called Purchasing Dept. to check status of order	Kawahara			
10:23 – 10:50	27	Discussion with Supt. about objectives for dept.	McWilliams			
10:50 – 11:00	10	Visited Personnel office to check status of applicants	Alice			
11:00 – 11:55	55	Met with United Way Committee	too many !			
11:55 – 12:10	15	Began work on dept. budget proposal				
12:10 – 12:50	40	Lunch	Dan, Patsy, Al			
—						
—						

an illustrative **time log** that is filled in conscientiously can be an excellent basis for seeing how your time is utilized.

Setting Priorities: A "Must"

Once you know where your time goes, you can analyze whether it's going in the proper direction. Not everyone can do all that he or she wants to do. The secret, then, is to spend time on those activities that are most meaningful and that contribute most significantly to your doing a top-notch job.

> *Harold Stevens said he couldn't find enough time to do everything he wanted to do because he was so busy. Yet, when he got home, he looked at his day and called it "wheel spinning." He didn't feel at all good about what he had accomplished. The point is that Harold, like many supervisors, had spent his typical day handling many low-priority rather than high-priority activities!*

Let's establish a rating system for classifying the priority of activities to be performed in a given day:

1. "A" priorities are the most important, most critical to your job.
2. "B" priorities are those of medium priority—important, but not like As.
3. "C" priorities are low-priority, routine, and/or *relatively* unimportant.

The efficient supervisor will spend a greater percentage of his or her time performing "A" activities. Note how well this worked for Charles Schwab, former president of Bethlehem Steel.

> *R. Alec Mackenzie, a noted management consultant, in his best-selling book, The Time Trap, tells an interesting story about how time management worked for Charles Schwab, then president of Bethlehem Steel. Schwab presented Ivy Lee, a management consultant, with the unusual challenge of showing Schwab how to get more done with his time. Lee asked Schwab for a sheet of paper and asked him to write down the most important tasks he had to perform the next day, then to number them in the order of their importance. He then told Schwab that, on getting to work in the morning, he should begin task Number 1 and stick with it until he finished it. Then he was to recheck his priority list and start on item Number 2. The important thing was to keep working on the most important task until it was done.*
>
> *"If this system works for you," Lee said, "have your other people also use it. Try it as long as you like. Then send me your check for what you think it's worth." Some weeks later, Lee received a check from Schwab for $25,000, along with the message that the lesson was the most profitable he had ever learned![8]*

Many of the "brush fires" to which supervisors devote a large percentage of their time are "B" or perhaps even "C" priority items. In the next section, we hope to help you learn to spend more of your time on your "As"!

Examine the list of activities shown in Figure 20–6. Identify an "A" activity and a "C" activity. What types of activities has Harold spent more time on?

Handling the Common Time Wasters

During a typical day, many activities, or **time wasters**, occur that are inefficient uses of your time (see Figure 20–7). These may include performing routine work that someone else could handle, excessive "socializing," or fighting a losing battle against paperwork, as shown in Figure 20–8.

Supervisory jobs vary a great deal in terms of the demands on the supervisor's time. That's why a time log is an important first step in diagnosing your time management habits. We've put together a broad list of "Do's" that may be helpful in using your time more effectively:

1. *Set priorities.*
   a. Establish "A," "B," and "C" priorities.
   b. Determine daily priorities.
   c. Focus effort on high-priority items.

FIGURE 20–7   TEN COMMON SUPERVISORY TIME WASTERS

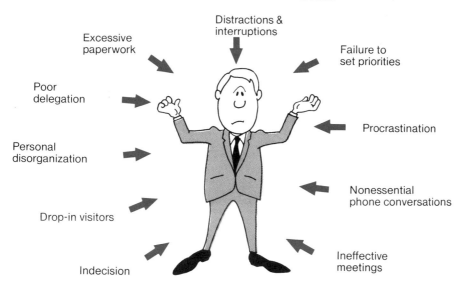

FIGURE 20–8 BURIED UNDER

2. *Don't procrastinate.*
    a. Break big jobs into smaller parts.
    b. Get started, even if on a minor part.
    c. Do the more unpleasant parts first.
    d. Reward yourself for doing things on schedule (break, candy bar).
3. *Manage the telephone effectively.*
    a. Have someone else take your calls and handle them if possible.
    b. Handle all return calls at set times of day.
    c. Accept calls only at certain times of day.
4. *Make your meetings effective.*
    a. Prepare an agenda.
    b. Announce the agenda in advance.
    c. Begin meetings on time.
    d. Stick to the topics on the agenda.
    e. Make decisions or come to conclusions.
5. *Learn to delegate.*
    a. Delegate details that are time-consuming.
    b. Delegate jobs that will help employees to develop.
    c. Delegate low-priority responsibilities.
    d. Delegate jobs that employees can perform better than you.
6. *Handle people who "drop in."*
    a. Close your door for periods of time.
    b. Keep books or materials on visitors' chairs to prevent them from sitting down and "locking in."

    c. Stand up and remain standing until visitor leaves.

    d. For long-winded persons, meet them at *their work area*, where you can leave when you're ready.

    e. Train your boss and work group to respect your time.

7. *Be decisive.*

    a. Set a personal deadline for making a decision.

    b. Once you have the facts, make the decision.

8. *Get organized.*

    a. Use a daily planner (see Figure 20–9).

    b. Implement a "filing" system.

    c. See 1(b) above.

9. *Stay on top of paperwork.*

    a. Handle papers only once!

    b. Handle papers at a fixed time each day.

    c. Handwrite short notes directly on original documents and forward them to the persons concerned.

    d. Have a secretary or assistant classify papers according to importance and route them for you.

10. *Avoid distractions and interruptions.*

    a. Keep a neat desk; work and papers piled on it are distracting.

    b. Try to set aside uninterrupted blocks of time.

    c. See 3(c) above.

    d. See 6(a) above.

    e. Face your desk away from view of others.

CHAPTER REVIEW

Stress involves any external stimulus that causes wear and tear on a person to the extent that it can possibly result in internal damage. Modern men and women react to stress like the cavemen, with either a fight-or-flight reaction. Obviously we cannot flee or fight in normal situations; so we need to develop other ways to cope with and manage stress.

When we are unsuccessful in coping with stress, the costs are enormous. Stress is a major cause of many illnesses, ranging from the common cold to heart disease. It also plays a role in absenteeism, accidents, and lost productivity. However, we should not assume that all stress is negative. Small and great achievements occur as a result of moderate amounts of stress. If we never faced anything that challenged us or caused us to look to our inner resources, we would all be like vegetables.

Major causes of stress can come from life events, personal psychological makeup, and organizational and work-related factors. The death of a spouse or a divorce

FIGURE 20–9 EXAMPLE OF DAILY PLANNING AID

To do today	Today's schedule	Time	Notes about scheduled events
DAILY PLANNER			April 23, 198–
1. Get photocopies for supt. meeting		8:00	
		8:15	
		8:30	
2. Fill out performance evaluations for new positions	Superintendent meeting	8:45	
		9:00	Need to give report on
		9:15	safety at April 30
		9:30	meeting -- 3 to 5
3. Write out procedure for handling maintenance request	Meet with Wilson for arbitration hearing	9:45	minutes long
		10:00	
		10:15	
		10:30	
4. Call Payroll about mix-up in overtime		10:45	
		11:00	Didn't get to --
		11:15	need to do tomorrow
		11:30	
		11:45	
5 Contact department heads about United Way		12:00	
		12:15	
		12:30	
		12:45	
	Crew safety meeting	1:00	At next meeting
		1:15	Anderson will give
Notes for Record		1:30	fire hazard demo.
Need to check status of P.O. #135 -- overdue	Interview applicant for forklift	1:45	
		2:00	Not bad. Seem to
		2:15	favor him over other
Call Maintenance about noisy air-conditioner blower		2:30	candidates so far
		2:45	
		3:00	
		3:15	
Harrison was 10 minutes late; next time, oral warning	Meet with Purchasing about new policy	3:30	
		3:45	Got this one squared
		4:00	away. No need for
		4:15	us to get Purchasing's
#2 Machine down 10 minutes		4:30	approval of items
		4:45	under $20

places tremendous stress on most individuals. Similarly, an extremely high-pressure work environment under prolonged autocratic leadership can cause difficulties.

A person's psychological makeup influences how that person handles stress. Type A behavior characterizes a person who tries to accomplish too many things in a short period of time and who tends to lack patience in dealing with people and time. Type B people tend to be calmer and more realistic in their assessment of the length of time it will take to complete an assignment.

Fortunately many of us can do a better job in managing stress if we develop certain strategies and behaviors. On a personal level, we can (1) exercise, (2) practice the relaxation response, and (3) gain a sense of control over our lives.

On the job, a supervisor can practice many of the concepts discussed throughout this book. Particularly helpful in reducing stress in a work unit is to practice the concept of balance through participative management when appropriate and to delegate effectively without losing control.

One of a supervisor's greatest resources is time. A time log is a necessary first step toward becoming a more efficient "time manager." This enables a supervisor to see exactly where his or her time is being spent. Effective supervisors spend a greater proportion of their time on "A" priorities—those that are ranked number one in terms of importance to the effective performance of their jobs. A number of time-saving tips are: (1) set priorities, (2) don't procrastinate, (3) manage the telephone effectively, (4) make your meetings effective, (5) delegate to others, (6) handle people who "drop in," (7) be decisive, (8) get organized, (9) stay on top of paperwork, and (10) avoid distractions and interruptions.

QUESTIONS FOR REVIEW AND DISCUSSION

1. Discuss stress from the standpoint of what it is, its costs, and its benefits.
2. What are the major causes of stress on the job? Off the job?
3. Compare and contrast Type A behavior and Type B behavior.
4. Explain why exercise and the relaxation response are helpful in coping with stress.
5. Gaining a sense of control over one's life has been discovered to be effective in managing stress. What are some ways to gain control over your life?
6. What can a supervisor do to prevent stress in his or her work unit?
7. Under what conditions would resigning from a supervisory position and seeking a position elsewhere become a worthwhile solution to excessive job stress? From the information in Case 20–1, do you think Paul Williamson should consider seeking a position with another company?
8. A time management expert called on supervisor Andrea Stone, whose hand was raised. "You say I should determine my priorities for the day and work only on those. That sounds good. But what happens when the vice-president walks in and says, 'I want you to look over this and give me your ideas by this afternoon.' What he's given me isn't on my list of priorities; in fact, it may not really be important at all. What do I do then?" asked Andrea. What do you think the time management expert's answer would be? Explain.

LEARNING EXERCISE 20–1
A PLANNING STRATEGY TO COPE WITH STRESS

Consider your life at the present time and list the things that are causing stress. Diagnose which factors are causing positive stress and which are potentially negative and harmful.

Develop an action plan that will enable you to cope with the negative factors more effectively. A good action plan looks ahead and deals with what, when, where, and how.

LEARNING EXERCISE 20–2
HOW VULNERABLE TO STRESS ARE YOU?

The following test consisting of 20 items was developed by psychologists Lyle H. Miller and Alma Dell Smith at Boston University Medical Center. According to how much of the time each statement in the test applies to you, score each item 1 (for *almost always*) to 5 (for *never*).

Stress Test*

_____ 1. I eat at least one hot, balanced meal a day.
_____ 2. I get seven to eight hours' sleep at least four nights a week.
_____ 3. I give and receive affection regularly.
_____ 4. I have at least one relative within 50 miles on whom I can rely.
_____ 5. I exercise to the point of perspiration at least twice a week.
_____ 6. I smoke less than half a pack of cigarettes a day.
_____ 7. I take fewer than five alcoholic drinks a week.
_____ 8. I have the appropriate weight for my height.
_____ 9. I have an income adequate to meet basic expenses.
_____ 10. I get strength from my religious beliefs.
_____ 11. I regularly attend club or social activities.
_____ 12. I have a network of friends and acquaintances.
_____ 13. I have one or more friends to confide in about personal matters.
_____ 14. I am in good health (including eyesight, hearing, teeth).
_____ 15. I am able to speak openly about my feelings when angry or worried.
_____ 16. I have regular conversations with the people I live with about domestic problems, e.g., chores, money, and daily living issues.
_____ 17. I do something for fun at least once a week.
_____ 18. I am able to organize my time effectively.
_____ 19. I drink fewer than three cups of coffee (or tea or cola drinks) a day.
_____ 20. I take quiet time for myself during the day.

*Source: "Vulnerability Scale" from the *Stress Audit*, developed by Lyle H. Miller and Alma Dell Smith. Copyright 1983, Biobehavioral Associates, Brookline, MA. Reprinted with permission.

Add up your scores for the 20 items. Then, to get your *final* score, subtract 20 from your total score. Any final score over 30 indicates a vulnerability to stress. You are seriously vulnerable if it is over 75.

LEARNING EXERCISE 20–3
CORRECTING THE TIME WASTERS

Examine the list of 10 supervisory time traps in Figure 20–7 on page 501. If you are presently employed, complete the exercise below. Identify the three biggest time wasters for you and then try to come up with three creative ways to deal with each of them. If you are not employed, interview a supervisor or manager and ask him or her to complete the exercise. Be prepared to discuss your findings in class.

Top Three Time Wasters	Corrective Steps
1.	a.
	b.
	c.
2.	a.
	b.
	c.
3.	a.
	b.
	c.

ENDNOTES

1. Claudia Wallis, "Stress: Can We Cope?" *Time* (June 6, 1983): 48–54.
2. A. P. Brief, R. S. Schuler, and M. V. Sell, *Managing Job Stress* (Boston: Little, Brown, & Co., 1981), 2.
3. Wallis, *op. cit.*, "Stress: Can We Cope?" 48.
4. *Ibid.*, 52.
5. Brief, Schuler, and Sell, *op. cit.*, *Managing Job Stress*, 86.
6. W. W. Suojanen and Donald R. Hudson, "Coping with Stress and Addictive Work Behavior," *Business* (College of Business Administration, Georgia State University) 31 (January-February 1980): 11.
7. Herbert Benson and Miriam Z. Klipper, *The Relaxation Response* (New York: William Morrow & Co., 1975), 114–15.
8. R. Alec MacKenzie, *The Time Trap* (New York: McGraw-Hill Book Co., 1975), 38–39.

SUGGESTIONS FOR FURTHER READING

Brody, R. "Keep Cool in Hot Spots." *Executive Female* 9 (July-August 1986): 33 + .

Charlesworth, E. A., and R. G. Nathan. *Stress Management*. New York: Ballantine Books, 1984.

Eckles, R. W. "Stress—Making Friend with the Enemy?" *Business Horizons* 30, No. 2 (March-April 1987): 74–78.

Jenner, J. R. "On the Way to Stress Resistance." *Training and Development Journal* 40 (May 1986): 112–15.

MacKenzie, R. Alec. *The Time Trap*. New York: McGraw-Hill Book Co., 1975.

"The Positive Side of Stress." *Marketing Communications* 11 (May 1986): 71.

21
CAREERS IN SUPERVISORY MANAGEMENT

OBJECTIVES

After reading and studying the material in this chapter, you should be able to:

- Recognize the need to plan for your career in supervisory management.
- Understand how to develop an effective career strategy.
- Know the career opportunities in supervisory management in the near future.
- Appreciate the need for a college education as the basis of a supervisory career.

IMPORTANT TERMS

career management
career planning
career development
career path

mentor *or* patron
networking
career strategy

CHAPTER OUTLINE
CASE 21-1. A CAREER IN SUPERVISION?

I. NEED FOR CAREER MANAGEMENT
   A. Why the emphasis on career management?
   B. Who is responsible for your career management?
      1. Role of mentoring
      2. Role of networking

II. CHOOSING A CAREER IN SUPERVISORY MANAGEMENT
   A. What is an effective career strategy?
      1. It should be flexible
      2. It should be based on experience
      3. It should be inclusive
   B. Steps in developing a career strategy
      1. Identify your opportunities
      2. Inventory your competencies and resources
      3. Clarify your ambitions and hopes
      4. Acknowledge your obligations
      5. Recognize your personal values

III. CAREER OPPORTUNITIES IN SUPERVISORY MANAGEMENT
   A. Favorable industries
   B. Favorable occupations

IV. OPPORTUNITIES IN SUPERVISORY MANAGEMENT FOR COLLEGE GRADUATES
   A. Why get a college degree?
   B. Trends in job opportunities for college graduates

Chapter Review

Questions for Review and Discussion

Learning Exercise 21-1. The Returnee

Learning Exercise 21-2. Chance for Promotion?

Suggestions for Further Reading

Hitch your wagon to a star.
Ralph Waldo Emerson

The emergence and decline of occupations will be so rapid that people will always be uncertain in them.
Norman Auon

One-half of you will work in jobs not even in existence now.
Dudley Hile (1964)

CASE 21–1
A CAREER IN SUPERVISION?

John Brantley was one of eight hourly personnel selected by AMP, Inc., to attend a presupervisory training course conducted for people who had been identified as having potential to move into supervision. The course, which consisted of 15 hours of class instruction, was taught by the company's training department. The topics covered were the role of the supervisor, communication, discipline, delegation, and others.

AMP, Inc., was rumored to be offering an attractive early retirement package for salaried personnel, and a number of supervisors would be in the age range that favored it. Therefore, John knew that being selected to attend the course was a sign that he might soon be offered a position in supervision. There was no question about it: The course definitely forced John to start thinking about the possibility of a new career.

Since he joined the company five years earlier with two years of junior college under his belt, John had worked in the warehouse as an inventory clerk and had spent the last two years as a quality inspector. He had never really planned for a career; things had simply fallen into place. Since supervision would certainly open up some different doors and mean a career change, John wondered if this was really for him.

Like John Brantley, many people never prepare for a specific career in supervision. It seems that an opportunity presents itself and it "just happens." Since you are reading this book, however, we must assume that you either are a supervisor or are at least thinking about the possibility of becoming one. This chapter focuses on several important aspects of careers: developing a career strategy, career opportunities in supervisory management, and opportunities in supervisory management for college graduates.

NEED FOR CAREER MANAGEMENT

Career management is the effort to combine ways of achieving organizational goals by helping employees achieve personal goals. It thus includes both career planning and career development. **Career planning** is the process of choosing occupations, organizations, and routes that will help you achieve your career goals. **Career development** is engaging in education, training, and other activities that will help you grow in order to reach your objectives. A **career path** is the route you take in moving upward in your field from one job to the next until your chosen position is achieved.

Why the Emphasis on Career Management?

Several factors are causing more and more people—employed and unemployed—to reexamine their career plans. These factors are changes in the work environment, increasing life expectancy (which leads to longer time in the work force), and new patterns of career opportunities.

In the past, people have followed one of two career routes: (1) specializing in a particular field and gaining depth in that area, or (2) generalizing in that field and gaining breadth in it or a related field. So they change directions not because they're forced to by lack of work, failure in the field, or other negative reasons, but because their interests are being heightened through greater self-awareness or widening horizons.

> *Cesar Reyes is a lab technician with the State Department of Health. He had completed two years of college by age 21 when he accepted the position with the state. For his first three years at this job, he took no college credit courses; but for the past two years, he has been taking night courses at a local university. When he completes his degree program, he plans to join a hospital, preferably in a management position, with an eye on ultimately occupying a higher-lever administrative slot.*

Who Is Responsible for Your Career Management?

While the primary responsibility for career management must rest on your shoulders, others will have a share in the decisions you make. If you presently attend or have attended college or technical school, your parents may have influenced your value systems and interests and perhaps helped you select a school or curriculum.

Your teachers and advisors may have helped you choose courses and may even have aided you in your job search.

If you're employed, your boss may have helped you. *If your employer isn't helping you in this respect, then you may want to consider a job move at this time.* But the ultimate responsibility for career planning and development is yours. Management can't force you to plan, for career planning is essentially a personal process of planning your life work. Therefore, you need to (1) do a careful self-analysis, (2) set realistic and attainable goals, (3) study career paths, and (4) develop a detailed plan of action to reach those career objectives in the optimum time frame.

THE ROLE OF MENTORING. The rate at which a person's career progresses in an organization can depend on having a **mentor**, or **patron**, who can lead and guide the person into the right places and situations at the right time. The mentor can contribute to faster progression than normal. It has been known for some time that, if you can find someone up the line to keep an eye out for you and occasionally "put in a good word" in the right places, your career will progress faster.

THE ROLE OF NETWORKING. Operating on the theory that informal communications are sometimes the most effective (see Chapter 6), a fairly new system is now changing recruitment and promotion practices. Similar to mentoring, **networking** is transmitting information on job leads and mutual support via informal contacts, instead of relying solely on formal procedures. This practice is especially useful to women and minority applicants and employees.

CHOOSING A CAREER IN SUPERVISORY MANAGEMENT

Assuming that you want a career in supervisory management, the best way to manage it is to develop a career strategy and carry it out in seeking your first meaningful full-time job. A **career strategy** is a plan of the various roles you intend to play at various stages of your career development. A role is the part in human relationships you're expected to play, or the way you're supposed to act in a given situation. In other words, a *career* is what you want to become; a *role* is the part you play at each stage along your *career path*; and a *career strategy* provides the objectives necessary to achieve those roles and develops the guidelines for achieving them.

Note in Case 21–1 that John Brantley didn't appear to have a given career strategy. As a result, his career path had no particular direction. At this stage in your career, do you have a career strategy? Do you have a career path in mind? If so, what roles will you play along this career path?

What Is an Effective Career Strategy?

A practical book on career advancement begins by stating, "You will be what you resolve to be."[1] This observation is quite true. When you resolve to reach a certain position in your career, you'll then begin to prepare to achieve it. You'll read about the position, study the courses leading to it, and prepare to reach it in others ways. You'll ask your parents, spouse, children, friends, and teachers to help you achieve your goal. You may *change* your goal as you progress, but you'll have a strategy for reaching the new goal.

What are some desirable qualities to seek in an effective career strategy? The career strategy probably should be (1) flexible, (2) based on experience, and (3) inclusive.

IT SHOULD BE FLEXIBLE. A career strategy should be flexible and take a long-range perspective. Obviously, the farther roles are projected into the future, the more uncertain they'll be. Yet an important advantage of this approach is that you can make alternative plans that you otherwise might not have considered. Your strategy can be changed as necessary, but do have one so that you'll have a goal to seek.

While in high school, Emily wanted to be a civil engineer; so she studied such subjects and physics, math, and drafting. But she needed a scholarship in order to go to college. Since she was working in a pharmacy, her boss helped her to get a small pharmacy grant. Thus, Emily worked her way through the first year. By then, she wanted to be an economist; so she planned her courses accordingly. After dropping out for a couple of years, she returned to study management. After graduation, she became an ordnance supervisor in a shipyard making naval vessels.

IT SHOULD BE BASED ON EXPERIENCE. From past experiences you can obtain information about your strengths, weaknesses, values, and needs. Whenever you have had an especially satisfying day, reflect on it and jot down your reflections. For example, what happened to make it good? What particular people or activities were involved? Was something new accomplished? The answers to questions like these can furnish clues to your future career opportunities. Many schools have excellent career guidance centers that can help you do this and other types of analysis of your abilities.

Note that John Brantley in Case 21–1 had spent two years in junior college but still had no clear career strategy. This is very common among college students. Why do you think this is so?

IT SHOULD BE INCLUSIVE. A career strategy should include not only what you hope to achieve in a job (see Figure 21–1), but also your hopes for family, community, and personal life. In other words, plan not only for your professional advancement but also for your personal growth and development. Courses in areas such as art, crafts, music, and literature, as well as participation in travel, sports, and leisure-time activities, should lead to a well-rounded life.

FIGURE 21–1 CHOOSING A CAREER STRATEGY

Other career factors that you should consider are (1) how much time you plan to devote to a job; (2) how to resolve potential conflicts between the job and your family; (3) in what company or industry you want to seek a career; and (4) how far you wish to advance in a company—whether to remain a technical specialist or operative employee or to move up to first-line supervisor or even higher levels of management.

Steps in Developing a Career Strategy

There are some fairly well-defined steps to follow in developing a career strategy. Regardless of how you actually do it, a career strategy should include at least the steps given below.

IDENTIFY YOUR OPPORTUNITIES. The opportunities will help determine the things you *might do*. Consider the technological, economic, political, and socio-cultural environments to see what new businesses and jobs might develop. Ask questions such as the following:

1. What kinds of resources (skills, values, and abilities) are increasingly in demand?
2. What areas of the economy, such as manufacturing, marketing, financial, or service, are most likely to use these resources?
3. What is the reward for someone with these resources?
4. What costs will be involved in upgrading your present skills?

INVENTORY YOUR COMPETENCIES AND RESOURCES. List the strengths that you can build upon and weaknesses that you can overcome. Consider factors such as abilities, time, money, skills, and the help you can expect from others. Some other key questions are:

1. Can my strengths be utilized in a variety of situations or in only a few areas?
2. Am I mobile, or am I limiting myself to a certain location?
3. How well do I manage myself?
4. Do I set measurable standards to be met in reaching my objectives?
5. Do I seek performance feedback in order to determine how well I am doing?

In other words, "Know myself." The simple self-analysis in Figure 21–2 should help you determine what you *can do*.

FIGURE 21–2   A SIMPLE SELF–ANALYSIS

Ask yourself the following questions:

■ What major projects, hobbies, and related things have I done in the past few years? (Identify those activities that gave you the most personal satisfaction and most nearly matched your talents and interests.)

■ What are my favorite activities—in the order of preference? (Relate them to specific skills you have.)

■ Have I consulted my campus career counselors? (Most schools have counseling services that offer career planning.)

■ Have I obtained advice from my professors and/or my supervisor at work? (Ask for their honest assessment of your strengths and limitations. Be prepared not to be hurt when a true assessment is given!)

Source: Adapted from Leon C. Megginson, Gayle M. Ross, and Lyle R. Trueblood, *Introduction to Business* (Lexington, MA: D.C. Heath & Co., 1985), Chapter 24, Quiz 24–1.

CLARIFY YOUR AMBITIONS AND HOPES. Be realistic in deciding on the following questions: What would I really like to do or become? What am I willing to sacrifice to achieve my dreams? Do I want to become an entrepreneur, to be a top executive, or to serve in supervisory management? These are the things that determine what you *want to do*.

ACKNOWLEDGE YOUR OBLIGATIONS. We try to live up to the expectations of people who've helped us, for they deserve some of our time, energy, and effort. Those debts you owe to your family and other groups will determine what you *ought to do*.

RECOGNIZE YOUR PERSONAL VALUES. The relative worth of importance we attach to people, things, ideas, or events influences our career choice because the work we do also affects the way we feel about ourselves. Thus, some questions to ask yourself are: What does "success" mean to me, and is it worth the effort? How much risk am I willing to take? Do I believe in the work ethic or in a more leisurely approach? The things you believe in will largely dictate what you are *willing or unwilling to do* (see Figure 21–3).

Realistic dates for completing specific phases of your career strategy should be established, along with specific criteria for measuring your progress. Make these measurements of your career objectives (and progress) quite specific so that it will be easier to decide whether or not you've reached them.

FIGURE 21–3

Source: Cartoon by Fred Maes. Reproduced with permission.

CAREER OPPORTUNITIES IN SUPERVISORY MANAGEMENT

Competition for careers in supervisory management is going to be intense during the late 1980s and early 1990s. However, there should be plenty of opportunities for those who develop and carry out a sound career strategy.

The older, traditional view of the supervisor was that of someone who had strong technical grounding and was capable of "pushing" or coercing people to perform. In many cases, technical skills were the primary basis for selection. Fortunately today's view of the supervisor's job is changing. Conceptual, human relations, and administrative skills are acknowledged to be at least as important as, if not more important than, the supervisor's technical background and ability. Today's supervisory job is more complex. Supervisors must conceptualize clearly the relationships between their departments and other departments, plan and execute change smoothly, lead a work group that increasingly consists of less homogeneous workers, and adapt to new organizational processes such as MIS, quality circles, and MBO. Thus, the supervisor's job is increasingly being viewed in broader, more professional terms.

In choosing your career in supervisory management, ask yourself some specific and penetrating questions such as the following: First, which industries are growing, creating more job opportunities? Second, which occupations provide growing opportunities? Third, but by no means least, in what part of the country do I want to work (and live)? The ensuing discussion should help you in making these decisions.

Favorable Industries

In 1987, nearly three out of four employed persons were expected to be working in service-performing industries—17 percent in government and 57 percent in services. Figure 21–4 shows the specific industries in which these jobs are expected to be concentrated by 1990. Notice how strong the demand will be in services, trade, manufacturing, and government. Within those groupings, health care, information processing, and computer-related industries will have the greatest number of job openings. On the other hand, teaching, farming, and service in private households will probably not generate many job openings.

Table 21–1 shows the percentage of all employees in selected industries who are managers and administrators. You can see that you have excellent chances to become a supervisor in (1) finance, insurance, and real estate, or (2) wholesale and retail trade, which have a high percentage of managers, or (3) services, manufacturing, and government, which are increasing in employment as reflected in Figure 21–4.

Favorable Occupations

The United States Department of Labor estimates that nearly 25 million jobs will open up by 1990, and around 1 out of 10 to 15 of these will be supervisory

FIGURE 21-4   THE SHIFT FROM GOODS-PRODUCING TO
SERVICE-PERFORMING JOBS IS CONTINUING

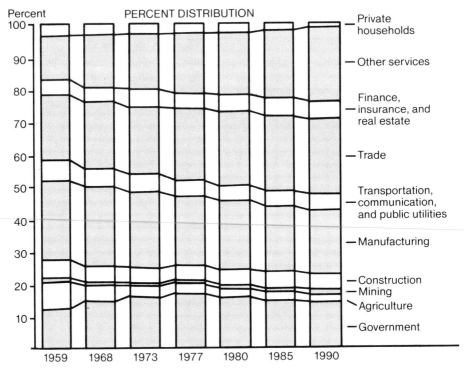

Source: U.S. Department of Labor, Bureau of Labor Statistics.

TABLE 21-1   PERCENTAGE OF EMPLOYED PERSONS IN EACH
INDUSTRY WHO ARE MANAGERS AND
ADMINISTRATORS

Industry	% Employees Who Are Managers
Finance, insurance, and real estate	19.6
Wholesale and retail trade	19.3
Construction	12.9
Public administration	12.8
Mining	11.7
Transportation and public utilities	11.0
Manufacturing	8.3
Services	7.9
Agriculture	1.1

Source: U.S. Department of Labor, Bureau of Labor Statistics, *Handbook of Labor Statistics*, Bulletin 2175 (Washington: U.S. Government Printing Office, December 1983), 55.

positions. But the job opportunities vary according to occupation. For example, by 1990, around 55 percent of all employees will be in white-collar jobs.

Table 21–2 shows that the fastest-growing occupations are in services, sales, clerical, professional and technical, and transportation. The slowest-growing occupations involve production workers, unskilled laborers, managers and administrators, and farm workers (which will continue to decline). Finally, the largest number of expected job openings will be in clerical, professional and technical, services, production, and managerial areas.

TABLE 21–2 EXPECTED EMPLOYMENT IN SELECTED OCCUPATIONS IN 1990

Occupation	Percentage Change (1978–1990)	Expected Number of Jobs (in millions)
Services	+ 32	19.2
Sales	+ 28	8.8
Clerical	+ 27	24.0
Professional and technical	+ 26	20.7
Transportation	+ 26	4.4
Production workers	+ 23	13.2
Unskilled laborers	+ 22	7.1
Managers and administrators	+ 21	11.3
Farm workers	− 18	2.2

Source: U.S. Department of Labor, Bureau of Labor Statistics.

From the standpoint of the total number of jobs available, though, what are the most favorable occupations?

Table 21–3 shows a more detailed listing of the increases expected in a number of specific occupations. Notice the large number of clerical job openings, new health-care jobs, and sales jobs. Once again, these jobs will require a large number of supervisors to manage them.

These figures point up a truth that should affect your career choices; namely, while the high-tech industries are glamorous and attention-grabbing, they aren't expected to generate many job openings because people will still use pen and pencil (see Figure 21–5 on page 523). Notice in Table 21–3 that, of the top 22 fastest-growing occupations, only five are related to high technology: computer-systems analysts, physicians, computer operators, computer programmers, and

TABLE 21-3 SELECTED OCCUPATIONS THAT ARE EXPECTED
TO GROW

Occupations Expected to Grow	Job Growth, 1980–1990
1. Secretaries	700,000
2. Nurses' aides and orderlies	508,000
3. Janitors	501,000
4. Sales clerks	479,000
5. Cashiers	452,000
6. Nurses	437,000
7. Truck drivers	415,000
8. Fast-food restaurant workers	400,000
9. General office clerks	377,000
10. Accountants, auditors	221,000
11. Automobile mechanics	206,000
12. Blue-collar supervisors	206,000
13. Typists	187,000
14. Bookkeepers	167,000
15. Stock clerks (warehouse)	142,000
16. Computer-systems analysts	139,000
17. Store managers	139,000
18. Utility repairers	134,000
19. Computer operators	132,000
20. Computer programmers	112,000
21. Electricians	109,000
22. Electrical and electronic technicians	107,000

Source: U.S. Department of Labor, Bureau of Labor Statistics, *Handbook
of Labor Statistics,* Bulletin 2175 (Washington: U.S. Government Printing
Office, December 1983), 55.

electrical and electronic technicians. And by the early 1990s, between 200,000
and 285,000 industrial robots are expected to displace around 200,000 jobs.[2]

So what can we conclude? In general, most employment opportunities—
especially in supervisory management—will be in clerical, health care, trade,
manufacturing, and government occupations. Also, the "smokestack industries"—
construction, autos, steel and nonferrous metals, chemicals, textiles, and machine
tools—aren't dead yet. The vitality, innovation, and creativity, as well as the
profit motive, of American entrepreneurs are leading to a revival in these and
other industries. And don't underestimate the role of small businesses. Between 80 and 90 percent of new jobs during the 1980s were generated by
small firms. Therefore, it can be concluded that your best chances for a supervisory position are with a small company, even if you have to found it yourself!
This is especially true of young people, women, older workers, and the handicapped.

FIGURE 21–5

Source: Cartoon by David Carman. *Tulsa World* (March 17, 1983), A-1. Reproduced with permission.

OPPORTUNITIES IN SUPERVISORY MANAGEMENT FOR COLLEGE GRADUATES

A quiet revolution occurred from the 1930s to the 1950s that vitally affected employment in the United States, especially of supervisors and other managers. A high school diploma usually wasn't required for employment before 1930, not even for a manager. But by the late fifties, it was required for the vast majority of management jobs. Now a similar revolution is taking place. A college degree is needed for most supervisory and management positions.

Why Get a College Degree?

There are still several sound financial and nonfinancial reasons for getting at least a baccalaureate degree, whether in business or in some other area. As shown in Figure 21–6, the higher the education attainment of the head of the household, the higher the household income. According to the U.S. Bureau of the Census, a bachelor's degree was worth more than $300,000 in extra lifetime earnings for a young man and $142,000 for a young woman in the early 1980s.[3] A male college graduate was expected to earn $1.4 million, a high school graduate $1 million,

FIGURE 21–6 EDUCATION MEANS DOLLARS

1986 MEDIAN HOUSEHOLD INCOME, BASED ON EDUCATION OF HEAD OF HOUSEHOLD

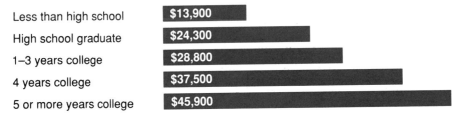

Less than high school	$13,900
High school graduate	$24,300
1–3 years college	$28,800
4 years college	$37,500
5 or more years college	$45,900

Source: Copyright ©1987, *USA TODAY* (March 9, 1987), 1A. Reprinted with permission.

and a high school dropout $845,000. For female students, the corresponding figures were $846,000, $634,000, and $500,000. There are few opportunities that offer as high a rate of return on investment as a college education. Isn't it worth the hassle?

Second, a degree is a "door opener" because job applicants are often screened out during recruitment and selection by the elimination of those who don't have a degree. Some other reasons for desiring a college degree are the personal and job satisfaction derived from it, a feeling of higher status and prestige, and the realization that "they can't take it away from me now that I've earned it."

Trends in Job Opportunities for College Graduates

Job opportunities for college graduates will continue to be available until at least 1990 (see Figure 21–7). Thus, students with a college degree will have a competitive edge over noncollege workers because they will have entry-level skills to offer and will be able to work in such a wide variety of fields. But the Bureau of Labor Statistics has pointed out that as many as one out of five college graduates will be in positions below their educational level or out of their field. Finally, colleges—at least colleges of business—are being pressured to train their students to be first-line supervisors. For instance, Edward Donley, chairman of Air Products and Chemicals, Inc., said "We need lieutenants before we need colonels and generals."[4] We believe this trend will accelerate in the near future.

FIGURE 21–7   REQUIREMENTS FOR COLLEGE GRADUATES ARE EXPECTED TO GROW FASTER THAN REQUIREMENTS FOR ALL WORKERS

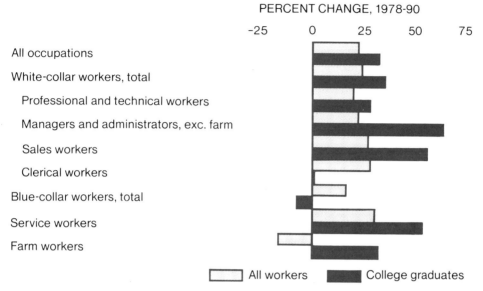

Source: "Tomorrow's Jobs for College Graduates," *Occupational Outlook for College Graduates,* 1980–1981 ed. (Washington: U.S. Government Printing Office, 1981).

CHAPTER REVIEW

Career management, which includes career planning and development, is becoming more important because of factors such as changes in the work environment, increasing life expectancy, and new patterns of career opportunities. Now people are changing careers not because they have to but because their interests are being heightened through growing self-awareness and widening interests.

While families, teachers, employers, and others are partially responsible for career management, the ultimate responsibility rests with us as individuals. We need to (1) do a careful self-analysis, (2) set realistic and attainable goals, (3) study career paths, and (4) develop a detailed plan of action to reach our career objectives in the optimum time frame. Mentoring and networking can also be helpful, especially to women and minorities.

If you desire a career in supervisory management, you should develop a career strategy and implement it in seeking your first meaningful full-time job. In general, a career is what we want to become, a career strategy is the plan of the various roles we play at various stages of our career development, and a career path is the route we follow in moving upward from one job to another as we progress toward our chosen position.

The desirable qualities of a career strategy are flexibility, basis in experience, and inclusiveness. The steps in developing such a strategy are (1) identify your opportunities; (2) inventory your competencies and resources; (3) clarify your ambitions and hopes; (4) acknowledge your obligations; and (5) recognize your personal values.

In choosing a career in supervisory management, you need to study the opportunities in various industries and occupations. The industries that will probably provide you with the greatest opportunities are services, trade, manufacturing, and government. Within these broad industry groupings, health care, information processing, and computer-related industries will provide the greatest number of job openings. Even the "smokestack industries," such as construction, autos, steel and nonferrous metals, chemicals, textiles, and machine tools, are recovering and will provide job openings.

The fast-growing occupations are services, sales, clerical, professional and technical, and transportation. Yet the largest number of actual job openings will be in clerical, professional and technical, services, production, and managerial areas.

There will be more opportunities in supervision for you if you get a college degree. Also, you'll probably make more money; have easier entry into employment offices; and have greater status, prestige, and job satisfaction.

QUESTIONS FOR REVIEW AND DISCUSSION

1. Why is career management increasing in importance?
2. Who is responsible for career management? Explain.
3. How would you distinguish among (a) a career, (b) a career strategy, (c) a role, and (d) a career path.
4. Briefly explain the processes of mentoring and networking.
5. What are the desirable qualities of an effective career strategy? Explain each.
6. What are the steps needed to develop an effective career strategy?
7. Note that, in Case 21–1, John Brantley had never really planned for a career—things "just happened." What are the pros and cons of this approach?
8. Which occupations do you think will be most favorable to you?
9. Why should you get a college education if you aspire to a supervisory position?

LEARNING EXERCISE 21–1
THE RETURNEE

A speaker asked a group of supervisors in a large hospital to recount a managerial situation that had caused them their greatest problem. A head nurse answered as follows:

> My problem has been trying to readjust to hospital life. In 1960, I left the nursing profession to be a housewife and mother. I returned to hospital work only seven years ago when I was asked to come in and "help out." Since then, I've had a problem adjusting to the changes that have occurred.

During those years at home, I remained a member of the professional associations and subscribed to two nursing journals in an effort to keep abreast of the changing trends. I also read anything that pertained to my profession.

After returning to work, I worked for a very smart head nurse. She was quite helpful in trying to get me acquainted with the latest equipment and methods. I suppose the hardest thing was getting used to the new type of people working in hospitals. When I had nurse's training, we were taught always to be "strictly professional" when on duty. So I had to adjust to the new relaxed attitude and permissiveness that prevailed in our hospital.

I thought I did very well and really enjoyed my work until I was asked to be head nurse in my department. I accepted the position reluctantly and with reservations. I love to work with people, but the job of being head nurse is a lonely one. I like to teach or instruct, but I don't like to be a supervisor and to have to watch and point out errors and mistakes that are made through carelessness.

Answer the following questions:

1. What does this situation tell you about the need for supervisors in the health-care field?
2. What does it show about the need for career development?
3. How would you advise the head nurse to think and act like a supervisor?

LEARNING EXERCISE 21–2
CHANCE FOR PROMOTION?

Before joining Adolfo Industries four years earlier, Mike Bronson had served a four-year hitch in the military. He was 27 years old, married, and had two children. Mike had the reputation of being the outstanding electrical technician on the staff—in fact, he was reputed to be tops in the entire company chain of 15 manufacturing sites. He handled with ease work on voltages that senior electrical technicians shied away from.

Mike's uncle, who has since retired, had worked in Adolfo's electrical mainte-nance department and had himself been an outstanding technician. He ran his own electrical shop as a hobby. Throughout high school Mike had worked with this uncle, learning the work. Thus, Mike became an expert at a relatively young age. So the company was eager to hire him upon his return from active military service.

The previous Friday, Jack Goings, supervisor of the electrical maintenance department and Mike's present boss, left the company unexpectedly because of personal problems. To Mike's surprise, the maintenance superintendent offered the position to him. The department consisted of 12 electrical technicians, a number of whom had been with Adolfo Industries for over 20 years. Mike's relationship with them was excellent. The company was unionized, and the contract prohibited "hands-on" repair work by anyone not a member of the bargaining unit.

As a technician, Mike expected to earn $52,000 this year, including overtime pay. As a supervisor, his salary would be $42,500 but he would not be able to do the work he loved. Mike pondered his decision, as he was given a week to consider the career move.

Answer the following questions:

1. What are the pros and cons of the offer made to Mike?
2. What additional information should Mike try to obtain in weighing the decision?
3. What do you recommend that he do?
4. If he were to take the position, what career advice would you give him?

ENDNOTES

1. John Shingleton and Robert Bao, *College to Career* (New York: McGraw-Hill Book Co., 1977).
2. Cindy Skrzycki, "Will Robots Bring More Jobs—or Less?" *U.S. News & World Report* (September 5, 1983), 25.
3. "How Much Is a Degree Worth? $329,000," *Tulsa World* (March 14, 1983), B-6.
4. Pat Ordovensky, "Stick to Basics, Execs Tell Business Schools," *USA Today* (January 30, 1984), 2-B.

SUGGESTIONS FOR FURTHER READING

Bolles, Richard N. *What Color Is Your Parachute?* Rev. ed. Berkeley, CA: Ten Speed Press, 1982. A career planning classic.

Hall, Dennis. *Careers in Organizations*. Santa Monica, CA: Goodyear, 1976.

Holland, James. *Making Vocational Choices: A Theory of Careers*. Englewood Cliffs, NJ: Prentice-Hall, 1973. One of the classics in career planning.

Jackson, Tom, and Alan Vitberg. "Career Development, Part 1: Careers and Entrepreneurship." *Personnel* 64 (February 1987): 12–17.

Megginson, Leon C. *Personnel Management: A Human Resources Approach*, 5th ed. (Homewood, IL: Richard D. Irwin, 1985). See especially Chapter 5, "Personnel Planning and Career Management."

Moore, Carl C., Edward L. Harrison, and Paul H. Pietri, Jr. "The First-Line Supervisor: Who Wants the Job?" *PIMA* 66 (March 1984): 18–19.

COMPREHENSIVE CASE 1 FOR PART VI
CHANGING TO A PARTICIPATIVE MANAGEMENT CULTURE*

A former junior engineer from the Deep South plant mentioned in Case 19–1 ("The Turnaround Chemical Plant") is now vice-president and division manager over several plants. His division is presently the most profitable in the corporation, and the plant discussed in Chapter 19 is now the most profitable within the division.

Unfortunately one of the (non-union) plants in the division was not doing well. Part of the problem was due to marketplace conditions, and part to the plant manager's

*This case is a follow-up to Case 19–1. Like that case, it is adapted from Donald C. Mosley, "System Four Revisited: Some New Insights," *Organization Development Journal* (Spring 1987): 20–24.

autocratic leadership style. At any rate, the plant was unprofitable. Morale was so bad at this non-union plant that the employees had bypassed the plant's management and contacted the division manager complaining about their treatment at the plant. After an investigation, the division manager concluded that the plant manager's autocratic leadership style was a *major* factor in the plant's poor results.

Twenty years earlier, one of the authors of this book had given the then young engineer a copy of Rensis Likert's *The Human Organization*. Since that time, the engineer has been a follower of Likert's work and a manager who appreciated the potential benefits of participative management. He now concluded that the solution to the non-union plant's problem would be to shift from an autocratic management style in the direction of a consultative style (System 3) or participative style (System 4).

Toward that end, as a division manager, he initiated the following actions: (1) he removed the autocratic plant manager and placed him in a staff role elsewhere in the corporation; (2) he replaced that plant manager with one who, he believed, shared his philosophy regarding participative management; and (3) he contacted one of the authors of this book and asked to meet with him and the new plant manager to explore the feasibility of shifting to a more participative management system.

The Entry and Approach

In retrospect, the similarity of the approach in 1985 to that in 1965 is interesting. The same external consultant was involved, and in both situations the goal was to shift the plants to a more participative management system. Both approaches developed a strength/problem profile that was used as the basis of a tailored development program. Yet there were several big differences. In 1985, the new plant manager was the primary agent of change, whereas, in 1965, the consultant had been the change agent.

In 1985, the OD program was just one of the factors in assisting the new plant manager to change the organization's culture and end results. For example, one of the first acts of the new plant manager was to recruit and hire a replacement employee-relations manager. This man, an experienced professional and a graduate of Cornell's School of Industrial Relations, served, among other roles, as the internal OD consultant.

Another difference was the use of Likert's Profile of Organizational Characteristics questionnaire in 1985. Also, strength/weakness profiles of key managers, which were a factor in 1965, were not developed in 1985. Finally, in 1985, task forces were assigned to develop action-planning recommendations to solve key problems.

Some of the key problems identified in the action research were:

1. The previously mentioned autocratic leadership style of the former plant manager and its impact on the plant.
2. Lack of cooperation between departments, especially between production and maintenance.
3. Significant problems with downward, upward, and horizontal communications.
4. The failure to confront and resolve recurring problems.

These key problems, along with market conditions, explained why the plant was still unprofitable.

The data from the action research served as the basis for a tailored management development program oriented toward shifting the management style toward Systems 3 and 4. Kurt Lewin's concept of behavioral change passing through three conditions of unfreezing, changing, and refreezing was definitely at work in the change effort. All participants examined the data, which revealed that, although the plant had some underlying strengths, there were significant and major problems preventing the plant from reaching its potential effectiveness.

All participants in the development program served on at least one task force that developed an action plan to solve a major problem. Especially outstanding were the action plans to improve communications and to decrease conflict between production and maintenance.

During the year, the consultant followed through by holding periodic meetings with the new plant manager and the new employee-relations manager to check on progress. The consultant was also called on for special assistance during this period. An in-depth analysis was made of the maintenance department that served as a basis for making some organizational changes. One study made by the consultant led to a recommendation that the plant shift to a Scanlon-type bonus plan that would reward team efforts. This particular recommendation was considered, but adoption of a bonus plan has not materialized at the time of this writing. In general, the consultant was available for consultation during this period and was called on for guidance on several occasions.

The Outcome

In June 1986, a year after the program was initiated, the plant was producing at its top performance level and making a profit for the first time in its history. Although improved market conditions were a factor, almost everyone concedes that the style of the new plant manager and his effective use of the OD program played a key role in the turnaround.

At the start of the OD program in May of 1985, the Profile of Organizational Characteristics questionnaire revealed that the plant was essentially being operated as a benevolent autocracy (System 2). An exception was the accuracy of upward communication, as shown by the eighteenth item in the questionnaire. Almost all organization members conceded that upward communication was "often accurate," but the information was ignored and no action was taken.

At the end of the first cycle of the OD program, completed in June of 1986, the questionnaire revealed that the management system had shifted from a benevolent autocracy to a consultative management system (System 3). The initiation of a new cycle of the OD program was focused on shifting the plant even further toward a participative-group management system (System 4). Figure 1 shows the before-and-after measurements using the Profile of Organizational Characteristics questionnaire.

FIGURE 1   PROFILE OF ORGANIZATIONAL CHARACTERISTICS

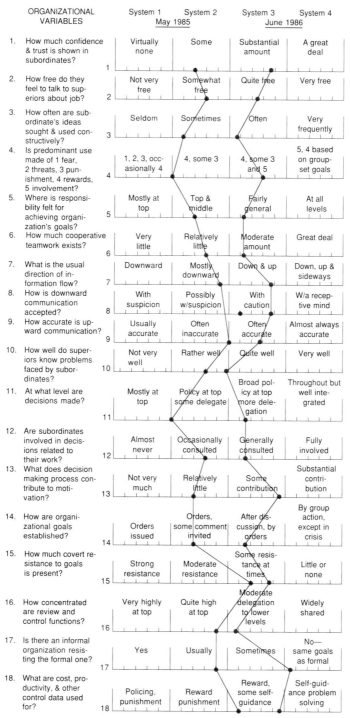

Source: Donald C. Mosley, "System Four Revisited: Some New Insights," *Organizational Development Journal* (Spring 1987): 23.

In addition to the questionnaire, two tailored instruments were used in the May 1986 evaluation phase of the OD program. The instruments and results are shown in Figures 2 and 3. Again, there has been significant improvement in one year's time. It is worth noting that the top two ratings in June 1986 were downward communications and confrontation of problems and opportunities. This highlights the role of the new plant manager and his effective use of task forces to work on problems and opportunities.

Answer the following questions:

1. Do you think this approach would work with many organizations that had both an autocratic management system and poor end results? Why or why not?
2. Identify the specific concepts found in Part VI of this textbook that made this change effort successful.
3. Why are organization members more motivated when working in a participative management system?

FIGURE 2   COMMUNICATION

On a scale of 1 to 10, in your opinion, how effective is each of the three basic communication flows in your organization compared to a year ago? Please write the appropriate number in each of the spaces provided.

1	2	3	4	5	6	7	8	9	10
Very Weak									Excellent

	May 1985	June 1986
Downward Communication—The effective transfer of information, including goals, objectives, policies, changes, performance feedback, etc., from top management to lower levels of the organization.	3.9	7.1
Upward Communication—The effective transfer of information such as performance reports, problems, suggestions, feelings, attitudes, gripes, etc., from lower levels to top management of the organization.	4.8	6.9
Lateral or Diagonal Communication—The effective transfer of ideas and information between and among departments, including interdepartmental cooperation, interdepartmental services relationships, committees, task forces, etc., comprising members of different departments.	3.7	6.5

FIGURE 3 PLANT ANALYSIS

On a scale of 1 to 10, in your opinion, how effective is each of the following areas compared to a year ago? Please write the appropriate number in each of the spaces provided.

1	2	3	4	5	6	7	8	9	10
Very Weak									Excellent

	May 1985	June 1986
Cooperation between production and maintenance	3.5	6.7
Teamwork between all departments	3.9	6.7
Attitudes and morale within the plant	3.1	6.9
Confrontation of problems and opportunities rather than "sweeping them under the rug and allowing them to grow and fester"	3.5	7.0

COMPREHENSIVE CASE 2 FOR PART VI
THE NEW MIS

Recently the Tolineau Company, a medium-sized manufacturer of heavy-duty work clothing, embarked on an extensive modernization program of plant and equipment. To realize the new plant's efficiencies in cutting overhead, the work force was reduced from 670 to 500 hourly employees.

One new person, Al Bell, a whiz with computers, was hired to implement the new computer and MIS system that was to serve as the central focus for the new streamlined organization. Bell, a relatively young man of 27, had received his master's degree in industrial engineering and had been hired five months ago from a national consulting firm. He reported directly to Alvin Sternes, the plant manager.

Pete Adams was head of production control. Adams had been with Tolineau since 1975. Adams's department was one of the major areas in which savings had been expected. Before the modernization, Adams had 30 people in his department. Because of the introduction of new methods and greater efficiencies, Bell now recommended that only 20 people were needed. Several employees had been transferred, and several had quit rather than undertake the training required to become familiar with the new system. As a result, several additional workers were hired. Despite the turmoil created, the new system went on line three months ago.

Since that time, Adams's job had intensified rather than become simpler. Bell had promised to rid Adams of the everyday problems of "putting out fires" and had said that the system would pretty much run itself. Indeed, if Bell had delivered as promised, the new system would truly be great. But the following important things happened to prevent that:

1. Adams's staff was not adequately trained to handle the new system. A four-day training program was originally established. Bell himself had been scheduled to conduct the classes, but last-minute commitments required the hiring of an outside training consultant to substitute for Bell. On such short notice, the consultant was available for only two days, and so a two-day "compressed version" of the training program was scheduled and presented. Bell indicated that he would supplement the short course with a follow-up training course of his own, but this has not yet materialized.

2. Of the 20 people retained in Adams's department who received the two-day training, four have since left the company, citing "better opportunities." (Two went with other firms, one went back to school, and the fourth hasn't been heard from.) Adams feels that the uncertainties of further personnel cuts, plus some fear of inadequacy in their future performance, contributed to the turnover. While the four replacements have not had formal training, they have been trained by other personnel in Adams's department.

3. The new system has not kept up with its promises. It has had quite a few bugs, many of which still remain. In some cases, erroneous inputs have resulted in mismatches between computed inventory and inventory actually on hand. Production runs of various sizes and cuts have been set up, only to find after a short run that the run wasn't needed. In other cases, the computer system itself has gone down, requiring a temporary return to the old system. However, with fewer personnel (some of whom hadn't worked under the old system), it was impossible for Adams's department to keep up. Thus, everyone's nerves have been frayed.

4. Bell himself has changed in temperament and behavior. Initially, Adams and the other managers were impressed with Bell's candor and openness. He solicited their input and took great care to keep them informed. Recently, however, it has become obvious that, instead of managing the new overall system, Bell is being driven by it. He has a short fuse and always seems in a rush. Moreover, he has not been as visible or as willing to help managers with their problems. He supposedly "took a full blast" about his system's failures from two key line managers at last week's meeting with the plant manager.

Adams wonders how long he and his personnel can hold up under the promises of the new system and the realities of a system out of control.

Answer the following questions:

1. Identify the errors that were made in the situation above.
2. What steps should have been taken in completing the new system?
3. What steps do you recommend now?
4. What should Pete Adams do?

GLOSSARY

accident-prone workers or **injury repeaters** —
workers with personality types and recognizable syndromes peculiar to them that cause their
safety to be jeopardized

accountability — the obligation created when a
person accepts duties and responsibilities

achievement or **proficiency test** — a type of
employment test which can fairly accurately
measure the applicant's knowledge of and ability
to do a given job

active listening — a listening technique which
requires the listener to make a response so as to
encourage feedback

ad hoc task forces — supplement formal organization and provide the opportunity for the
concepts of ownership and synergy to be operative

administrative skills — the ability to establish
and follow policies and procedures and to process paperwork in an orderly manner

advisory authority — a type of authority concerned with serving or advising line departments

affirmative-action programs (AAPs) — programs encouraged by the Equal Employment Opportunity Commission to put the principle of
equal employment opportunity into practice

agency shop — an agreement whereby all employees must pay union dues even if they choose
not to join the union

alcoholism — a disease resulting from drinking
alcoholic beverages to the point where normal
functioning is impaired

alternatives — possible courses of action that can
satisfy a need or solve a problem

appraisal interview — a type of interview
wherein the supervisor communicates the results
of performance appraisal to employees

apprenticeship training — training which blends
the learning of theory with practice in the techniques of the job

535

aptitude test — a type of employment test which is used to predict how a person might perform on a given job and which is most useful for operative jobs

arbitrator — the third party who makes a binding decision over a dispute between management and the union

authority — the right to command others to act or not to act in order to reach objectives

authority obedience or **task management** — a leadership style based on the leader's having a high concern for production and using a Directive approach

bargaining agent — the employees' representative who deals with management over questions of wages, hours, and other terms of employment

body signals — nonverbal messages such as slumped posture, clenched fist, raised eyebrows, and so on

budget — a forecast of expected financial performance over a period of time

cafeteria benefit plans or **smorgasbord benefit plans** — benefit plans which provide each worker with an individualized benefit package

career development — the process of engaging in education, training, and other activities that will help one grow in order to reach one's objectives

career management — the effort to combine ways of achieving organizational goals by helping employees achieve personal goals

career path — the route taken in moving upward in the field from one job to the next until the chosen position is achieved

career planning — the process of choosing occupations, organizations, and routes that help in achieving career goals

career strategy — a plan of the various roles one intends to play at various stages of one's career development

centralized organization — an organization in which a strong central staff makes most of the important decisions that concern all levels or units within the organization

change — the process of altering, modifying, or transforming one state, condition, or phase to another

channel — the means used to pass a message in the communication process

chief executive officer (CEO) — individual responsible for the overall operations of the entire organization

closed shop — an agreement whereby all prospective employees must be members of the union before they can be employed and all current employees must join the union to retain their jobs

closure — reaching a decision about a given agenda item in a meeting

coaching and selling style — a leadership style which is usually best employed with individuals or groups that have potential but haven't realized it fully

cohesiveness — the degree to which group members pull in the same direction and have unity

collective bargaining — the mutual obligation of the representatives of the employer and the union to meet at reasonable times and places and to confer in good faith over wages, hours, and other conditions of employment

communication process model — a model which shows the five components of communication (sender, message, channel, receiver, and feedback) and their relationships

comparable worth or **pay equity** — an evaluation of work by a formula of points for the amount of education, effort, skill, and responsibility required for an individual job

computer-assisted design (CAD) — refers to computerized systems that enable designers to utilize computer screens in designing three-dimensional parts and systems

computer-assisted manufacturing (CAM) — refers to special computers that assist automated machines or equipment in performing the necessary processes or sequences of actions for production

computer network — a system for linking computers so that information can be shared among them

concept of balance — the theory that states that in many work-related decision areas, the best condition is a state of equilibrium between extremes

conceptual skills — the ability to acquire, analyze, and interpret information in a logical manner

conference — a meeting of two or more people to discuss matters of common concern

consumer price index (CPI) — an index which measures changes in the price of a group of goods and services that make up the typical consumer's budget

contingency planning — thinking in advance of problems or changes that may arise in order to be prepared to deal with them smoothly when they do arise

continuum of leadership behaviors — a leadership model representing a continuum of power to show the relationship between the use of authority by a supervisor and the area of freedom for subordinates

controlling — the management function of comparing actual performance with planned performance and taking corrective action, if necessary, to ensure that objectives are achieved

cost-of-living adjustments (COLAs) — an arrangement in which wages rise in direct proportion to increases in the consumer price index (CPI)

counseling — professional guidance of one individual by another, using psychological techniques

country club management — a leadership style based on the leader being supportive and somewhat permissive in order to keep employees happy and satisfied and avoiding pressure in getting the work done

craft union — a union of workers in a specific skill, craft, or trade

Crawford slip technique — technique used in problem solving that will generate new ideas by using fluency and flexibility

cross-addiction — the condition wherein alcoholics are also addicted to other chemical substances

corporate culture — refers to the set of values, beliefs, and behavior patterns that form the core identity of an organization

data processing system — system which focuses on producing or processing information such as sales orders, inventory reorder reports, and employee time cards

database management — systems which provide supervisors with a powerful tool for record keeping in areas such as daily absenteeism, quality per employee or component, and hourly output per employee

decentralization — a concept referring to the extent to which authority is delegated from one level of the organization to another

decision making — the conscious consideration and selection of a course of action from among available alternatives to produce a desired result

deferred judgment — the idea of delaying judgment while generating ideas

delegating style — a leadership style which is usually difficult to follow, even when individuals or groups are exceptionally mature and capable, because of the leader's reluctance to delegate in certain situations

delegation of authority — the process by which managers and superiors grant authority downward to the people who report to them

disciplinary layoff or **suspension** — a layoff which involves a loss of time and pay for several days to workers

discipline — training that corrects, molds, or perfects knowledge, attitudes, behavior, or conduct

distribution — marketing and distributing the product

downward communication — type of communication that originates with managers and supervisors and passes down to employees

drug abuse — a condition in which the use of drugs interferes with the employee's capable level of performance

due process — a judicial procedure which guarantees a hearing for the individual accused of violating an established rule or law to determine

the extent of guilt, and which imposes the established penalties only after the hearing is conducted

economic order quantity (EOQ) — a formula
which considers material utilization rates, consequences of running out of materials, the length
of time typically needed to receive orders, costs
of carrying materials in inventory, and costs of
ordering more materials
ego or **esteem needs** — the level in Maslow's
hierarchy of needs that is concerned with such
needs as self-confidence, independence, recognition, appreciation, status, and so on
empathy — the ability to put oneself in the other
person's place
employee-assistance programs (EAPs) — counseling programs for employees
employee-comparison method — a traditional
method of performance appraisal wherein supervisors are required to rank each of their subordinates in comparison with one another as to their
performance and value to the organization
employee associations — professional or governmental, white-collar, agricultural, and service
employee organizations which function as unions
employee benefits — the financial rewards and
services provided to employees in addition to
their regular earnings
employees' bill of rights — the section of the
Landrum-Griffin Act concerned with the protection of employees from possible abuse by some
unscrupulous managers and union leaders
equity theory — the theory of motivation that
is concerned with reducing feelings of inequity
when they exist
exempt employees — employees, including executives, administrative and professional employees, and outside sales personnel, who are not covered by the provisions of the Fair Labor Standards Act
expectancy theory — the theory of motivation
that is concerned with the belief that a particular
act will be followed by a particular outcome

experience rating — rating including the employer's unemployment rate within the state and the
record of unemployed workers
experiential learning — the procedure through
which one learns by doing and uses mistakes as
an opportunity to know how to prevent them in
the future

fact-finding meeting — a type of meeting held
to seek out relevant facts about a problem or a
situation
feedback — the response that a communicator
receives from the receiver of the message
financial resources — the basic resource consisting of money, capital, and credit needed by an
organization
financing — providing and using funds
flexcomp — a method of providing employees
with flexible benefit packages
flexibility — the ability to use free association to
generate or classify ideas in categories
fluency — the ability to let ideas flow out of your
head like water over a waterfall
formal roles — expected behaviors among group
members which are written out in job descriptions
functional authority — a restricted kind of staff
authority over a given function, regardless of
where that function is performed in an organization

goals — specific ends or aims
graduated scale of penalties — a system of
punishment which becomes progressively more
severe as the violation is repeated
grapevine — the rumor mill in organizations
grievance procedure — a formal way of handling
employee complaints, usually outlined by specific steps to be taken
group-centered approach — the approach used
at meetings in which group members interact
freely and address and raise questions to one
another, with no one dominating the discussions
group dynamics — refers to the social process by
which people interact face to face in small groups

hardware—the equipment needed to operate a computer system, including devices such as central processing units, storage devices, printers, and terminals

hierarchy of needs—the concept based on two principles: (1) that people's needs may be ranked according to importance; and (2) that once a need is satisfied, it isn't a primary motivator of behavior

hierarchy of objectives—a body of objectives ranked according to those determined by top-level management down to those determined by other levels of management

hot-stove rule—the concept which compares the disciplinary system to a hot stove in that the discipline should (1) carry advance warning, (2) be immediate, (3) be consistent, and (4) be impersonal

human-relations model—the model of participative leadership whose premise is to use participation as a technique to make people feel happy and important and lower their resistance to formal authority

human-relations skills—the ability to understand other people and to interact effectively with them

human-resources model—the model of participative leadership whose premise is that participative leadership used for important matters leads to improved decision making and departmental effectiveness

human resources—a basic resource composed of people needed by an organization

hygiene factors—the factors that can forestall any serious dissatisfaction or drop in productivity, but cannot motivate by themselves

impoverished management—a leadership style based on the leader's complete abdication of the leadership role

incentive wages—a method in which the employee is paid according to the amount of goods and services that the employee produced

industrial relations—labor relations or union-management relations

industrial union—a union of all eligible workers in a particular industry

informal communication—type of communication which exists separately from the formal, established communication system

informal roles—behaviors for group members which are not stated in writing but develop as a result of the dynamics within the group

information-exchange meeting—a type of meeting held to obtain information from group members and allow them to provide information to one another

information-giving meeting—a type of meeting held to make announcements of new programs and policies or to update the present ones

intangible standard—a type of standard that relates to human characteristics and is therefore difficult to measure

intermediaries—go-betweens who act as mediators between low-level employees and high-level managers

internship training—system in which on-the-job training at a cooperating business is combined with education at a school or college

intolerable offenses—disciplinary problems which are of such drastic or illegal nature that they severely strain or endanger employment relationships

intuition—the unconscious basis for reaching a conclusion as influenced by one's cultural background, education, training, or knowledge of the situation

IQ test—a type of employment test designed to measure an applicant's capacity to learn and solve problems and to understand relationships

job analysis—the process of gathering information and determining the elements of a job by observation and study

job burnout—physical and/or mental depletion significantly below one's capable level of performance

job descriptions—written statements that spell out the primary duties and responsibilities of specific jobs

job evaluation—a process used to determine the relative value of jobs to an employer in order to determine more objectively the earnings of employees doing given jobs

job posting—the procedure of posting available job openings on a bulletin board to give current employees a chance to bid on them

job specification—the statement containing the personal characteristics required of a person to perform a described job

job stress—a condition arising from the interaction of people and their jobs, characterized by changes within people that force them to deviate from their normal functioning

KISS principle—a general guide to public speaking which stands for "Keep It Short and Simple"

labor relations—the relationships between managers of organizations and their unionized employees

labor union—an organization of workers banded together to achieve economic goals through improved wages, working hours, and working conditions

lateral-diagonal communication—type of communication that takes place between individuals in the same department or in different departments

law of effect—a law which holds that those activities that meet with pleasurable consequences tend to be repeated, whereas those activities that meet with unpleasurable consequences tend not to be repeated

leader-controlled approach—an approach used at information-giving meetings or meetings of large groups in which the leader clearly runs the show and the open flow of information among members is impeded

leadership—the process of influencing individual and group activities toward goal-setting and goal-achievement

leading—the management function of directing, guiding, and supervising subordinates in the performance of their duties and responsibilities

life cycle theory of leadership—a situational theory of leadership which holds that leadership behaviors should reflect the maturity level of subordinates

line authority—a type of authority concerned with the power to directly command or exact performance from others

line organization—an organization structure in which each person has clearly defined responsibilities and reports to an immediate supervisor

line personnel—personnel who carry out the primary activities of a business such as producing goods or selling products and/or services

lockout—the closing by a company of its premises to employees in order to achieve its demands

mainframe computer—largest type of computer system which has the capability to store enormous amounts of information and to process data at the fastest speeds

maintenance-of-membership clause—an agreement whereby an employee, once he or she joins the union, must maintain that membership as a condition of employment

major life event—anything that causes a person to deviate from normal functioning

major violations—disciplinary problems that substantially interfere with orderly operations

malicious obedience—the act of an aggrieved employee doing exactly what he or she is told even if the order is faulty and will result in getting things fouled up

management—the art of working through people to achieve objectives by means of effective decision making and coordination of available resources

management by exception—the management style by which the supervisor focuses attention on the most critical control needs and allows employees to handle most routine deviations from the standard

management by objectives (MBO)—a system whereby managers and their subordinates jointly establish objectives and develop a systematic approach for monitoring results

management information systems (MIS)—an integrated system, usually computer based, that provides information to management to assist in decision making

managerial functions—the acts or operations expected of a manager in a given situation

Managerial Grid®—Blake and Mouton's leadership model which portrays two concerns: people and production

maternity leave—time off with pay for the pregnant employee

maturity level—the state of a follower's drive or need for achievement as a result of experience, education, attitudes, and willingness and ability to accept responsibility—which should be considered only in relation to a specific task to be performed

mediator—the third party who tries to bring disputing parties together in an attempt to solve an impasse

mentor or **patron**—one who can lead and guide an employee into the right places and situations at the right time

merit—a basis for promotion which refers to an employee's ability to perform the job better than others

message—words or nonverbal expressions that are capable of transmitting meaning

microcomputer—the smallest type of computer, which resembles a typewriter keyboard and has a television-like screen (called a CRT) to display the data

middle-of-the-road management—a leadership style which places some emphasis on people and some emphasis on production

middle management—the management level responsible for a substantial part of an organization such as a division or department

minicomputer—smaller version of the mainframe which originally had less speed or capacity than the mainframe, but today is more powerful than the mainframe of the 1960s

minor infractions—disciplinary problems which do little harm or result in few serious consequences when they happen in isolation

minutes—the recorded important points discussed and agreed upon at a meeting

monetary standards—tangible standards expressed in terms of dollars and cents

motivation—the act of inducing a person or a group to work to achieve the organization's objectives, while also working to achieve individual objectives

motivators—factors that have uplifting effects on attitudes or performance

negative discipline—an outer force which often causes a person to change outwardly in an isolated situation or to change only for events that continue to occur over a period of time

networking—transmitting information on job leads and mutual support via information contacts

nominal grouping technique (NGT)—a technique very effective in developing creativity and generating useful information

nonexempt employees—employees covered by the Fair Labor Standards Act who must be paid the basic minimum wage

norms of behavior—certain behaviors which define what is and is not acceptable behavior within a group

numerical standards—tangible standards expressed in numbers

object signals—nonverbal messages given by the type of office furniture used, protective helmet, plush carpet, wall plaques, and so on

objectives—broad, general ends or aims

occupational stress—factors that interfere with an employee's job performance

on-the-job training—training which involves the employees in actually performing the work under the supervision and guidance of the supervisor or a trained worker or instructor

operations—production of the products or services

opportunity—a chance for development, progress, or advancement

organization—a group of people working together to achieve a common objective

organization change—the way an organization adapts to its external and internal environment

organization development (OD)—a planned effort, managed from the top, that is designed to increase an organization's effectiveness and health

organizational activities—consist of operations, distribution, and financing

organizing—management function of deciding what activities are needed to reach objectives, dividing the human resources into work groups, and assigning each group to a manager

outplacement or **disengagement**—terms used for counseling people who are laid off or terminated

ownership—the notion that soliciting participation from people affected by a problem or decision results in involvement, commitment, and a strong desire to ensure that the decision is implemented effectively

paired comparison—a variant of the employee-comparison method of performance appraisal in which an employee is compared to other employees in the work group

parity principle—management principle which states that when responsibilities and duties are assigned, adequate authority should be delegated to meet the responsibilities and carry out the assignments

participating and supporting style—a leadership style which is best used with mature individuals or groups

participative management—taking part or sharing in problem solving or decision making

paternity leave—leave which permits new fathers to take unpaid leave to help take care of the new baby

peer rating or **mutual rating system**—a traditional method of performance appraisal wherein employees evaluate their fellow employees in their own ranks

perception—the process by which one selects, organizes, and gives meaning to the world around oneself

performance appraisal—the process used to determine to what extent an employee is performing the job in the way it was intended to be done

performance objectives—guidelines established to help achieve standards of performance in specific areas

personality test—a type of employment test which is designed to measure an applicant's emotional adjustment and attitudes to see how that person might fit into the organization

physical resources—a basic resource composed of buildings, furnishings, machinery, equipment, tools, materials, and supplies needed by an organization

physical standards—tangible standards expressed in terms of quantities of work, quality, durability, size, and so on

physiological or **biological needs**—the lowest level in Maslow's hierarchy of needs which concern basic needs for food, water, air, and so on

picketing—the act of walking back and forth, usually carrying signs, by employees outside their place of employment to tell the public why they are striking

planning—the management function of selecting future courses of action for the organization as a whole and for each of its subunits, and deciding how to achieve the desired results

policy—a type of standing plan which is a guide to decision making

polygraph (lie detector)—a device used to measure changes in breathing, blood pressure, and electrothermal response under extensive questioning of a person

positive-reinforcement theory—the theory of motivation which is based on the law of effect and uses rewards as reinforcement

positive discipline—an inner force which promotes emotional satisfaction instead of emotional conflict

preliminary interview—a type of employment interview during which the application form is completed and general observations of the applicant are made

prevailing wage rate—wage rate which approximates the union wage scale for an area in a given type of work

preventive controls—actions taken before or during the course of a job to prevent things from going wrong

principle of supportive relationships—a theory that the supervisor's leadership and interactions must be such that each employee views the experience as supportive and one that maintains the employee's sense of personal worth and importance

private-industry councils (PICs)—councils headed by company executives and local business people who help employers with training activities

probe—a form of active listening which is more specific than the reflective statement by directing attention to a particular aspect of the speaker's message

problem—a source of anxiety or distress

problem-solving meeting—a type of meeting which combines the purposes of information-giving, information-exchange, and fact-finding

procedure—a type of standing plan which outlines the steps to be performed when taking a particular course of action

productivity—a measure of inputs as compared to outputs

proficiency and skill test—a type of employment test which measures an applicant's ability to perform a particular trade, craft, or skill

program—a type of single-use plan which involves a mix of objectives, policies, rules, and small projects

programmed decisions—decisions that are routine and repetitive and can be handled in a systematic way

progressive discipline—the use of a graduated scale of penalties

project—a distinct smaller part of a program

project or **matrix organization**—an organization structure in which both functional departments and project teams exist

promoting—moving a person from a lower- to a higher-level job

protected groups—women and minorities whom employers should make good-faith efforts to recruit under affirmative-action programs

punishment—the negative result which a person receives after committing an undesirable act or omission

quality-of-work-life (QWL) program—a program that systematically studies such factors as working conditions, jobs performed, supervision, company policy, and so on, that affect the conditions of the work place and its environment

quality assurance—the entire system of policies, procedures, and guidelines that an organization installs so as to attain and maintain quality

quality circles—groups of 5 to 12 workers and their supervisory leaders who meet regularly (once a week or twice a month) to identify ways to improve quality and productivity

quality control—the system of measurements that is designed to see if the desired quality is being met, which typically uncovers problems after they have occurred

rate range—consists of a minimum and maximum range of wage rates for a given job, with employees paid at different rates depending on how well they perform

rating scale—a traditional method of performance appraisal which rates an employee on a number of characteristics on a point scale

receiver—the ultimate destination of the sender's message

reflective statement—a form of active listening in which one repeats what another person has just said

reframing—an aspect of management education emphasizing management training and development programs

relationship behaviors—leadership behaviors that provide people with support, give them positive feedback, and ask for their opinions and ideas

relaxation response—a meditative technique that helps relieve tensions, enables one to deal more effectively with stress, lowers blood pressure, and in general improves physical and emotional health

responsibility—the state of being accountable for carrying out tasks and duties that have been assigned

right-to-work laws—laws which give employees the right to join or refuse to join a union without being fired

risk—the possibility of defeat, disadvantage, injury, or loss

robot—a machine, controlled by a computer, that can be programmed to perform a number of repetitive manipulations of tools or materials

roles—the manner in which various managerial activities are carried out by managers, characterized by quick and frequent changes

rule—a type of standing plan which gives final and definite guidance

safety or **security needs**—the level in Maslow's hierarchy of needs that is concerned with protection from danger, threat, or deprivation

self-fulfillment or **self-actualization needs**—the highest level in Maslow's hierarchy of needs that is concerned with the realization of one's potentialities, self-development, and creativity

sender—the person who communicates a message

seniority—an employee's length of service in a company

"Siamese twins" of management—the management functions of planning and controlling which are most closely related

single-use plans—types of plans that are developed to accomplish a specific purpose and are then discarded

single rate—the same wage paid for a job, regardless of the level of performance

situational leadership—a leadership model which shows the relationship between the maturity of followers and the leadership style based on the leader's task behaviors and relationship behaviors

social or **belonging needs**—the level in Maslow's hierarchy of needs that is concerned with the needs for belonging, association, acceptance by colleagues, friendship, and love

software—programs that issue directions to perform manipulations of data

space signals—nonverbal messages such as huddling close, being distant, or sitting close to someone

span-of-control or **span of management**—a management principle which holds that there is a limit to the number of people a manager can supervise effectively

spreadsheet—software which turns the computer into a large piece of paper with columns that can be manipulated in any number of ways, such as to show inventory levels needed to accommodate various production outputs

staff personnel—personnel who have the expertise to assist line people and top management in various areas of business activities

staffing—the management function of selecting, training and developing, using, and paying and rewarding people to do an organization's work

standard—a unit of measurement that can serve as a reference point for evaluating results

standing plans or **repeat use plans**—a type of plan used repeatedly over a period of time

status—a characteristic which refers to a group's "pecking order" and varies according to factors such as seniority, expertise, job classification, and job location

stereotyping—the tendency to put similar things in the same categories in order to make it easier to deal with them

strategic control point—that point in an activity where performance is measured sufficiently early that the necessary corrective action can be taken to accomplish the objective

stress—any external stimulus that causes wear and tear on one's psychological or physical well-being

strike—the withholding of services from their employer by employees in order to get something

structured interviews—interviews which are standardized and controlled with regard to questions asked, sequence of questions, interpretation of replies, and weight given to factors considered in making the value judgment as to whether or not to hire the person

structuring and telling style—a leadership style which is used with an individual or group that is relatively low in maturity for a given task

supervisory management—first-line management or first-line supervision

synergy—the concept that the whole is greater than the sum of the parts

System 1—management system in which top management primarily uses an autocratic style, makes all the decisions, and relies on coercion as the primary motivating force

System 2—management system in which higher management makes most of the decisions, although some minor implementing decisions may be made at lower levels

System 3—management system in which higher management still reserves the tasks of direction and control, but ideas are at least solicited from lower levels

System 4—management system in which higher management views its role as that of making sure the best decisions are made through a decentralized participative group structure

tangible standard—a type of standard that can be expressed in easy-to-measure terms

task behaviors—leadership behaviors that involve clarifying the job; telling people what, how, and when to do a job; providing follow-up; and taking corrective action

team—a collection of people who must rely on group cooperation if the group is to experience the most success possible and achieve its goals

team management—a leadership style based on the leader having a high concern for both people and production and using a participative approach

technical skills—the ability to understand and be able to perform effectively the specific processes, practices, or techniques required of specific jobs

technological unemployment—the situation in which employees can no longer perform their jobs because educational or skill demands have increased beyond their capacity

termination-at-will—a rule whereby an employer can dismiss an employee for any reason unless there is more explicit contractual provision preventing it

Theory X—a leadership theory based on the assumptions that the average person (1) has an inherent dislike for work; (2) must be coerced, controlled, directed, or threatened to work toward achieving organizational objectives; and (3) prefers to be directed, wishes to avoid responsibility, has relatively little ambition, and wants security above all

Theory Y—a leadership theory based on the following assumptions: (1) that work is as natural as play or rest; (2) that the human being will exercise self-direction and self-control when committed to objectives; (3) that the average person learns to accept and also seeks responsibility; (4) that the capacity for imagination, ingenuity, and creativity is widely found in the population; and (5) the intellectual potentialities of the average person are only partially utilized in modern industrial life

time management—the ability to use one's time to get things done when they should be done

time signals—nonverbal messages such as being on time, being tardy, being available, and so on

time standards—tangible standards which are expressed in terms of the speed with which jobs should be done

time wages or **day work**—a method in which the employee is paid for the amount of time spent on the job, regardless of the output during that period of time

top management—the management level responsible for the overall operations of an organization

training needs survey—survey in which supervisors state their needs on a prepared form by using interviews

transferring—involves a change in responsibilities and duties, either with or without a change in pay

Type A behavior—individual behavior characterized by (1) trying to accomplish too many things in a short time, and (2) lacking patience and struggling against time and other people to accomplish one's ends

Type B behavior—individual behavior characterized by (1) tending to be calmer, (2) devoting more time to exercise, and (3) being more realistic in estimating the time it takes to complete an assignment

unfair labor practices—practices that either management or labor unions are prohibited from engaging in under law

unified planning—the process of establishing plans at all organizational levels to be in harmony rather than at cross purposes

union-management relations—labor relations or industrial relations

union authorization card—a card to be signed by an employee who authorizes a particular union to be his or her collective bargaining representative

union shop—an agreement whereby all employees must join the union within a specified period or be fired

union steward—a union member elected by other members to represent their interests in their relations with management

unity of command principle—a management principle which states that everyone in an organization should report to and be accountable to only one boss

unprogrammed decisions—decisions that occur infrequently and require a separate and different response each time, making it difficult to establish a systematic way of dealing with them

unstructured interviews—interviews in which the pattern of questions asked, the conditions under which they are asked, and the bases for evaluating results are not standardized

upgrading—the process of retraining unskilled or semiskilled workers in their present positions

upward communication—type of communication that is initiated by employees and passed upward to their immediate supervisors

vocal signals—nonverbal messages characterized by the emphasis placed on certain words, pauses, or the tone of voice used

vocational-technical education programs—a program in which vocational-technical schools, business schools, and junior colleges conduct regular or special training classes

vocational interest test—a type of employment test designed to determine an applicant's areas of major interest as far as work is concerned

vocational rehabilitation programs—programs which provide counseling, medical care, and vocational training for physically and mentally handicapped individuals

wage surveys—surveys which determine the "going rate" for jobs in the local labor market and in the industry

word processing—software which turns the microcomputer into a ready-to-use typewriter at which the supervisor can prepare memos or documents, easily make modifications or corrections, and print the final document on the printer

work sampling or **work preview**—a type of employment test which consists of having an applicant do a task that is representative of the work usually done on the job

INDEX